A Higher Education

The Council for National Academic Awards
and British Higher Education 1964–89

A Higher Education

The Council for National Academic Awards and British Higher Education 1964–89

The Council for National Academic Awards can be described as 'a national network for quality assurance'. It was established in 1964 as a guardian of academic standards in the non-university sector of higher education in the UK. In the last quarter-century it has encouraged the development of degree courses across the full range of disciplines, excluding medicine and veterinary science. *A Higher Education: The Council for National Academic Awards and British Higher Education 1964 to 1989* was commissioned by the CNAA to commemorate its silver jubilee. The history covers a period of very rapid expansion in higher education outside the universities, mirrored in the growth and development of the CNAA. The Council was established with the role of awarding degrees and safeguarding the quality of degree courses in polytechnics and colleges, and so its successes and strengths — as well as its problems and difficulties — reflect very closely the preoccupations and events of higher education since 1964.

Dr Silver describes how the CNAA helped to broaden the range of degree courses beyond the traditional subjects, the way it maintained and enhanced standards in a swiftly changing academic world, and its part in widening access to higher education. He draws on interviews as well as the extensive records of CNAA and some of its institutions. Through the story of the body whose awards are now held by nearly 1 per cent of the population, he paints what is, in effect, the changing landscape of British higher education in the last twenty-five years.

Harold Silver, currently researcher and consultant, is a visiting professor at Oxford Polytechnic and senior project associate at Pennsylvania State University. He is also chairman of a group advising the Government of the Bahamas in the reorganization of their higher education. He was Principal of Bulmershe College of Higher Education, Reading, until 1986 and before that held a University of London chair of education and social history. He is the author of many well-known books on the history of education, including *Education as History* (1983) and, most recently, *Education, Change and the Policy Process* (1990) Falmer Press. He has written a regular column for the *Times Higher Education Supplement*, and was a member of CNAA's Council for four years until 1986. He was awarded a CNAA higher doctorate in 1986 for his work on the history of education.

A Higher Education

The Council for National Academic
Awards and British Higher Education
1964–89

Harold Silver

The Falmer Press
(A member of the Taylor & Francis Group)
London ● New York ● Philadelphia

UK	The Falmer Press, Rankine Road, Basingstoke, Hampshire, RG24 0PR
USA	The Falmer Press, Taylor & Francis Inc., 1900 Frost Road, Suite 101, Bristol PA 19007

First published 1990

British Library Cataloguing in Publication Data
Silver, Harold, *1928 –*
  A higher education: the Council for National Academic Awards and British higher education 1964–1989. — (Education policy perspectives).
  1. Great Britain. Degree courses. Validation. Organisations: Council for National Academic Award
  I. Title   II. Series
  378.199
  ISBN-85000-700-4
  ISBN 1-85000-701-2 pbk

Library of Congress Cataloging-in-Publication Data
Silver, Harold.
  A higher education: the Council for National Academic Awards and British higher education 1964–1989/Harold Silver.
  p. cm. — (Education policy perspectives series).
  Includes bibliographical references.
  ISBN 1-85000-700-4
  ISBN 1-85000-701-2 (pbk.)
  1. Degrees, Academic—Great Britain—History. 2. Council for National Academic Awards (Great Britain)—History. 3. Higher education and state—Great Britain—History. 4. Education, Higher—Great Britain—History.
  I. Title   II. Series
  LB2391.G8S54   1990
  378.2'4'0941—dc20

Jacket design by Caroline Archer
Crest by courtesy of CNAA

Typeset in 10/12 point Garamond by
Bramley Typesetting Limited, 12 Campbell Court, Bramley, Basingstoke, Hants.

Printed in Great Britain by
Taylor & Francis (Printers) Ltd, Basingstoke

Contents

List of Abbreviations		vi
Chapter Notes		viii
Acknowledgments		ix
Introduction		1
Chapter 1	Inventing Higher Education	7
Chapter 2	Launching an Alternative	21
Chapter 3	Making the CNAA	44
Chapter 4	Confronting Policies	65
Chapter 5	Shaping a System	90
Chapter 6	Redrawing Boundaries	113
Chapter 7	Interpreting Partnership	144
Chapter 8	Experiencing the CNAA	166
Chapter 9	Making Judgments and Being Judged	184
Chapter 10	Making Responses	220
Chapter 11	Pasts and Futures	260
Appendices		273
Index		284

List of Abbreviations

AAC	Academic Advisory Committee
ATTI	Association of Teachers in Technical Institutes
BTEC	Business and Technician Education Council
CAA	Committee for Academic Affairs
CAIP	Committee for Academic and Institutional Policy
CAP	Committee for Academic Policy
CASS	Committee for Arts and Social Studies
CAT(s)	College(s) of Advanced Technology
CATS	Credit Accumulation and Transfer Scheme
CDP	Committee of Directors of Polytechnics
CEO	Chief Education Officer
CI	Central Institution (Scotland)
CN or CNAA	Council for National Academic Awards
CST	Committee for Science and Technology
CVCP	Committee of Vice-Chancellors and Principals
DES	Department of Education and Science
DipAD	Diploma in Art and Design
DipHE	Diploma of Higher Education
DipTech	Diploma in Technology
DMS	Diploma in Management Studies
DSU	Development Services Unit
FE	Further Education
HE	Higher Education
HMCI	Her Majesty's Chief Inspector
HMI	Her Majesty's Inspector
IT	Information technology
LEA	Local Education Authority
MoE	Ministry of Education
NAB	National Advisory Body (on Local Authority — later Public Sector — Higher Education)
NACEIC	National Advisory Council on Education for Industry and Commerce

NATFHE	National Association of Teachers in Further and Higher Education
NCDAD	National Council for Diplomas in Art and Design
NCTA	National Council for Technological Awards
OU	Open University
PCFC	Polytechnics and Colleges Funding Council
PNL	Polytechnic of North London
PSHE	Public sector higher education
RAC	Regional Advisory Council
RISE	(Committee on) Research into Sandwich Education
SCOVACT	Scottish Council for the Validation of Courses for Teachers
SED	Scottish Education Department
UCB	University College Buckingham
UGC	University Grants Committee
UQ	*Universities Quarterly*

Chapter Notes

The full reference for any source is given the first time it is cited in each chapter.

Page references are given for published sources only.

Titles are italicized for published sources only.

The 'Note on sources' in Appendix B indicates the location of the primary sources used. Where no location is obvious from the Note or the reference it is in the possession of the author.

An outline chronology is contained in Appendix A.

Interviews by Martin Davis (MD) or the author (HS) are on tape or in transcript in the possession of the interviewers. No direct quotation from living interviewees has been used without their consent.

Where any doubt is possible about a primary source being a CNAA document the reference is preceded by the letters CN, or in the case of the NCTA — NC.

File numbers are not given where the source and date are self-evident.

The following abbreviations are used in the Notes:

B Poly	Brighton Polytechnic
CEdmin	Minutes of the Committee for Education
Cmin	Minutes of Council
CN	Council for National Academic Awards
GB	Governing Body (of the National Council for Technological Awards)
GBmin	Minutes of the Governing Body
HS	Harold Silver (interviews by)
L H Ed min	Lord Hives Education Miscellaneous file
MD	Martin Davis (interviews by)
NPoly	Newcastle Polytechnic
NC	National Council for Technological Awards

Acknowledgments

This book was written at the invitation of the Council for National Academic Awards (CNAA), which has throughout given unstinting support, at the same time imposing no constraints or pressure of any kind on the conduct of the research or the shape or content of the resulting publication. No organization could have been more generous with someone invited to probe, record and judge.

In addition to the people interviewed and listed in Appendix C, all of whom were generous with their time and help, there were many who provided assistance in a variety of other ways. Edwin Kerr was of enormous help in launching the project. Many former and present officers of the Council made available their personal collections of material. Colleagues in the institutions whose views of the CNAA were sought in their records gave considerable help — librarians and archivists, directors and senior staff in giving ready access to records and people. The collaboration of the CNAA's own archive and library staff was indispensable and always forthcoming. Michael Lewis and his colleagues at the Committee of Directors of Polytechnics (CDP) gave ready access to the CDP's records. For their comments on a draft of the manuscript I am deeply grateful to Ann Ridler, Norman Lindop, Bill Gutteridge, Bridget Rogers and Malcolm Frazer.

Many others graciously offered help which in the event could not be taken up. This project occupied two people for a good deal of their time over a three-year-period, and given the range of the CNAA's activities and records, and the many directions the narrative and analysis could take, it was impossible to interview, meet and correspond with all the people who were ready to share their experience and with whom contact would have enriched — and perhaps even corrected — the research. Unfortunately, permission to consult the relevant records of the University Grants Committee (UGC) was not given.

Two specific acknowledgments are particularly important. First, to Martin Davis, at the time Senior Lecturer at Coventry Polytechnic and now HMI, and author of a PhD thesis on the CNAA at Loughborough University of Technology in 1979. His thesis and resultant articles were themselves important, but equally so were the interviews that he conducted during his research. Some of those he interviewed are deceased, others have long ago moved on to other things. Although it was possible for me to reinterview some of those concerned, some of the interviews he conducted were of major interest. He was willing to make available both the tapes and transcripts, and all the interviewees agreed to my having access to this material. My debt to Martin Davis and his work is acknowledged at appropriate points in the book.

Secondly, to Pam Silver, who has worked as Research Associate throughout the project. Her name does not appear as co-author only because she has not been involved in the writing, and is in that sense not responsible for the product. Without her, however, this history of the CNAA could not and would not have been written.

Although so many people were helpful in so many ways the only responsibility for the outcome is mine.

Harold Silver
Oxford
November 1989

Introduction

The Council for National Academic Awards (CNAA) has been, since its creation in 1964, the most public and explicit organization in the history of British higher education. It has been so for several reasons. Its Charter and Statutes virtually required it to be, by establishing as its aim the guardianship of the standard of degrees and other awards in the institutions whose courses it was to validate. Being accountable to do so, it established procedures by which not only to achieve this aim, but also to be able to defend publicly the basis of its accountability. It has therefore been able to speak with confidence for standards in the sector and in its associated institutions. It has also had to deal with a considerable and complex range of polytechnics and colleges, discipline areas, interdisciplinary programmes, curriculum structures, modes of teaching and assessment, research and a diversity of traditions and developments. In constantly changing economic, political and policy environments it has had to lay down ground rules, give approval and disapproval, review and encourage others to review, and negotiate around processes of documentation, dialogue and report. Continuity and change have both required description, analysis and justification. Responsiveness to policy initiatives at many levels of the educational system has meant consultation and debate, the promotion and defence of what for a quarter of a century was known as 'public sector' higher education.

From its inception the CNAA inherited the mantle of the National Council for Technological Awards (NCTA) in providing awards for students in non-university higher education institutions, notably in science and technology. An outline chronology is contained in Appendix A. Its role widened with the designation of the polytechnics in the late 1960s, the appearance of diversifying colleges and institutes of higher education in the mid-1970s, and its amalgamation with the National Council for Diplomas in Art and Design (NCDAD). It acquired responsibility for the Diploma in Management Studies (DMS), and it expanded into the social sciences, business studies, teacher education and the creative and performing arts. It initiated, supported or encouraged interfaculty and modular courses, research degrees, credit transfer and a range of other openings into wider provision and access. The CNAA became a unique voice for public sector higher education, and for developments in higher education more broadly. There have been other validating bodies alongside the CNAA — including some universities — but it has been a crucial spokesman for the sector, and it has managed its relationships within and outside the sector accordingly. The polytechnics and colleges themselves have had to establish, explain and justify their roles and objectives in ways that the universities and colleges of the nineteenth and twentieth centuries rarely, if at all, had to do. They, and the CNAA, have had persistently to explain or debate their roles in relation to research or industry and the professions, non-traditional students or 'peer review'. The very vocabulary of 'Council', 'polytechnic' and 'college of higher education' has required the CNAA to be constantly explicit on its own and their behalf.

The complexity of the CNAA and of the processes and events in which it has been involved dictate the choices to be made in approaching its history. With the CNAA, as with other organizations and institutions, there are differently perceived histories, different historical emphases. There are different views of its machineries and of the work of the large and diverse constituencies which it has comprised, its relationships with the validated institutions, its influence in the development of specific subject areas, its position in the networks, politics and controversies of higher education. There are different views of its roles and procedures across time. Views differ amongst and within institutions and subject areas, categories of officers and of members. Although this history of the CNAA touches these and other differences of emphasis and perception, its self-imposed limitation is one of an essentially policy focus. It is concerned primarily with the sources of the CNAA's own policies, the contexts and directions of its policies, its options and ambiguities, the means and hazards of its policy implementation — and failures to implement. It is also concerned with the policy context of higher education in general, the CNAA's positions amidst the busy changes of public policy, and its responses and contributions to the policy processes of governments, public agencies and the higher education community itself. The choice of such a policy focus does not lessen the complexity of the history, but it does move the emphasis away from some of the detail of internal mechanisms and modes of operation.

One of the penalties of focussing on policy is the inevitable interest in change. The policy focus drives the analysis into a dominant concern with how things emerged and were shaped and became part of the organization's purposes and operations. It diverts attention to a large extent from what is well-established, from how things continued and were sustained — though there is often a need to explain why things might have been expected to change, but did not. There is a danger, therefore, that the new appears to take precedence over the established. The CNAA, for instance, took over from the National Council for Technological Awards a firm and continuing commitment to validating and encouraging courses in science and technology. These were not unchanging subject areas in scale, course content, research or the emergence of new branches and sub-branches, and as such they required the continuing advocacy and critical attention of boards and committees. Once established, however, the CNAA itself, followed by the polytechnics, became concerned with subject developments which radically changed the profiles of many institutions and of the CNAA itself. With the polytechnics, the colleges of higher education, and other validated institutions, the CNAA moved into the new problems of different subjects, subject combinations and interdisciplinary studies.

In terms of defining and implementing policies the CNAA became, in the late 1960s and 1970s, increasingly preoccupied with these enlargements of interest and responsibility. In explaining the determinants and shape of the CNAA's policy concerns in this period, therefore, the analysis gives priority to such substantial changes. Science and technology were not diminished in the continuing work of validation and advocacy, but they entered policy arenas in particular instances — for example, when the CNAA confronted the controversial question of 'general' or 'balanced' studies, or in response to a public policy initiative such as the appointment and report of the Finniston Committee on engineering education.

An 'in-house' history would give greater weight to the structures, operation and personnel of committees, the tensions and subtleties of organizational behaviours and administration, the sustaining efforts of Council and officers, chairmen and members. Amidst these details, however, the policy directions would be less emphasized and clear. None of these 'in-house' threads is entirely neglected here, but they are not the shaping dynamic. Emphases and details that many who have taken part in the 'sustaining efforts' might expect to find are often embedded in the underlying structures against which other developments are presented.

A further difficulty in reduced attention to the specifics of committees and personnel lies in the judgments apparently involved in what is selected as illustration. Naming one committee appears to undervalue others; an applauding or critical comment on one institution reflects on others. To illustrate a trend or a moment in the 'culture' of the CNAA there are here, for example, cameo studies of officers or members, and these may appear arbitrary and invidious, or some kind of 'team' selection. They are intended, in fact, to be no more than indications of what it was like to be a board chairman, a registrar, a validator, at various points in the CNAA's history. They are to suggest how processes worked, how policy was developed and implemented, how changes were introduced.

In approaching the history of the CNAA as a piece of recent history or policy history there is therefore the particular problem of 'angles of vision'. Historical distance simplifies patterns of description and explanation. The analysis has to cope with the question — whose history? Whose angle of vision has been preserved in the records? How can the opinions of other constituencies be engaged? Recent history offers the opportunity to identify such perspectives directly: oral history becomes accessible. How reliable are these and other primary and secondary sources? How can in-built bias and false memory be evaded? One set of problems may be substituted for another. In the case of the CNAA the problem is acute, given the range and volume of documentation and the numbers of participants, and the multiplicity of angles from which it can be viewed and judged.

The Council itself was created with a roughly tripartite membership of 'public sector', university and 'other' (industry, local authorities . . .), with all that this means in terms of divergent views of the policy needs of different constituencies. Her Majesty's Inspectors (HMI), acting as 'assessors' on the Council or its committees, are likely to have reflected views of directions of policy and practice in the context of possibilities and policy developments of other kinds. Members of CNAA boards and committees have had subject-specific, profession-specific or similar frameworks of judgment. Officers of the CNAA have had policy views coloured by their knowledge of the wider working of the organization, its prospects and limitations, the internal politics of its decision-making processes. Other views from outside — employers' organizations, vice-chancellors . . . — have had their shaping environments. The polytechnics and colleges of higher education have had both shared and divergent interests. Policy is not the prerogative of governments and national councils. It is also a function of academic boards and departments, course teams and conferences. The focus on policy in the case of the CNAA does not dispense with complexity, it selects one kind of complexity at the expense of others.

One question of emphasis or bias is the author's own shaping backgrounds. This arises in the present case because of my own involvements with the CNAA, having been Principal of a CNAA-validated college, a member of Council and many of its committees, and a participant in research activities sponsored by the CNAA. As a Principal I know how easy it has been to judge and to misjudge the CNAA. As a member of its Council I know how easy it has been to hold strong but inadequate views. Such realizations do not mean escape from backgrounds, but they help to minimize them. They have at least contributed to the intention to locate different 'angles of vision'. These have been found in different locations. The CNAA gave open access to its records, with obvious safeguards of confidentiality regarding correspondents and institutions. The CNAA's records, whether at the Public Record Office or in the possession of the CNAA, are a major resource for research into the history not only of the CNAA itself, but also of academic disciplines, professions, institutions, processes of teaching, learning and examining, the development of the public sector and issues of higher education in general. As such they have formed the most crucial basis for this study. Interviews were conducted with a substantial number of people who have been active in different ways in the CNAA over the past quarter of a century. Documentary records were consulted in other places — including three polytechnics and two colleges of higher education. These and some of the interviews were particularly important with regard to differences of opinion over specific issues, or acute controversies in which the CNAA was involved. It is clear, amidst these complexities, that neither the CNAA nor I have expected this to be *the* history of the CNAA. It is, of course, *a* history of the Council for National Academic Awards.

Chapter 1

Inventing Higher Education

In the autumn of 1950 H.C. Dent, editor of *The Times Educational Supplement*, paid a one-day visit to what might well have been Atlantis. In fact it was to the Technical University of Delft. People talked about the famous institutions of higher technological education — Zürich, Charlottenburg, MIT . . . — but, Dent wrote, 'What *are* these places like? Those people who commend them must know, but I often wonder how many among their audiences do; and I cannot recollect having seen a detailed description of a single one in print'. So in a single day Dent visited parts of Delft, including the laboratories, of which he recorded his 'feelings of awe as I walked through these vast halls', where there was 'great vitality, deep scholarship, and a keen awareness of the dangers inherent in a community limited mainly to exploration of one field — albeit a broad one — of knowledge'.[1] During and after the Second World War there were currents of anxiety, reflected in Dent's visit, about Britain's failure to develop this kind of education, and about the adequacy of higher education in Britain to meet the demographic, economic and social demands of the post-war world.

Until the 1960s 'higher education' meant the universities, although the phrase was not in common use. Not until the appointment of the Robbins Committee in December 1960 'to review the pattern of full-time higher education in Great Britain' did a conception of higher education embracing sectors other than the universities become widespread currency. The Anderson Committee, in its report on *Grants to Students* in 1960, only a few months before the appointment of the Robbins Committee, never used the phrase 'higher education', but referred throughout, for example, to universities and higher technical education, or to university and comparable course students.[2] In 1961, opening a discussion whose billing contained 'higher education' in the title, Sir Edward Boyle wondered how many people realized 'just how rapidly our national pattern of further education is already changing. Until quite recently, the universities had almost a monopoly of further education in Britain', and his discussion of universities and other institutions of 'further education' only rarely incorporated a reference to 'higher education.[3] The University Grants Committee (UGC), in its report on the period 1957–62, commented on its post-war responsibility for helping to prepare plans for university development 'adequate to national needs', but in discussing those needs and pressures for the expansion of science and technology it made no reference to institutions other than universities. In its following report, however, covering the period 1962–67, the basic change heralded by the Robbins Committee was heavily underlined:

> It was one of the major features of the Robbins Report that it viewed the pattern of full-time education in Great Britain as a whole. It dealt not only with the universities but with those colleges, within the purview of the Ministry of Education and the Scottish Education Department, that provided courses for the education and training of teachers or systematic courses of further education beyond the advanced level of the General Certificate of Education or beyond the Ordinary National Certificate or its equivalent.

The recommendations of the Robbins Committee had significantly changed 'the demarcation lines which had previously existed between universities on the one hand and teacher training colleges and further education colleges on the other'. After the Robbins Report and ensuing government action 'it was no longer possible, even if one had been so inclined, to view the universities as a completely detached group in the educational structure of the country'.[4] Following a number of pressures, including the demand for higher technological education and the demand for, and the existing momentum of, expansion, there had at this point been a fundamental change of vocabulary and perception. The landscape was no longer the same.

The particular thread of education in science and technology is crucial in the developments of the late 1950s and early 1960s which led to the creation of the Council for National Academic Awards and a 'non-university' sector within the emergent pattern of higher education. It is important to emphasize, however, that the period between the late 1940s and the early 1960s contained the most sustained and penetrating attempts in Britain in this century to reconsider the nature and purposes of the universities. The reconsideration was motivated by war and demography, by changing social expectations and the construction of a 'welfare state', by worldwide economic changes and the fragile position of Britain's economy, by the growing centrality of science and technology in national planning.

During the Second World War British universities were faced with the beginnings of what was clearly an important 'struggle to maintain autonomy'[5] amidst the pressures for responsiveness to wartime and post-war needs. In Britain as elsewhere the nature and extent of expanded provision and access raised — acutely in the late 1940s and 1950s — questions of funding and of government involvement in the processes of planning and sustaining expansion. In this, as in many other respects, the issues facing British universities and the institutions that were laying claim to recognition as higher education were international issues. The late 1940s in fact saw the beginning of a modern internationalization of dialogue and debate about higher education. In the British discussions of policy and practice that were to follow there is constant reference to, and contact with, higher education in the United States, its increasingly mass scale, its different curricula and structures, its graduate work and technology — sometimes with approving and often with pejorative judgments. The American experience seemed, however, an inescapable touchstone in the literature of higher education in the 1950s and 1960s, with *Universities Quarterly* and other journals constantly returning to American teacher education, student numbers and quality, vocational programmes . . . European and international conferences of university administrators and teachers, under the auspices of UNESCO and others, discussed provision, adult education, the problems and purposes of universities. The universities of the Commonwealth debated their traditions, directions and dilemmas. At a congress of the Commonwealth universities in 1948 the international nature of the tensions aroused by greater government intervention became particularly clear.

Introducing Sir Walter Moberly, Chairman of the University Grants Committee, who was to open discussion on the congress theme of 'Relations of the state and universities', his Australian Chairman commented:

> . . . those who selected the topic of relationship of the state and the universities for our first subject of discussion acted wisely and well, for it is the problem which more than any other is keeping all those of us who are responsible for University adminstration awake.[6]

Moberly himself went on to delineate the British conditions in which autonomy was clearly not, and did not need to be, absolute. He underlined the importance of a high degree of university autonomy and the importance of the UGC as a mechanism guaranteeing both that autonomy and responsiveness to a necessary degree of public supervision of university affairs — themes which were to surface the following year in the larger argument of Moberly's book *The Crisis in the University*. What was emerging was a range of concerns covering all aspects of the university and its relationships with the parent society, and involving a review of the basic purposes of the university system. Moberly's analysis of the crisis, whilst Christian in motivation, underlined the deepening anxieties, the 'causes of our present discontent', 'spurious remedies', the complexities of tradition and new horizons, the balancing of aims:

> It is clear . . . that the university must combine these aims, the occupational and the cultural. In framing its Degree Course, it must have in mind preparation for life. But it must remember that, for the vast majority of its students, life will be life in a job.

He argued against being 'excessively absorbed in immediate needs' and neglecting more fundamental ones:

> We need above all things to cultivate our sense of values. But it must be said emphatically that this does not mean a plea for more 'Arts' and less 'Science' . . . Technical narrowness is found among 'Arts men' at least as frequently as among 'Science men', and a complacent acquiescence in their own one-sidedness even more often.

Moberly's basic assumption was that the universities faced a crisis resulting in part from their own confusion, pusillanimity and evasion of the issues. In developing new policies they needed to become a 'battle ground where the real intellectual issues of our time are fought out', to restore communication 'between the isolated mental worlds which different groups have come to inhabit', constantly to explore their values as a basis for action.[7] Moberly's book was the basis of prolonged debate, both illustrating and articulating a deep unease about the position of the universities in a changed and changing society. Responses to the book were in terms of the moral dilemmas of the post-war world and an appropriate philosophy of education and of life, but there were other kinds of response. Moberly's 'crisis' was perhaps 'the moral crisis of the Western democracies', but in the book 'he hardly mentions the number of students, the shortage of buildings and teachers, whether the universities have any responsibility for the national production crisis, whether there may be a financial crisis in the university.[8]

The important feature of these debates of the late 1940s and 1950s was in fact this combination of concern about immediate difficulties, about new pressures and appropriate policies, and about long-term principles. A document produced by a group of signatories under the auspices of Nuffield College, Oxford, in 1948, gave a clear indication of the contexts within which these emphases had to be reconciled. It considered the implications of the demand for a substantial increase in the number of science graduates and did so — as did much other discussion of the time — in terms of the options for increased university size or altered internal balance. It looked at pressures for 'more specialized instruction or research and more facilities for the training of members of this profession, or recruits to that branch of applied research, or entrants to some field of social activity hitherto untouched by universities'. The pressures were for quick results and to be '"professional" in a narrow sense'. It concluded that the functions of universities 'must be considered as a whole, and an attempt made to lay down principles by which new claims can be balanced against old duties, and one new claim against another'.[9] 'New claims and old duties' could well have been the motto for all the concerns of higher education in the following decades. Central to those concerns was to be the Nuffield preoccupation with the meaning and place of the 'professional' in the university, and then in the pattern of higher education which at different times came to include the colleges of advanced technology, the polytechnics and the colleges and institutes of higher education — and the CNAA. The Nuffield group considered that a university, while maintaining a reasonable range of studies, should not allow itself to be turned into a specialized institution 'serving the needs of one profession or one field of research'. The limits for a university were difficult to define:

> If Law, why not the very similar profession of Accounting? If Forestry, why not Horticulture? If Engineering, why not Navigation? If Agriculture, why not Commerce? If Architecture, why not Building? If Music, why not Dramatic Art?

The case for inclusion in the scope of a university depended on the profession's interest in 'a study of the underlying sciences or other branches of knowledge (in which the university will already be engaged)'. The kind of questions formulated by the group was to be crucial to the thinking that went into the development of the polytechnics, for example, from the late 1960s. There is a certain prescience in the way the Nuffield argument is conducted. Much of the 'higher professional training' that in America was conducted in universities could be devolved on specialized institutions. The Percy Committee on Technical Education, the Loveday Committee on Agriculture and some members of the McNair Committee on Teacher Education had proposed to make the necessary provision for all or part of professional education outside the universities: 'such a development would relieve the universities of a pressure which it might be difficult otherwise either to resist or sustain'. The document later returned to the theme, underlining that a clearer definition of the function of universities would relieve them of work which could be done as well or better 'by secondary schools or institutions of professional and technical training'.[10] Throughout the 1950s the universities were to grapple with such issues, anxious about the repercussions of the expansion of the system and the scale of individual institutions, the distribution of decision-making power amongst government, the UGC and the university, the ability of the universities to increase their output of graduates in science and their need to respond to the demands for technological manpower — without distorting what they considered their underlying values and purposes. Gradually the position of the teacher training colleges and the technical colleges engaged in advanced work (including external degrees of the University of London) assumed greater prominence in discussion of the future of 'specialized', 'professional' and general higher education. By the second half of the 1950s debate about the content of higher education remained intense, the search for solutions to the tension between new claims and old duties was intensifying, and new directions and policies were being formulated. The period from 1956 to 1963 was to be the most productive in these two decades of post-war reexamination of the roles of the universities and the increasingly visible contenders for admission to a new diagram of 'higher education'.

Discussion of the universities, their purposes and futures, was prominent in the journals. *Universities Quarterly* had established itself as a forum for the debate of fundamental issues as well as current specifics — and in 1958 Lord Simon of Wythenshawe triggered off an impassioned debate by proposing a Royal Commission on the Universities, countered by his critics the following year as being a blueprint for overzealous planning.[11] *Nature* carried editorial discussion of such themes as 'The purpose of university education' or 'The function of universities' — often reflecting conference or parliamentary debate.[12] *Twentieth Century* in 1956 ran a special edition on 'Redbrick universities'.[13] Before the end of the decade Eric Ashby had published his influential *Technology and the Academics*, discussing the traditions and functions of the universities in Britain and Europe, and specifically Britain's failure to understand and develop science,[14] C.P. Snow had given his famous lectures on the two cultures,[15] and the Fabian Society had published a pamphlet by Graeme Moodie pointing out that although the universities were distinctive and needed to be handled with care, a Royal Commission on them was not a threat to their basic freedoms.[16]

Talk of a Royal Commission accelerated in 1960 (and Lord Simon and others were carrying the proposal into the Houses of Parliament[17]) and from 1960–61, with the appointment of the Robbins Committee, not on the *universities* but on *higher education*, the range of the public discussion, and of the evidence prepared for Robbins, widened. Lord Hailsham, Minister for Science, was arguing strongly for a recognition of the proper dual role of the university:

> . . . side by side with their function as the teachers of human society as a whole, the universities have also the task of providing vocational training . . . many academics are far too fastidious to speak of it openly . . . The plain truth is that if it had not been for this function, the universities would have neither been brought into being nor survived.

The growth of further education outside the universities, he also argued, had encouraged 'a certain element of built-in snobbery' in the universities, which had excluded or 'placed below the salt' disciplines which in other countries were rightly included on an equal footing with other university studies. It was this general theme of expansion and diversity of provision that prompted John Vaizey to suggest that one of the great problems was a lack of machinery for considering the 'whole problem of higher education' — which Hailsham believed the new commission of enquiry would address.[18] The new universities already being developed at the beginning of the 1960s were the theme of discussion at a Home Universities Conference in 1960, where topics included the changing student population, the frequent rejection of a liberal education as being out of date, and the relevance of questions about new universities and their purposes to all universities. The Principal of the new University College of Sussex asked: 'Will the universities have a monopoly of the nation's talented youth? If they share them with other post-school institutions, how?'[19] H.C. Dent's book, *Universities in Transition*, which he completed at the end of 1960, described itself as being addressed to the layman rather than to the academic: 'today interest in university education is far from being confined to academic circles. It is widespread among the general public'. One of Dent's anxieties was that expansion, however necessary, risked breaking up the university's sense of community. Increasing the range and promoting to university status the specialized, non-university institutions would not in fact make them universities: 'great range without cohesion would not make a community'.[20]

From 1961 the Robbins Committee was receiving a broad sweep of evidence which reflected its own wide remit and the spectrum of issues and concerns that had been gathering momentum in the 1950s. There were those who emphasized to the Committee that there was in the population no 'fixed distribution or "pool" of intelligence', and that the numbers of students capable of higher education could be increased without lowering standards or increasing wastage. There were those urging that the universities had an obligation to new professions such as teaching and social work as well as to older, established ones.[21] Some were arguing against excessive specialization and vocational content, and in favour of more personal and general education on science and technology courses.[22] Sir Sydney Caine, Director of the London School of Economics, assumed that the Committee would take 'a completely fresh look at "higher education" and its various divisions', and pressed the view that 'the existing differences between universities and other institutions of full-time higher education, including colleges of advanced technology and teacher training colleges, need to be very much reduced'.[23] The Ministry of Education (renamed the Department of Education and Science after the Robbins Committee had reported) submitted evidence in 1962 which looked at 'the future pattern of higher education in England and Wales'. This evidence is clearly and directly relevant to the decisions that were made in the period following the Robbins Report. The Ministry firmly rejected suggestions that all higher education could be included in the university sector, so as to 'simplify control and to reduce invidious distinctions of status between universities and other places of higher education'. Making the universities 'comprehensive' would be bringing together institutions with very different courses from those 'traditionally provided in British universities'. The Ministry concluded that:

> . . . a certain homogeneity of interest is desirable if an educational institution is to flourish, and to widen the range so much as this proposal involves might well damage either the universities themselves or the interests of the subordinate colleges. It would benefit both the country and the universities if the universities . . . were to identify themselves more closely with the higher education

system as a whole. But it seems very doubtful whether the development of the large number of institutions of higher education now outside the university ambit would be best served, at any rate during the next twenty-five years, by bringing them *all* administratively within it.[24]

There is reflected in this the cautious approach to expansion which sought to capitalize on the universities' willingness to expand, but which was at the same time anxious not to disturb too far the traditional curricula, clienteles and values of the university. At the heart of the reconsideration of the university and increasingly of 'higher education' were questions about what could legitimately be considered to be 'higher education', what were the essential characteristics of its 'divisions', whether or how to reduce the differences, and what values across higher education or within its parts needed to be protected or reappraised. Such questions were sharply summarized at a conference of mainly Christian university teachers in 1961 by the Vice-Chancellor of the University of Leeds. If, by the end of the 1970s, the English universities could cater for approaching 200,000 full-time undergraduates, might there not be another 300,000 or so for whom some other form of college education would have to be provided? Could the English universities 'take on the whole job and deal with the whole 500,000 satisfactorily on behalf of the nation?' His answer to that question was *no*, but then there was a second question:

> Can the universities, in the interests of the future of universities, dare *not* to take on the whole job? So far the universities have, without disadvantage to themselves, shared the higher educational field with vocational colleges — technical and teacher training. Would they dare to share it with a host of *general* higher education colleges, dealing with larger numbers possibly than themselves?[25]

Those pressing considerations remained at that point without an answer, but these were questions the Robbins Committee was having to address, and in their recommendations and in the subsequent move to a 'binary' policy in the second half of the 1960s, policies — if not fundamental answers — had to be found.

One of the questions addressed by the Committee was the future of the University of London's external degrees. The University had, since the late 1850s, provided this route to degrees for students unable to attend universities, and all the University provided was an examination system. The numbers were considerable. At the time of the Robbins Committee there were 11,000 external students in the United Kingdom registered for first degrees, half of them in the technical colleges (and the latter numbers were to double by the end of the decade, with the largest increases in the arts and social sciences). Continuing the nineteenth-century tradition, a high proportion of these students were part-time, but the demand for full-time courses was growing. The Robbins Committee summarized this external degree system as one which had provided 'the possibility of academic quality for many thousands of people who had no opportunity of entering a university. It has provided a means whereby advanced work can be properly examined in institutions not yet of full university status, both at home and abroad'. The system's 'honourable place in academic history is a matter of common consent', but for the new conditions of expansion the Committee found it 'not a permanently suitable arrangement for developing institutions'.[26] For such development the Committee looked in other directions.

In the transition from analysis of the role of the university to a pattern of higher education and its components, the pressures of expansion in general played one important role, the others were those of science and technology.

In similar ways to the impact of pressures for change and response deriving from expansion, those for an increase in higher scientific and technological education and manpower went to the heart of the university enterprise and pointed to a variety of solutions and redefinitions. Although the place of science in British universities had been established in the late nineteenth and twentieth centuries — more slowly and less certainly south of the border than in Scotland — the place of technology had not. Debates about the position of 'professional' education in the university in the nineteenth century had focussed on the traditional areas of preparation for the liberal professions — the church, law and the state, and medicine — but also in general terms on claimants to new professional status and an academic base. At different speeds engineering, architecture, social work and others penetrated the university, but during and after the Second World War the driving force of technological and economic change thrust the demand for appropriately qualified personnel into the centre of discussion about university development. What kept those 'responsible for university administration awake' was the combined and interlocking pressure of governments and the demands of science and technology. In Britain, the Percy Committee reported in 1945 on *Higher Technological Education*, and the following year the Barlow Committee reported on *Scientific Manpower*. The Percy Committee was anxious to lengthen and raise the status of engineering education — including the 'works practice' that was later to become the practice of 'sandwich courses'. In addition to an increase in the output of university-trained engineers, the Committee recommended a new kind of course in the technical colleges, one which focussed more on the 'art' of technology, was freed from the restrictions of external degrees, and would result in 'the development of a type of higher technological education which is, for the most part, new to this country'.[27] What the Committee was, in fact, proposing was the creation of a National Council of Technology to be responsible for the awards and the standards in the colleges, once released from the demands of external London degrees.

The aim was to make the colleges themselves responsible for planning courses and teaching and assessing students. The Committee was making a dual incursion into what was eventually to become the 'binary' system of higher education. Neither the Percy Committee, nor the Barlow Committee which went in a similar direction, envisaged that any new award would be a 'degree', though the new courses and their awards would be parallel or equivalent to university degrees. Both committees were arguing for a substantial increase in higher education provision for science and technology, and numbers in the universities began in fact to increase — and in science the number of students doubled in less than five years. The development of an 'alternative' route for the education of technologists was not to take place for a decade.

The nature and extent of these specific expansionist demands on the universities fuelled self-analysis and controversy. The basis of the demands in the 'needs of the state' or 'national needs', in UGC vocabulary, was understood — particularly in wartime — but seen as a possible, and even an imminent, threat to university independence. The existence of the UGC as a buffer between government and the universities was some protection against such encroachments. The UGC acknowledged the validity of new demands on the universities arising from changes 'precipitated by war' and 'the further post-war developments in the social and economic structure of the country'. It was conceivable, however, that such demands might distort the balance of the universities, lead to the neglect of important subjects and the dangers of 'uncritical acceptance':

> We have always considered it essential, therefore . . . that such demands should be channelled by the government through us . . . and . . . that individual universities should have the last word in deciding whether to undertake a particular activity . . . [28]

Those comments preceded a section in a UGC report on science and technology. The background in the post-war period was not only fear of the distortion of the balance of work. It was also a deep suspicion of science and technology and their impact on university values — and it should be underlined that this was a period when the scientist and the technologist were commonly bracketed by anxious critics as indistinguishable. Specialists in other fields regularly accused scientific and technological studies of being specialized. In a 1947 lecture (widely read when published the following year), Sir Richard Livingstone talked about 'scientific and mathematical specialism' as the most dangerous form at the undergraduate level. The limitations of science, in not being concerned with human values, were particularly serious 'because the influence of science and the need for scientists will increase'.[29] Also in 1948, a professor of moral philosophy from Scotland addressed the Congress of Commonwealth Universities on the 'cultural crisis . . . the fundamental issue of our time', which was a breakdown expressed in 'the rapid growth and spread of the technological mind'. He was not castigating technology, he maintained, but attacking 'that habit of thinking and behaving as though all problems were technical problems; as though all difficulties could be solved by more technical knowledge and skill'. Technology should be subservient to a culture concerned with the priority of intrinsic values:

> . . . the technological obsession *is* the crisis in our Western culture
> . . . The spread of the technological obsession within the university itself, in its own spirit and outlook, is more insidious and unfits it for its primary cultural function.

Things had already gone too far. Any subject could be a vehicle of cultural education, but when 'shut in on themselves' subjects became merely a training in 'technical pedantry'.[30] Such fears clearly affected the whole curriculum, but the particular grounds for the fears were clear enough.

A symposium in the *Universities Quarterly* in 1949 showed how deeply controversy around these issues was running, with strong expressions of view of the traditional role of the university in preserving and extending knowledge, and one comment (by a professor of physics) that Oxford and Cambridge had largely abandoned this view 'in favour of purely vocational training and investigations designed to solve *ad hoc* problems of the day . . . the applied sciences, as at present taught and developed, are out of place in a university'. The opposing view was expressed that 'training for professional skills had been a characteristic function of the universities' from earliest times, and that the university could well promote:

> the scientific study of materials, construction techniques, or forms of propulsion . . . provided that the social importance of the technology be established and that the discipline is such that the undergraduate is not given a mere technical skill.[31]

In the pages of the *Universities Quarterly* anxious debate about these issues flowed on. A section devoted to 'Higher education in technology' in 1952 found the Vice-Chancellor of the University of Leeds arguing for technology as a discipline for the universities:

> the homes of learning, the most privileged seats of education, the guardians of standards. Will their charmed circles open to welcome new inquiries and as yet imperfectly established disciplines? Or will they remain intransigently conservative?

And in the same section the Chairman of Council of the City and Guilds of London Institute argued the case put forward by the National Advisory Council on Education for Industry and Commerce to upgrade some technical colleges 'to be indisputably of university standard', in order to solve the problem of insufficient technological education.[32] Sir John Cockcroft continued the attack on behalf of technology in the next issue: 'We ought to get rid of the once strongly held feeling that education for technology is a lower form of education than education in the arts'.[33] The very persistence of the debate casts doubt on the appropriateness of the reference to 'once'. The Vice-Chancellor of the University of Bristol talked of the future of technological education having been 'in the news' since the report of the Percy Committee, 'and even before', and argued the distinctions between science and technology, and between universities and technological institutions.[34] Here and elsewhere the late 1950s and early 1960s encountered continuing discussion of the purpose of the university, the nature of alternative provision, the distribution of resources, curricular balance and values, and the locus of power to make decisions — questions sharpened dramatically by the concerns regarding science and technology. Perceptions of the nature and roles of the university were central to the future planning of provision in these fields, and judgments about the institutions and sectors capable of making the provision. As *Nature* said in 1957:

> . . . the distribution of our resources between the universities, the colleges of technology and the technical colleges — the whole structure of technological and technical education — is ultimately determined by our idea of the place and purpose of a university.[35]

What that place and purpose were was discussed perhaps most influentially the following year by Eric Ashby in his book *Technology and the Academics*, with its central message of the failure of British universities to understand and adapt to the scientific revolution, its rejection of a false distinction between specialized science and technology and liberal arts subjects, its urgent statement that 'if the university repudiates the call to train technologists, it will not survive; if it repudiates the cultivation of non-practical values, it will cease to merit the title of university', its claim that technology was 'inseparable from humanism' — and its examples of how this could be best demonstrated and organized in courses of study.[36] A sociologist's analysis of the universities in 1960 underlined that, in Britain, their 'mediaeval and aristocratic traditions . . . have hitherto acted as a powerful brake against movement towards the technological society'.[37]

This sketch of the pressures, opinions and controversies in and surrounding the universities suggests some of the elements from which a new map of higher education began to be drawn. It explains some of the hesitations, reservations and alternatives out of which the first major steps were taken towards a new, 'non-university' base for higher technological studies in the mid-1950s, and then, with the creation of the CNAA, the basis of a wider system of 'public sector' higher education nearly a decade later. The first step was the establishment of the National Council for Technological Awards.

Notes

1 H.C. Dent (1951) 'The technical university of Delft', *Universities Quarterly*, 5, 3.
2 Ministry of Education (1960) *Grants to Students*, HMSO.
3 Sir Edward Boyle (1962) opening discussion on 'Intellectual responsibilities in higher education', *Universities Quarterly*, 16, 2, p. 127.
4 UGC (1964) *University Development 1957-1962*, HMSO; and (1968) *University Development 1962-1967*, HMSO, pp. 79-80.
5 Geoffrey L. Price (1978) 'The expansion of British universities and their struggle to maintain autonomy: 1943-46', *Minerva*, 16, 3.
6 Sir John D.G. Medley (1951) in *Sixth Congress of the Universities of the British Commonwealth: Report of Proceedings*, Association of Universities of the British Commonwealth, p. 11.
7 Sir Walter Moberly (1949) *The Crisis in the University*, SCM Press, pp. 172, 177 and 293-8.
8 Lord Simon of Wythenshawe (1949) 'University crisis? A consumer's view', *Universities Quarterly*, 4, 1.
9 Nuffield College (1948) *The Problems Facing British Universities*, Oxford University Press, pp. 87-9.
10 *ibid.*, pp. 90-1, 95-6 and 100.
11 Lord Simon of Wythenshawe (1958) 'A Royal Commission on the universities?', *Universities Quarterly*, 13, 1; and (1959) symposium in *Universities Quarterly*, 13, 2.
12 *Nature* (1955) 'The purpose of university education', 176, 4485; and (1958) 'The future of universities', 182, 4650.
13 *Twentieth Century* (1956) 159, 948.
14 Eric Ashby (1958) *Technology and the Academics*, Macmillan.
15 C.P. Snow (1959) *The Two Cultures and the Scientific Revolution*, Cambridge University Press.
16 Graeme Moodie (1959) *The Universities: A Royal Commission?*, Fabian Society.
17 *Nature* (1960) 'University education in Britain', 187, 4739, p. 720.
18 Lord Hailsham (1961a) 'Functions of universities', *The Engineer*, 212, 5519, p. 735; and (1961b) New and larger universities?' (opening a Gulbenkian conference), *Universities Quarterly*, 15, 2.
19 *Conference of the Universities of the United Kingdom 1960. Report of Proceedings* (1961), Association of Universities of the British Commonwealth, pp. 44-56 and 84-5.
20 H.C. Dent (1961) *Universities in Transition*, Cohen & West, pp. 5 and 123.
21 Committee on Higher Education (1963) *Evidence — Part Two*, HMSO, (memorandum from P.E. Vernon, 1961; memorandum from Jean Floud, 1962).
22 *ibid., Evidence — Part One A* (memorandum from National Union of Teachers, 1961); *Part One E* (memorandum from Trades Union Council, 1961).
23 *ibid., Evidence — Part One A* (memorandum from Sir Sydney Caine, 1961), p. 138.
24 *ibid., Evidence — Part One E* (memorandum from Ministry of Education, 1962), p. 1905.
25 Sir Charles Morris (1962) 'The function of universities today' in W.R. Niblett (Ed.), *The Expanding University*, Faber & Faber, p. 23.
26 University of London (1970) *The Future of the External System: First Report*, pp. 2-3; Committee on Higher Education (1963) *Higher Education: Report*, HMSO, p. 140.
27 J. Heywood (1969) 'An evaluation of certain post-war developments in higher technological education', MLitt thesis, University of Lancaster, pp. 100-7.

28 UGC, *University Development 1957–62*, p. 154.
29 Sir Richard Livingstone (1948) *Some Thoughts on University Education*, Cambridge University Press, p. 14.
30 John Macmurray in *Sixth Congress of the Universities of the British Commonwealth*, pp. 102–4.
31 M.L. Oliphant and John Adams (1961) quoted in Dent, H.C. *Universities in Transition*, pp. 117–18.
32 C.R. Morris (1952) 'The universities and technology', *Universities Quarterly*, 6, 2, p. 122; Sir Frederick Handley Page (1952) 'The higher technology' *ibid.*, pp. 126–8.
33 Sir John Cockcroft (1952) 'Technology in the universities', *Universities Quarterly*, 6, 3, p. 246.
34 Sir Philip Morris (1954) 'The higher education of scientists and technologists', *Universities Quarterly*, 8, 3, pp. 278–87.
35 *Nature* (1957) 'Education for modern needs', 180, 4596, p. 1150.
36 Eric Ashby (1958) *Technology and the Academics*, pp. 77–8 and passim.
37 A.H. Halsey (1960) 'The changing function of universities in advanced industrial societies', *Harvard Educational Review*, 30, 2, p. 125.

Chapter 2

Launching an Alternative

Pressures, national and international, increased between the Percy Committee's 1945 recommendations and the government's announcement in July 1955 that it intended to establish the NCTA, as it did by the end of the year under the chairmanship of Lord Hives, Chairman of Rolls Royce. In 1950 the National Advisory Council on Education for Industry and Commerce had strongly argued the case for a necessary expansion of technological education and, in terms similar to those of the Percy Committee, recommended that a Royal College of Technologists be created to make appropriate, non-degree awards and guarantee standards in institutions other than the universities. Acceptance of the proposals by the Labour government in 1951 was reversed by the Conservative government elected later that year. In 1952, however, the process of promoting advanced level courses in technology in the colleges began to take shape, with a Ministry of Education decision to raise an existing 60 per cent grant for the provision of such courses in local authority colleges to 75 per cent, and under this impetus advanced course provision gained momentum.[1] From 1955, with the creation of the NCTA, the specific demands for increased higher technological education had outcomes which affected the pattern of 'higher education', and converted hypothetical debate about the potential of the non-university tradition of further education into one about the relationship and roles of the parts of the 'system'. Questions of definition and status now took different forms. Why could the NCTA not award *degrees* for work parallel to that in the universities? Was it, in fact, better for the future of recruitment to technology that the new awards should be specific to technology and different from the existing pattern of undergraduate degrees? How did the new awards square with the existence of University of London external degrees in some of the colleges? In what ways would the awards of the NCTA be different from university degrees — in standard, admission requirements, curriculum and methods of teaching? Should the NCTA be empowered to make higher awards, in parallel with university masters' and doctorate degrees? How extensive and rationalized should the NCTA and its related institutions be? Answers to at least some of these and contigent questions began to be found quickly once the NCTA was in place, and in the framework of a government White Paper on *Technical Education* in 1956.

The NCTA was operational in December 1955. Under its Trust Deed, finally approved a year later, it was 'to create and administer awards for students in technical colleges'. To accomplish this the Minister had constituted for the Council a Governing Body, a Board of Studies in Engineering and a Board of Studies in Technologies other than Engineering. After a decade of confused discussion about what it was possible and appropriate for the universities to do in this field, and the desirability and feasibility of enhancing the roles of the colleges, this Trust Deed was to be a kind of foundation document for an alternative system. It was not, however, to point a clear, unilinear path through to the CNAA and a binary system of higher education. It nevertheless delineated a set of purposes and procedures that were to act as guidelines for developments outside the universities for more than a quarter of a century. The crucial statement regarded the roles of the NCTA's two boards of studies, which, under the direction of the Governing Body, were to have duties comprising:

the consideration of the following matters and such other matters as the Governing Body may from time to time prescribe:-

(a) the curricula and syllabuses of courses proposed by the technical colleges for the awards and, in particular, the standard of the college work in pure science and in technologies related to the courses for which approval is sought;

(b) the standard of admission to the said courses;

(c) the qualifications of the teachers conducting the said courses;

(d) the accommodation and equipment available for the said courses; and

(e) the principal conditions of the conduct of examinations including the approval of external examiners to act with the teaching staff of the colleges providing the said courses.[2]

Although the NCTA was to have oversight of the new developments in the colleges, these were clearly to be responsible for proposing the content of courses, and it was this pattern of responsibilities that was to mark the process off from the centrally examined structure of the existing University of London external degree. The London external was not concerned with, for example, teachers' qualifications and college facilities. The new arrangements were clearly designed to implement a policy of promoting and monitoring higher institutional as well as course standards in the colleges. When Lord Hives met with the new boards of studies for the first time in December he hoped that their work would stimulate 'public and industrial interest in the work of technical colleges and provide them with a means to develop a fuller and higher standard of education. It may well be that upon your work will depend the whole future of the education given in our technical colleges'.

Hives summarized for the members of the new boards what he considered the essential role of the NCTA. It was to provide the 'peak qualification' in engineering and technology for students in technical colleges, on courses 'at what we will call the "undergraduate" level. The standard reached therefore must be that of a first degree of a university'. The colleges were to plan their own courses and arrange for examinations 'in the manner of internal courses of a university'. He underlined how different this was from the London external degree, given the amount of freedom the colleges were to have. Before they could have this freedom a college had to satisfy the NCTA:

(a) that the course for which recognition is sought is suitable;

(b) that it can be operated under satisfactory conditions as regards staff, accommodation and student amenities;

(c) that the examinations are appropriately and properly conducted.

An NCTA board was to be 'not an examining body, but a "recognizing" body'.[3] With that Trust Deed and such emphases the history of a system of higher education parallel to that of the universities was beginning to be written.

The new 'undergraduate' award was to be a Diploma in Technology (DipTech). Sir Harold Roxbee Cox, who became Chairman of the NCTA in 1960 and then the first Chairman of the CNAA (as Lord Kings Norton from 1965), recalled that 'most of us' in the NCTA had originally wanted to call the award 'Bachelor of Technology, or similar titles':

> We were told, however, by very high authorities that, whilst possibly the title doctor was not the exclusive property of the universities, bachelor and master were. Rather than engage in a long argument, we thought up a new name.[4]

There was, indeed, a good deal of internal dissent about the name of both the award and the organization itself. The first meeting of the Governing Body postponed decisions on the word 'Diploma' and drew attention to the confusion that could be caused by the word 'Awards' in the title.[5] Lord Hives told the boards of studies that the term DipTech was 'horrible'.[6] The pros and cons of the Diploma title, particularly as the award established itself with the employers, continued to be rehearsed throughout the life of the NCTA, and in a summary of the position for the Governing Body when it was preparing its evidence to the Robbins Committee in 1961, Frank Hornby, the Chief Officer, wrote:

> It may be the balance of opinion of members of the Governing Body that it is desirable for means to be sought to change the title of Dip. Tech. to B.Tech.: the Secretary's opinion after five years close contact with people from all fields concerned with the award is that this replacement might well be a set-back rather than a step forward.[7]

What was established from 1955 was that the combination of technology and local authority colleges was a viable alternative to university undergraduate courses, but different — one of the key differences being the integration of the college course with industrial experience — the sandwich course.

The DipTech scheme had been established on the advice of the National Advisory Council on Education for Industry and Commerce (NACEIC), which had stipulated in what became in fact a draft of the Trust Deed that the awards should be available in respect of courses solely in those colleges approved by the Council.[8] By the time the White Paper on *Technical Education* was issued in 1956 twenty-four colleges were receiving the 75 per cent grant introduced in 1952 for advanced work. There were also part-time advanced courses in 150 or so local colleges, and other advanced courses were likely to emerge. The intention was to promote the development in England and Wales of Colleges of Advanced Technology (CATs), and to improve Scotland's existing Central Institutions (CI).[9] It rapidly became clear that although the NCTA was to continue to make the DipTech available for courses in colleges which satisfied the conditions, only a small number were to be designated as colleges of advanced technology in terms of the White Paper. They were to be those engaged exclusively in work at advanced level, whether in full-time, part-time or 'sandwich' courses. Following ministerial speeches and reports in the press in April and May, Lord Hives began to receive anxious letters from members of the boards of studies and others regarding the restrictive effect of what now appeared to be the proposed designation of 'about eight' CATs.[10] The DipTech did, however, have wider currency than the designation of the CATs — of which there were, in fact, ten — seemed to imply. Between September 1956, when the Council first began to consider courses, and the spring of 1960 100 courses had been recognized at twenty-three colleges.[11] A large number of technical colleges and their supporters, however, had been disappointed by the disjunction between the total of twenty-four institutions named in the White Paper and the final limitation of college of advanced technology status to ten.

The Council rapidly established its criteria and procedures. Courses were to be on the sandwich principle, with alternating periods in college and industry. They were to cover, as the first report emphasized, 'liberal studies and informal activities' also, though initially the Council had been prepared to accept a statement of intention on the part of a college to develop 'a liberal approach to the curriculum'. The industrial training was to be integrated with the course as a whole. The Council was prepared to accept inadequate facilities if building and other plans were intended to remedy deficiencies by the time renewal of recognition was sought after five years. At a press conference to present the report, Lord Hives commented that technical colleges had been regarded as 'second strings', and even leading colleges had buildings, staffing and equipment inferior to the universities. The government had made it clear that the intention now was that the major colleges should 'stand alongside the universities as fully effective partners'.[12] Procedures for initial application and then renewal were spelled out in detail. The Council was faced, in fact, with a wide range of deficiencies which led to reservations about approval, conditions to be met on renewal, or rejection of applications. The Governing Body received detailed reports from the visiting parties which went to the colleges to consider course applications. Some reports read in the style: 'The accommodation and staff for the course are satisfactory'.[13] Others indicated the opposite. A detailed report on a visit to Rugby College of Technology, for example, in 1956 was highly critical of a proposed course in engineering, and additionally the library facilities, facilities for private study and project work, and laboratory provision for mechanical engineering were all poor. Other laboratories, workshops and equipment were mediocre, staff common rooms and work rooms were of average standard, and there was no accommodation for special amenities — which were awaiting new buildings. The course was not recognized.[14] Some of the CATs had a struggle to get recognition for courses, and some failed to secure it first time round. At its meeting in January 1958 the Governing Body considered sending a confidential report to the Minister of Education describing the 'deficiencies in accommodation, equipment and staff' which had led to so many courses being rejected, but decided in the event to leave it to the Chairman to send a personal letter.[15] If a new 'sector' of higher education was emerging it was with considerable difficulties, and legacies of second-class status that it was going to be extremely difficult to overcome.

Although it was for the colleges to propose the courses, the NCTA established what its expectations were — not only in terms of facilities and staffing. It had views about the shape of courses appropriate to the mission which it had been set. The detail varied according to the discipline but there were prominent common elements, notably three that the Council declared formally that it wished to encourage — the sandwich structure, projects and liberal studies. The colleges' freedoms were to be earned within a variety of expectations, guidelines and directives.

The Council and its leading spokesmen brought the sandwich structure to the centre of their conception of an education that was both academic and practical, and in some respects it was the Council's most characteristic achievement. Lord Hives, at least at first, thought privately that sandwich courses 'had been running in this country for forty years and if they really possessed all the merits that are now being claimed for them it seems to me that this would have become apparent long ago'.[16] In public however the NCTA and its senior representatives strongly endorsed the principle of alternating and relating college and industrial experience — a process which had indeed a history — albeit a limited one — in Scotland and England.[17] Industrial training — 'an aggregate of at least one year of industrial training in addition to the academic study' — became a requirement, and the Council emphasized that 'it is also of fundamental importance that the academic study and industrial training should be as closely related to each other as is practicable so that the two together provide an integrated course of study and training'.[18] Exactly how this was to be achieved exercised both the colleges and the Council. Sir Walter Puckey, who chaired the Board of Studies in Engineering, played a prominent part in debates about the nature and structures of sandwich courses, publishing an address in 1957 which asked a range of questions about the balance of theory and practice and other aspects of such courses. In 1962 he launched a major discussion with a letter to the Governing Body suggesting the need for research into the structure of courses and the nature of integration of industrial training and academic study.[19] A variety of different sandwich structures had evolved — mainly variations on 'thin' (alternating period of six months in college and six months in industry) and 'thick' (normally the third year in industry) arrangements for the four-year course. The search for integration, or even for coordination — was, as the Governing Body realized, a difficult one. They had before them in 1960 a copy of an article in *Technology* which emphasized that the sights for the DipTech had been set high:

> Most American cooperative programmes offer no more than industrial experience. The DipTech is supposed to provide not merely industrial training, but industrial training integrated with the technical instruction given in the colleges. Few people yet realize what an extraordinarily ambitious plan this is. American professors with years of experience of cooperative work will stand silent with admiration — or disbelief — on hearing it explained.[20]

Applying the requirement more strictly, as the Council determined to do in 1960, meant having a clearer idea of what precisely was meant by integration, and asking the colleges for 'more detail than heretofore' did not solve the problem.[21] Puckey's 1962 letter touched off two lengthy debates on the Governing Body, resulting in an enquiry into what relevant research was being conducted by the colleges on 'educational aspects of the courses leading to the Diploma in Technology'. At a third meeting this information, from ten colleges in England and Wales, was presented. Only two of the responses related to the sandwich nature of the courses: John Heywood at Birmingham CAT was researching the experience of sandwich courses with a view to recommending improvements, and Marie Jahoda at Brunel College was researching 'sandwich courses and students' attitudes to work'.[22] In spite of this continuing concern, there were underlying problems and weaknesses. In 1964, just before the NCTA ceased to exist, the Industrial Training Panel reported on the training of engineering students and concluded:

> The purpose of industrial training as an integral part of the courses leading to the Diploma in Technology is far from clear in the minds of either college or industrial staff. This is not surprising in view of the uncertainty which has existed within the Council. In many cases the main part of the training is something of a ritual based on modified craft training concepts.[23]

Nevertheless, the Council believed that the sandwich course it had promoted both in engineering and in other technologies, including subjects such as applied chemistry and applied physics, had pioneered a major new departure in British higher education. The Governing Body told the Robbins Committee in 1961 that although its limited experience had not made it possible to 'fully explore' the merits of the integrated sandwich system, it was confident 'that this type of course is already playing an important part in higher technological education and that it will become of increasing importance in the future'.[24]

Participation by students in a 'substantial project' was also an NCTA requirement. In its annual report in 1960 the Council spelled out in detail the variety of ways in which projects might fit into courses, and the roles of projects both in providing an extended experience of experimental work and reporting, and in bridging college work and the industrial period or periods, out of which many ideas for projects originated. The Council underlined to the Robbins Committee how the process of developing ideas for a project, and conducting the enquiry and being examined on a final report fitted into the whole sandwich philosophy.[25] The Council interpreted its mission from the outset as one of preparing engineers and other technologists with a grounding in industrial practice, and capable of applying their knowledge in order, as Sir Walter Puckey put it, 'to execute things well . . . the courses should produce men who have a sound appreciation of technical principles and yet have the ability to apply those principles to a better degree than, generally speaking, has been so far'.[26] The sandwich course and the project were directed towards that end.

The third, and more controversial, major direction taken by the NCTA, was its requirement for a component of liberal studies. Underlying the policy adopted was the feeling, often explicit, sometimes disputed, that courses of study in technology and science, particularly in the colleges, had been narrow and illiberal — a criticism which in the prevailing climate of opinion was also sometimes levelled against university courses. University departments and the universities themselves were often addressing questions of course and student narrowness, introducing interdisciplinary seminars or university-wide courses of voluntary lectures, new course formats or teaching approaches. These were, however, marginal and sporadic, and mainly in the 1960s. The main thrust of attempts to translate debate about the 'cultures' into curricula was in 'technical education'.[27] The public attention given to the place of the technologies in a 'liberal education' had its maximum policy impact precisely at the time at which the NCTA was formulating and beginning to implement its own policies. An influential book on *Liberal Education in a Technical Age* was published in 1955 by a committee under auspices including the National Institute of Adult Education, and it argued for the extension of technical studies into areas of social, historical and ethical study. The 1956 White Paper on *Technical Education* argued for a broader, liberal approach to technical courses. Ministry of Education Circular 323, *Liberal Education in Technical Colleges*, continued the call for a broader treatment of technical and scientific subjects, including by the addition of suitable subjects — a policy which in the event proved an easier option than altering teaching approaches to technical subjects. Although the target of these policy declarations was mainly technical education at a lower level, the NCTA rode the policy tide. 'Liberal' or 'general' studies were to be a required part of courses submitted for DipTech recognition. The requirement, as the colleges themselves were to discover, was open not only to an enormous range of curricular interpretations, but also to widely different responses by staff and students.

The commitment to liberal studies was clear from the outset, though with some of the confusion that the concept almost inevitably provoked. At the end of the first year the Council's report talked not only of 'liberal studies' but also of 'a liberal approach to the curriculum', and at the press conference Lord Hives talked of introducing 'a more liberal atmosphere into the education'.[28] In January 1957 the Governing Body's Executive Committee emphasized that 'Liberal Studies must occupy a prominent place in the syllabus of any course leading to the Diploma in Technology', though the colleges needed to be given room for flexibility and experiment. It asked for the Joint Steering Committee of the two boards of studies to prepare a paper for consideration. The Joint Steering Committee met at the end of the month and discussed the liberal studies requirements in detail. These were to occupy some 10 per cent of the total course time, and could take a variety of forms (examples given included human relations, communication, industrial history, music, art and a foreign language). The aim was to enable students to express themselves clearly and take their place in the community. Technological and scientific subjects could be broadened, and the potential of libraries, seminars, directed study, project assignments, overseas contacts and residential facilities could be explored. The statement containing these recommendations was approved by the Governing Body in February with only one alteration. The boards of studies had considered written examinations to be not necessarily suitable, but tests needed to be devised 'to ensure that students have made satisfactory progress in this section of the course'. The Governing Body amended this to read that the tests should ensure 'that students give adequate attention to this aspect of the courses'.[29] The question of compulsory liberal studies and students' 'progress' or 'adequate attention' was to raise considerable controversy and problems in the colleges, most of all where the subjects offered were what the CNAA was later to call 'contrasting' rather than 'complementary'. The NCTA had in many cases to negotiate on the interpretation of its guidelines by the colleges. As early as November 1956 it was questioning whether Battersea College of Technology was making adequate provision, and after some dialogue accepted Battersea's version of two-and-a-half hours per week of 'perimeter studies'.[30] In the same month, Anthony (later Sir Anthony) Part, Head of the Further Education Branch at the Ministry of Education, and assessor on the NCTA Governing Body, was lecturing in Newcastle. His theme was 'liberal education in technical colleges', and he summarized both the difficulties and the direction. He disagreed that there were 'liberal subjects and illiberal subjects and that technology is one of the latter'. His emphasis was on liberal or illiberal teaching, and:

> let me now freely admit that I believe a lot of the teaching in technical colleges today cannot be described as liberal in the sense in which I am using it in this talk, except from the important point of view that it is providing the students that technical competence which I have suggested to be essential to self-respect. Some of it, indeed, can fairly be described as instruction rather than education.

Referring to the DipTech he then underlined:

> It is not often that an opportunity occurs for real pioneering in education. The advanced sandwich course, I believe, offers one. And it includes potentially all the necessary ingredients for a liberal education.[31]

The NCTA itself considered that it was providing a framework within which the broad and competent technologist could be educated, and within that framework 'many interesting and encouraging experiments' were taking place in the colleges.[32]

In establishing all of these basic parameters for the DipTech the NCTA was postulating a future for the colleges under its tutelage. They were to have freedoms and responsibilities; they and their controlling local authorities needed to be guided, cajoled and helped to improve the quality of their environments and their curricular delivery. The Council was delivering messages to the Ministry, the professions, the colleges and the public about the needs, possibilities and deficiencies.[33] The Council was therefore, in developing a new direction for the colleges, shaping uncharted roles for itself in interpreting and implementing its foundation document. It was self-consciously distancing itself from the London external degree pattern, which had served a vital function from 1858 in enabling individual students to gain access to higher qualifications, but which could not now serve the purpose of developing the colleges and broadening the availability of advanced courses in technology. Many of those involved with the NCTA understood that it was replacing an external system which was now an obstacle to progress for the colleges. Sir Anthony Part's reflection was that one motive for creating the NCTA was dissatisfaction with the London system, which gave little scope for the colleges and did not encourage them to mature. His Further Education Branch at the Ministry told the NCTA at the start that the London external degree:

> not only suffers from the rigid nature of its external control, but is limited to students who have matriculated; it is also limited in the scope of the subjects provided. It was therefore considered to be unsuitable as a permanent qualification for the major colleges whose functions more and more are bound to be complementary to the universities.[34]

The colleges themselves, of course, were aware of the opportunities that had been opened up, were eager for NCTA recognition of their courses, and ultimately for the new status that their selection for the limited concentration of completely advanced level work implied. The search for an appropriate status and image involved more than the financial support needed for appropriate facilities and staffing, and more than NCTA approval for DipTech proposals. It involved, for example, consideration of the relative balance of full-time and part-time courses, with a temptation to undervalue the latter in favour of the former:

> ... many of them were effectively saying at the end — well you know, here we are, we're institutions with largely full-time degree work, why can't we be the same as universities?[35]

A second feature of the status issue was the muted but growing interest in the development of 'postgraduate' work and research. The NCTA had a view of research which was directly related to the quality of courses and teaching and it was not normally 'willing to renew the recognition of a course ... unless a proportion of the staff of the department of the college concerned is carrying out research work, consultative work for industry, or the organization of post-diploma courses'. For a department to be effective members of staff needed to be contributing to the advancement of knowledge in their subjects.[36] The reality, however, was continually disappointing, as reports on visits to colleges testified. Nevertheless, as H.C. Dent recognized in 1961, the CATs and the second tier of Regional Colleges, were 'undertaking more and more research. There seems every likelihood that before long they will become as fully committed to it as are the universities, and, like them, will consider its pursuit as essential for the quality and vigour of their teaching and other academic activities'.[37] It was in the direction of filling out the profile of the colleges and providing opportunties for its diplomates that the NCTA began in 1958 to look at the feasibility of establishing an award higher than the diploma.

The Governing Body considered and published proposals for such an award, Membership of the College of Technologists (MCT) in 1958, and the 'College' was established the following year. Membership was to be via 'a programme of work successfully carried out jointly in industry and at a college', requiring industrial experience and academic study for at least three years, and teachers in technical colleges, amongst others, were encouraged by the Council to become candidates.[38] There were mixed reactions to the development. The Minister of Education wrote welcoming the scheme. *The Times Educational Supplement*, in a report discussed by the Governing Body, considered that the Council would be 'better occupied getting the DipTech firmly established'. Staff Inspector French shared this view, reflecting later that it was a hard enough job for the institutions to lift themselves to truly first-degree standards, and anyway, once you reached first degree level it was the PhD that had the 'worldwide accolade'.[39] The college associations disliked the concept of a College of Technologists, which was to make the award, and the colleges themselves would be less identified with the award than was the case with the Diploma of Technology. The response in terms of numbers of candidates was meagre. By 1964 there were 106 registered candidates for Membership, and since the first award in 1962 the total number gaining Membership had been eight.[40]

Across the eight years of the NCTA's operations the strategies adopted by the Council and the directions taken by the colleges in association with it in fact raised questions about the degree of autonomy beginning to be enjoyed by them, or likely to become available to them. The NCTA, by the time it considered its evidence to the Robbins Committee, had no unanimous view about the future of the CATs, and indeed there was difference of opinion about whether they should be discussing the colleges at all. Sir Walter Puckey held out for the view that the NCTA was concerned with the future of the DipTech only, and that the NCTA's attention should not be directed towards the future of the colleges, which varied considerably in the rate at which they might attain autonomy. Some of the colleges with which the Council was dealing 'might, in fact, never reach a suitable stage of development'. Lionel (later Sir Lionel) Russell and Dr (later Sir) Peter Venables disagreed: the NCTA and the Robbins Committee shared an interest in the future of the colleges, and the DipTech and the colleges could not be discussed in isolation from each other. Parallels and differences were drawn with the universities, old and new, and the main point of agreement on the Governing Body was that some form of coordinating body for higher technological education would continue to be necessary.[41]

Behind this debate lay previous attempts to clarify the NCTA's and government policy towards the CATs. Frank Hornby, as Secretary of the NCTA, had in May 1960 written a 'personal and confidential letter' to Antony

Part at the Ministry, beginning by mentioning that 'from time to time we have had odd snatches of conversation about the possibility of CATs granting their own awards'. Peter Venables had recently commented on this at an awards ceremony at his Birmingham college, and Hornby had 'a growing feeling of uneasiness'. Was this the right time to air the matter publicly? The Council's standards had not been unduly rigorous but a number of the CATs had nevertheless 'had difficulty in reaching those standards even after considerable assistance and sympathy from the Council and others'. The number of diplomates was still small (168). Colleges had taken little advantage of the Council's policy to allow experiment. The letter indicates very clearly the position in the colleges that was being reflected in these 'conversations':

> Sometimes I have gained the impression that the college's sole objective is to gain the Council's recognition of a course with the minimum amount of effort and original thought; it is in these cases that the Council's control has been regarded as irksome because they are not content with anything slip-shod . . . where the standards are high college staff do not find that the Council have in any way inhibited academic freedom . . . courses have been recognised at some CATs only as recently as the middle of last year and even then on a good deal of promise rather than achievement, and yet there is agitation for colleges to have an early decision about their own award.

Part's response was to invite Hornby for a discussion (and they did indeed meet a few days later). Part's letter contained his own interpretation of the present position:

> . . . even if the issue were to become a live one, there would be no question either in our minds or those of the Principals of the CATs of any sudden transition. What the Principals are, I believe, after is that it should be agreed in principle that one day, when each CAT has developed sufficiently, it should be able to grant its own awards.[42]

The Governing Body's recommendation to the Robbins Committee was in fact to build on the academic freedom that the colleges of advanced technology had been given, and to allow the existing CATs and any further ones so designated in the future ultimately to grant their own awards. It urged that the higher technological education provided in the colleges *and by the universities* 'should be coordinated by a national body established for the purpose'.[43] There was no eagerness on the part of the National Council to press for the colleges to obtain university status, and whatever the 'agitation' in the colleges may have been, the concern of the Governing Body and its boards was to ensure that the momentum of higher technological education should be sustained and enhanced. In the internal discussions within the Ministry and the Inspectorate there were differing views, with some favouring the NCTA concern maintaining the momentum of recent years, while others felt that traditional university status was the best solution, a view which eventually won the day.[44]

Confused though much of the discussion of 'autonomy', 'academic freedom' and the right to grant 'awards' was, by the time the Robbins Committee came to consider its evidence and proposals between 1961 and 1963 images of the future were being made available based on the expectations and aspirations generated by the NCTA and its relationships with the colleges. Such images, projected by the NCTA and the CATs, were influenced by the degree of recognition they had secured in the early 1960s. For a variety of specific and general purposes the Governing Body of the NCTA worked to obtain formal recognition of the DipTech and was anxious to publicize the recognition it was given. In 1961 the annual report summarized various kinds of recognition. The Burnham Technical Committee had from the outset recognized a holder of the Diploma as eligible for the graduate addition to salary; it was accepted by the Scientific Civil Service on the same terms as a university degree; the Committee of Vice-Chancellors and Principals (CVCP) had recommended that holders of the Diploma should be treated on the same terms as university graduates when applying for higher degree courses. The report the following year recorded that the Department of Scientific and Industrial Research had decided that the Honours DipTech should be accepted according to the same rules as university honours degrees. CVCP recognition, in 1958, had emphasized that holders of the Diploma 'should be able to undertake their advanced work either in technical colleges or in universities, according to the nature of the opportunities available and the interest and ability of the students concerned'.[45] Recognition by employers was inevitably variable, and there were often difficulties in finding enough places for students to have their industrial experience. One form of the sandwich course arrangement was for students to be 'industry-based' rather than 'college-based', but as total numbers of students increased the proportion on industry-based arrangements gradually declined. In March 1964 the percentage of industry-based engineering students had fallen to 67 per cent from 83 per cent in 1961, and those in technologies other than engineering had fallen from 47 per cent to 25 per cent.[46] In the case of the professional bodies, the NCTA met with ready acceptance from all except the Institution of Mechanical Engineers, which insisted that in the early stages the Institution had to lay down conditions in order to satisfy itself of the colleges' standards. It began by laying down ten conditions under which it would accept a DipTech in Mechanical Engineering for exemption from the Institution's own examinations, though by 1959 it had reduced these to two. In an exchange of views with a deputation from the NCTA (which suggested that the conditions amounted to a lack of confidence in the Council's ability to maintain its proclaimed standards), it proposed to drop the conditions in two years or so.[47] There were no such problems with the other engineering institutions, or with other bodies.

The success of the NCTA in establishing itself depended in large measure on the relationship between education and industry as anticipated in the composition of the Governing Body and the two boards of studies (and others who took part in panels), and on the commitment of those involved. The first Governing Body contained industrialists, well known figures in the field of science and technology education, CAT principals and one leading Chief Education Officer, Lionel Russell, CEO for Birmingham; a total of twelve people. Between them the two boards contained more than fifty people, including other college principals and staff, university and industrial researchers, and people from a range of public and private industrial enterprises. For particular purposes, such as the Industrial Training Panel, members were also drawn from a wider range of industrial and other organizations. Many of those involved in these committees and in the subject panels that were established were later to play similar roles in the CNAA, and this was to be particularly important in the case of university members, whose presence was an important public indicator of the seriousness with which the NCTA approached the question of academic standards. This was true also of the external examiners approved by the Council: in 1961–62 the five approved in electrical and mechanical engineering included two university professors and a reader, a professor from Heriot Watt College, Edinburgh, and the head of a CAT department of civil and mechanical engineering. A tradition was begun in the NCTA and continued into the CNAA of appointing as Chairmen leading figures in industry and the public services. The two Chairmen of the NCTA, Lord Hives and Sir Harold Roxbee Cox, were Chairmen of Rolls Royce and Metal Box respectively. With this balance of membership the Council gained not only the degree of credibility it needed to carry out its roles, but also the commitment of a range of people from diverse and relevant backgrounds. At the first meeting of the Governing Body Lord Hives told the Minister of Education, there to welcome the members, that 'he and the members of the Council had taken on their task with enthusiasm'.[48]

The Governing Body's small Executive Committee, under the chairmanship of Sir Harold Roxbee Cox as Vice-Chairman of the Governing Body, was given the responsibility of appointing a Secretary. The person appointed, Frank Hornby, was a former science teacher and Assistant Education Officer for Nottingham. As Secretary to the Governing Body Hornby defined a role for himself, suggesting policy, relating to the Ministry and its assessors on the Council, working closely with the Chairman and running the small new organization. Chosen from a considerable number of applicants, Hornby was, in the view of Lord Kings Norton (Roxbee Cox) 'brilliant' and an 'undoubted success'.[49] He was committed to establishing the NCTA and its awards as rapidly as possible, and the public recognition of the DipTech owed a great deal to Hornby's dedication throughout the life of the Council — and he was to carry the same commitment through into the first eight years of the CNAA.

Enthusiastic though the participants in the Council's work may have been, they were operating in the climate of opinion that was at best ambivalent about the development of technology. Lord Hives could talk of the DipTech as a means of 'raising the standards generally in the technical college world and infusing a new spirit into it',[50] but the process of elevating the new sector required more than the enthusiasm of the participants. *Education*, in June 1956, talked of technical education as being 'now fashionable. It is riding on a tide of opinion, constantly aided by one big technocrat's speech after another. Figures from Russia and the USA reinforce the call for more'.[51] Technical education was perhaps 'fashionable' in the sense that a White Paper appeared, the NCTA had been created, the process was expansive, demand for more was being strongly expressed, and the dangers of foreign competition (to reach a peak in 1957 with the launch of the Soviet sputnik) were being underlined. But it had taken a decade from the Percy Committee to produce the NCTA, and 'fashion' did not necessarily mean national commitment. Fashion for some meant fad. Growth in the 1950s in the technical college sector was from a starting point of profoundly low esteem. Criticism of the universities' record and attitudes indicated boundaries beyond which the fashion did not reach. The feelings of some of the leaders in the industry are revealed with great clarity in an exchange of correspondence between Sir Roy Fedden, a leading aeronautical engineer, adviser to British government departments and NATO, and at this time Aircraft Consultant to the Dowty Group, and Lord Hives, in late 1956 and 1957. Fedden was distressed at the state of education for engineering in general and for the aircraft industry in particular. He was particularly unhappy at the failure of the grammar and public schools to take the need for high quality scientists and engineers seriously. In late 1956 he drafted memoranda addressed to the schools, to parents and to industry, asking basically what was 'the best way to get a fair share of our grammar and public school boys for the great task of British engineering?'.

The traditional hierarchy of British education, Fedden pointed out in the draft he sent to Hives, had been left 'entirely cold' by the first industrial revolution, even while glad enough to benefit from its results:

> Grudgingly, however, it was brought home to the powers that be that Engineering was a great calling that had to be reckoned with, but it never thought of giving it the esteem of other professions such as, for example, medicine or the law. There are many people in this country even today who cannot see their way to do this, and unfortunately most of them move in very influential circles . . . no other great nation is handicapped in this way . . . our present culture is basically antipathetic to engineering and science.

This theme and variations on it pervade the twenty-four pages of Fedden's document. He met with Hives for a discussion, and in notes for the meeting he again emphasized the difficulty of attracting 'bright public school boys' on to schemes such as the NCTA sandwich courses (which he misleadingly referred to as 'Hives' National Diploma'), and the importance of establishing the award at the right level. He wondered 'if the Ministry of Education is working on really sound lines in this respect'. After the meeting, he wrote:

> Although it is popular for the top level people in our great schools and universities to publicly state and give lip service to the view that they are in favour of diverting a fair proportion of their top level boys to applied science or, in our language, honest-to-God mechanical engineers, in their hearts they do not feel this way at all, but I think they are better than they used to be about it, and we have just to keep hammering away at them all the time.

Hives wrote to Fedden in 1957 — after some six years of Conservative government — saying that the essential thing lacking was leadership, 'and I see no signs of it, in the administration of today'. Lack of leadership was 'the cause of our national problem'. Policies were suffering from 'mediocre administration'. Hives was commenting on a book Fedden had written on air power, and in his response Fedden expressed even more strongly the anger and frustration of the technologist:

> . . . the trouble in the air is only symptomatic of the poor leadership we are suffering from in this country on most governmental matters . . . our basic culture, classical education, and inordinate belief in tradition has to bear a good deal of the blame . . . unless we are prepared to face up to the fact that what has suited Britain well in the past will not make her 'tick' in the technological age, we are lost . . .

And then the real indication of the strength of feeling:

> In 1933, when Baldwin was Prime Minister, and we were in about as bad a position as we are today, a small band of forthright men in Britain formed themselves into a thing called the OTHER CLUB. There were about two dozen of them and they met every month for dinner. They did their best to support Churchill, see him through when he was 'in the wilderness', and make some preparation for the coming war. It may be a forlorn hope, but my suggestion is that something of a similar nature might be set up by some independent people not connected with the aircraft industry or the government who would be prepared to show leadership and not pull their punches.[52]

The picture of higher education and education in general, of policy for technology and technical education, has to have in perspective the meanings of the fashionable and the public statement, leadership and lip service, tradition and failure, national policy and national problem.

If the NCTA was one element in the struggle to place education for a technological age more squarely on agendas for action, so also were the universities. Post-war statistics of the university output of graduates in science and technology make it difficult to be precise about the proportion in technology, and the kind of technology (whether, in the words of the 1956 White Paper, they were of a 'general nature', or 'more closely linked with the careers available in the region'[53]). The number of students in science and technology increased from 13,000 in 1938-39 to 27,000 in 1952-53. The number actually graduating in 1956 was just over 6000, of whom 4200 were in pure science ('many' of whom, indicated the White Paper, ultimately enter industry), and about 1850 were in technology. Lord Hives's comment in 1957 was that the technical colleges were producing about 20 per cent of the supply of scientists, but 70 per cent of the supply of technologists. Plans for expansion did not yet make it clear what the university expansion was going to be, but the colleges were to increase their annual output of technologists from 5000 to 9000. The White Paper began its section on the role of the universities: 'The training of technologists is shared between the universities and the technical colleges. Each has its own distinctive contribution to make to the development of technological education, and the aim is to expand facilties for both'. Five years later the Scientific Manpower Committee was reporting that within the projected university total of scientists and technologists there was still likely to be a shortage of the latter, and in 1963 the Committee continued to underline that there would remain 'a relative shortage of technologists and there are likely to be major shortages in particular disciplines'.[54]

The role and impact of the NCTA have to be seen, therefore, in these wider contexts of conflicts of values, national policies and disappointments, and the calculation of the respective roles of the universities and the new 'sector' — as well as in terms of college development and student numbers. With regard to the last of these, the Council was, by 1963-64, registering over 3000 new students a year, had approaching 9000 students attending 122 courses leading to the Diploma, and had conferred over 3000 Diplomas since its first conferments in 1958.[55] It had sought to establish rigorous but flexible frameworks in which the colleges could develop, and it had brought direct pressure to bear on government and local authorities to improve the facilities and environments of the colleges. It had paid particular attention to the quality and problems of staffing. It had placed the sandwich course and its implications at the centre of its concerns. Reflecting on that experience in 1969, Lord Kings Norton, by then Chairman of the CNAA, talked of the DipTech as having achieved 'a succès d'estime'. The sandwich arrangement was 'not a new invention, but previous examples had gained no more than occasional and generally ephemeral local fame'. He concluded that 'the manifest success of the sandwich courses in the applied sciences under the NCTA had major consequences'[56] — some of which will emerge in discussion of the work of the CNAA, including in new subject areas. The NCTA, he later reflected, was 'an experiment'.[57]

The experiment was not, of course, without its difficulties and weaknesses. The DipTech as equivalent to a degree but not a degree was a source of at least ambivalence or considerable irritation. The reason for its not being a degree had to do with a variety of factors, including university opposition,[58] conservatism, caution, and a positive belief in a new award for a new type of programme. Kings Norton's analysis of the position in the mid-1950s remains a highly pertinent one:

> It would be shutting one's eyes to truth not to admit that, in common esteem, the universities were the high road and the colleges the low. But in 1956 a process started which, under the guidance of thoughtful people, many of whom will be anonymous in history, in and under governments of different complexions, has developed into a major educational change.[59]

How major the educational change was will be for further discussion, including the concept of high roads and low roads. The NCTA certainly began the important process of involving substantial numbers of people from industry and the professions, the universities, local authorities and other areas of public life (anonymously in history) in the procedures it adopted for establishing, maintaining and being publicly accountable for the standards of its awards. It launched the process, with virtues and difficulties that were to continue beyond its own lifetime, of detailed and closely scrutinized proposals for new courses and the renewal of courses — a process that was intended to be one of evaluation and self-evaluation. How far this process produced real changes in curricula and teaching methods, as represented in documentation and as experienced in practice, is open to the doubts we have previously heard expressed by Frank Hornby.[60] What is certain, as Kings Norton put it, is that 'a process has started'.

By the time the Robbins Committee was receiving evidence and producing its report, the question of the future of the colleges of advanced technology and other institutions had become prominent — not only under pressure from within the colleges themselves, and reflected more widely than in the conflicting views expressed on the Governing Body of the NCTA. The situation was one of a continuing expectation of the expansion of higher education, expectations which went far beyond the ambit of the Robbins Committee itself. New universities were already being created at the beginning of the 1960s. The Labour Party's study group on higher education, the Taylor Committee, reported before Robbins and recommended that 'higher education' should become synonymous with 'universities', and that the colleges of advanced technology, the teacher training colleges and certain specialized national colleges should all become universities.[61] The month before the Robbins Report appeared Michael (later Lord) Young was arguing the case in *The Observer* for a 'national university to provide for those currently without access to higher education, and bringing in the existing technical colleges, the BBC and ITV and other adult education bodies, including university extra-mural boards'. The same month, Harold Wilson made a speech in Glasgow outlining the possible development of a 'University of the Air', and the government set up an advisory committee under the chairmanship of Jennie Lee to consider the proposal. Its report appeared as a White Paper, entitled *A University of the Air* in February 1966, and the Open University (OU) was to follow. Curriculum changes were taking place — not only in the new programmes of the new universities and the CATs, but also in the established universities. The Ministry of Education proposed to the Robbins Committee that the new developments should take account of wider ranges of subjects and new student clienteles.[62]

The central proposals of the Robbins Committee, so far as this discussion is concerned, were those which related to the colleges in the comprehensive higher education picture that the committee envisaged. There was to be a new role for the CATs as technological universities, conferring their own degrees, and:

> in other colleges a new system for degrees should be established, covering business studies, languages and other subjects as well as science and technology. We consider that among what are now Regional Colleges there will be found scope for some further elevation of institutions to the status of universities. These and our other recommendations . . . should together give new impetus to the development of vocational higher education in Great Britain, and in particular, should remedy weaknesses in the nature and organization of technological education and research.[63]

The proposals, including for a Council for National Academic Awards to replace the NCTA and to cover 'areas of study outside the field of science and technology',[64] was welcomed by the NCTA and in the CATs, caused feelings from anxiety to dismay in the colleges left outside the remit and the recommendations of the committee, and opened up a continuing debate about the shape of the 'higher education' that was now being defined and moulded. Pratt and Burgess suggest that in 1956 no-one thought of the CATs as becoming universities, 'yet by 1962 this transformation was largely thought to be inevitable, and it was complete by 1966'.[65] Crosland and the Labour government did not accept the Robbins view that the elevation of the CATs would be the beginning of a continuous process of expanding a 'unitary' system of higher education by constantly absorbing colleges as they grew in maturity and status. In the event, what Crosland and his advisers preferred was to formalize into a discrete sector what had been taking shape since the 1956 White Paper, but from which the CATs had escaped. The 'binary' system that emerged was one of the logical outcomes of the 'public sector' that the White Paper had begun to construct out of 'technical' or 'further' education traditions. Crosland chose, rather than created, the binary system.

Robbins reported in October 1963, and by the beginning of the following month the government was moving quickly to establish the Council for National Academic Awards, which had been central to the Robbins expansionist plans, and which the government had endorsed in its statement on the Robbins Report on 24 October. The CNAA was to award degrees, and it would widen the range of subjects available under its auspices beyond science and technology. In a Ministry of Education memorandum it was underlined that there would be greater representation of colleges on the new body, and that haste was necessary because the period 1965–68 would be 'years of crisis' in the increased demand for places in higher education. J.A.R. Pimlott wrote to Hornby on behalf of the Ministry on 4 November indicating that the government had decided to start 'early discussions with the universities and other interests', enclosed a copy of the Ministry's memorandum and asked if the NCTA was in agreement with the proposals and wished to make any comments. The Ministry offered to arrange a discussion with the NCTA, and this consultation began with Frank Hornby and Lionel Russell meeting officers of the Ministry to discuss administrative problems involved in forming the new Council.[66] Early in 1964 the NCTA drew up a memorandum to the new body, outlining existing NCTA procedures, the criteria for judging standards in approving and reapproving courses, and examination arrangements. It drew attention to such matters as the reasons for turning down courses — mainly 'on the grounds of the outlook of the college and/or staff matters' — and the fact that the integration of industrial experience and academic study was 'still only imperfectly understood'.[67] The CNAA was to be different in many ways, but to a very large degree it was to take over principles and practices that the NCTA had pioneered. By 1963 'higher education' had been invented, and the transition from the NCTA to the new Council was a major element in recognizing the concept and putting it into operation.

Notes

1 M.C. Davis (1979) 'The development of the CNAA 1964–1974: A study of a validating agency', PhD thesis, Loughborough University, p. 14.
2 *Declaration of Trust, The National Council for Technological Awards, 22 November, 1956*, section 3 (1).
3 Lord Hives, address to the first meeting of Boards of Studies, 15 December 1955, pp. 2–4, NC Box 52 (LH EdM).
4 Cox to Freshwater, 3 May 1963, NC Box 6, 102 Policy, File 3.
5 Council minute ('Governing Body' was used after the first meeting) 19 December 1955 (Lord Hives told the Minister, Sir David Eccles, at this meeting that 'he disliked the term "Diploma" ').
6 Address to the first meeting of Boards of Studies, p. 6.

7 GBmin, 4 October 1961, memorandum by the Secretary, p. 4. These arguments were analyzed in full in Marie Jahoda (1963) *The Education of Technologists*, Tavistock, pp. 197–202.

8 NACEIC, Proposals for creating awards in technology at technical colleges in England and Wales, NC Box 52 (LH EdM), undated.

9 Minister of Education and Secretary of State for Scotland (1956) *Technical Education*, chapters III and IV.

10 NC Box 52 (LH EdM), various correspondence.

11 NC *Report for the Period April 1959 to March 1960*, p. 4.

12 NC annual reports, and report and statement with GBmin, 4 December 1957.

13 Report of a mathematics subject panel visit to Battersea College of Technology, GBmin, 9 July 1958.

14 Report of a visit to Rugby College of Technology and Arts, GBmin, 15 November 1956.

15 GBmin, 24 January 1958. The Chairman wrote four days later drawing attention to criticisms of staffing and accommodation and concern over the rejection of a high percentage of courses, NC Box 6 (Hives to Geoffrey Lloyd, 28 January 1958).

16 Lord Hives (1956) The White Paper on Technical Education, a commentary, NC Box 52. The document is unsigned and undated, but the internal evidence is clear.

17 Tyrrell Burgess and John Pratt (1970) *Policy and Practice: The Colleges of Advanced Technology*, Allen Lane, p. 85.

18 NC, *Memorandum on Awards Conferred*, 1956, revised 1961, p. 3.

19 Sir Walter Puckey (1957) *What is Meant by Practical Training?*, Institution of Production Engineers; GBmin, 19 March 1962.

20 GBmin, 6 July 1970.

21 NC, *Memorandum on the Industrial Training of Students following Courses Recognised as Leading to the Diploma in Technology* (1960). The Industrial Training Panel, which produced the memorandum, was chaired by Sir Walter Puckey, and the *Technology* article was commenting on this document and its attendant difficulties.

22 GBmin, 18 July 1962.

23 NC (1964) *Report of the Council's Industrial Training Panel on the Training of Engineering Students following Courses Leading to the Diploma in Technology*, p. 3.

24 NC, Evidence given by the Governing Body of the Council to the Committee on Higher Education, 18 October 1961, pp. 8 and 16.

25 NC, *Report for the Period April 1959 to March 1960*, pp. 5–7; Evidence to the Committee on Higher Education, p. 14.

26 NC, minutes of the Joint Steering Committee of the Boards of Studies, 30 January 1957.

27 For a more detailed account of the liberal studies development in technical education see Harold Silver (1988) *Intentions and Outcomes: Vocationalism in Further Education*, Longman, pp. 30–2. For the 1960s approach in higher education see Harold Silver and John Brennan (1988) *A Liberal Vocationalism*, pp. 77–80.

28 NC, *Report for the Period 1959 to 1960*, and Lord Hives, Press conference, with GBmin, 4 December 1957.

29 NC, Report of the Executive Committee 11 January 1957; minutes of the Joint Steering Committee of the Boards of Studies, 30 January 1957. For a report of research on student and staff attitudes to liberal studies see J. Heywood (1969) 'An evaluation of certain post-war developments in higher technological education', MLitt thesis, University of Lancaster, pp. 377 and 389–99.

30 GBmin, 9 July 1958.

31 NC, Box 52 (LH EdM). The speech was given at King's College, Newcastle, on 19 November 1957.
32 NC, Evidence to the Committee on Higher Education, p. 13.
33 For an example of the press interest in the DipTech and the colleges see reports of a speech by Sir Harold Roxbee Cox at Nottingham and District Technical College on 5 March 1957, in which he indicated that no college yet visited came up to appropriate standards of libraries, laboratories, playing fields, halls of residence and so on. The speech was reported extensively in, for example *The Guardian* on 16 March, *Education* on 22 March, *Engineering* on 29 March, and the *Engineering and Boiler House Review* in April.
34 Sir Antony Part, MD interview; Ministry of Education, Facilities for Technical Education in Technical Colleges, January 1956, p. 5, NC Box 52 (LH EdM).
35 Mr H.W. French, MD interview. Mr French was, at the time of the creation of the NCTA, HMI for Further Education, became a Regional Staff Inspector in 1956, Chief Inspector from 1965-72, and Senior Chief Inspector from 1972-74.
36 NC, Evidence to the Committee on Higher Education, p. 11.
37 H.C. Dent (1961) *Universities in Transition*, Cohen & West, p. 121.
38 NC (1958) *An Award Higher than the Diploma in Technology*, pp.4-5.
39 GBmin, 20 November 1958; French, MD interview.
40 GBmin, 18 March 1959, letter from J.E. Richardson, 27 February 1959, on behalf of the Joint Policy Committee of the Association of Principals of Technical Institutions and the Association of Technical Institutions; NC *Report for the Period April 1963 to March 1964*, p. 5.
41 GBmin, 4 October 1961. The minutes contain a detailed account of the views of individual members. Hornby wrote a detailed memorandum for the meeting containing a discussion of autonomy (p. 2).
42 NC, Box 6, 102 Policy file 1, Hornby to Part 11 May 1960; Part to Hornby 13 May 1960.
43 NC, Evidence to the Committee on Higher Education, pp. 20-1.
44 Sir Cyril English, private communication.
45 NC, *Report for the Period April 1960 to March 1961; Report for the Period April 1961 to March 1962*; GBmin 19 May 1958 (copy of letter from CVCP to universities, 1 May 1958, appended).
46 NC, *Report for the Period 1963 to 1964*, p. 7.
47 Record of a meeting held at the Institution of Mechanical Engineers, 20 February 1959, with NC GBmin, 18 March 1959.
48 GBmin, 19 December 1958.
49 Lord Kings Norton, HS interview.
50 Hives, press conference, GBmin, 4 December 1957.
51 *Education*, 'Training in depth', 1 June 1956.
52 NC, Box 52 (LH EdM), Sir Roy Fedden to Lord Hives, 16 November 1956 enclosing the draft (quotations are from the Introductory Note and section I, pp. 1-2); Fedden, 'Points for discussion with Hs, on December 13th (1956)', p. 1; Fedden to Hives, 27 December 1956; Hives to Fedden, 21 August 1957; Fedden to Hives, 27 August 1957.
53 *Technical Education*, p. 13.
    University Development 1957-62, HMSO, pp. 154-6.
55 NC, *Report for the Period 1963 to 1964*, p. 5.
56 CN, Chairman's file 1964-74, Lord Kings Norton, speech at inaugural ceremony of Newcastle Polytechnic, 13 October 1969.
57 Lord Kings Norton, MD interview.
58 Part, MD interview.
59 Lord Kings Norton, speech at Newcastle Polytechnic.
60 For further discussion of this issue see Heywood, *An Evaluation of Certain Post-war Developments*, pp. 143-9.

61 Labour Party (1963) *The Years of Crisis*, March (seven months before the publication of the Robbins Report). For press reactions see Harold Silver (1987) 'From great expectations to bleak house', *Higher Education Quarterly*, 41, 3, p. 208.
62 Committee on Higher Education (1963) *Evidence – Part One F*, HMSO, p. 1891.
63 *ibid., Report*, p. 146.
64 *ibid.*, pp. 142–3.
65 Burgess and Pratt, *Policy and Practice*, pp. 172.
66 GBmin, 21 November 1963 (Pimlott's letter and the Ministry memorandum are attached); GBmin, 9 December 1963.
67 NC, Box 51, Memorandum from the NCTA to the CNAA, February 1964.

Chapter 3

Making the CNAA

Between the Robbins Report and the government's acceptance of its main provisions for the expansion of higher education, and the formal establishment of the CNAA less than a year later, the new organization was negotiated and structured with considerable speed. Since the new body was to award degrees at comparable standards to those of the universities, and was in many ways to operate in parallel with the universities, consultation with the universities was seen to be particularly essential and urgent. A meeting was held on the last day of December 1963, with representatives present from the UGC, the CVCP, the Ministry of Education and the Scottish Education Department (SED), under the chairmanship of Sir John Wolfenden from the UGC. He described the establishment of the CNAA as a matter 'of great urgency'. The meeting discussed the composition of the new Council and its likely functions. Sir Herbert Andrew from the Ministry thought that the NCTA had done more detailed work than the CNAA 'would probably be able to cope with, and the new Council might well have to concentrate on broad policy issues'. The CVCP was anxious about the proposal to have Ministry 'asssessors' at meetings of the Council and its boards, as on the NCTA, but they were assured that the role of the assessors was not to interfere with the autonomy of the body, but to perform a liaison role between the Council and other parts of the educational system. The CVCP 'saw considerable dangers' in the proposal that the CNAA should be able to award higher degrees: 'on both academic and financial grounds it was important to keep within reasonable limits the number of institutions providing courses and facilities for higher degrees'. Additionally, the CVCP saw great pressure being exercised for the award of higher degrees for work done 'in non-academic institutions, which often had extensive research facilities, for example, industrial research laboratories or government research establishments; this would create great difficulties and embarrassment for the universities'. The Ministry and SED representatives demurred, but suggested that higher degrees might be left to the new Council to agree, on condition of a two-thirds vote in their favour. It was agreed that the work on drafting the Charter would begin as soon as possible, and that further consultation with the universities would then take place.[1] When the draft Charter was presented informally to members of the new Council in July 1964, they were reassured by John Pimlott, assessor from the Ministry, that the UGC, and through it the CVCP, had been properly consulted.[2]

The speed with which the Ministry and other bodies involved felt obliged to act had to do particularly with the increasing demand for higher education places. The UGC talked of setting up the Council 'with the least possible delay', so that the colleges concerned could 'make their maximum contribution to the demand for courses of degree level in the years immediately ahead'. At the same time, in November 1963, the Ministry was setting the timetable for the Council to be able to 'make an effective contribution to the "bulge" problem by 1965/66'. There was 'no time to be lost'.[3]

The meeting that took place on 31 December, as other consultations, including with the NCTA, focussed on the memorandum prepared in the Ministry of Education, summarizing the Robbins proposals and outlining a suggested scheme. It proposed a tripartite membership of the Council, which would include university (and CAT) members, those from colleges associated with the Council's awards, and members from industry, commerce and local government. This memorandum began the process that was to result in the charter, and central to the process from the outset was John Pimlott, then an Under-Secretary at the Ministry, and described as 'gentle and serious'.[4] With responsibility for preparing the ground for the CNAA, Pimlott did the drafting, and was present at the 31 December meeting and other meetings where the creation of the CNAA was under discussion. In addition to proposals for the constitution, transfer of NCTA responsibilities and other matters, the memorandum underlined the role of the future boards of studies in ensuring that the Council's awards were 'equivalent in standard to university awards', and that in approving courses they would have to consider all those matters which had, in fact, been at the heart of the NCTA's activities: curriculum; standard of work in the subjects concerned; arrangements for related practical experience as appropriate; admission standards; teachers' qualifications; accommodation and equipment, arrangements for examinations and the appointment of external examiners, and 'the suitability of the College in other relevant respects'.[5] Following these initial consultations, Pimlott more or less single-handedly drafted the charter.

The Royal Charter, as approved and presented to the CNAA by the Secretary of State at its first meeting in September 1964, defined the broad purposes of the CNAA as 'the advancement of knowledge and learning, the diffusion and extension of the arts, sciences and technologies and the promotion of liberal, scientific, technological, professional industrial and commercial education'. In order to achieve these it would have the power 'to confer academic awards and distinctions on persons who have successfully pursued courses of study at education establishments other than universities'. Specific mention was made of the Council's ability, in determining the conditions governing awards, to include 'where appropriate arrangements for training and experience in industry or commerce associated with such courses'. The Council would be able to confer degrees, diplomas, certificates and other academic awards and distinctions; grant degrees to holders of the DipTech or an Associateship of a Central Institution in Scotland; confer research degrees for work carried out in educational or research establishments other than universities; confer degrees on holders of Membership of the College of Technologists; award honorary degrees, and perform all the functions of a body politic. The accompanying Statutes laid down a Council membership of seven persons appointed after consultation with representatives of the universities, seven with teaching experience in establishments of 'further education other than Universities', five from industry or commerce, and two with experience as members or officers of local education authorities, together with three coopted members, chairmen of what began as boards of studies and became committees, and the Chief Officer. The committee responsibilities were defined in roughly the terms outlined by Pimlott in his initial memorandum, and the crucial reference to the standard of the CNAA's awards, echoing (with the substitution of 'comparable' for 'equivalent') the formulation in the memorandum, stipulated that the committees would ensure:

> that the Degrees, Diplomas, Certificates and other academic awards and distinctions granted and conferred by the Council in the subjects assigned to the Board are comparable in standards to awards granted and conferred by Universities.[6]

For two decades the life of the CNAA and its related institutions, their relationships and aspirations, the resolution of problems and failure to take particular directions, were governed to a considerable extent by reference to and interpretation of the content of the Charter and Statutes.

The first membership of the Council was announced in the House of Commons in July. It included Michael Clapham, Director of ICI, who was later to succeed Lord Kings Norton as Chairman; Dr Helen (soon to be Professor and Dame Helen) Gardner, from the University of Oxford; Dr Kathleen (also soon to be Dame Kathleen) Ollerenshaw, Manchester City Councillor; Sir Lionel Russell, Chief Education Officer for Birmingham; Professor G.D. Rochester, who was to figure prominently as Chairman of the Committee for Research Degrees; the Vice-Chancellor of Exeter University, the Principals of Paisley College, Ealing Technical College, Brighton College of Technology and Leicester College of Technology and Commerce, department heads from colleges in Nottingham and Woolwich, two members from the CATs, and other university, industrial and local authority representatives. In addition to the preliminary meeting of Council held in July, a Planning Committee began to meet at the beginning of August.

The Committee began its work by recommending to Council that it should grant degrees for courses in pure as well as applied science, and that the Council should itself consider whether — in addition to sandwich courses — it should approve full-time courses without industrial training. It paid special attention to its power to grant retrospective degrees to holders of an Associateship of a Central Institution in Scotland, and to a report of the National Advisory Council on Education for Industry and Commerce on *A Higher Award in Business Studies* (the Crick Report) which could provide a basis for inviting colleges to submit proposals for business studies courses — with priority to be given to sandwich courses. When a board of studies for arts and social studies was established it would need to devote 'much thought' to a policy for those subjects, separate and in conjunction with technological fields — and it was advised to consult the University of London. Priority would need to be given to establishing first degrees, but degrees at masters and doctorate level would need to follow. Later meetings of the Planning Committee made recommendations about the constitution of the Committee for Science and Technology (CST), the Committee for Arts and Social Studies (CASS), and the associated subject boards. In October it proposed particularly that a Business Studies Board be set up without delay. There was discussion of the possibility of an existing Diploma in Management Studies (DMS) becoming part of the Council's structure, and consideration was given to the possibility that approaches might be forthcoming from Scottish colleges to approve courses in teacher education and art and design.[7]

Of immediate concern to this Committee, and to the Council when it began to meet, was the transition from the NCTA, the need for the NCTA to continue to operate until the CNAA machinery was in place, interim arrangements for the approval and reapproval of courses, and retrospective degree awards for holders of the DipTech and the MCT. The Department of Education and Science (DES) (as the Ministry of Education had recently become) offered a set of priorities to the CNAA at its preliminary meeting in July:

to take over the DipTech scheme from the NCTA and replace DipTechs by its own degrees;

to consider the award of degrees to students at present following associateship courses in Scottish central institutions;

to consider the introduction of degrees in business studies, as recommended in the Crick Report;

to settle its policy towards applications for the approval of degree courses in other fields; and

to consider the position of MCT students in relation to awards of the Council.[8]

That meeting had asked the NCTA to continue its work relating to the DipTech until the CNAA was ready to take over, and close attention began to be paid to the need to formulate any changes rapidly for the benefit of the colleges. In all cases this priority list presented need for urgent action, either because there were students whose position needed to be clarified, or colleges anxious to submit proposals in existing areas of DipTech experience, or in new areas.

Quintin Hogg (later Lord Hailsham), as Secretary of State for Education and Science, attended the first meeting of Council, handed over the Charter, and described the event as an historic occasion, this being the first time that powers to award degrees had been given to anyone other than universities and the Archbishop of Canterbury: it marked a 'turning point in the development of higher education in regional and other colleges of further education engaged in advanced work'. (It is interesting to note the intersection at this point of the vocabularies of 'higher', 'further' and 'advanced' — and the uncertain and often confusing relationships of these vocabularies were to continue, although the pattern of 'higher education' was to become rapidly strengthened.) The Secretary of State underlined that the Council's task would be:

> to help the colleges to make their full contribution to higher education by providing a range of degrees of unimpeachable standard and quality which reflected the diverse needs of the colleges and the distinctive character of their work. Colleges had a part to play in higher education complementary to that of the universities and the opportunities were great.

He mentioned business studies and modern languages as areas offering scope for 'novel development', and hoped that with encouragement from the Council the colleges would find other opportunities for 'experiment and innovation'.[9] The DES had by this time issued a memorandum to local education authorities and establishments of further and adult education outlining the purposes and functions of the new Council, and at this first meeting a draft public statement was discussed, amended and approved for circulation. Statement No. 1 became, therefore, the Council's first formulation of policy, though much in it was tentative — including whether the Council would be adopting pass degrees, what the degree titles were going to be, the types of courses that would be encouraged in arts subjects and social sciences, and how the Council's support for the development of part-time higher education would be implemented. The statement acknowledged the impact of the NCTA and its DipTech awards, and the influence — recognized by the Robbins Committee — of the NCTA's work in developing the CATs to their high standards. In its intention to continue and widen the work of the NCTA, the Council understood the complex policy position it now faced:

. . . the Council will need to consider a number of matters of the highest importance relating to the development of higher education in this country and there is no doubt that many of these matters will require prolonged and careful consideration. Thus it would be unrealistic to expect the Council to announce in the immediate future its final policy on all the aspects of higher education with which it will have to deal.

Reinforcing the sense of urgency generated by the demographic situation, the statement recognized the importance of the proposed degrees to solving the problems that would arise 'during what the Robbins Committee described as the "short term emergency", during the years 1965-1968'.[10]

Two other features of this and other early meetings of the Council point to continuing aspects of its work. First, there was to be the constant issue of what it meant to be a national Council with powers to award degrees, and not to be or be called a 'university'. Explaining the position of the CNAA in British higher education was to be a source of unending national and international difficulty. The question of *degrees* had been won inside the Ministry of Education with Pimlott coining the phrase 'equal awards for equal work', and he and Staff Inspector French had worked to persuade people that normal entry qualifications plus the equivalent of an honours degree course merited the award of a degree.[11] There was uncertainty in many minds, however, as to how permanent the CNAA was going to be, and widespread interest in establishing difference at the same time as comparability or equivalence. There was, however, pressure in the opposite direction, and the CNAA Chairman went with Frank Hornby to the Minister of State to ask if the CNAA would be allowed to use the word 'university' in its title.[12] How deep the doubts ran was clear at the first meeting of Council when the Chairman reported that the Duke of Edinburgh had expressed his willingness to accept an invitation to become President of the Council, though it was reported that 'His Royal Highness had criticized the Council's title and had suggested alternatives'. The Chairman had replied 'saying that he personally held similar views to those of His Royal Highness but that nevertheless, a change in title of the Council at this stage would probably not be advisable'. The Council decided both that it would extend a formal invitation to the Duke of Edinburgh to become President, and would consider a change of title 'after the Council had established itself'.[13] From this time on there were discussions with the CVCP, the Secretary of State and others about a possible change of name, including to 'National University', but the position remained unchanged.[14]

The second important aspect of the Council's work from the beginning was its extension to cover awards in Scotland. Sir Lionel Russell's view was that the coverage of Scotland, in parallel with that of the UGC, gave the CNAA 'standing'.[15] The Associateship of the Scottish Central Institutions had not had anything like the same system of validation that had been built up for the DipTech in England and Wales (it had, in fact, been validated by the SED), and the CNAA was in the early stages to encounter difficulties with some of the courses and institutions approaching the CNAA for approval. In the event the Council was to accept a Planning Committee recommendation to regard only the honours associateship as being equivalent to a DipTech and qualifying for the retrospective grant of a degree. New courses were invited for submission, to begin in 1965/66. The Council's first policy statement underlined that 'what is said in this statement about the Council's degrees applies to Scotland as well as England and Wales'.[16]

The CNAA had from the outset to combine continuing what were now the traditions of the NCTA with the exploration of appropriate machineries and processes appropriate to its new responsibilities. It had to mark out the directions in which it was prepared to go in endorsing the activities of institutions and in approving courses in new subject areas, and establish a framework and atmosphere in which policy could be determined. The long-term needs of the colleges and an emergent, expanding student population needed to be married with the urgencies of immediate action. Although differences appeared in the ways the committees and boards operated, by and large the procedures remained unchanged for some years. The pressure of demand and the ability of the CNAA to operate on the basis of adequate information meant that the Council was reluctant to accord any priority to proposals coming from institutions with no previous DipTech experience, and in some cases were not in the group of Regional Colleges (those defined as the second-tier institutions below the CATs when the Ministry was making its plans in the mid-1950s).

One of the Council's focal points for getting down to new subject areas was the establishment of a Business Studies Board, proposals for which were discussed in December, and by March 1965 the Board was holding its first meeting, under the chairmanship of W.F. Crick, whose NACEIC report had pointed towards the kind of priority that the CNAA was now attaching to the area. The Board intended to proceed with caution, offer as much guidance as possible, and hoped that the CNAA, like the NCTA before it, 'would influence standards of courses, teaching, and accommodation in colleges and to this end they intended to set high standards from the beginning, acknowledging at the same time the need, especially in the early stages, for flexibility'.[17] There was no doubt about the new Board's commitment to the sandwich principle. There was no difficulty in getting down to work on science and engineering, given the carry over of experience and personnel in the area, although in a second policy statement in March 1965 the Council admitted it was unlikely to be able to consider all the courses intended to start in September, in the fields where numbers were greatest — mechanical, production and civil engineering, building and surveying.[18]

To begin the process of developing work in arts and social studies, a study group met in April, primarily to make recommendations about the composition of the Committee for Arts and Social Studies, but also about its functions. It agreed that the Committee should be 'a broadly-based, balanced and effective policy-making body', reflected in a membership of university, college and other — including employers' — interests. The Committee of thirty-one members, two assessors and two officers was convened in November.[19] In addition to the possibility that had been mentioned that the Council might be faced with teacher education proposals from Scotland, it began to receive other enquiries about the possibility of CNAA validation. The second meeting of the Council, in November 1964, considered a letter from the Principal of Oastler College, Huddersfield, asking if the CNAA would consider proposals for a BEd. In March 1965 it received a similar request from the Principal of the Cambridge College of Arts and Technology. The Robbins Committee had made proposals about the future of teacher education, and the CNAA — while prepared to enter the field — was anxious to tread carefully in a sensitive area. Its reply to Oastler was that it could not formulate proposals in this field until government policy on the Robbins recommendations was known. Hornby's reply to an enquiry from Chorley Day Training College was that under the Council's Charter there was 'no restriction on the fields of study in which it may offer degrees', and when he addressed a meeting at Chorley in November 1965 he indicated that if there was limited interest in CNAA validation for teacher education this could be handled by the establishment of an Education Board under the Committee for Arts and Social Studies, or if 'the demand for degrees in Education became quite substantial, then I would see reason for the Council to set up a Committee for Education'.[20] In the event, it was the latter that was to take place.

It is clear that some, including Hornby, would have liked time to debate and plan with some care, but it is equally clear that the pressures for swift action were considerable. Demography, students on or about to enter courses, the expectations of past students and institutions anxious to award degrees in existing fields and develop into new ones, combined to put considerable pressure on the new organization, its decision-making structures and officers. At this stage the Council had only a handful of officers to service its pyramidal structure, in which boards reported to committees and committees to the Council. In its first annual report the CNAA could report that eighteen subject boards had been established, with another four on the way. The Council had already reached decisions on whether or not to approve sixty-seven courses that had been submitted in business studies, science and technology — entailing thirty-four board meetings and thirty-nine visits to colleges. At the beginning of the academic year 1965–66 there were over 4000 students enrolled on eighty-nine courses leading to the Council's degrees (including 129 students on five courses leading to the new BA degree in business studies). A year later the report could name other new subject areas in which degree courses had been approved, including agricultural engineering and nautical studies (both, it was emphasized, not previously covered by degrees of universities). The total number of enrolled students was now over 7000 — including seventy-four registered for research degrees. Dr (from 1969 Sir) Derman Christopherson, Vice-Chancellor of the University of Durham, was about to become Chairman of the Committee on Education, whose main initial functions would be to advise on policy in its field of study, and then begin considering courses. Further policy statements had by now been issued, including one on higher degrees in July 1966 — following Statement No. 3, which had set out the conditions for the Council's first degrees. The latter were to be BA and BSc, the former MSc, MA, MPhil and PhD, on the university model — and proposals for distinctive nomenclatures for CNAA awards had not been favoured.[21]

There was, Lionel Russell felt, nothing uncertain about the CNAA in setting to work on its new tasks. Establishing the CNAA was felt to be a 'great event': after some fifteen years the Robbins Committee had resolved the problem of degrees in establishments other than universities.[22] The confidence was generated in part by the speed of action, in part by the strong support of government departments and — despite some of their initial misgivings — the universities, and in part by a degree of continuity of committee and board membership and officers. Key figures on the Council and its committees had been similarly placed and active in the NCTA — including the Chairman, Lord Kings Norton, and the first Chairman of the Committee for Science and Technology, Dr James Topping. The chairs of the boards in civil, mechanical and engineering were occupied by former members of the NCTA Board of Studies in Engineering, and the chairmen of the physics and metallurgy boards had been members of the Board of Studies in Technologies other than Engineering and one of the subject panels respectively. The carry over of other members was substantial. The CNAA took over the premises of the NCTA. Hornby became its first Chief Officer, and the first Senior Assistant Registrar responsible for courses in science and technology was Gordon Hunting, who also transferred over from the NCTA. The first non-NCTA appointment at senior officer level was that of Jean Rossiter, appointed from a training background in the electricity industry to be Assistant Registrar responsible for courses in arts and social studies. Appointed as from 15 March 1965, she attended the first meeting of the Business Studies Board four days later. The initial complement of senior officers was completed the following year, with the appointment of Francis Hanrott from a post as Assistant Education Officer in Hertfordshire to be Registrar and Secretary. With all the modifications and new departures, the CNAA had available to it a considerable reservoir of experience relevant to its new operations. The collaboration of the Council's Chairman, officers and committee chairmen — notably the first group of chairmen, Dr J. Topping from Brunel, Professor H.C. Edey from the London School of Economics, Professor G.D. Rochester from Durham, and Dr Christopherson

— was an essential element in establishing both the machinery and the credibility of the organization.

The Council went through some hesitations and disagreements, and made some false starts. The Robbins Committee had suggested, for example, that the CNAA might award degrees at pass and honours level. The draft of the CNAA's first policy statement committed it to exploring the need for pass degrees, but the first Council meeting expressed the view that such a commitment was undesirable at the time. It forecast the need for degrees 'of different types or at different levels' and agreed to consider the case for 'ordinary degrees'. There was clearly strong resistance to the concept of a pass degree with its assumption of separate entry with lower qualifications.[23] For the next five years or so there were to be disagreements — notably between the committees for Science and Technology and Arts and Social Studies — about the desirability or nature of different degrees at different levels, different entry qualifications and different tracks through the degrees. In arts and social studies there were people opposed to ordinary degrees on the grounds of the unreliability of 'A' level examinations as predictors of university performance, and on other grounds. Under stronger pressure from science and technology, however, the Council settled down to a pattern of honours and ordinary degrees, the latter intended to be 'a worthwhile qualification in its own right. It is not awarded for indifferent performance on an honours degree course'. As described in 1966, the position became that:

> In the majority of cases, ordinary degree courses are offered by colleges side by side with honours degree courses and there is a common first year which has a diagnostic function. In some cases the student may elect to follow the ordinary rather than the honours course because, for example, he wishes to study a wider range of subjects or to take a less specialized course. The Council expects also that the teaching of the ordinary degree student will be different in approach, for part of the course at least . . . [24]

In the 1970s, after years of unease about this position, the Council adopted a structure comprising 'degrees' and 'honours degrees'.

The outstanding false start involved a star, or asterisk. At its second meeting the Council discussed titles for its awards, including the possibility of a BATech or BScTech to indicate a degree programme comprising academic study and industrial or practical experience. It was felt, however, that the suffix 'could well convey the impression that a sandwich course was less highly valued than a full-time course', but there was an eager search for some other distinctive title to be attached to a sandwich course. One suggestion was that the normal BA or BSc title should be followed by some symbol, including a star or asterisk. This was, in fact, adopted at the next meeting, and a statement was issued indicating that the Council would award the degrees of BA* and BSc* to indicate successful completion of a sandwich course. It conceded that there were opposing views about this policy, but that it was agreed both that sandwich courses should continue to be encouraged, and that a proliferation of degree titles was inadvisable. The star or asterisk was greeted, according to *The Guardian*, with a certain amount of derision in the colleges (and it considered the compromise reached as by no means the worst of the new Council's teething troubles). Two weeks later, in mid-February, under the headline 'Asterisk with degree "snobbish" ', *The Guardian* reported that the North Staffordshire College of Technology was opposing the proposal to use the asterisk, and reported one of the College governors as saying this was yet another 'typical British attitude to put as many people as possible in different tiny categories'. At its meeting in March the Council acknowledged the widespread criticism of the scheme, and dropped it.[25]

In the first two years or so, in determining its policies and priorities and responding to others', the CNAA was also having to establish the pattern of its relationships with other organizations, its principles for the development of subjects and professional programmes, and the dynamics of its relationships with colleges. On the first of these, interaction with the DES, local education authorities (LEAs) and the university sector were to be prominent, though in different ways. With the DES, as we have seen, there were issues to be explored at various levels, including the Council's assessors and the Secretary of State. Hornby commented that he had access at all levels: 'I floated around quite a lot in the hierarchy of the DES'.[26] Pimlott, French, English and others kept closely in touch with the development of the CNAA, and from Hornby's correspondence it is obvious that in the early days, either on his own or on the initiative of the Chairman or the Council, he took soundings of likely DES and HMI support or otherwise for moves in particular directions.

In the case of the CVCP the position was different. Having been consulted both about the Charter and the membership of the Council, the university sector was well represented in the Council itself. University support in that respect, as in other ways — including the commitment of individuals to the work of the new body and to its colleges as examiners — was obviously important for the credibility of the procedures, the courses and the general attempt to establish and improve standards. Although, as Christopherson, for example, considered, university influence was not *felt* strongly in the CNAA,[27] the role of the universities had been built in to the Council's work from the moment the Robbins Committee reported. In 1966 the DES underlined that Robbins had recommended that 'the universities should participate in the work of the new Council in "giving important assistance in establishing standards and generally helping the colleges in their academic progress" '.[28] As a member of the Electrical and Electronic Engineering Board wrote in 1979:

> If it was not for the very active cooperation of the university sector both at an official level and at the level of individual university

members of staff, then the CNAA could not have been set up in the first place. Much less could it have developed and evolved as it has done . . .

The Board had had 'a considerable university presence', making an 'immense contribution' to the CNAA, and deriving indirect benefits for the work of the universities themselves.[29] In setting up the CNAA, the CVCP reported, the government had 'had the support of our Committee', but the support had not been unequivocal, and the CNAA's relationships with the Committee inevitably reflected some of the ambivalent attitudes within the CVCP. In the consultation phase, as we have seen, there were strong and contradictory views in the CVCP. At its meeting in December 1963 discussion had arisen 'on the question of the power of the proposed Council to award higher degrees, and it was considered at that meeting undesirable to restrict the CNAA's powers in this respect in the Charter'. It was agreed to inform the UGC that it 'wished to modify its previous view on this point and that it would not regard it as appropriate that the Charter should contain a clause restricting the Council's power to award higher degrees'. By the time the Committee was discussing the draft Charter in April, however, it again reversed its opinion and opposed a reference to research in the Charter, on the grounds that research under CNAA auspices would deflect PhD students from universities to institutions where they could both 'study for a PhD and also earn a salary'. Objections were also expressed to a failure to limit the degrees the CNAA would be able to award, and to its power to award honorary degrees. The following month the UGC wrote to the CVCP to explain why it had decided that the reference to research should remain in the Charter.[30] The CNAA, knowing the background, aware of the ambivalence, and needing CVCP 'active cooperation', trod carefully, and in particular sought CVCP help in filling positions on its committees and boards. In the views of some, especially in the colleges, what resulted was a strong thread of educational conservatism. At a conference in 1970, where thirty-two of the thirty-four participants were from colleges or what were by then polytechnics, the views of the experience to date — following a paper on the development of the CNAA by Frank Hornby — were summarized as follows:

> A debate began here which lasted throughout the conference, and this concerned the lack of encouragement from the CNAA subject boards for colleges to experiment with their courses . . . the surest way of getting a course approved is to present it as a traditional academic course, both in terms of content and structure. The situation is at stalemate given the predominant membership on the subject boards of traditional university teachers. Mr Hornby admitted that the situation worried him . . .[31]

When it came to applications for validation of BEd courses at colleges currently belonging to an Institute of Education, the CNAA would be 'well advised', in Hornby's view, 'to have the view of the university concerned. The latter is an obvious and sensible procedure'.[32] The relationships were intricate, and careful. Attitudes were complex. The universities resisted postgraduate expansion in the CNAA institutions, at the same time as recognizing CNAA first degrees (as they had the DipTech) for access to higher degrees and research. The UGC thought it 'reasonable' for non-university institutions to embark 'sparingly' on postgraduate work, and for graduates of non-university institutions to pursue postgraduate work by transferring to universities.[33] Recognition of the CNAA's undergraduate degrees for entry to university postgraduate courses was if nothing else a means of ensuring that the colleges and polytechnics did not develop their own postgraduate activities.

Interaction with the local education authorities was different again, in that this was for the most part as a result of rejection of courses or adverse reports by visiting parties to colleges, dialogue with LEA representatives about resources, and contacts by LEAs with the CNAA officers either in response to criticism of *their* colleges or to discuss the perceived weaknesses or misdemeanours of *their* college principals or others. Hornby instanced a visit from one Chief Education Officer who came to object strongly to what the CNAA had said about two of his colleges — 'we had a barney'.[34]

Establishing relations with the colleges, somewhere between stringent paternalism and laissez-faire flexibility, was a complex process, because of the wide range of institutions and courses with which the Council was called upon to deal, the meaning to be established of standards 'comparable' with those of universities, and the sense of precedent that pervaded much of the CNAA's early work in this respect. The CATs had by 1962 been transferred out of local authority control and their independent governing bodies received direct grant from the Ministry of Education until they were transferred to the UGC following the recommendation of the Robbins Report. The remaining colleges with which the CNAA now dealt ranged from regional colleges which had hoped to be given CAT status and were barely distinguishable from them as universities, to those colleges endeavouring to embark on advanced work for the first time. Questions of status were now vitally important for many institutions. At the end of 1964 two comments using the same vocabulary reflect perceptions of the colleges whose degrees were now to be validated by the CNAA. Hornby, speaking at a conference of technical college lecturers in December 1964, said he had been alarmed to be asked 'if it is the intention of the Council to pitch its degrees at sub-university level. It will not, and it cannot do so . . . '. The previous month, speaking in the United States, the Director of the University of Oxford's Department of Education had been outlining the issues in British higher education, and the quotation marks of the printed version presumably reflect the tone of voice in the address:

We have already set up . . . a Council for National Academic Awards

> which is empowered to grant 'degrees'. This will presumably act
> as a sort of national accrediting agency to validate courses in a large
> number of what are at present 'subuniversity' institutions . . .

Confusingly, these were 'of an academic quality, equal to that of a university degree course'.[35] The CNAA's relations with the colleges involved issues about its own status and about that of the institutions, and there were strong political undercurrents in the perceptions of the relationships as seen from Whitehall, county halls, the CNAA and the colleges.

One of the elements in this complex politics was the relationship between particular colleges and their university neighbours, with the possibility of 'transbinary' mergers beginning to take shape, as universities, local authorities and colleges began to weigh the respective advantages, potential and drawbacks of competition and amalgamation. Within the DES there was already, following the departure of the CATs, a hardening view that it would be wrong for such amalgamations to deprive the new sector of some of its likely 'flagship' institutions, such as Lanchester in Coventry, where negotiations on amalgamation with the University of Warwick ultimately proved abortive. All of these questions of status, institutional and sector differences and directions were to be reinforced by the politics of teacher education.

The most direct factor in the relationships between the CNAA and the colleges was, of course, the question of the quality of the institutions as perceived by the CNAA's visiting parties, boards and committees, and the resulting acceptance or rejection of proposals for courses. The initial success rate of applications was not high, many being rejected, returned for revision, postponed or otherwise given a measure of cold water. In 1966–67, for example, the Council considered 136 proposals for undergraduate courses, and approved fifty-four. Many, if not most, courses approved were subject to conditions — normally relating to improvements required by the time renewal would be sought after a period of five or so years. At a meeting in July 1965, which set the pattern of the Council's decision-making, Bolton Institute of Technology failed to obtain approval for an honours degree in civil engineering, Leeds College of Technology failed with a proposed honours course in building, Leicester College of Technology failed with an honours degree in mathematics and an ordinary degree in applied chemistry, and Rugby College of Engineering Technology failed with proposals in production engineering and mechanical engineering. At the same meeting, however, Leicester was successful in applied chemistry, Rugby in electrical engineering and applied physics, Watford College of Technology in printing, and Wolverhampton and Staffordshire College of Technology in computer technology. The conditions attached to approval normally related to improved staffing or facilities, syllabus revision or amended examination arrangements. Acting on committee, board and visiting party recommendations, however, the Council went further in some cases. Wolverhampton, for example, was issued a warning regarding 'the College as a whole'. The Committee for Science and Technology recommended that 'the College be warned that in order for the approval of courses to be extended beyond 1967 the Council will expect to see significant progress in the implementation of plans for the development of the College as a centre for advanced work'. The Council endorsed the warning, adding the words — 'including the development of research in mechanical engineering and computing'.[36]

The clearest picture of the role and problems of the CNAA at this stage — and for some time to come — came at this same meeting with the case of Constantine College of Technology, Middlesbrough. A party of seventeen members and two officers, chaired by Dr (later Sir) Alan Richmond, visited the College in June 1965 to consider renewal of a DipTech course in mechanical engineering as an honours degree, and to consider proposals for honours degrees in civil engineering, metallurgy and mathematics, as well as preliminary consideration of a proposed honours course in instrumentation and control. The College was beginning to occupy new building extensions and was purchasing extensive new equipment. In mechanical engineering, however, little had been brought into use for teaching purposes, and there was little space for future development, including in research. The mechanical engineering course not only did not 'provide a satisfactory basis for an honours degree course', but also gave no evidence of the developments that might be expected if renewal were sought in five years' time. Staff 'outlook' was deficient, and research claimed to be in operation had produced no publications in the previous six years. In civil engineering the visitors did not feel that 'the staff as a whole fully appreciate what is the appropriate treatment for an honours degree course' or knew how to select students for it. There was little research in progress, and proposals for industrial training were unsatisfactory. In metallurgy the proposed aims were 'impossibly wide', the objectives had not been 'fully thought out', and the staff needed strengthening at senior level. The proposals for instrumentation and control had not been adequately formulated. The report of the visit, therefore, recommended that all of these courses be not approved, and the Council in July endorsed decisions of the Committee for Science and Technology not to approve them. The visiting party and the Mathematics Board had, however, recommended approval of the honours course in mathematics, since the College had a nucleus of appropriate staff and was proposing to appoint the necessary additional ones. CST and Council, nevertheless, turned this down also. The visiting party had expressed the belief that:

> the Council should consider whether some colleges, such as this College, might be better advised to begin work at degree level by first developing ordinary degree courses rather than, as at present, going straight to honours degree courses.[37]

The condition of the colleges, lack of experience, over-eager aspirations, and the Council's own concern with realism and standards, therefore, combined to produce often harsh and unpalatable decisions. The CNAA was being driven into making judgments about colleges as well as courses, laying down conditions about environments and future overall directions, as well as about course syllabuses. The CNAA's judgments in many cases meant college reappraisal of the realism of proposals, or anxious responses which related to the plans of college staffs, governors or local authorities.[38] The Principal of Constantine College, for example, responded to the Council even before it formally considered the recommendations of its visiting party and Committee, asking for the decision on mathematics to be reversed. On the other courses, the Principal, heads of departments and the College Academic Board had held 'four long meetings and action has already been taken to meet the Council's criticisms' (this action was outlined in an appendix to the letter). In addition:

> the Board of Governors have met as a matter of urgency to consider the Council's criticisms of the proposed courses, and of other matters concerning the College, and I understand that it is their intention to take whatever action may be required after the enquiries have been completed to enable these honours degree courses to be established as soon as possible at the College. The decision of the Council not to reapprove the mechanical engineering course was a bitter blow to the aspirations of the College.[39]

Whether or not there were strands of conservatism in the CNAA's emergent processes, at this formative stage of its development getting down to work meant formulating procedures for the assurance of standards, and judgments on the specifics of courses and institutions.

Some of the problems were to remain salient in the early years of the Council — in relation to research, for example, emphasized in various ways from the beginning. Among the qualities expected of staff, said Statement No. 3 in 1965, was at least in some cases the undertaking of research,[40] but on the general issue of research there was some resistance within the DES (Hornby believed that Pimlott, for example, did not understand research[41]) and ambiguity, to say the least, from Ministers about the colleges' research role — an issue to which we shall return. There were also immediate problems of relative authority within the CNAA on the part of the Committees for Science and Technology and Arts and Social Studies. The role and ethos of CST was imported ready-made, so to speak, from the NCTA, against the background of its commitment to improving student access and take-up in higher technological studies. CASS was in a sense grafted on to this and was seen by some, in Hunting's words, as a 'rogue element'. Professor Gutteridge, reflecting on the carry over from the NCTA, considered that 'it took some years for CASS to acquire parity of influence within the organization'.[42] Hornby detected among some of those members who had made the transition from the NCTA a certain loss of interest as the remit of the new organization widened.[43] Others, including Lord Kings Norton and Dr Topping, felt that the atmosphere in the CNAA was the same as in the NCTA.[44] There were new kinds of problems as the CNAA tried to adapt to new conceptions of standards and new subject ranges, including outstandingly the issue of the role of liberal or general, complementary or contrasting, studies in degree level courses, and in business studies and other areas of arts and social studies in particular.

There were underlying policy and related issues which the CNAA could address only tangentially, given its dependence on directions and attitudes adopted elsewhere — DES policy in general and in areas like teacher education in particular; the 'binary' decisions from 1965, and therefore also the long-term temporary or permanent role ascribed to the CNAA — alongside other validating bodies — in maintaining a 'public' sector or promoting institutions out of it; the balance, therefore, between its guardianship role and that of nurturing 'autonomy' or 'independence' — which was to prove the most fundamental issue for the CNAA in the 1970s and 1980s; the legitimacy and status of the CNAA and its associated institutions.

Whether the Ministry of Education and then the DES had coherent or consistent policies for higher education in the mid-1960s is not of primary concern here. Carswell's picture of the policy-making process across this period suggests that it was fragmentary and ad hoc, and Hornby's view was that it was essentially 'inept'.[45] There was little doubt in the minds of any of the participants that something crucial to higher education had taken place following Robbins and government acceptance of the recommendation to set up the CNAA. For Hornby it was a 'unique event', the most far-reaching outcome of the Robbins Report.[46] The Chief Education Officer for Leeds thought that graduation by a route other than a university was 'nothing less than a minor revolution in the academic world, which, in its ultimate effects, may prove to be a major one'.[47] A 'supersenate', in Maurice Kogan's formulation, had been created for the non-university sector.[48] The policy directions of this novel and relatively independent body were in the nature of things, however, not unambiguously independent. Decisions on the creation of polytechnics and a binary structure for higher education directly shaped the CNAA's activities. The greater public accountability of the sector than that of the universities was to make the CNAA particularly visible amidst changing national policies affecting finance and resources, courses and institutions.

Sir Lionel Russell was in one sense right that at the beginning there were no uncertainties about the CNAA — it had a job to do and set about it with readily available commitment and expertise and no small amount of confidence. It is also clear, however, that there were strong latent tensions in the whole operation. The conference of college and polytechnic staffs which discussed 'CNAA degrees and the colleges' in 1970 endorsed the CNAA's role in undergraduate and postgraduate courses, research and moves towards more general college assessment and a 'shared commitment' with the institutions offering courses. The report of the discussion ends, however, with a statement which describes the position of the CNAA from its creation: 'on the one hand a Council which is committed to the development of a distinctive system of higher education pursued nationally but with policies which provide individual colleges with the maximum flexibility and autonomy'.[49] The new universities of the early 1960s and the CATs when given university status had Academic Advisory Committees (AAC) to provide initial steerage, support and guarantees of appropriate development on the way to autonomy. Though the CNAA had something of the same role to play this was complicated by the pursuit of a 'distinctive system of higher education' nationally, the diverse levels of development of a substantial number of institutions, and the interplay of interests and perceptions. The Council was offering the colleges both a considerable measure of freedom and rigorous external scrutiny of their intentions and possibilities, at a level and in a detail — as well as across a range of institutions — not undertaken to the same extent by Advisory Committees. The CNAA was in the business of replacing the London external degree, responding to a sense of demographic urgency, operating in the interstices of a status-ridden and status-conscious higher education system. As it warmed to its work in the early part of 1965, its confidence in being able to occupy an important space in higher education was strengthened by comments on both sides of the House of Commons during a debate on higher education and teacher education in March. Sir Edward Boyle, for the Opposition, believed that 'we should give the highest possible standing to the Council for National Academic Awards' and his view, like that of the Secretary of State, Tony Crosland, was that there could be a development of teacher education in the colleges, validated by the CNAA. Crosland hoped for a growing range of arts and social studies courses in the colleges, with the help of the Council: 'there is great scope for imaginatively devised courses which depart from the traditional patterns without any sacrifice of quality'.[50] In less than two years the Robbins Committee had reported, its recommendations for the CNAA had been accepted, consultations had taken place, the new organization had been set up, its initial policies had been decided, the work of the NCTA in science and engineering had been taken over, new subject areas had been opened up or explored, courses had been approved, criteria of judgment had become explicit and public, and the landscape of higher education had been radically altered.

The expansion and diversification of higher education, the Robbins Committee, the CNAA, the binary system and the creation of the polytechnics that followed soon after, were all responses to British conditions and needs, but were at the same time part of what was to emerge as an international development, not only towards greater access to higher education, but also towards greater — and often profoundly ambiguous — system planning and diversity. In many countries expansion of access —

itself a response to the pressures of demography and democratization — meant expansion of existing institutions and sectors, but in others it meant the creation of new sectors, or both. In the United States in the 1960s this meant the expansion of existing institutions, but also the conversion of the old normal schools or state teachers' colleges into state colleges and later into state universities in many instances — with moves towards greater state-wide coordination or control. In Australia it was to mean the creation of a sector of Colleges of Advanced Education, following a recommendation of the Martin Committee in 1965 — a sector which, as in Britain, had the ambiguous role of supplementing, and deflecting excessive demand from, the more prestigious universities. In Europe the process was widespread. In the Federal German Republic the Fachhochschulen (previously called Ingenieurschulen) were reclassified as 'higher education' at the end of the 1960s. France created the Instituts Universitaires de Technologie, while other countries redesigned their higher education to incorporate teacher education or technical institutions under new names or with new roles and relationships — though in no case with any easy transition to a new status. New short-cycle or alternative modes of study were often involved in the changes, and all were in some way responses not only to demographic pressures and student demand, but also to economic and technological change and competition, manpower forecasting and new needs for professional and managerial leadership. The ambiguities in such developments stemmed invariably from the uncertainties of the expansion, as against the protection, of the historical roles and values of existing institutions — which normally meant the universities, or in the American case the established private or major land-grant universities. The ambiguities stemmed also from uncertainties about planning and the market, and the responses differed internationally according to traditional levels of centralized or decentralized control, methods of funding and definitions of mission. The level of ambiguity was nowhere more apparent than in the aftermath of the Robbins Report and the reinterpretation of its central message for the system as a whole by Crosland and his advisers, in terms of a divided or binary system, rather than the 'unitary' views of the Robbins Committee and Robbins himself. The CNAA took shape in both this national and this international context.

Notes

1 Note of a meeting on 31 December 1963, CVCP, C 29/4.
2 CN, minute of meeting of members of Council, 17 July 1964.
3 UGC, letter to CVCP from Chairman of UGC, 8 November 1963, CVCP agenda paper, 22 November 1963, C 29/4; Ministry of Education (1963) 'Proposed Council for National Academic Awards', November, CVCP C 29/4.
4 John Carswell (1985) *Government and the Universities in Britain*, Cambridge University Press, p. 69.

5 Ministry of Education, 'Proposed Council'.
6 CN, *Charter and Statutes*.
7 CN, minute of Planning Committee, 6 August, 21 October and 15 December 1964.
8 CN, minute of Planning Committee, 6 August 1964.
9 Cmin, 30 September 1964.
10 CN, draft Statement No. 1, with *ibid*.
11 French, MD interview. The phrase 'equal awards for equal performance' occurs in the Robbins Report, p. 265.
12 Hornby, MD interview.
13 Cmin, 30 September 1964.
14 M.C. Davis (1979) 'The development of the CNAA 1964–1974: A study of a validating agency', PhD thesis, Loughborough University, pp. 88–9.
15 Sir Lionel Russell, MD interview.
16 CN, minute of Planning Committee, 21 October 1964; Cmin, 30 September 1964.
17 CN, minute of Business Studies Board, 19 March 1965.
18 Cmin, 24 March 1965.
19 CN, minute of Arts and Social Studies Committee Study Group, 27 April 1965; minute of Committee for Arts and Social Studies, 5 January 1965.
20 Cmin, 26 November 1964, and attached letter from G.E. Wilson, 18 November 1964; Cmin 24 March 1965 and attached letter from D.E. Mumford, 3 March 1965; Hornby to G. Price, 17 March 1965 and notes of Hornby's speech at Chorley College 3 November 1965, CN Chairman's file 1964–74.
21 CN, *Report for the Period 30 September 1964 to 30 September 1965*, pp. 5–10; *Report for the Period 1 October 1965 to 30 September 1966*, pp. 5–9.
22 Sir Lionel Russell, MD interview.
23 Committee on Higher Education (1963), *Report*, HMSO, p. 43; Cmin 30 September 1964.
24 CN *Report 1965–66*, p. 9.
25 Cmin, 26 November 1964, 22 February and 24 March 1965; *The Guardian*, 1 and 15 February 1965.
26 Hornby, MD interview.
27 Sir Derman Christopherson, MD interview.
28 DES (1966), *Reports on Education No 30: The Council for National Academic Awards*, p. 1.
29 B.F.N. Briggs (1986) 'By CNAA degrees', *IEE Proceedings*, 132, Pt A, 4, pp. 188–9.
30 CVCP (1967) *Report on the Quinquennium 1962–1967*, p. 13; minutes of meeting 13 December 1963, 24 April and 19 June 1964 (UGC letter dated 29 May 1964).
31 Coombe Lodge Report 3 (1970) (18): *CNAA Degrees and the Colleges*, p. 3. The issue is discussed in M.C. Davis (1980) 'Performance at national level: The CNAA as a validating agency' in D. Billing (Ed.), *Indicators of Performance*, Society for Research into Higher Education, Guildford, p. 36.
32 Hornby, speech at Chorley College, 3 November 1965.
33 UGC (1968) *University Development 1962–1967*, HMSO, p. 82.
34 Hornby, MD interview.
35 Hornby, address to the ATTI FE Educational Section meeting, 30 December 1964, CN Chairman's file 1964–74; A.D.C. Peterson (1966) 'English higher education: The issues involved' in Earl J. McGrath (Ed.), *Universal Higher Education*, McGraw-Hill, p. 231. Peterson did, however, become a member of the CNAA's Committee for Education.
36 Cmin, 29 July 1965; CSTmin 26 July 1965.
37 Report of a visiting party by members of subject boards to Constantine College of Technology, 3 June 1965; Cmin, 29 July 1965.

38 Reports of visits to Ealing (14 May 1965), City of London (31 May 1965), Hatfield (12 July 1965), Lanchester (14 June 1965), Woolwich (5 May 1965), Regent Street (21 July 1965), Manchester (7 July 1965); minute of Business Studies Board, 25 May 1965; Recommendations of the Business Studies Board on Courses Examined, 28 July 1965; Cmin, 25 July 1965.
39 J. Houghton to Hornby, with CSTmin, 23 July 1965.
40 CN, Statement No. 3, p. 10.
41 Hornby, MD interview.
42 Hunting, MD interview.
43 Hornby, MD interview.
44 Kings Norton and Topping, MD interviews.
45 Carswell, *Government and the Universities*, pp. 19, 68–9 and 126–8.
46 Hornby, addresses 9 January and 11 September 1965, Chairman's file, 1964–74.
47 G. Taylor (1965) 'Tapping mature brainpower', *TES*, 29 January.
48 M. Kogan (1986), *Education Accountability*, Hutchinson, p. 78.
49 Coombe Lodge, *CNAA Degrees and the Colleges*, pp. 25–6.
50 Extracts from discussion in the House of Commons, with Cmin, 11 June 1965.

Chapter 4

Confronting Policies

The CNAA had been created as a policy instrument to increase access to 'higher' or university-level education outside the universities, and simultaneously to guarantee or raise standards in appropriate institutions. Irrespective of the certainties or ambiguities in the roles that it had begun to develop, the CNAA was also — as a policy instrument — incomplete. It could oversee the substantial new academic development but it could not determine the shape of the sector of higher education it performed only one part in developing. The government's decision — a rough mixture of logic and irrationality — to establish a 'binary' system of higher education completed, at least for the foreseeable future, the policy diagram which contained the CNAA. From the second half of the 1960s the CNAA was increasingly involved in the award of degrees for students on courses which it had approved, in a sector of education whose boundaries were being drawn from elsewhere.

A central feature of the government's binary policy and the concept of a 'public sector' was the decision to concentrate a good deal of advanced work in a new generation of 'polytechnics' — a title borrowed from an earlier response to technological and economic demand — the generation of polytechnics created in London in the last two decades of the nineteenth century. The polytechnics of the new binary policy were to be a key group of partners for the CNAA from roughly the beginning of the 1970s: the Assistant Director of Hatfield Polytechnic spoke of the polytechnics and the CNAA as 'inseparable . . . Theirs is a symbiotic association'.[1] Operationally, the CNAA was crucial to the binary policy and to the establishment of the polytechnics, but the CNAA had no part in shaping the policy itself. The 'rough mixture' from which the policy derived was neither advocated nor forecast by the Robbins Committee, nor an inevitable outcome of the creation of the CNAA. It was one option chosen by Tony Crosland and his advisers from 1965.

The question to be faced after the Robbins deliberations was whether the solutions they had proposed for the CATs constituted a model for future action. Was 'promotion' to university status to be the goal of all 'developing' institutions in association with the CNAA? Having settled one set of problems and delineated a pattern for higher education, had Robbins left the way open for a succession of what Eric Robinson called 'small cadet universities'[2] — some of which were in fact very similar to the CATs, and others of which might see no future except in aspiring to enter the university sector? On the other hand, was the local authority segment of higher education constantly to lose its premier institutions to the universities, and be left with a permanently subordinate pattern of further education colleges doing a proportion of advanced work?. The options and the commitments were various, and some form of rationalization, clarity or working hypothesis became essential once the Robbins proposals for immediate action were endorsed. It is clear that on the Conservative side, before defeat in the 1964 General Election, Edward Boyle was attracted to a binary solution and in March of that year put a paper on it to a Cabinet committee.[3] By the time Tony Crosland became Secretary of State (following Michael Stewart, Labour's first Secretary of State for Education) he was overcoming his initial resistance to the binary idea, and was quickly to become a firm advocate.[4] There is little doubt also that within the DES the binary solution had been canvassed for some time, and throughout the life of the Robbins Committee interest in it was being shown in the Association of Teachers in Technical Institutes and elsewhere. The Robbins proposals, however, pointed towards a system of CNAA tutelage for those institutions which might have university aspirations but which had not, like the CATs, yet earned their spurs.

The choice of a binary direction, along which there would be two types of higher education, was far from what the Robbins Committee had intended. Robbins insisted that the Committee had not intended to erect a barrier of that kind, and deplored Crosland's establishment of 'a rigid line between them never again to be crossed'. He confessed:

> I just can't understand what has happened. Here you have a Labour government which is attempting, for good or for bad, to introduce the comprehensive principle into the schools . . . At the same time, they are deepening the existence of lines of division in higher education and actually announcing . . . that these divisions are to be permanent.[5]

In the House of Commons Sir Edward Boyle argued similarly the case for a 'continuing place for the non-autonomous sector within our national system of higher education', but, he reflected, 'I was careful to preach no "doctrine of eternal separation", as Lord Robbins called it'.[6] In the meantime, however, Crosland was propounding and enacting an increasingly committed version of the binary policy, the philosophy and the detail of which were worked out and announced essentially between April 1965 and April 1967. In April 1965 he argued the case for maintaining two separate sectors, without automatic movement 'upwards' from one to the other. The 'public sector' had its own traditions and characteristics, and could respond to the need for vocational or professional preparation. It would be unhealthy to have a sector constantly depleted by institutions moving into what he called 'the University Club', and it was desirable to have a sector 'under social control, and directly responsive to social needs'. It was a buoyant pronouncement, suggesting that the new sector would be Britain's answer to the industrial and vocational needs served in some other countries by long-established, high-status technological institutions.[7] Over the next two years the language of the policy was toned down, but the policy itself was sharpened. It came to include the policy for polytechnics, that is — a measure of concentration — announced in the 1966 White Paper, and more or less finalized in a Parliamentary statement in April 1967, when Crosland announced confirmation of a list of twenty-eight polytechnics in England and Wales, leaving open the possibility of two more. The White Paper had stipulated that once the list was announced there would be no further designation of polytechnics for at least ten years. Notes for Guidance were distributed together with the Parliamentary statement, indicating how individual schemes were to be prepared with the object of creating 'institutions which can be developed as comprehensive academic communities offering a wide range of disciplines and catering for full-time, sandwich and part-time students at all levels of higher education'. Guidance was given on the government and academic organization of polytechnics: the system of government needed to be suitable for institutions serving national as well as regional and local needs, and to be attractive to staff who would be able to 'share fully in their government and management as academic communities'. Governing bodies needed to have 'a large measure of autonomy', and appropriate responsibilities needed to be delegated to Directors, Academic Boards and the staff directly concerned. A note on research in polytechnics was to have considerable significance in the history of the polytechnics. It began:

> The main responsibilities of the polytechnics will be as teaching institutions, but it will be necessary to make provision for research which is essential to the proper fulfilment of their teaching functions and the maintenance and development of close links with industry . . . The Secretary of State believes that Polytechnics — and indeed other colleges which are suitably staffed and equipped — should be able to make a valuable contribution to the research needs of industry on their own distinctive lines and particularly in specialist fields of direct interest to industry in their areas.

The Secretary of State hoped that qualified members of the teaching staff would pursue research that would contribute to the 'better performance of their teaching duties', but he did not envisage that 'in the ordinary way it will be necessary for members of the academic staff to devote the whole or most of their time to research'.[8] Underlying these policy statements, and spelled out clearly in January 1967 in another speech by Crosland, was a portrayal of the distinctive history and character of the technical colleges — an emphasis which suggested both the positive virtues and potential of the polytechnics and the public sector in general, and the uncertainties and limitations involved — as highlighted by the ambiguities of the statement on research.

The 1966 White Paper made it clear that the polytechnics were not to have a monopoly of higher education in the public sector, but they were to have priority development in resource allocations for this purpose. The polytechnics were from this point onwards to have greater opportunities for development than other colleges, as a result of the operation of two factors. First, the procedure for approving the establishment of courses — before their being submitted for academic validation by the CNAA — was administered by HMI through the Regional Advisory Councils (RACs), and this procedure was operated in favour of the polytechnics. Secondly, the pooling system for higher education expenditure amongst local authorities was one which protected those authorities in which the newly-designated polytechnics happened to be situated. As one former polytechnic director comments: 'the polytechnics made good use of their favoured position', but 'the course approval policy was about the only positive assistance the DES gave; their capital programme allocations never matched the role given to the polytechnics'.[9]

Although the CNAA acquired this new set of privileged partners, it also retained those institutions which shared to one extent or another in the provision of higher education. The other colleges were equally committed to the provision of full-time and part-time advanced education, and to the pattern of combined advanced and non-advanced education which enabled students to progress easily through the system. The CNAA's commitment was as much to sustaining and enhancing advanced further education in these institutions as in the polytechnics.

There are two important aspects of the emergence of the binary policy and the concentration of a significant proportion of advanced level work in polytechnics — attempts to explain the policy and its philosophy, and responses to it. Crosland's own public explanations rested, as we have seen, on the argument from separate traditions — though there is no inevitability about preserving separate traditions. He also argued from the virtues of a sector under 'social control' (though given the later usage of that term what he clearly meant was 'greater public control'), and the possibility of greater responsiveness to economic or other national need. Other explanations have, however, to be considered. Robbins thought they included a form of resolution of a conflict for power between the DES and the local authorities.[10] Carswell describes an 'informal coterie' which met at Crosland's house, 'with a standing membership of Labour sympathisers drawn from the educational world', and to which senior civil servants were occasionally invited. It was here that the resolution was reached 'that no further institutions of higher education could be wrested from local authority control'. Crosland had realized 'the impossibility, as he saw it, of a Labour Secretary of State taking institutions from urban local education authorities which were predominantly controlled by Labour, and bringing them under the same regime as the universities'.[11] Although that sense of political strategy may be true, it is not the whole explanation of the binary policy in general, or of the polytechnic part of it. Crosland no doubt shared with Boyle a sense of the need to reexamine the basis of higher education and ensure that the concept of social responsiveness was not forgotten among the range of its purposes. Parliament, in Boyle's formulation, 'does not take a narrowly vocational view of educational advance . . . But except for that small minority who are going to spend a lifetime in academic pursuits, there must come a time when education for the great majority needs to become more vocational, more concerned with professional training'. Part of the justification 'for greatly increased expenditure on universities must be their success in strengthening the professional infrastructure of our society'.[12] One element in Crosland's policy was clearly the belief that at least to some extent the future of the vocational or professional 'infrastructure' lay with a sector with an explicit commitment to promoting it. It is likely that there was also a sense that higher education on a wider basis could be provided more cheaply outside the universities, though it is likely that at the time any such view would have been based on guesswork rather than hard information. The Vice-Chancellor of Brunel University, Dr Topping, with his long experience of the NCTA, thought 'it may be cheaper in the non-university sector, but we do not know'.[13] Eric Robinson expresses the view that Michael Stewart's decision not to implement the Robbins proposal to put teacher training under the universities in fact 'committed the Wilson government to a "binary" policy in higher education'.[14]

The binary policy, which is central to the history of higher education from its elaboration in the second half of the 1960s, and intimately related to the history of the CNAA's own policies and operations, is explained by many or all of these factors, but cannot be separated from perceptions of the roles and attitudes of the universities that we have previously discussed, and which were part of the decision-making environment of the mid- and late 1960s.

Despite the universities' expansion, including in science and engineering, there were still strong — and perhaps even growing — doubts about their ability to respond appropriately to the needs of a rapidly changing society. At senior levels of the universities, including at the CVCP, there was resentment at the interpretation of the universities in general as somewhat effete and isolated institutions. In 1965 Robbins, for example, reflected on the possible views of the DES:

I don't know what the Department thinks about the universities. I do think, however, that there are still prevalent many gross misconceptions of what universities do and what they should do in the modern age: and it may be that some of these misconceptions still drift about the corridors of the Department.

The binary policy was perhaps a product of the search for power by the DES and the LEAs, but partly also a result 'of mistaken conceptions of what is appropriate for universities to do in the modern age'. There were still people who saw the life of a modern university as 'some community of pure scholar-students pursuing their work regardless of its bearing on their subsequent careers, and of staff having the sole duty of inculcating appropriate habits of thought and advancing knowledge with no practical application'.[15] Christopherson, who, apart from his roles in the CNAA, also had a CVCP perspective, recalls that Crosland's chief adviser at the DES, Toby Weaver, the Deputy Secretary, was, 'we thought, continually representing to the Minister a totally false impression of what the universities were like'.[16] Boris Ford, strongly opposed to the binary policy and the new role of the CNAA, described the policy as deriving its impetus from 'an oddly outmoded view of universities as remote, anti-professional and unresponsive to social needs'.[17] Whether or not Crosland actually shared this view of the universities it is possible, as Carswell points out, to deduce from Crosland's 1965 Woolwich speech that the universities were somehow 'placed in isolation, seeking after truth, persuing learning for its own sake, and getting a lot of money for it'.[18] As the binary policy gained momentum, it remained possible to have that impression. From within the universities there were stern voices of anti-vocationalism and resistance to public demands for responsiveness, strengthening the impression.

The binary policy can to some extent be interpreted, therefore, as either an attack on, or at least a misreading of, the universities — as seen from the universities themselves. Writing in 1966, Edward Boyle felt it necessary to defend the House of Commons — and Crosland in particular — from the accusation of being hostile to the universities: 'there is little envious ill-will towards the universities in the present House of Commons'. He did not see Crosland hinting at wanting to 'nationalize' or exert control over the universities, and he did not see the DES as being 'jealous of the universities as is sometimes suggested'.[19] In September 1966 *The Guardian* published an article by Brian MacArthur under the title, 'Running down the universities'. It began: 'There is deep concern in the universities about the government's present policy on higher education'. Many vice-chancellors believed that the universities were being run down 'in order to build up the state system of higher education of colleges and polytechnics, headed by the Council for National Academic Awards'. Students were being deliberately channelled into the state system;

> What worries me, said one Vice-Chancellor, is that the policy of the government is to leave the universities autonomous, as they are, with the implication that they are irresponsible, to stew in their own

juice, while an attempt is made to build up a rival system, via the CNAA.[20]

The fact that, for various reasons, Crosland opposed suggested 'transbinary' mergers — including Lanchester and the University of Warwick, Brighton and the University of Sussex — strengthened the feeling that the new public sector was being protected or singled out for special development.

It is possible, nevertheless, to take quite a different view of the relationship between the binary policy and perceptions of the universities — a view which would have resonances in the developing higher education systems of many other countries. This is that the policy was not an attack on the universities so much as a defence of their interests — whether or not correctly understood by officials and ministers. This is the view that the creation of a second, lower-status sector of higher education, capable of absorbing large numbers of less able, full-time and part-time students, would protect the universities and their traditional roles and processes from being swamped and distorted. This is a policy intention that has been attributed to Toby Weaver, and which (as Sir Toby) he largely confirmed in an article in 1982. The universities, he suggested, were 'for the most part . . . perhaps irreversibly, tight groupings of subject specialists properly intent on the possession, expansion and transmission of the knowledge they guard'. The problem was how to protect that function 'compatibly with meeting the educational needs of the population'. The wider function of a higher education, which Weaver defined as education for 'capability, creativity or communion', was incompatible with the organization of the universities. In the key part of his argument, he faces the need for a solution:

> . . . the increasingly articulate demand of society, voiced by parents, employers, politicians and the students themselves is for just this wider service — wider in aims, wider in curriculum and wider in access. I believe that the polytechnics and other public service institutions should leave to the universities the essential functions of pursuing and transmitting specialist knowledge through research and scholarship and that, drawing on this knowledge should concentrate on the no less difficult and important task of meeting this wider demand from potential learners from 18 to 80.

He recognized that he could be accused of a conservative, 'indeed reactionary', direction for the universities, and of condemning the public sector to second-class status, but 'unrepentant I shall believe that in the long run this represents the logical development of both the Robbins principle and the binary policy'.[21]

It is possible to regard the perceived characteristics of the universities as both strengths and weaknesses, to applaud or to regret their commitment to the 'guardianship' of knowledge and their resistance to performing the 'wider service', and in both cases to end up with the binary policy. It is unlikely that Weaver's views in 1982 were significantly different from those he held when he was involved in creating that binary policy in the mid-1960s, and it is likely that his arguments reflect one of the elements in the decisions made. The origins of the decisions are probably complex, and inevitably the responses were diverse. Many thought the policy confused or at least unfortunate in not allowing what Peter Venables called the 'natural evolution' of institutions to university status.[22] Boris Ford thought that Lord Robbins and his Committee had to accept some of the blame 'for the ease with which the grey eminences at the Department have been able to enlist radical ministers like Sir Edward Boyle and Mr Crosland in support of policies that are socially and academically reactionary'.[23] There were those — and Ford was one — who thought the binary system and the role of the CNAA would prevent a more natural local or regional grouping of institutions. Ford believed, in fact, that putting colleges with the CNAA rather than their local university meant for students that 'academically they might as well take the train to London'.[24] Lord Kings Norton had a different view of alternatives to a rigidly conceived binary divide:

> My personal hope is that we shall move away from a formalised dichotomy of university and non-university institutions, and that there will be a less obvious division: two groups of educational organisations with parity of esteem in the public mind. I hope it is not too fanciful to think in terms of the old universities, the civic universities, the former colleges of advanced technology, and the polytechnics grouped like the colours in a spectrum each with its distinctive character but with no barriers.[25]

Even where the binary policy was welcomed — for instance in the Association of Teachers in Technical Institutes (ATTI) and the local authorities — there were often reservations, either about the rigidity of the binary boundary, or about the possibility of the 'public sector' acquiring suffecent resources or status. The Inner London Education Authority expressed anxiety about the ability of the polytechnics to reconcile the DES pressure for them to retain their sub-degree work and the CNAA search for an academic environment appropriate to degree-level work.[26] The CVCP indignantly pointed out that all universities were vocational and responsive, and that 'higher education' consisted of three parts, not two, the third being the colleges of education.[27] Sir Lionel Russell, with a view from within the CNAA and the local authorities, said that he had never understood Crosland's Woolwich speech and why he made it, and had doubts about the concentration in polytechnics because of the disappointment it meant to other colleges.[28] At a meeting of the CNAA Council the Vice-Chancellor of the University of Exeter said that he was 'not enthusiastic' about the binary policy, and that many other vice-chancellors shared his view.[29]

In the consideration given to the new policy, the position of the CNAA inevitably came under scrutiny, particularly what now appeared to be the permanent and powerful role it would develop in relation to the formally established public sector. Robbins summarized the intentions of his Committee in this regard as being to encourage a 'more or less continuous spectrum in the developing system of higher education', and within that spectrum to have institutions that would gradually acquire university status: 'our recommendation of the creation of the National Council for Academic Awards was designed to be part of such a continuous sytem'.[30] Describing the CNAA in 1965, Venables said of the wider powers given to it than those of the NCTA, that it was apparent that 'it is government policy for the CNAA to exert a central role in the rapid development of a quasi-university system within "the public sector". It may at least be surmised that such a role was not envisaged for the CNAA by university representatives in the discussions which led to its being proposed and established'.[31] Lionel Elvin, Director of the University of London Institute of Education, had, as a member of the Robbins Committee, framed its recommendations for the teacher training colleges (as they were called before the committee's recommendation that they be renamed colleges of education) to be brought within the universities' ambit. He was also strongly opposed to the CNAA being responsible for the development of a rival system to that of the universities, rather than the safety net for the universities that he had envisaged.[32] Instead of an awarding body for the 'small cadet universities' as conceived by Robbins, the CNAA had become a 'permanent major degree awarding body for very large institutions . . . of a new kind' — and therefore, as Eric Robinson suggested in 1973, the universities now had to share the apex of the educational system with the polytechnics and the CNAA.[33] While Robinson applauded the development, Boris Ford condemned the transition of the CNAA from a body simply working with institutions which had 'not yet been upgraded and which could not obtain a degree through a neighbouring university' and therefore working in tandem with the universities, to a body which had become 'a fully blown alternative to the university system'.[34] The Vice-Chancellor of the University of Manchester, speaking in Canada, was cautious and ambivalent. The CNAA, he explained, would take pressure off the University of London, and if other universities were not prepared to enter the field of external degrees 'they could not complain at the creation of the new body'. What had not been foreseen was the linking of the CNAA with a public system of higher education 'as rigidly conceived as it is implemented by present governmental policy'. He was not blind to the dangers of 'a private and a public sector in higher education, both largely financed from the public purse'. He was not going to become unduly agitated about all of this: 'vigilant, yes, but not agitated'.[35]

It has been important to review the establishment of a binary system and some of its implications, as although the CNAA was created in 1964, it was the binary policy and its implementation that set the seal on the CNAA's operations for the next two decades. The CNAA's own response to the binary policy was remarkably muted, given probably that the policy in effect simply enlarged and extended the CNAA's existing and developing pattern of activity. Its Charter was unaffected, the range of its subject interests was in any case growing, and the basic nature of its validation relationships with colleges was not affected in the short term by the designation of any of them as polytechnics. In January 1966, following receipt of a DES memorandum on the future of the further education system (containing the suggestion of the designation of thirty or so 'polytechnic centres'), the Council 'welcomed the proposal of concentrating resources in a limited number of major centres', as this would 'greatly assist the achievement of higher standards for the Council's degrees'. It hoped that the final proposals would be flexible enough to allow advanced work to continue, however, in other colleges where the need existed in other centres of population. The DES memorandum suggested that the new institutions be called 'polytechnic institutes' (another throwback to the late nineteenth-century institutions) but the Council expressed a preference for 'polytechnic colleges' — and neither nomenclature in fact survived.[36] The Council's response to the policy and to the creation of the polytechnics was expressed most firmly in relation to research. The notes of guidance accompanying the Secretary of State's announcement on the polytechnics in 1967 were considered by the Council to be 'considerably more liberal than the original draft which had been amended since the Chairman of the Council had made representations about the matter to the Secretary of State'. Although it was still a disappointing document and discouraging, it was agreed that the terms of the statement would enable the colleges to 'develop research in the way that they wished'. When Pimlott addressed the Council on the White Paper in September 1966, members of the Council had been 'very disturbed by Mr Pimlott's statement that research would not be a primary activity of the colleges'.[37] An emphasis on its own policy for research was to be one of the CNAA's most tangible responses to the development of a public sector of higher education.

The CNAA's developmental policies focussed, as intended, on the range of subjects which colleges proposed to offer, and on the questions of quality with which the Council and its committees were concerned from the beginning. The functioning of the polytechnics, as their schemes began to be accepted and formal designations made, was to become of increasing interest to the CNAA, and the issues surrounding relationships were to become increasingly prominent, with regard to such matters as the roles of Academic Boards, resource allocation and internal evaluation.

Following a statement to Parliament and his Woolwich speech in March and April 1965, Crosland set up an informal planning group under the Minister of State, Reg Prentice, 'to discuss the future pattern of advanced work in the further education system' and 'the related question of the best arrangements for the government of such colleges'. Frank Hornby was invited to be a member of this group — like the others also, in his personal capacity.[38] The group in fact discussed the questions of polytechnic internal government and other questions covered in Crosland's Parliamentary statement on the polytechnics and the administrative memorandum of April 1967. Although the CNAA was not itself formally involved in this planning, it was involved in the consultations, and at various points it linked in with the continuing policy developments. As the Chairman of the CNAA wrote in 1970:

> It has been suggested recently by a press commentator that without the CNAA there would be no polytechnics, and undoubtedly if the Council did not exist some similar body would be necessary to give the new institutions the opportunities they need for their full development.[39]

By the time the polytechnics were formally designated (the first provisional designation of eighteen polytechnics was announced in May 1968 and the designations continued into the early 1970s), the CNAA already had several years of experience of validation procedures, of evaluating the quality of courses and their institutional environments. Although the CNAA was not now to oversee a rolling programme of promotions to the 'university club', how much autonomy the new polytechnics would want and acquire — from their local authorities and the CNAA — was to be a feature of debate from the creation of the first polytechnics, and from the decision to set up a Committee of Directors of Polytechnics in December 1969 and its formal establishment in April 1970. In one critical sense none of the new policy-making affected the CNAA: its purpose remained to validate degrees and other awards in institutions other than universities — whether or not they were designated as polytechnics. The CNAA was overwhelmingly concerned with the approval or otherwise of courses submitted to it. In ensuring that these were of comparable standard with that of the universities, the CNAA became inevitably — though its Charter did not make this explicit — concerned with those institutional features, beyond the details of the course itself, which affected judgment of the quality of the student experience. In this respect the CNAA's central concerns would have remained the same whatever policy governments formulated, so long as there were 'non-university' institutions seeking approval for their courses under the terms of the CNAA's Charter.

The creation of the polytechnics was, however, to influence the range of subject areas validated by the CNAA — notably by the subsequent history of courses in art and design. From its inception through the late 1960s and into the 1970s the courses proposed to, and approved by, the CNAA remained predominantly in science and technology. In September 1968 the CNAA had approved a total of 213 courses, of which 175 were undergraduate courses and 12 were MSc courses. Of the 15,547 students enrolled on CNAA courses three-quarters were in science and technology. By this stage the Committee for Science and Technology had twelve subject boards, and was approving courses in new subject and interdisciplinary areas, many described as of 'considerable industrial importance' — including for the first time instrumentation and control engineering, and computer systems engineering. In 1967–8 interdisciplinary courses were approved in environmental engineering (involving collaboration between scientists, engineers, architects, public health officers and industrial management), engineering geology and geotechnics, and statistics and computing. The six MSc courses approved in that year were in areas directly relevant to industrial research and development, including diesel engine design, molecular science of materials and operational research.[40]

In the late 1960s, in the arts and social studies areas there were more good intentions than successful proposals. Even at the time the study group that was planning the establishment of the Committee for Arts and Social Studies met in April 1965 there were proposals waiting to be processed in business studies, languages, sociology, psychology, administration, economics, law and 'combined subjects', with business studies leading the field in both honours and ordinary degree course proposals by a wide margin. By September 1968 the nearly 4000 students enrolled on arts and social studies courses included students of librarianship and the sociology of education, textile marketing and social and public administration. Twenty-three of the courses approved by this point were sandwich courses, and 12 per cent of the students enrolled had qualifications other than the General Certificate of Education (as compared with 33 per cent in science and technology).[41] The following year the Council reported that 'the average number of first year enrolments in arts and social studies is forty-seven per course entry while in science and technology it is twenty-seven. This situation reflects the great demand for degree places in Arts and Social Studies and a number of the colleges could have admitted many more well qualified students if they had the resources to cope with them'. In business studies there were generally six or so applicants for each place.[42]

The Committee for Arts and Social Studies confirmed at its third meeting, in April 1966, that 'it was established that courses submitted to the Council would not necessarily have to be directly vocational in nature'. The only criterion was that 'all courses approved should be comparable in standard to those of a university'. It then, in October, expressed its concern that a high proportion of courses in subjects other than business studies were being turned down, and it suggested that one of the reasons making it difficult for such courses to be approved might be that 'the Council's present structure of honours and ordinary degrees was not so appropriate for courses in those fields' as in science and technology. The controversy over ordinary and honours degree pathways was to smoulder between CASS and CST, and the CASS pressure for the ending of the policy was countered consistently by CST with the argument that in science and technology it was appropriate to have two types of course, and that in general it considered students with lower abilities and attainments were more suitably educated 'in courses specially designed to make a different intellectual demand'.[43] CASS was also encouraging the development of part-time degrees, a policy which won an expression of DES approval for these and other CNAA efforts in this direction, since they would appeal to married women wishing to return to study (and presumably helping to solve a shortage of school teachers).[44]

The rapidity with which the CNAA sought to respond to the demand for business studies courses can be judged by the fact that the Business Studies Board, which began to meet in March 1965, had held five meetings by July. The Crick Committee, which had been appointed in 1961 and reported on *A Higher Award in Business Studies* in 1964, had originally been looking for an equivalent of the DipTech, but had waited for the Robbins Report before issuing its recommendations. It did so around its central conception of what an appropriate 'high level' qualification in business studies should offer:

> an advanced education which, while comparable to a university honours degree course in quality and standard, differs from it in method. While the aim is to offer a good general education in subjects relevant to business, the method is the systematic linking of academic study with practical experience. This points to the sandwich form of education and training as being the only suitable form for the courses we have in mind.

Economics, sociology, mathematics, law and accounting were suggested as the essential subjects, and although colleges could provide liberal studies also, 'we would stress the importance we attach to a liberal treatment of the whole curriculum'.[45] There was no doubting the eagerness of many colleges to respond to the challenge and the opportunity, and the Board — containing a number of lively young university people and interested employers — was torn between its anxiety to go ahead quickly and the need to ensure that it established what it called at its first meeting 'lasting standards'. Something like 80 per cent of proposed courses were turned down when first submitted in the late 1960s. Between March and July 1965 the Board looked in detail at the first six courses before it, conducted visits and pondered policy. There was, the Board felt, a need to reconcile two 'separate images' of a degree course in business studies, 'that of intellectual rigour presented in the university pattern, and that of a new range of studies designed to meet the needs of the business world'. The early meetings of the Board were preoccupied with the details of visits, attention to the content of courses — including, for example, law, office organization and communication studies — and the balance of what was being proposed. At the sixth meeting members agreed that 'as a result of their examination of the first six courses they had established certain standards for assessment and were now able to make an objective judgment upon the courses submitted'. They decided therefore that at their next meeting they would devote themselves to matters of 'general policy affecting courses in business studies', and they did in fact, in September, consider a draft memorandum on courses leading to first degrees, and questions regarding board membership and procedures for the consideration of courses.[46] The Board, which became the Economics and Business Studies Board in 1966, continued to be concerned primarily with the detail of proposed courses, examination arrangements and revisions to courses not approved. It also began to look at proposals for MA courses, and at its November 1966 meeting, for example, it expressed the view that a proposed MA in Business Administration at Portsmouth College of Technology did not meet the CNAA's criterion that the content should be substantially postgraduate in character: too much of it was introductory work, insufficiently rooted in the basic disciplines.[47] The approach adopted by the Board and its parent bodies was both a response to the Crick recommendations and acceptable to the appropriate institutes for exemption and to the employers. Its influence on the colleges, including the future polytechnics, was also important. HMI Baker, who had been a Ministry of Education assessor on the Crick Committee, commented in 1968:

> The CNAA will exert — indeed has already exerted — a significant influence over the thinking of teachers in the polytechnics. In the past the attitude of the majority of teachers has been one of 'tell us what you want and we will provide it'. Today they are asked to think out their own courses in their own way, and to justify their thinking before a visiting panel of experts from the CNAA committee.[48]

Not everything in the CNAA's and the colleges' procedure was conducive to innovation, but the ripple effect from groups of staff having 'to think out their own courses' was probably one of the most immediate invitations to innovation in the early years of the CNAA.

The CNAA and its board structure were beginning to respond to proposals for courses in what the annual reports termed 'rarer subjects' or subjects 'not traditionally covered by universities', including printing, business law, town planning, surveying and a range of technologies. In January 1968 the Council considered information from Huddersfield College of Technology (soon to become Huddersfield Polytechnic) that it intended to submit a degree course in music. HMIs had already expressed a view that there was a prima facie case for the proposal, and the Council agreed that it would mean setting up a music board or at least an exploratory committee — and the DES music panel had offered suggestions of possible members.[49] Degrees in pharmacy were approved to the point at which an article in the *Times Educational Supplement* in 1971 could comment:

> About one third of the 1971 crop of pharmacy graduates will hold C.N.A.A. degrees. Since 1964 six polytechnics and colleges have taken the opportunity afforded them by the Council for National

Academic Awards to design and develop courses culminating in the
C.N.A.A. B.Sc. degree.

It quoted from the *Pharmaceutical Journal*, which had commented that
CNAA degrees were to be comparable with those of the universities, and
'teachers in pharmacy are confident that this is, and will remain so'.[50]

One of the important new professional areas that grew under CNAA
auspices was librarianship. A sub-committee then a Librarianship Board was
established in 1966. The Board had long debates about whether the content
of degrees in the areas should be *for* or *in* librarianship, what the academic
content of study should be, and what career opportunities would be open
to students if they were not *subject* graduates. Interlock with the
requirements of the professional association was a crucial theme, and the
Library Association expressed its willingness to accept CNAA degrees for
postgraduate entry. Various possible approaches to course syllabuses were
outlined in 1967, and a paper submitted in that year by one member of the
Board on deliberations that had taken place in the Library Advisory Councils
indicated that 'they would welcome the development of CNAA first degrees
in librarianship or in librarianship associated with other disciplines'. There
was an explicit determination to ensure that all course elements studied and
assessed were at degree level, and there were criticisms of 'traditional'
submissions. A review of the Board's work in November 1971 indicated that
in the previous five years it had approved six courses in librarianship and
two in information science at a total of six colleges. The Board had from
the start been conscious of its pioneering role.[51]

Although the main CNAA developments in teacher education and in
art and design belong to the 1970s, the history of both really begins in 1965.
Hornby, as we have seen, was in that year emphasizing both the approaches
to the CNAA by many colleges to explore validation of teacher education
courses, and the caution with which the CNAA moved. By May 1966 the
Council agreed to treat teacher education, because of the existing roles of
the universities and institutes of education, 'with care and circumspection',
and the Council's Chairman was to keep the CVCP informed of
developments. He wrote to the CVCP, in fact, explaining that the CNAA
would be considering courses 'in Education', that it intended to approach
the whole question with care, and that although the Council 'was not taking
the initiative in seeking to extend its work in the field of Education, several
colleges of education had made informal approaches which could not be
ignored . . . I can assure you that the Council will not move very far without
consulting representatives of all the interested parties, including the institutes
of education'.[52] These consultations were, in fact, already well under way.
A meeting between the CNAA and the DES had taken place in June 1965,
and there were further meetings. In January 1966 Hornby met with
representatives of the Conference of Institute Directors, and in February
1966 the Association of Education Committees asked the CNAA to look

sympathetically on approaches from colleges of education. A key development in 1966 was the decision by the DES to begin teacher training in five of the technical colleges. By 1970 there were to be education departments in seven polytechnics in England and one in Northern Ireland. The CNAA knew from the first meeting of its sub-committee to discuss courses in education, in July 1965, that the DES was moving towards a policy of teacher education in some technical colleges, and that the DES thought it reasonable that they should come to the CNAA for validation.[53] The DES also believed that the colleges of education should seek validation from the universities before turning to the CNAA. Protracted discussions began with Worcester College in 1966, as the test case of the CNAA's intentions and possibilities. Worcester was disappointed with the University of Birmingham's responses to the College's degree proposals and submitted an application to the CNAA. The new Committee agreed to ask the University of Birmingham to comment on the application, visits were made to the College, and discussion of the proposals and their implications continued. In 1970 Worcester decided not to continue with the CNAA application because Birmingham was reviewing its BEd and the new arrangements would probably be acceptable to the College.[54]

Worcester, in Christopherson's expression, 'was the experiment'.[55] The CNAA had to decide not only the merits of the particular case, but whether it would be willing and able (under its Charter) to validate a teachers' certificate as well as a degree, and how it might relate to the Area Training Organizations which had some responsibility for the teaching practice component of existing courses. Of a different nature was a proposal from Enfield College of Technology, the first such to be considered, for a part-time BA in Social Science for qualified teachers. This also led to protracted discussions, including meetings and visits jointly with the Sociological Studies Board before the course was finally approved. Other proposals for teacher education courses were submitted before the end of the decade, but none was approved. St Osyth's College of Education at Clacton-on-Sea proposed a BEd in 1969 and by December of the following year it had been turned down on the grounds that the College did not have an 'appropriate academic structure', more thought about the objectives of the course (it was for teachers of Home Economics) was needed, the staff needed strengthening, the library expanding and laboratory facilities improving.[56] The first course to be approved was in fact in Scotland, and was submitted to the CNAA with the support of the Scottish Education Department in 1970. The proposal, from Notre Dame College, a Catholic college in Glasgow, was received sympathetically, but was not approved at a visit to the College in December. A meeting was arranged with the College Principal and officials of the SED to discuss the College environment, staff numbers and 'capacity'. Enough progress had been made by March 1971 for a BEd ordinary degree to be approved.

Didsbury College, Manchester, Dunfermline College, Edinburgh, and others were talking with the CNAA in 1970, in the former case about a certificate as well as a degree, but national policies on teacher education were now coming under the microscope, and there were no other approvals in this field until after the James Committee on teacher education had reported in 1972. In 1971 the CNAA gave evidence to the James Committee expressing its willingness to take on the validation of the Teachers Certificate if there was a need for it to do so.[57] For six years or so the CNAA had moved with caution — indeed, only one of its officers, Francis Hanrott, had any previous experience involving contact with teacher education, and he was given responsibility for the various levels of negotiation. The teams that visited Worcester, Notre Dame and elsewhere were large ones, and in some cases — proposals for movement and dance at Worcester, for example — the territory was new.[58] University — and particularly institute of education — suspicion of the entry of the CNAA into the field also spurred the universities to take up the challenge to validate the BEd that Robbins had thrown down. By the time the James Committee met, the CNAA was not only prepared, but experienced enough, to respond rapidly to opportunities and demands.

In art and design the position was somewhat different. The National Council for Diplomas in Art and Design (NCDAD) (the Summerson Council) was established in 1961. The question of the relationship with the CNAA was provoked in 1965 by an approach to the CNAA from the Scottish Woollen Technical College at Galashiels to validate a degree in textile design. The NCDAD did not operate in Scotland, and it could not award degrees — working, as the NCTA had done, on the basis of a Deed of Trust, not a Charter. If approved, would the Galashiels course be a precedent? Would the Diploma be devalued? Would there be two bodies operating in the same field? Discussion in the NCDAD raised the question of the possibility of its seeking a Charter, but also the possibility — some thought the spectre — of amalgamation between the NCDAD and the CNAA. Some — including the ATTI — were in favour of an amalgamation. Opinion in the NCDAD was generally hostile, among other reasons because it was feared that degrees in art and design would mean raising the entry qualifications. Two meetings were held, involving the Chairman and Chief Officer of the CNAA, the Chairman and other representatives of the NCDAD, and the DES. The CNAA's preoccupation was with future arrangements regarding proposals for combined courses in technology and art and design, but the question of possible amalgamation was bypassed, not to be reopened from 1966 until the early 1970s. The historian of these events believes that the CNAA may not have shown sufficient flexibility: 'if the same attitude as was adopted in the early 1970s by its new Chief Officer, Edwin Kerr, had been taken, amalgamation might have occurred sooner'.[59]

Of considerable relevance for the future of art and design were the decisions regarding the establishment of the polytechnics. Some of these institutions were to be the outcome of local amalgamations — including colleges of art. The polytechnic proposals suggested the possibility of federation as well as amalgamation, but in practice the DES was hostile to federation, and none was approved. The colleges of art, therefore, were in many places faced with the proposal to become departments of designated polytechnics, and from the outset the NCDAD and the colleges were opposed, even violently opposed, to the development. In November 1966 the NCDAD wrote to the DES in response to its draft memorandum on the government and academic organization of the polytechnics:

> The Council is of the opinion that the proposals in the main set forth
> in the Department's document . . . are inimical to the best interests
> of advanced art education. The Council is of the opinion that a
> federated system of colleges should be permitted . . .[60]

Extensive correspondence took place between the National Council and the colleges, as well as with the local authorities and the Secretary of State. Pressures from the DES and what in some cases amounted to directives from local authorities, led the colleges concerned to move away from outright hostility to testing out what degree of autonomy and protection for art and design would be forthcoming within the polytechnic structure. At the West of England College of Art, for example, the Chairman of the Governing Body and some other members were — like the Principal and staff of the college — strongly opposed to the proposed merger into Bristol Polytechnic, but the proposals ultimately went forward 'without acrimony'. The Principal wrote in November 1967 that the only recourse was 'to ensure that every possible safeguard should be written into the constitution of such a scheme', and following local negotiations he considered that 'we have gone as far as we are able so far to safeguard the courses and attitudes of this College and we have confidence that the LEA are making every effort to ensure that Diploma in Art and Design (DipAD) courses and developments will be given the fullest support, and will not be undermined in any way by the Polytechnic proposals'. At Liverpool the Principal wrote, also at the end of 1967, that within the new polytechnic 'there will be complete autonomy in respect of the academic work of the Faculty of Art and nothing that has been said causes me to have any misgivings on this score'.[61]

While negotiations with the CNAA had been discontinued, the position of art and design within some newly emerging polytechnics inevitably raised the question of the status of the diploma alongside degree awards, and of multiple validation of degree-level awards. By the beginning of the 1970s the relationship was therefore again under scrutiny. In November 1970 the CNAA was informed that the NCDAD had written formally to request a joint meeting to explore 'interrelationships'. Stewart Mason, Chairman of the NCDAD, was at the same time proposing to write to polytechnics and colleges with DipAD courses, in advance of a meeting of the London Colleges Alliance the following month, to raise the possibility of the two bodies 'getting closer together', and suggesting that they would 'probably amalgamate'. David Lloyd Jones at the DES was shown a draft of the letter and objected to the reference to amalgamation, as 'precipitating certain apprehensions'. Mason's rejoinder was that he was not going 'to be gagged' about amalgamation. The battle, he wrote, 'is not one for the future but is on NOW . . . I am not going to write to the Colleges themselves one week with bureaucratic non-talk and then come into the clear the following week . . . if there is going to be an outburst I believe the sooner we get it over the better. It is like going into Europe — the important thing is by reiteration to make people think, whether they are for it or against it, that it is inevitable'.[62] At its meeting in February 1972 the CNAA endorsed an initiative by the Chairmen of the two bodies to suggest entering into discussions about the possibility of an amalgamation[63] — which finally came about in 1974.

Although in some subject areas there were complaints that proposals from the colleges were too 'traditional' (and a belief by some colleges that this was the best way to ensure success with the 'traditional' members of subject boards), there were developments unrelated to specific subjects that were new and — in validation terms — difficult. This was particularly true of interdisciplinary and unit-based or modular courses. These presented problems for the validation process, and raised sharp questions about coherence — particularly from members of visiting teams suspicious of departures from standard university structures. Some of the officers concerned were also unsure at the time that such courses had been sufficiently thought through.[64] There were proponents in the colleges, however, who believed both in the virtues of the courses and in the likely positive impact on departmental separatism in the institutions. Business studies and town planning were examples of early interdisciplinary courses approved by the CNAA. City of London Polytechnic and Oxford Polytechnic were two of the institutions which sought to combine an interdisciplinary approach with a modular structure. By 1970 the former was negotiating an ambitious first degree scheme with the CNAA, which was explained by the Vice-Provost as more fully meeting the needs of students, employers and society, and was presented in the belief that 'polytechnics should develop a degree pattern which includes an increasing amount of interdisciplinary study'. The City of London plan was for students in the first semester (sixteen weeks) to take three basic courses, followed by a second semester in which three introductory courses stemming from the basic courses would be followed. Advanced course units would then be taken, with a combination of twelve of them in one subject area leading to an honours degree, twelve in two subjects to a joint honours, and various other 'less demanding combinations' to ordinary degrees:

> If it is felt that this smacks too much of the 'green shield stamp' approach, it should be realized that it is intended that the scheme will operate with a substantial element of vocational and tutorial guidance using specialized staff.[65]

Discussing the need for greater student mobility and the advantages of unit courses for a 'national degree system', the Dean of the Faculty of Educational Studies at the Open University suggested that the basis of a unit-based, credit transfer system already existed since 'inside the CNAA we already have one of the elements required: that, we have a national degree system. The CNAA is constitutionally able to approve suitable courses without altering its charter'.[66] Modular degrees were to become more widespread in the 1970s as the colleges of education — including those validated by universities — diversified, but some of these substantial programmes introduced by polytechnics and gaining CNAA approval were pioneering new curricular patterns at the undergraduate level.

By the beginning of the 1970s the sandwich course commitment was accompanied by a variety of difficulties. There is no doubt about the commitment. As Sir Alan Richmond recalls it: 'we were very hot on sandwich courses, almost dogmatic about it for a time'. In the early years of the CNAA it was almost impossible for a course in engineering to gain approval unless it was a sandwich course: 'there was a big argument within CNAA when the first courses on the university pattern started to emerge'. Brighton caused controversy by proposing to teach full-time and sandwich students together for part of the time. The integration of industrial experience and the college course was 'always very important but always very tenuous in analysis and judgment'. Some made a good job of the sandwich element, but many paid it lip service.[67] In 1967–68, the Council's Training Panel looked at the problems and set up two sub-committees to be concerned with the practical training element of sandwich courses in arts and social studies, and in science and technology. The Panel's aim was to help colleges to establish more effective integration of the practical training and academic study, and more effective supervision of training and assessment of students' work.[68] The question of the assessment of practical training was a difficult one. The assessment did not contribute to the student's final classification, and whether and how it might do so was neither clear nor a welcome issue in the colleges. The Coombe Lodge conference of mainly polytechnic staff in 1970 heard the Chairman of the Training Panel argue the case for assessment, though also for much discussion and the introduction of a scheme slowly. The report of the discussion that followed his lecture indicates the strength of feeling: it was 'received by the conference with total scepticism'. Members viewed the creation of the Industrial Training Panel as an attempt 'to force upon colleges what they already vociferously deny they want'. The majority saw little future for college-based sandwich courses, let alone the assessment of the industrial part. Colleges were experiencing great difficulty in finding industrial placements for students. Administrative complications and the high cost of running the course had resulted in a 'heavy swing of opinion away from the sandwich to the full-time course'.[69] There was in the polytechnics and colleges, as there had also been in the colleges of advanced technology, some general discussion about the validity of sandwich courses as such, given the possibility that they might be a means of perpetuating outdated practices. Some leading figures in engineering, for example, were in two minds about sandwich courses and about the quality of practically-oriented polytechnic graduates in competition with more 'imaginative' university graduates.[70] Although there were some reservations of this kind in both industry and the institutions the balance of opinion was with the sandwich course, and within the Committee for Science and Technology and its boards the commitment to sandwich courses remained strong. Despite the problems and doubts, sandwich courses remained a central feature of the polytechnics — even as some institutions began to press for full-time courses to replace or to accompany them.

In terms of difficulty and controversy it was, however, the CNAA's policy of complementary and contrasting studies, enshrined in Statement No. 3, that occupied the centre of the stage within the CNAA almost from the adoption of the policy until 1971. What the statement laid down — following the NCTA tradition — was that all courses had to include 'studies which by complementing or contrasting with the main subjects studied will help to provide a balanced education'. Science and technology students might be introduced to social and economic problems, and arts students might 'gain an appreciation of science and technology in modern life'. It was often possible, the statement continued, to bring out in all courses:

> the fact that scientific method, in the sense of a critical and sceptical approach to enquiry and a readiness to test hypotheses, enters at many points into so-called arts subjects, and that equally the spirit of speculative enquiry, the exercise of creative imagination and the capacity for making value judgments are important in the activities of the scientist and technologist.[71]

Both the policy and the range of practices in the colleges raised questions. Those who taught the 'liberal studies' components were often accused of being unsympathetic to 'the activities of the scientist and technologist'. The CNAA's policy was viewed as ad hoc and unresearched. Students were often resistant to these components of their courses. Within the CNAA the controversy was, to say the least, lively. When a joint committee of CST and CASS was set up during the debates, it was chaired by Sir Alan Richmond, who described it as 'the most difficult committee I have ever chaired in my life'.[72]

The basic issue was compulsory complementary and contrasting studies for arts students. Many of the university members of CASS and its boards were opposed to the principle, especially as it had been adopted before the arts and social studies had any real influence in the CNAA. Critics saw the policy as a legacy of the NCTA and applicable perhaps to technical but not higher education. The concerns became explicit in 1967 when CASS considered Statement No. 3, and suggested that a joint sub-committee with

CST was needed to discuss the issues.[73] Views continued to be expressed in CASS regarding the inappropriate nature of the CNAA's principle when applied in particular to interdisciplinary and wide-ranging courses like business studies and town planning. Some subject board chairmen were adamant that they were not prepared to implement a policy that they had had no hand in shaping. In the Joint Committee that was set up the conflict was, in Hanrott's words, 'played cool', but it was conflict nevertheless. There were threats of resignation over what some saw as an issue of academic freedom.[74] The debate continued within CASS and CST and in a sub-committee of each. The issue was discussed, in fact, at ten meetings of CASS, and three meetings of each of the sub-committees.[75] It was clear that the policy could not survive in its existing form, and in 1970 agreement was being reached on a new approach. The CNAA announced that its policy of requiring the inclusion of complementary or contrasting studies in courses in order to provide a balanced educational experience had been 'under review', and that changes would shortly be announced intended to respond to recent developments in the colleges and allow greater flexibility.[76] In January 1971, after the considerable discussion in its committees, the Council adopted a new formulation, dropping the stipulation of a specific requirement. Courses were still expected to provide 'as balanced an educational experience as possible', and to aim at developing in students a number of abilities:

> to think logically, communicate clearly, and read critically and with understanding. To make the student aware of the limitations of his disciplines and their methods and to provide opportunities for him to understand, make, and criticize, value judgments. To give the student an understanding of the significance of science and technology in modern society, of the contribution they can make to improve material conditions and in widening man's imaginative horizons and his understanding of the universe.[77]

While the CNAA had been debating and arriving at a new policy statement, a considerable diversity of approaches had developed in the institutions. Some had strong traditions of liberal studies inherited from the NCTA arrangements. Some had made the original policy an enthusiastic part of their provision. Some — in areas like librarianship — had little or no provision in complementary and contrasting studies.[78] The removal of the requirement, while retaining the broad objectives, ended the controversy as a question of principle and placed the responsibility on the subject boards and their panels to monitor the ways in which institutions and their courses interpreted the changed policy. Compulsory 'liberal studies' was, however, not to remain a distinctive feature of CNAA degrees as they had been of the Diploma in Technology.

By the early 1970s the CNAA had established and reviewed policies; framed a pattern of degrees and made the revisions which resulted, for example, in the adoption of the degree and degree with honours, branching from a common foundation, to replace the essentially two-track ordinary and honours structure; and arrived at a broad and growing diversity of subject areas to validate, with a potential to make a major contribution in additional areas. It had also introduced postgraduate diplomas and higher doctorates to supplement the undergraduate, masters and doctoral degrees it had decided on at an early stage. It had set up a Committee for Research Degrees in 1965, as well as a study group on research degrees to look at policy for this activity, and had developed research degree relationships with industrial firms and research establishments.

The CNAA had become not just the 'safety net' validating body envisaged by the Robbins Committee and others, but also a major factor in the implementation of the new binary policy and the promotion of colleges, not to 'university status' by inclusion in the existing pattern of universities, but to a major element in a binary approach to what constituted 'higher education'. It had entered into these relationships with the new category of institutions while retaining its role for the validation of degree-level courses from whatever direction they might come outside the universities. Whether or not this was all a move towards a system of 'state universities' on the American model, was a genuine attempt to provide an alternative and distinctive system, or was a retreat from and a weakening of the Robbins approach to a 'unitary' system of higher education was to remain a matter of debate at the policy level. In procedural terms also there was to be no shortage of room for ambiguity.

Notes

1 J.A.P. Hall (1969) 'CNAA and the philosophy of polytechnic education', Coombe Lodge Study Conference Report, *The Development of the New Polytechnics*, p. 5.
2 Eric Robinson (1973) 'The future of teacher education in the polytechnics' in Donald E. Lomax (Ed.) *The Education of Teachers in Britain*, John Wiley, p. 118.
3 P.R. Sharp (1987) *The Creation of the Local Authority Sector of Higher Education*, Falmer Press, p. 39.
4 *ibid.*, pp. 39–40.
5 Lord Robbins (1965) interview with Boris Ford, *UQ*, 20, 1, pp. 6–7.
6 Edward Boyle (1966) 'Parliament and university policy', *Minerva*, 5, p. 9.
7 Anthony Crosland, speech at Woolwich Polytechnic, 27 April 1965 in John Pratt and Tyrrell Burgess (1974) *Polytechnics: A Report*, Pitman, pp. 203–4.
8 Polytechnics. Parliamentary statement by the Secretary of State for Education and Science on 5 April, 1967; Appendix A: Government and Academic Organization of Polytechnics; Appendix B: Research in Polytechnics; Appendix C: Designation of Polytechnics (these constituted Administrative Memorandum 8/67), CN Box 54.
9 Sir Norman Lindop, private communication.
10 Lord Robbins, interview with Ford, p. 9.
11 John Carswell (1985) *Government and the Universities in Britain*, Cambridge University Press, p. 93.

12 Boyle, 'Parliament and university policy', p. 17.
13 Reported in *The Times*, 10 December 1966.
14 Eric Robinson (1988) 'The polytechnics: 20 years of "social control"', *Higher Education Review*, 20, 2, p. 19.
15 Lord Robbins, interview with Ford, p. 9.
16 Sir Derman Christopherson, HS interview.
17 Boris Ford (1966) 'Crisis in higher education: Has Crosland made a basic error of judgment?', *New Statesman*, 21 January, p. 84.
18 Carswell, *Government and the Universities in Britain*, pp. 75–6.
19 Boyle, 'Parliament and university policy', p. 13.
20 Brian MacArthur (1966) 'Running down the universities', *The Guardian*, 1 September.
21 Toby Weaver (1982) 'Policy options for post-tertiary education', *Higher Education Review*, 14, 2, p. 17.
22 Peter Venables (1965) 'Confusion, concentration and clarification in higher education', *Comparative Education*, 2, 1, p. 12.
23 Ford, 'Crisis in higher education', p. 84.
24 *ibid.*, p. 86.
25 Lord Kings Norton (1970) 'The CNAA and the polytechnics', *The Guardian*, 12 February.
26 ILEA response to 1967 Memorandum on Polytechnics, Notes from the Chief Education Officer, pp. 4–6.
27 CVCP (1967) *Report on the Quinquennium 1962-1967*, London, p. 14.
28 Sir Lionel Russell, MD interview.
29 Sir James Cook, Cmin, 26 January 1966.
30 Lord Robbins (1980) *Higher Education Revisited*, Macmillan, p. 99.
31 Sir Peter Venables (1965) 'Dualism in higher education', *UQ*, 20, 1, pp. 17–18.
32 Lionel Elvin (1972) 'Jettisoning James', *Times Educational Supplement*, 15 December, p. 5.
33 Robinson, 'The future of teacher education in the polytechnics', p. 118.
34 Ford, 'Crisis in higher education', p. 83.
35 William Mansfield Cooper (1966) 'Change in Britain' in William Mansfield Cooper, *et al.* (Eds) *Governments and the University*, Macmillan, pp. 14–15.
36 Cmin, 26 January 1966.
37 Cmin 5 May 1967 and 30 September 1966.
38 NC Box 53, Crosland to Hornby, 10 May 1965.
39 Lord Kings Norton, 'The CNAA and the polytechnics'.
40 CN, *1967–8 Report*, pp. 81–9 and 37–8.
41 *ibid.*, pp. 8 and 37–8.
42 CN, *Report for 1968-9*, p. 14; E.I. Baker (1968) 'The future of business studies', *Trends in Education*, 9, p. 25.
43 CASSmin, 22 April, 21 October and 15 December 1966, and 27 April 1967.
44 CASSmin, 15 December 1966.
45 NACEIC (1964) *A Higher Award in Business Studies*, HMSO, pp. 2 and 9–12.
46 Minutes Business Studies Board, 19 March, 2 and 23 April, 25 May, 2 July and 30 September 1965.
47 Minutes Business Studies Board, 18 November 1966.
48 Baker, 'The future of business studies', p. 27.
49 Cmin, 23 January 1968.
50 Natasha Kidwai (1971) 'CNAA degrees for more pharmacists', *Times Educational Supplement*, 21 May.
52 Librarianship Board, Summary of the Board's Work to Date, with Board minute, 8 November 1971.
52 Letter from Lord Kings Norton, 9 June 1966, with CVCP agenda, 17 June 1966.

53 Minutes of Sub-Committee for Courses in Education, 29 July 1966; attached is DES statement of April 1966, Departments of Education in Technical Colleges.

54 CEdmin, 6 April 1967 and 26 January 1968 (including reports of two visits to Worcester), 5 July and 11 December 1968, 27 March 1969 and 7 July 1970.

55 Sir Derman Christopherson, MD interview.

56 CEdmin, 27 March 1969 and 10 December 1970.

57 CEdmin, 30 March 1971.

58 Hanrott, HS interview.

59 Robert Strand (1987) *A Good Deal of Freedom: Art and Design in the Public Sector of Higher Education, 1960–1982*, CNAA, pp. 47–52.

60 CN Box 54, file 'Miscellaneous correspondence . . .', F. Walsh, Secretary of NCDAD, to Miss K.A. Kennedy, DES, 29 November 1966.

61 CN Box 54, Memorandum by the Principal, West of England College of Art, Bristol, 28 November 1967; Letter from the Principal, Liverpool Regional College of Art, to the Chief Officer, NCDAD, 6 December 1967. See same file for correspondence with DES and others.

62 CN Box 54, Lloyd Jones to Mason, 16 December 1971; Mason to Lloyd Jones, 29 December 1971.

63 Cmin, 22 February 1972.

64 Rossiter and Hanrott, HS interviews.

65 R.M.W. Rickett (1970) 'Future pattern of degree work', *TES*, 4 December, pp. 230–1.

66 Walter James (1970) 'Unit courses in a national degree system', Coombe Lodge Report 3 (18): *CNAA Degrees and the Colleges*, p. 6.

67 Sir Alan Richmond, HS interview.

68 CN, *1967–8 Report*, p. 9.

69 R.C. Winton (1970) 'Assessment of performance in industrial training', Coombe Lodge, *CNAA Degrees and the Colleges*, pp. 7–15; 'Discussion arising', *ibid.*, p. 15.

70 W.F. Gutteridge, HS interview.

71 CN, *Statement No. 3*, 1965.

72 Sir Alan Richmond, HS interview.

73 CASSmin, 27 April 1967.

74 Hanrott and Richmond, HS interviews.

75 M.C. Davis (1979) 'The development of the CNAA 1964–1974: A study of a validating agency', PhD thesis, Loughborough University, p. 145. The controversy is discussed by Davis, pp. 136–47.

76 CN, *Annual Report for 1969–70*, p. 9.

77 Cmin, 11 February 1971.

78 For an account of the content of CNAA courses see T. Whithead, (1971) 'Complementary and contrasting: Survey of the liberal content of C.N.A.A. degrees' in F.D. Flower (Ed.) *Complementary or Contrasting: Liberal Studies in Higher Education*, Association for Liberal Education. Other contributors to the volume recount case studies and Hornby contributes a general discussion.

Chapter 5

Shaping a System

The CNAA's central concern was with standards, with the negotiation, approval and reapproval of courses through explicit validation procedures, with the quality of the student's academic environment. The balance it had to seek between guarding standards and promoting institutional development was worked out in the constant attention to the details of courses and the means of their delivery, in subject areas pioneered by the NCTA, and in the new — and sometimes unique — programmes being considered and approved. By the end of the 1960s the CNAA was able to review its own substantial experience in establishing and maintaining degree level standards. Its validation procedures were being debated — not least among polytechnic directors — in the context of the newly, if not unambiguously, acquired status of some of the more experienced institutions. The balance established by the CNAA could not be a permanent one as institutions grew and changed, and as all the partners in the exercise responded to changing policies and experience. It is important at this point to have in view the position reached at the beginning of the 1970s by the validation procedures of the CNAA, the procedures of the colleges and polytechnics themselves, and the issue of institutional 'autonomy' or 'independence'. These were three salient and interconnected issues for the CNAA and its institutions at the end of the 1960s and the beginning of the 1970s. They were to persist, amidst changing circumstances and judgments into the 1980s.

The CNAA did not, as the historian of one institution put it, 'make it easy'.[1] The validation procedures were designed to be rigorous, and all levels of the CNAA took the question of rigour extremely seriously. The Council was at this stage receiving not only reports from its committees but also the reports of visiting parties. It remained difficult to obtain CNAA approval for courses at first submission, and officers and members of boards and panels were frequently engaged in lengthy attempts to give advice and assistance. One of the difficulties in the procedure for the institutions was the constraint on planning of not knowing — often for long periods of time — when or whether courses would be able to begin, or even whether they would be allowed to continue. Even major institutions with developing reputations were unsuccessful in their first-time submissions — and this was bound to be particularly true in arts and social studies where members were anxious to ensure appropriate standards of course content and all that related to it — including staffing and other resources. At one meeting in 1967, for example, the Committee for Arts and Social Studies turned down degrees in applied social science at Hatfield, town and country planning at Lanchester, international marketing at Woolwich, applied social studies at Constantine, European studies and textiles and marketing at Huddersfield, and applied languages at Sunderland.[2] Some committee, board and panel chairmen acquired a reputation for being especially rigorous, and in some cases angry responses from institutions focussed on the alleged biases or eccentricities of panel members as much as on the nature of the judgments made about the courses. The general consensus, however, was probably that teams and committees had to be seen to be operating tough but fair standards. University members of boards in particular were regularly to agree that the process was more rigorous than those in their own universities. In 1970, the manager of professional and commercial training at the Ford Motor Co., offering a 'consumer's view' of the polytechnics, described how he began to consider 'the use of polytechnics' when even the CNAA was new. He needed a 'hardness test' for both. The outcome of the test is revealing:

> Two would-be polytechnics unwittingly supplied a gauge — syllabi softer than butter, one in business studies and one technological. Being fascinated with the problems of developing highly professional staff, and having many years of experience in recruiting from almost every British campus, I could not accept them as good building stone and felt obliged to turn them down. So did the C.N.A.A. Later I was to see this body investigating a syllabus elsewhere. They passed it, but their audit was gruelling.[3]

The 'gruelling', or at least rigorous, element in the approval process made it frequently a long one, and was often accompanied by the traumatic shock or disappointment of rejection. It appeared to be, and in many respects was, an adversarial situation, despite efforts by officers and members not to make it so. It was a learning situation for all concerned, and in the processes of meeting and debating, reporting and being reported on, there was a substantial measure of self-scrutiny — in relation not only to the content of courses, but also to the procedures being followed within institutions and in the CNAA.

Pressures on the CNAA's machinery were growing, and at the beginning of 1968 it complained that it was being overburdened with unsuitable applications. Before obtaining CNAA approval, courses had to have authorization under further education regulations from the Regional Advisory Councils, the machinery used by the DES for this purpose. In response to the CNAA's complaint the DES agreed to circularize colleges warning them that they had to be prepared to satisfy CNAA requirements, and indicating that the DES would not be prepared to entertain new courses in excess of likely demand.[4] The validation procedure had become what one of the officers described as a 'treadmill',[5] sometimes with two or three visits a week. While members were also sometimes heavily involved, the compensation was often seen as the academic and professional networks established through the board and the visits. The extent of the process can be judged by the fact that in 1970–71 there were 117 meetings of subject boards, 113 visits, 253 courses considered and 159 approved (of the ninety-four rejected thirty-four were still under consideration at the beginning of the next academic year).[6] The process depended on the willingness of large numbers of members to serve voluntarily in the various capacities concerned. The nature of the involvement was by no means uniform, but some idea of it can be judged from a single case.

Maxwell Smith, at the Brixton School of Building from 1963, joined the Surveying Board of the CNAA some five years later. This Board was formed from two previous panels — Quantity Surveying and Estate Management — and he was a member or Chairman of the Board for twelve years, as well as being a member of the Committee for Science and Technology by virtue of his Board chairmanship. The Board itself involved at least three meetings a year, plus briefings with the secretary, membership of ad hoc meetings and working parties, and the preparation and conduct of visits (as Chairman he initially went on all visits). The process was particularly time consuming as this was, in that period, one of the CNAA's busiest boards in terms of the number of proposals processed. There was close affinity between the CNAA and the professional associations concerned, principally the Royal Institution of Chartered Surveyors, of which Smith had been an active member and Chairman of its Education and Membership Committee. This was particularly important as it was a field in which full-time education was only just emerging, and the development coincided with the early days of the CNAA. Although the Board was time consuming, therefore, the involvement was not extraneous to the central professional concerns of education for surveying. He also saw the process from both ends. Brixton itself was one of only two colleges which had nationally recognized diplomas in the field (it was one of only four specialist institutions in the field), and as a member of the School he experienced the 'shock of rejection', when its degree proposals were turned down in 1967–68. Hornby on the occasion rebuked Brixton for not looking properly at the CNAA's regulations — and the College was subsequently to have its proposals approved. Smith's reflection was that the work:

> involved discussions in all sorts of disciplines (within the professional body, with the educational institutions and within the CNAA itself, many of which were decidely uncomfortable at the time). Any measure of 'success' must be qualified: but I am

unrepentant in my support for peer group review systems of the kind that CNAA established.[7]

He was never as happy, it should be added, about the CNAA's *institutional* scrutiny, which he considered to have dealt out a 'rough justice'.

From the beginning, indeed, the CNAA had been concerned with the college as a whole, though there were no specific powers in the Charter to oblige it to do so. Frank Hornby describes how, at the first meeting of the Council the question was asked: 'were we concerned with the college?'. Lord Kings Norton, who had been primed, said: 'of course, very much indeed, and I take it we always shall be, don't we?'. He put the question round the room and people concurred. The responsibilities of the head of department and of the college entered into the picture. Quinquennial, institutional review visits became more prominent, and Hornby commented: 'I shoved this as hard as I could go'.[8] Hanrott was made responsible for the first 'Council' visits, at which they saw some quite 'unsuitable environments', information from these visits being fed at first into the subject boards rather than into the Council itself'.[9] There were visits of this kind at which institutions were told flatly not to come back to the CNAA for validation, for a variety of reasons. There were places where it was effectively not the Principal but the local authority that was running the college — a tradition of detailed local authority control over further education institutions that it was difficult to break even in developed institutions. Difficulties on a visit to Paisley were connected with the involvement of the local authority. At Liverpool, the Principal was not allowed to choose his own secretary.[10]

From these early visits the CNAA developed a keen interest in the role of the institution's academic board. In many of the colleges this was a new concept, or one that was implemented only cursorily. Many of these institutions had in their histories as further education colleges operated with strong hierarchical traditions, and these structures had often been accompanied by very authoritarian behaviour by their principals. What the CNAA was looking for, therefore, was evidence of a changed organizational and adminstrative environment, an academic machinery that could exercise responsibility for the continuing scrutiny and health of courses, and this was particularly important in the case of the newly-designed polytechnics, given the emphasis on academic boards and 'a large measure of autonomy' for institutions under their governing bodies in the government's 1967 statement on polytechnics. The question was often a difficult and delicate one given radically different perceptions of what was necessary or right in the changed circumstances, the different styles of polytechnic directors and their senior staffs, different approaches to organizational development. In Hornby's view, for example, Hatfield 'had a sort of Academic Board but it was not a very coherent one',[11] and yet Hatfield's Academic Board was at that stage probably the farthest advanced in its production of a development plan. A Council visit to Hatfield made adverse judgments on its organization and administration that conflicted basically with the views and approaches of the Polytechnic's Director and his colleagues.[12]

Another set of problems at the level of institutional approval was created for the CNAA by the decision of the University of London to run down its external degrees, and the CNAA's agreement to take up the reins where possible and appropriate. The problem was to be with those institutions which had no previous connection with either the NCTA or the CNAA, and where the London degree had been a part-time one. The first of these 'non-polytechnics' in that position to approach the CNAA was High Wycombe College of Technology[13] in 1972, and concern about the 'college as a whole' in this and other cases was to become part of the Council's expanded range of involvement and interests following the report of the James Committee in that year. Dissatisfaction with and criticism of validation procedures were paralleled by a recognition that the CNAA had succeeded through those procedures in gaining a wide measure of recognition and acceptance for its degrees, and for the institutions where they were offered. The CNAA, in the words of one commentator in 1971, was far from perfect, 'but it is the best procedure for devising innovative courses we have found so far'.[14]

The CNAA was establishing its own organizational shapes. In terms, for example, of the membership of its committees, it began modestly in including college representatives on its committees and boards. In July 1966 these contained eighty-six from colleges with CNAA courses (thirteen of them from Lanchester, by far the largest contingent from a single institution), and fifty-three from colleges without such courses. Since the CNAA approved external examiners, it is worth noting that in 1968–69 the number of examiners from universities was 461, with eight from colleges and forty-three others.[15] The CNAA machinery in the late 1960s and 1970s was powered substantially by its university membership, with major inputs from its 'industrial' members, including its first Chairman, Lord Kings Norton, and Michael (later Sir Michael) Clapham, who took over as Chairman in 1971. The Council itself came under criticism in the late 1960s as containing too few members from the colleges and polytechnics, especially members other than principals and directors.

The Council's agendas for the late 1960s were preoccupied not only with the validation procedure and its outcomes, but also with relations with the University of London and its external degree, and with the binary policy, teacher education and the Council's committee and board sub-structure and operation. The Council's name, as we have seen, was another preoccupation, and in 1968, while the issue was still a live one, members were asked to submit suggestions, and the following were made, either at a meeting or in writing:

Royal Council for University Awards
Prince Philip University Council
University Council for Colleges of Higher Education

National Council for University Awards
The Elizabethan University
University of Westminster
Elizabethan University Council
The Shires University
University Council of the Polytechnics
Council for National Academic Degrees
Royal (or British) Council (or Institute) for University Degrees
The Polytechnic University
The National University Council for Degrees and other Awards[16]

In addition to its regular meetings and activities the Council was also responsive to other policy issues, setting up sub-committees of its own and taking part in working parties elsewhere, including those discussions generated by the Schools Council and other bodies on the sixth-form curriculum and related issues. It established liaison committees on, for example, matters to do with schools, and it developed liaison arrangements with the Open University and others. The Council's senior officers were involved in frequent contacts with other bodies: meetings were held on an officer basis with the UGC and the CVCP, the DES, and the professional bodies in those fields covered by the CNAA's validation work. Michael Lane was appointed as a Senior Assistant Registrar in 1970 — in his case in science and technology — and whatever the differences amongst them they operated broadly in similar ways. Lane was Secretary at various times to between twelve and fifteen subject boards, and all of his work was very strongly committee-related. This meant, among other things, correspondence with the colleges, a great deal of travelling, and a small but growing advisory role. It meant a close working relationship with the chairmen of the boards, who were key figures in the developing CNAA. Officers were allowed to take part in board discussions, and they saw one of their main roles as being to help prevent negative decisions from being taken for trivial reasons. In the early days there was, he felt, a 'gentleman's club' atmosphere about the CNAA, and the main work was done by the boards — with no real role for the higher level committees. He, like his colleagues, had informal conversations with HMIs — who sometimes wanted to become too involved in visits, where they were 'in attendance'. On behalf of the CNAA he was a member of the Standing Conference for University Entrance, the Schools Council Science Committee, a working part of the Science Research Council, and others.[17]

With fifty or so subject boards and panels operating by the beginning of the 1970s there were serious problems of managing and regulating the processes concerned. In 1968 the Council moved from the premises in Park Crescent it had inherited from the NCTA to larger offices in Devonshire Street (formerly occupied by the Tavistock Institute of Human Relations). The work of the officers was obviously intensive and complex, and the boards played the key role in determining in practice what constituted CNAA policy. Because of their relationships with the institutions, and the professional networks that developed around them, the boards were in fact becoming powerful instruments. A 1971 CNAA document on the work of the subject boards, while describing the process with some care, also expressed warnings about excessive detail and going beyond the board's remit. For example, the reading lists supplied by colleges were intended 'merely to illustrate how the aim of the course will be implemented . . subject board members are encouraged to view syllabuses and reading lists in this light, and not to undertake a detailed critique of each one'. The assessment of the suitability of the college to undertake CNAA degrees was carried out by the Council, and board members would be kept informed of the Council's views when relevant: 'it frequently becomes unnecessary for a subject board to consider any matters other than those directly related to the operation of a particular course of study.'[18] Officers, members, committees, boards, and the Council itself, were defining their own and one another's roles.

The CNAA's involvement with Scotland was on a smaller scale than in England. The designation of the Polytechnic of Wales was to provide the main focus of the CNAA's work in the Principality, and the creation of Ulster College, The Northern Ireland Polytechnic, did the same in this province. Describing the Central Institutions — the main provider of higher education in Scotland outside the universities and the colleges of education — a Director of one of the CIs wrote in 1971 that 'during recent years the most significant development has been the growth of CNAA courses — including in business studies, architecture, various sciences and branches of engineering, marketing, computing with operational research and pharmacy'. Courses in other colleges included opthalmic optics and science with industrial studies.[19] The approach to the CNAA in 1965 from the Scottish Woollen Textile College for the associateship in textile design to become a degree raised the questions we have already discussed regarding the position of art and design, but it also raised the question of submissions from colleges where entry standards had not been at the level of the DipTech, and where issues of the college environment needed to be discussed. Some of the CIs were establishing themselves as being at the level of the English polytechnics, but in some respects were more specialized. They moved more slowly in arts and social studies, and indeed were not authorized to develop degrees in the humanities as the English polytechnics were doing. If this was a restriction, it was also a strength in focussing attention on the content of courses in science and technology and related areas of study. In 1972 *The Scotsman* carried an article by Colm Brogan on the demise of the London external degree and problems of 'sub-university' status of colleges. It began:

> Mention the initials CNAA to a committed and teaching technologist and the result is instant. Eyes light up, the conversation becomes more intense, team spirit takes on all the zeal of an ideology, facts flow, and one ends up getting the impression of being a part of . . .

a Great Dawn. All in all, very understandable, for CNAA . . . equals
a new status for Scotland's more advanced technological colleges.

Instead of imposing a university model 'what CNAA does . . . is to forget
the university bit, and concentrate on evolving standards that will gain
acceptance as of degree status. Surely a much more sensible attitude to
resources all round?' Although the CNAA system had been in operation since
1964, 'it is only recently that it has made almost total inroads as far as the
central, advanced colleges of technology in Scotland are concerned'. Paisley
and Napier were the examples chosen, the latter pointing to the 'wholehearted
acceptance by industry of CNAA degrees', and emphasizing the difficulty
of gaining course approvals.[20]

In the late 1960s and early 1970s the activities of the CNAA were
obviously related closely to the complex developments of the polytechnics.
Successive Secretaries of State formulated their own versions of what the
polytechnics should be, and in doing so established a substantial amount
of ambiguity. There was no doubt in the minds of the directors of the
polytechnics as they received their formal designations from the end of the
1960s that the polytechnics were to remain distinctive. Ministers believed
the same, asserting as had been asserted when they were created that they
were in some way different from the universities. They were, as Secretary
of State Ted Short said in 1968, 'strongly identified with the LEA system':

> Any kind of progression from the LEA system into a university of
> the kind accomplished by the CATs would be completely alien to
> the concept . . . the polytechnics were centres of comprehensive
> tertiary education for those over the age of 18 . . . they must offer
> a full range of courses, including some with modest entry
> qualifications designed for mature students . . . It was important
> . . . for polytechnics to develop as viable alternatives to universities
> in areas where they overlapped, and not as pale reflections.[21]

While Short and others emphasized the 'full range of courses', his
predecessor, Patrick Gordon Walker, had recently offered a different
formulation:

> In some ways the polytechnics will be like universities. The intention
> is, for example, that they should concentrate on higher education.
> Where other levels of work are being done they will be given up
> as soon as satisfactory alternative arrangements can be made.[22]

Lower level courses were, in fact, being transferred to other further
education colleges, but in that situation what was meant by a concept of
'comprehensive' tertiary education with a full range of courses, including
for those with modest entry qualifications?

In practice the polytechnics were initially mainly second-choice
institutions for students unable to obtain entrance to universities, but as their
reputations grew and they launched courses different from or not available

at universities, they attracted more able students. There was a struggle for the polytechnics to define, in private and in public, what the characteristics of the polytechnics were and should remain. They were, in the eyes of many people, 'primarily teaching institutions',[23] second-chance institutions, concerned more than the universities with the applications of knowledge. Eric Robinson pinpointed the differences in terms of their financing and degree-awarding powers, their legal independence and range of studies, the existence of professors in the universities, and the strong further education links of the polytechnics. George Bosworth, Director of Newcastle Polytechnic, thought that those who advocated a form of education in the polytechnics that was different from that in the universities had been 'singularly uncommunicative on the nature and extent of the difference'. He offered the suggestion that the universities were 'subject-orientated' and that the role of the polytechnics should be to prepare people 'to enter sectors of activity rather than extending the availability of subject-orientated courses of a highly specialist kind'.[24] The polytechnics, other colleges validated by the CNAA, and the CNAA itself in scrutinizing courses for approval, certainly took seriously the question of employment outcomes for students. They took their teaching role seriously enough also to inaugurate staff development programmes of various kinds. The first graduates from degree courses validated by the CNAA were beginning to enter industry and the professions, and to study for postgraduate awards in the universities, and were thus establishing the credibility of CNAA degrees — including in non-science subjects.

An industrialist's view of the polytechnics, and incidentally of the CNAA, was offered in 1970 by Sir Arthur Norman, President of the Confederation of British Industries. Given their prior, distinctive relationship with industry and commerce, the polytechnics were in a position to provide courses 'that are more relevant to industrial and commercial needs than the traditional academic courses at universities'. He recognized the complexity of both 'industry's view' and the changes in higher education — including the development of university courses 'more closely allied with national needs for qualified manpower', and pointed to some particular possible roles for the polytechnics:

> Industry will especially be looking to the polytechnics to provide a further and much needed stimulus to innovations already taking place in higher education; in particular, in the development of mixed degree courses, modular courses coupled with practical experience, and of the sandwich system of education and training generally, and in the opening up of opportunities for women in all branches of higher education, not least science and technology.

In the diversification of roles between the universities and the polytechnics, the latter would develop the 'highest levels of education' closely linked to employment in industry and commerce — in which 'the Council for National

Academic Awards would be the central pivot'.[25]

Perceptions of the polytechnics, as of the CNAA and of the changing roles of the universities, fuelled and continued to refocus debate about the liberal and the vocational in higher education. That debate was now not only about traditions and values, but also about the structure of higher education itself, and the declared or perceived missions of the new institutions and the whole new sector. The defence and definition of, or hostility towards, the polytechnics, was partly associated with questions of standards, partly with the nature of vocational emphases, and in fact with the connection between the two. The polytechnics were having to carry into the 1970s a defence and assertion of their particular — though not necessarily homogeneous — values and procedures, and in doing so made necessary a constant reaffirmation of the vocational or service roles that had aroused fierce passions throughout the nineteenth and twentieth centuries as new institutions and new sectors had come into existence in many countries. As the Director of Leeds Polytechnic put it in 1971: 'the very existence of the new polytechnics must signify the end of the general assumption that a liberal education is the only peak to which a higher education can aspire'.[26] The recurring question was: in what ways were the polytechnics the same as the universities, and in what ways different? Differences might be imposed, most notably in the case of the continuing ambivalence of Ministers and the DES about research, following the CNAA Council debates and actions around the 1966 White Paper. Differences were constantly defined by the polytechnic directors and others in terms of the funding differentials between the two sectors. Differences were described in polytechnic prospectuses and submissions to the CNAA in terms of tradition, employment-orientation, relationships with industry and employers generally, and commitment to effective teaching. However much both sectors might underline their commitment to high-quality education for students and other values of higher education as a whole, the struggle to define and remove boundaries at the same time led to uncertainty and ambiguity, tension and even 'ill-will'[27] between the sectors.

By the early 1970s the CDP, the individual polytechnic directors and voices in and around the CNAA were proclaiming the achievements of the new sector, despite the difficulties of course recognition or underfunding. From the polytechnics themselves the constant message was what had already been achieved, and the potential — in educational, economic and other terms — for doing more if given adequate support from government and local authorities. In 1968 Brian MacArthur suggested in *The Times* that of the two major educational developments under the Wilson government since 1964 the movement towards a national system of comprehensive education had received most attention: 'yet the development of the polytechnics, some of which will start with around 5000 students, is potentially the more revolutionary'.[28] Within the institutions, however, there was a growing sense of revolution unfulfilled: the decisions taken by government did not amount to policy, and the roles nebulously defined for the polytechnics could not be carried out and development sustained without public policies underpinned by finance. Critics pointed out that at the time of the White Paper and in the process of polytechnic designation there had been little or nothing in the shape of academic planning. Michael Locke pointed out that criticism sometimes levelled at the CNAA in fact constituted a critique of 'the lack of a polytechnic policy'. Also towards the end of 1971, Tyrrell Burgess was discussing 'what went wrong with the polytechnics' under the title 'The lost opportunities'. The blame lay with the DES, which had thought that 'establishing polytechnics was just an administrative exercise'. Little thought had been given to the question of what sort of institutions they were going to be:

> Only a few years earlier, the new universities had all been started through academic planning boards which established in general terms their objectives . . . Each polytechnic should have been required to work out its educational objectives and the means by which it proposed to achieve them . . . The Department, however, believed that there was no sense in planning, indeed no way of planning, until the new directors and governing bodies were installed . . . There was no reason why the existing staff of the institutions concerned could not have produced academic development plans. . .

As William Gutteridge had pointed out in 1969, the ability of the new polytechnics to match up to the universities was drastically hampered by their lack of resources of all kinds:

> The fact that the polytechnics have largely grown out of a technical college tradition, geared to different ends, means that they have practical problems of a kind unfamiliar to the universities today. Both by comparison and in absolute terms, there is serious underprovision of necessary administrative, and clerical help.

There was a shortage of well-qualified academic staff, poor library and other facilities, heavy teaching loads and other obstacles to academic development and student recruitment.[29]

In these circumstances each polytechnic evolved as best it could in the various contexts within which it had to operate — for finance, primarily its local authority; for permission to develop a course, the Regional Advisory Council; for course approval, the CNAA and other validating bodies. The polytechnics faced different local conditions, and established their own different policy priorities. Ulster College, the Northern Ireland Polytechnic, started from scratch — with two colleges of education and a college of art joining later, in 1971. It saw the CNAA connection as being 'with the substance, not the shadow', and CNAA degrees as being not 'a caste mark to be sought or scorned but . . . an opportunity to shape courses that will help those who follow them to live with the caprices of economic and social change'.[30] At the time of formal designation, in April 1971, Teesside Polytechnic (formerly Constantine College), had 1117 full-time students, and a complement of nearly 8000 including part-time students of various kinds. It had seventeen degree courses in operation, and was setting itself a target of 6–8000 full-time student equivalents by the early 1980s. It had at last been able to start building a hall of residence which had been in abeyance for six years, and the Director was underlining that student accommodation was in short supply in Teesside, and 'unless something is done by the provision of flats, hostels, etc., to supplement the supply of digs, I can see this being a factor which could really inhibit our development'.[31] Oxford Polytechnic, deriving from a further education institution with poor facilities, had a struggle to establish itself with the CNAA. By May 1969, the Oxford College of Technology, as it still was, had submitted six courses for CNAA approval, had received three visits, and had had nothing approved. The Chief Officer was instructed by the Council to have discussions with representatives of the Oxford authority. The Council pointed to 'serious weaknesses of academic control and coordination in the College', and thought it 'in need of external advice, perhaps through an academic advisory committee'. At the same meeting, the Council received reports of visits to Borough Polytechnic (soon to become South Bank Polytechnic) by three of the Council's boards and by the Council itself, and the combined visiting party had 'expressed complete satisfaction about the organization of the College' and its facilities, with the exception of its inadequate computing facilities.[32] Lanchester Polytechnic was by the end of the 1960s one of the premier public sector institutions, with one in six of all CNAA degrees (more than any other college or polytechnic). It had been operational as Lanchester College of Technology since 1960, conceived by the local authority in Coventry as a major institution, and had rapidly developed a reputation as such, expanding rapidly, and playing an important part in the committees and boards of the CNAA.[33]

Most of the polytechnics were created by institutional mergers. Bristol, for example, was formed from the Bristol Technical College, the College of Commerce and the West of England College of Art. The first meeting of the Academic Board of the Technical College took place in April 1966, and considered a proposal to develop courses for CNAA awards as soon as possible, given that Plymouth was already doing so. As the Bristol local authority set about creating a polytechnic in 1967, the Technical College was still trying to establish a policy regarding CNAA degrees in the context of the South West, including the emergence of a second university in the area. Its Academic Boad was emphasizing the the importance of research, otherwise there was 'little hope of recognition for CNAA degrees.[34] By the time the three colleges were meeting as a prospective polytechnic, from May 1969, it was clear that CNAA courses could not begin until 1971 at the earliest. Hanrott visited the Polytechnic in December to meet with senior staff and answer questions about procedures for the approval of CNAA courses, and throughout 1970 the Polytechnic was preparing submissions. An Academic Development Officer was appointed and an Academic Development Committee set up, and in 1971 the Polytechnic was approved by the CNAA as a centre for its awards for the next five years. The Polytechnic was anxious to ensure, however, that its commitments to diploma and other work were not overshadowed by the CNAA departure (and it is important in this respect to remember the fears nationally of colleges of art entering into polytechnic amalgamations). The Academic Board was 'concerned with ensuring that CNAA degree work did not form too large a proportion of the total Polytechnic commitment'.[35]

Brighton Polytechnic was established in April 1970 with the formal designation ceremony being held in February 1971. It had resulted from a merger between a Brighton Technical College and Brighton College of Art. The Technical College had been disappointed in not being nominated a college of advanced technology, and the Principal wrote in 1965 that 'prior to the publication of the Robbins Report we confidently expected to be designated as one of the colleges of advanced technology . . . We have been a college of technology in everything but name'.[36] A series of contacts with the CNAA from 1965 produced the controversies over the attempt to introduce full-time courses in various disciplines, and to combine them with sandwich courses, with Brighton's first full-time courses in engineering being approved at the end of that year. By 1968, with the CNAA withdrawing approval of the honours degree in quantity surveying, the College had not overcome some of its early difficulties. A CNAA visit to the College in 1969 was critical of a range of matters, including the operation of the Academic Board. The College was itself uneasy about the lack of 'coordinated opinion' among three engineering boards which had recently visited it, and an Academic Board sub-committee considered that undue emphasis had been given to the question of policy for full-time and sandwich courses, 'to the detriment of more important issues involved in the preparation of courses of degree level'.[37] A June visit resulted in a report particularly critical of the Academic Board's lack of policy for the coordination of departments and for the planning and control of resources, and in July the College was informed of the Council's concern about the relationship between full-time and sandwich courses. The Principal responded initially by agreeing to redesignate courses as full-time, and explaining that the Academic Board had come into existence after departments had been constructed to match DipTech requirements, but had in fact gone a long way towards the Council's view — further than the report on the June quinquennial visit had acknowledged. In October the Principal wrote further to express the Academic Board's disagreement with the visitors' findings. The Board, he pointed out, had met monthly for the past two years, and controlled the work of the College. Heads of departments had thereby been deprived of 'a large measure of independence'. A Planning Committee had been meeting weekly in 1969, but the College had not wanted to be too rigid in imposing teaching methods. A development plan had been accepted by the governing body and HMI as realistic, but clearly reorganization would be necessary when the Polytechnic came into existence.

One of the university members of the June visiting party wrote in some detail about his impressions of the College. He thought it appeared less like a college than a 'set of separate departments'. Collaboration over academic policy was nil, and over other matters it seemed minimal. They did not seem to have any idea of what a sandwich course was about; they seemed to pretend that their students were all mature men with industrial experience. Many of the staff were 'rather pugnacious characters — it's a pity this dynamicism can't be channelled into a less reactionary form'. The College had good features but there was a 'lack of central planning and a lack of collaboration. I doubt whether they should run sandwich courses until they have learned what the words mean'.[38] There were other difficulties that Brighton and other polytechnics had to face, apart from such academic and organizational ones, at the point of transition to polytechnic status. The planning at Brighton revealed some of the unease in relations with the local authority. An initial scheme not to include the College of Art in the Polytechnic was turned down by the DES. The CNAA was aware of strong controlling tendencies by the local authority, and indeed the Director of Education, who was retiring, was known to 'have ideas about becoming Director of the Polytechnic'. The response of the CNAA officer who visited Brighton was 'frankly incredulous . . . the position in Brighton is a difficult one and an unpromising basis for the launching of a new polytechnic'.[39] Major improvements were being noted two years later, and it was expected that these would be carried further when the Polytechnic was transferred to the East Sussex Local Authority following county boundary changes. New accommodation was being built, and a new faculty structure was coming into place. The Principal and other staff of the College and then the Polytechnic were playing a part in committees of the CNAA: in 1971, for example, the Academic Board congratulated one of its members on being invited to chair the CNAA Physics Board. The College tried, and failed, to persuade the CNAA Council to nominate an academic member of the College's Governing body.[40]

The Hatfield Polytechnic, which began life as a technical college in 1952, was one of the first to be designated — in 1969. As soon as the 1966 White Paper was published, however, the Principal, six department heads and the Registrar went into a retreat in a local hotel and began the process which resulted in a development plan, the first, policy-focussed part of which appeared in December, written by the Principal and Polytechnic Director designate, Norman (later Sir Norman) Lindop. This was a conscious attempt to produce what had been known largely in the United States as a 'mission statement'. Information was sought from other polytechnics-designate, and some other polytechnics — Sheffield, for example — were attempting similar plans in the late 1960s.[41] The 1966 decision of the Hertfordshire Education Committee to nominate the College as a polytechnic was the challenge taken up by the development plan. The CNAA had already approved a dozen of Hatfield's courses for honours degrees, and it was to have twenty degree courses by 1968,[42] establishing a pattern of honours degree, degree and sub-degree courses. The central aims of the new polytechnic should be, 'within the context of a committed involvement with industry and commerce and public affairs, to educate all our students so that they acquire: high professional competence; an appreciation of the unity of knowledge; a strong sense of social responsibility and moral awareness, both in professional practice and in private life, and a determination to use their skill and knowledge for the enrichment of human life'. In seeking to make these aims operational, the plan set out the general characteristics of the proposed polytechnic: it was to be a 'broadly-based institution catering for a wide range of higher education for the over-18 age groups', giving priority to sandwich courses, but providing courses other than degree courses for those able to benefit from 'advanced courses of a specialist nature'. The institution would have national, regional and local commitments. The plan set out to establish what was distinctive about polytechnics, and what was specifically so about Hatfield. In general terms a polytechnic, while sharing many of the functions of universities, would emphasize the close relationship 'between the type and content of the courses provided and the role which its graduates are expected to fulfil . . . the closest possible links with industry, commerce and the professions, the research institutions and the schools . . . the development of a truly comprehensive academic structure . . . the provision of a range of part-time courses, and the provision of postgraduate, post-experience, refresher and retraining courses. The special features of Hatfield were its strong tradition of integrating general studies within technological studies, and of synthesis of academic studies in engineering, through the development of design and creative talents; 'meaningful research', particularly in certain fields of chemistry; close integration with industry in relation to student projects, and the inclusion of computer and information studies in undergraduate courses. The Polytechnic would seek to integrate library and computer facilities, recruit women students in all subjects, develop links with particular overseas regions, focus on retraining courses and exploit its geographical position to develop new kinds of extra-mural studies. The 1966 plan, and two subsequent parts dealing with academic organization and administrative structure, and library and information services, looked in detail at such areas as target size and accommodation, the curriculum, research policy, outside relationships, academic standards, governance and structure.[43]

By 1972 Hatfield had over 1800 full-time students and 1000 part-time students, a quarter of whom were working for bachelors or masters degrees and the others for higher technician or professional qualifications. It had 300 residential places (and had had those for only a year). It was building on its strengths in aeronautical engineering and other areas, and had developed one of the country's first degree courses in computer science. It saw itself as primarily a teaching institution and Lindop underlined that 'we are at pains to ensure that we recruit staff who share our view of the primacy of teaching', and the Polytechnic was requiring new and inexperienced staff to attend an in-service training programme of about 250 hours in their first year. Although there would be pressures and prospects for independence ahead, Lindop emphasized that the CNAA had been 'one of the most significant features in our development'. It had 'provided the opportunity for colleges like Hatfield to serve their apprenticeship and come of age in the academic sense'. The transition from London external degrees to a 'virtually internal system', had meant great benefits:

> ... the staff of the College have realized that the future and reputation of the institution were in their hands and they have undergone the transmutation which occurs when full academic responsibility is placed upon professionally competent individuals.[44]

These differences amongst institutions, and amongst their environments and perceptions of direction and identity, were to account in part for the differences of speed and conviction with which they raised the question of independence or autonomy — or, in the terminology of the time, academic freedom. For the CNAA's relationships with the polytechnics in the 1970s the uncertainties surrounding this question, and the different interpretations of it by different polytechnic directors and within the CNAA itself, were to be of central importance. The role of the CNAA, as we have suggested, in sustaining a balance between guiding the sector and accounting for the quality of its degrees on the one hand, and delegating 'full academic responsibility' on the other hand, was inevitably a difficult one to fill. Its machinery had to be capable of carrying out the role in relation to those institutions now designated as polytechnics — which, as we have seen, were far from homogeneous — and in relation to a large variety of other institutions with one or another proportion of its work at the level of CNAA degrees. From its first policy statement it was clear that the initiatives for college courses and development was to come from the institutions themselves. Many of the colleges with which CNAA committees and visiting parties were dealing — including the new polytechnics — had traditions of autocratic management which the DES did a great deal to undermine with the notes for guidance it issued in connection with the proposed designation of polytechnics. The CNAA was from the beginning anxious to ensure progress towards greater democratic government in institutions, particularly, as we have seen, in the creation and proper functioning of academic boards. James Topping reflected: 'Yes, [the CNAA] had a great deal of influence on the development of academic boards. Quite often we found we went to places where there wasn't such a thing'. Lanchester College of Technology was the first of the future polytechnics to have established an Academic Board, in 1962. When Glamorgan College of Technology, the future Polytechnic of Wales, was visited by the CNAA in 1967, it had recently set up an Academic Board, and the visiting party felt that 'very belatedly the College is developing towards an academic structure' and towards the kind of academic independence now 'established for some time in most other Colleges'.[45]

Given the responsibilities the CNAA shouldered by virtue of its Charter, given its anxiety to ensure that its procedures safeguarded standards as fully as possible, and given the diversity of the institutions with which it had to deal, the CNAA moved cautiously in its discussions about relinquishing or reducing control over any aspects of the work its procedures were designed to monitor. From the early 1970s debate about autonomy, validation and partnership was to gain momentum. From the outset, as we shall see, the CDP adopted strong, but often confused and contradictory, policies aimed at securing greater autonomy for the polytechnics. The CNAA's first serious consideration of the issue as a matter of policy was in 1968-69. In November 1968 the Council considered a memorandum on 'Future relationships between the Council and the Colleges'. This document, written by Hornby, emphasized that the Council had set up a procedure for dealing with proposals which began with a detailed scrutiny of documents from the college and involved painstaking work by the subject boards, so that the Council 'might establish the standards of its degrees'. There was now, however, a need to streamline the procedure:

> . . . as CNAA degree work expands in a college concurrently with the growth of a college academic community capable of accepting further freedoms and responsibilities, there may well come a point where much of the detailed work now necessary can be dispensed with and a somewhat different relationship established between college and Council.

The CNAA would have to take account of the different rates of institutions' development, but a move in this direction would enable committees and boards to have 'more time at their disposal to explore new developments and policy'. The Council received the memorandum, and set up a sub-committee to consider it, with Lord Kings Norton in the chair. The sub-committee reported back to the Council in July 1969 that within its Charter, or minor modifications of it, changes should be possible with a result that a college, 'as it reaches an appropriate state of excellence, should be subject only to that minimum of control by Council consistent with the duties imposed by its Charter'.[46] Putting this principle into operation was to prove more difficult and contentious than may have been foreseen, and it was to be several more years before the CNAA was to consider changes in practice and begin consultations towards a new balance of 'minimum of control' with the duties imposed by the Charter.

By 1971 the Council was confronting more fully the implications of the earlier discussion. Hornby, as Chief Officer and Vice-Chairman of the Council, issued the further particulars to candidates for the post he was intending to vacate the following year. The Council, the notes explained, aimed 'to afford colleges conducting courses the same freedoms as universities have in the framing of curricula and syllabuses and the selection, teaching and examination of students'. As the colleges 'grew in excellence', their measure of freedom would increase. It was essential 'that the Chief Officer should be entirely in sympathy with these aims'. The Council not only considered proposals for degrees and other awards, it gave assistance and advice in the early stages of the formulation of courses, and in amending them if they were rejected by the Council. The Chief Officer needed to contribute to this work and to help the Council maintain the influence in higher education it had developed in the previous six years, and to develop public awareness of the Council's aims and activities. The main emphasis of the notes was on the role of the Chief Officer and the Council in developing academic standards and institutional freedom.[47] At the meeting when the Council approved this document it also received a paper entitled 'Academic freedoms which might be granted to colleges', directed towards 'relaxing controls'. The paper was, however, limited in scope, since it was felt that there were major changes in higher education ahead — the James Committee on Teacher Education was sitting, for example — and the items most prominent in the document were a proposal to reduce the amount of paper work for renewals of course approval, and the possibility of delegating authority for the registration of MPhil students. A discussion at a second meeting underlined the relationship between possible changes and the forthcoming heavy work load at the CNAA. A revised version of the paper was produced for a November meeting, at which a new committee with the same name as the 1968 committee was set up. This time, however, its brief included considering the possibility of major changes to the Charter, and proposing them if necessary. The meeting made it clear that the main reason for changes in relationships between the Council and the colleges was 'the need to give greater independence to colleges rather than the pressure of work at the Council'. The intention was to move away from detailed course scrutiny as colleges 'grew in excellence'. It had now become clear both that significant moves towards greater academic independence for the colleges meant Charter changes, and that proposals for improvements in relationships had to be worked out in greater detail.[48] The more detailed proposals were forthcoming in 1972, and were to initiate the consultation process over 'partnership in validation'.

It is important, in reviewing the early history of the CNAA's relationships with the colleges, to emphasize the consistent role played by Frank Hornby in pressing for greater academic independence. He was concerned with this as an issue almost from the beginning. He had discussions with the CDP about the issue, and the establishment of Research Degree Committees in the polytechnics was one of the first freedoms to be given to them 'under the Hornby plan'.[49] From the late 1960s he was convinced that the CNAA should shed the more experienced colleges and help the others to be ready to be shed.[50] He told a Coombe Lodge conference that he hoped for a curtailment of the role of the CNAA, and that the polytechnics would be bound to have Charters in the long run.[51] He believed, however, that in the short run — whatever time that might be — they had much to gain 'from the support and strength which they derive from the CNAA' — and a look at American accreditation had reinforced his view.[52] Although the question of autonomy was a complex and confusing one, Hornby contributed to the process of keeping seriously on the agenda that part of the CNAA's role which involved delegating responsibility within the limits currently imposed on the CNAA, and expanding those limits as it became possible.

By the early 1970s the CNAA was in various respects consolidating its position, looking at future developments and beginning to respond to criticism and pressure. It was beginning to take over from the London external degrees, and had already established a substantial range of subject areas in which it could work. Having begun as what Hanrott describes as an 'adventure in higher education',[53] it was both encouraging of innovation and cautious in its development. It was interested in curriculum development and course planning, research and staff training, resources and teaching methods. In some areas, teaching methods for example, the dialogue between the Council's committee and panels and the colleges was more substantial than in others. New teaching methods were more easily discussed in business studies or applied social science than in an area like engineering with an established body of knowledge and longer traditions of teaching. The Council had by this stage resolved the issue of its degree classification, so that separate degrees with separate admission for honours and ordinary students were no longer to be offered.[54] The Council was increasing the number of part-time courses available, and confronting questions of employment opportunities and the ability of students to meet 'the caprices of economic change'. From 1969 it was awarding honorary degrees. The criticisms it was encountering had to do, for instance, with the composition of the Council (whether or not there was adequate representation of polytechnic teachers or local authorities), or with the slow rate at which it was held to be devolving authority to the institutions. The number of students on CNAA courses was increasing rapidly, and exceeding its own and the institutions' forecasts. *The Times Higher Education Supplement* began an editorial on the CNAA in 1972 with the statement: 'The Council for National Academic Awards must be one of the few unqualified success stories in higher education in the past eight years — sharing that honour perhaps with the Open University'. It considered the success to be tangible, for example in the number of degree courses, but also intangible, given the difficulty of measuring 'the effect of the liberation of many colleges from the more restrictive control of London external degrees'. The CNAA had come a long way since 1964: 'from being a shy bureaucracy it has become an important and an innovatory force in higher education'.[55] It commented in the same year that, 'while recognizing the considerable contribution that Mr Hornby has made in building up the Council to its present position of eminence within the colleges, it was now time for the CNAA's influence to be more widely felt'. It was in a unique position to analyze educational trends and the development of specific subject areas: 'the publishing of such information would give guidance to colleges and reduce the isolation that many inevitably feel'. A more imaginative interpretation of the Charter than was appropriate for the 1960s was needed for the 1970s.[56] There were suggestions that the CNAA might — alone or in conjunction with the Open University — be turned into a National University.[57]

In 1971 Michael (two years later to be Sir Michael) Clapham succeeded Lord Kings Norton as Chairman of the Council, and Edwin Kerr was appointed to take over from Frank Hornby in 1972. Clearly these early years of the organization had been intensive and exciting for many people. For Kings Norton they had been 'exciting at the time', and 'always amicable'. For Jean Rossiter it was a 'most exciting period', for Maxwell Smith they were 'enormous fun'. For Christopherson it was an 'exciting time, especially for engineers', since engineering was at the time underrepresented and low priority in the universities.[58] Although there was some criticism of the CNAA as being overpopulated with university representatives, for most people associated with the CNAA there was considerable gratitude for the role played by many university people in establishing and supporting the CNAA and in helping and defending the polytechnics. Some were prominent in their disciplines, some became chairmen of CNAA committees or boards. Donald MacRae, a professor of sociology, for example, was seen as lending substantial support to the development of the polytechnics. Maurice Peston a professor of economics, Harold Edey, a professor of accounting, and many others accepted the CNAA system, worked on its behalf, and — in Hanrott's formulation — 'people in polytechnics did not always appreciate how much they owe to them'.[59] Peston told members of the Parliamentary Select Committee and others that CNAA degrees were better than many in the universities.[60] Kings Norton was aware of the quality of the people with whom he worked — Christopherson, Richmond, Hornby . . . — and felt that Sir Lionel Russell was the person whose judgment he most admired.[61]

The CNAA was now dealing with the new generation of polytechnics but also with Scottish institutions, and institutions as diverse as the Royal Air Force College, Cranwell, and the London Bible College. It was concerned with the status of itself as an organization and of the degrees it awarded: the question of status was, in Christopherson's words, 'there, but not written in minutes!'[62] All of the issues involved in the development of the CNAA as an element in the shaping of the new sector were present in some form in countries also developing 'alternative' sectors of higher education. Apart from the American connection, Australia was featuring in the CNAA's discussions and relationships. Hornby was invited to a conference on Australian Colleges of Advanced Education in 1971, and met with Australian visitors at the CNAA.[63]

Hornby was anxious that the CNAA machinery in general and the office in particular should remain modest in scale. Neither he nor the Council was fully aware of the pressures for expansion that were to intensify from 1972, or of what might be involved in a response to such injunctions as those of the *THES* to make the influence of the CNAA more widely felt.

Notes

1 Michael Locke (1978) *Traditions and Controls in the Making of a Polytechnic 1890–1970*, Thames Polytechnic, p. 83.
2 CASSmin, 27 April 1967.
3 R.H. Sheldon (1970) 'Industry tests the product', *Tmes Educational Supplement*, 4 December.
4 Cmin, 23 January 1968.
5 Overy, HS interview.
6 CN, *Annual Report for 1970–71*, p. 9.
7 Maxwell Smith, HS interview.
8 Hornby, MD interview.
9 Hanrott, MD and HS interviews.
10 Sir Alan Richmond, HS interview.
11 Hornby, MD interview.
12 Sir Alan Richmond and Sir Normam Lindop, HS interviews.
13 Cmin, 20 July 1972.
14 John Pratt (1971) 'The pressures towards university status — and how to cope with them', *Education and Training*, 13, 10, p. 336.
15 Cmin, 19 July 1966; *Report for 1968–9*, p. 26.
16 Cmin, 16 July 1968.
17 Lane, HS interview.
18 CN, The work of a Subject Board and how it is carried out, 1971.
19 Peter Clarke (Director of Robert Gordon's Institute of Technology), *Times Educational Supplement*, 3 December 1971.
20 Colm Brogan (1973) 'New status for advanced technical colleges', *The Scotsman*, 19 May.
21 Ted Short (1968) reported in *Education*, 132, 4, pp. 648–9.
22 Patrick Gordon Walker in March 1968, reported in Peter Scott 'At last the new polytechnics', *Times Educational Supplement*, 31 May.
23 Norman Lindop (1974) 'The future of the polytechnics' in Institute of Mathematics and its Applications, *The Future of the Polytechnics*, p. 71. See also William van Straubenzee (1970) Joint Parliamentary Under-Secretary of State for Education and Science, 'The polytechnic world of the '70s', *Times Educational Supplement*, 4 February.
24 Eric Robinson (1968) *The New Polytechnics*, Cornmarket, pp. 35–46; George Bosworth (1971) 'The role of the polytechnics', *Further Education*, 3, 1, pp. 13–14.
25 Sir Arthur Norman (1970) 'Industry and the polytechnics', *The Guardian*, 10 February.
26 Patrick Nuttgens (1971) 'Save the polytechnics from university straitjacket', *Times Higher Education Supplement*, 19 November, p. 14.

27 The phrase is John Carswell's in *Government and the Universities in Britain*, Cambridge University Press, 1985, p. 127.
28 Brian MacArthur (1968) 'Role of polytechnics is defined', *The Times*, 2 March.
29 Michael Locke (1971) 'Looking for a way out of the system', *Education and Training*, October; Tyrrell Burgess (1971) 'The lost opportunities', *The Guardian*, 1 November; William Gutteridge (1969) 'What are the polytechnics?', *New Society*, 23 October, p. 641.
30 Derek Birley (1971) 'Starting from scratch in Ireland', *Times Educational Supplement*, 3 December.
31 *Teesside Journal of Commerce*, 'Polytechnic recruits nationwide', April 1971, p. 97.
32 Cmin, 6 May 1969; Hornby, in CN Box 53, refers to Oxford's 'weakness'.
33 Sir Alan Richmond, HS interview.
34 Bristol Technical College, Academic Board minutes, 25 April 1966, 4 May 1967, 15 February 1968.
35 *ibid.*, 21 May and 3 December 1969, 11 March and 13 May 1970, and 13 January 1971.
36 Brighton Polytechnic (1978) *A Hundred Years of Higher Education in Brighton*, p. 40.
37 Brighton College of Technology, report of Academic Board ad hoc sub-committee, 4 June 1969.
38 CN 1003 (Courses 71), 20 June 1969.
39 *ibid.*, note of a discussion between the Principal and Hanrott, 22 November 1968; Hanrott to Hornby, 9 December 1968.
40 *ibid.*, note by Hornby of visit to G. Hall, newly-appointed Director of Brighton Polytechnic, 6 September 1971; Brighton Polytechnic Academic Board minute 13 May 1971; Principal to Hornby, 17 January 1968.
41 Sir Norman Lindop, HS interview.
42 Hatfield Polytechnic, *Annual Report 1976–7*, introduction by Norman Lindop.
43 Sir Norman Lindop, HS interview; Hatfield College of Technology (1966) *Development Plan*, December, and Parts II and III, 1967.
44 Norman Lindop (1972) 'Hatfield Polytechnic today' in W. Roy Niblett and R. Freeman Butts (Eds) *Universities Facing the Future*, Jossey-Bass.
45 Topping, MD interview; Richmond, HS interview; Cmin, 17 July 1961.
46 Cmin, 13 November 1968 and 14 July 1969.
47 Cmin, 25 May 1971.
48 Cmin, 3 August and 16 November 1971.
49 Rochester, MD interview.
50 Rossiter, HS interview.
51 F.R. Hornby (1970) 'The development of the CNAA', Coombe Lodge Conference Report, *CNAA Degrees and the Colleges*, p. 2.
52 F.R. Hornby (1971) 'CNAA policy for the polytechnics', letter, *Times Educational Supplement*, 17 December; Frank Hornby (1972) 'Academic independence and the polytechnic', *Times Higher Education Supplement*, 21 January.y.
53 Hanrott, HS interview.
54 Jim Proctor (1971) 'Emphasis on individual achievement in new CNAA policy for honours awards', *Education and Training*, December.
55 *Times Higher Education Supplement* (1972) 'Progress of the CNAA', 2 June.
56 *Times Higher Education Supplement* (1972) 'More imagination needed', 4 August.
57 R.C. Denny (1971) reported in *Times Higher Education Supplement*, 'Polytechnics should merge into a National University', 24 December; Philip Venning (1972) '"Merge OU in a national university"', *Times Educational Supplement*, 28 July; Dennis Longley (1972) 'Scheme for a national Polytechnic

University', *Times Higher Education Supplement*, 27 October. See also Philip Venning (1973) 'Edwin Kerr: Ready for the A level war', *Times Educational Supplement*, 16 March, for a reference to a proposal by Professor Gerry Fowler for a merger between the CNAA and the Open University.

58 Lord Kings Norton, HS interview; Rossiter, HS interview; Maxwell Smith, HS interview; Christopherson, HS interview.
59 Hanrott, HS Interview.
60 Rossiter, HS interview.
61 Lord Kings Norton, HS interview.
62 Sir Derman Christopherson, HS interview.
63 Cmin 17 November 1970; Hanrott, HS interview; Rossiter, HS interview.

Chapter 6

Redrawing Boundaries

In the early 1970s the CNAA moved from constructing a system to redrawing boundaries. In establishing major new configurations of subjects, courses and areas of professional preparation it was caught between pressures to expand and to retract boundaries. The next chapter will consider the protracted demands and efforts to redefine the balance of CNAA-institution relationships — towards greater partnership or complete institutional autonomy. Here it is important to look at extensions of the CNAA's wider involvement with subjects and institutions. It did not diminish its established commitments, but the impression gained from the annual reports for the early 1970s is that the CNAA was preoccupied with the validation of an ever expanding number of newly-associated institutions and a widening range of subjects — from Chinese studies to computer technology, from housing studies to occupational hygiene. At the beginning of the 1970s the Council had four committees and sixty-four boards and panels, and a staff of thirty-six, with an inevitably increasing workload. The subject areas with the most rapidly growing number of courses were business studies, combined studies (science), mechanical engineering, social science, town planning, and combined studies in arts and humanities. Roughly two-thirds of all students enrolled were in science and technology, the fields which remained particularly dominant in part-time first degree courses. In 1973–74, for example, 872 students were enrolled on fourteen part-time courses in arts and social studies, as against 2178 on sixty-eight part-time courses in science and technology. It was natural, however, that the CNAA's discussions — as distinct from its day-to-day validation activities — should focus, in the first half of the 1970s, on the most substantial new developments — either initiated by the CNAA or in response to initiatives elsewhere. The most significant areas of development in this respect proved to be teacher education, art and design, the creative and performing arts, and management studies.

One of the most noteworthy outcomes of the James Committee Report of 1972 on teacher education was, in fact, the central involvement of the CNAA with the validation of courses of teacher education, with the new Diploma of Higher Education, and with the diversification of the colleges of education. Not that the James Committee was convinced that the CNAA would or could accept a validating role for the colleges and the field of study. The CNAA, as we have seen, was cautiously approaching a possible role in teacher education from 1965, and with the beginnings of its Committee for Education the following year. In the early 1970s that committee was, in one officer's words, 'a committee waiting for a job'.[1] And as the Chief Officer, Edwin Kerr, told a conference on teacher education in 1976, 'if a meeting on teacher education had been held four years ago, the Council would not have been invited to attend'.[2]

What the James Committee placed on the agenda of public discussion — even though its own recommendations were in general not widely popular among teacher educators — was the reshaping of the education of teachers. Its proposals included ways to eliminate the certificate and introduce a new structure of undergraduate and in-service education, incorporating an integrated phase of probationary service. The first two years of education were to be the academic years, and there were proposals for these two years also to be seen as discrete and eligible for a Diploma of Higher Education. A National Council for Teacher Education and Training, with a regional structure, would have responsibilities which included validation, though this might 'quite rapidly' be assumed by the CNAA and, in some cases, by universities.[3] The Committee was generally critical of the universities' past role, and clearly hoped that the CNAA might be persuaded to take on what might prove to be a very substantial validating function. Few of the specifics of the James proposals were implemented in the forms envisaged, but government acceptance of the principle of a degree structure to replace the certificate became the focus of debate and planning in the colleges and departments of education.

For the CNAA the question was now clear and urgent. Was the Council willing to embark on a major new undertaking in a field in which it had only limited experience, none of it in the validation of teacher education itself? The Committee for Education was crucial to the CNAA's internal discussion, but the issues were wider than its remit and a special committee to consider the response to the James Report was set up. Throughout 1973 and 1974 the Council was engaged in debate about the DipHE and the BEd, relationships with the colleges of education, standards, procedures, and liaison with the universities. Discussions of many kinds took place with the DES, and even as Chief Officer-designate, Kerr had seen Margaret Thatcher, Secretary of State for Education and Science, to discuss the possibility of CNAA involvement. In July 1972 the Council's response to the James Report and subsequent debate was to affirm categorically that it would be willing to establish the award of a Diploma of Higher Education, and a three-year degree including practical professional experience:

> The Council . . . believes strongly that a first degree course in Educational Studies lasting three years may be designed to lead to

an Honours award . . . the concept of a three-year degree course in Educational Studies, leading to an Honours or an unclassified degree, will be acceptable provided it combines an adequate period of practical experience in the classroom with a requisite minimum of academic studies.

It was important that the colleges should have 'considerable freedom' to interpret the overall requirements, and the Council itself would determine the title of the new degree. The Council was opposed to the idea of setting up interim validating bodies, and it would be willing to share validation with the universities. The Council was aware of the 'high degree of priority and urgency' to be attached to this work, but in making the commitment it pointed out also that leaving freedom to colleges to devise and conduct their courses meant that 'the consequent interaction between College and Council can stretch over a fair amount of time'. It considered that the James Committee had not taken sufficiently into account the experience and potential of the polytechnics in teacher education.[4] The conception of a three-years *honours* course incorporating as many as fifteen weeks teaching practice was the component of the response that produced the most controversy inside the CNAA. For the purpose of teacher training regulations the CNAA would now need to become a 'relevant organization' on the same footing as the Area Training Organizations.

Given the parallel problems that the CNAA and the universities would face as validators of the DipHE and/or the new BEd, Edwin Kerr and Sir Kenneth Berrill, Chairman of the UGC, took the initiative to propose that the two organizations should convene a conference to discuss the DipHE and the BEd. The conference took place at the Polytechnic of Central London in January 1973, with Kerr and Berrill each chairing one of the sessions. The conference agreed to set up a joint study group to look at the particularly urgent question of the DipHE, to be followed by a similar study group on the BEd. The BEd report was issued in December, after a second conference had discussed the DipHE report in June. The report accepted that the entry qualifications for the new degree and its standards should be as for other first degrees, but a majority of the group could not accept that it was possible to combine a professional and academic education to honours standard in three years. It recommended that the honours course for full-time students should be four years in length, and it called on the DES to explore and resource such a departure — which was eventually to prove to be the pattern adopted.[5]

The anticipation of having to respond to a considerable amount of interest from the colleges, and of the 'fair amount of time' the interactions would take, both proved to be accurate. By February 1973 the Chief Officer was reporting to the Council that the CNAA had already had discussions with over fifty colleges — about a third of the total.[6] In 1972 Christopherson, as Chairman of the Committee, saw that 'there was going to be a flood',[7] and that the work of the Committee was going to become much more like that of other CNAA committees. The pressures on the CNAA as colleges showed interest in coming to it for validation were of various kinds. It was a new subject area for the CNAA, and a rapidly changing one, and the colleges had no previous experience of the CNAA. Since a high proportion, normally at or near 100 per cent, of their work was in teacher education, looking at BEd proposals meant in fact judging the institution as a whole, and the CNAA knew from the outset that many of the colleges hoping for validation would not be adequately staffed, experienced and resourced to teach at degree level. An additional problem for the CNAA was its own structure — given the complexity of the BEd and DipHE proposals that were being designed. The CNAA could not establish boards for every subject component of degrees in education, and in the event for the first few years the Committee for Education, using a range of specialist panels in support, itself carried out the validation work. When it also rapidly became clear, following the 1972 White Paper, *Education: A Framework for Expansion*, that there was to be in fact a massive reduction in teacher education and an opportunity to diversify to fill the gaps created, the CNAA began to be faced with proposals for degrees in other subjects, often combined or modularized degrees, and often with an attempt to build both a BA and BEd degree on top of a two-year Diploma. The proposals were numerous, almost always complex, and generally extremely ambitious. In all of these situations, therefore, the pressures on the CNAA included the need to conduct preliminary discussions, to explain the CNAA procedures, to advise and guide, to ascertain the local conditions with regard to the university, to explain rejection, and to encourage or discourage resubmission. The colleges themselves, of course, took part in these processes often with some trepidation and nervousness, not knowing how well the CNAA would understand them as institutions or how sympathetic it would be to their approach to teacher education.

In the session 1972–73 the expected workload of the Committee as judged in October 1972 consisted of fifteen proposals for full-time or part-time BEd courses, as well as one for a full-time Diploma in Educational Technology and a Further Education certificate. Trent Polytechnic and the Polytechnic of North London had come forward with proposals for full-time BEd courses. Sunderland and Huddersfield Polytechnics were discussing honours degree courses in science and education. Part-time BEd courses were being proposed by The Hatfield Polytechnic jointly with two colleges of education, Manchester Polytechnic, Gipsy Hill College of Education, and others. Didsbury, St Osyth's, Worcester and others which had previously had discussions with the CNAA were either already back in discussion, or were soon to be so. Didsbury and Berkshire College of Education (soon to be renamed Bulmershe College of Higher Education) were to be the first to submit 'major' complete schemes for full-time BEd courses. Some submissions were to clear the initial hurdles relatively quickly, even when they fell at the first one. Manchester Polytechnic's part-time BEd, for example, was turned down by the Committee in January 1973 with a recommendation that it should be resubmitted. The Committee was informed in May that this was happening, and in July it was approved.[8]

The increasing numbers of colleges approaching the CNAA had to do in part with difficulties over validation by universities — particularly those which were unwilling or reluctant to validate honours degrees — and in part with the attraction of the CNAA as a validating body which could consider a range of courses, including those in the areas of proposed diversification. Some ran into trouble as they severed their lifelines with universities, only to find their initial proposals to the CNAA turned down. For the CNAA itself there was also the problem of the transitional situation in which the new BEd degree would run in parallel with the existing certificate courses, and the Committee laid down that 'the new BEd must be established as an award of degree standard, distinct from the Certificate course which it is intended to replace'. Normal entrance requirements for degree courses should apply, and parallel courses should make differentiated demands on students.[9] The CNAA was in fact now beginning to approve a variety of different types of education course, including certificates as part of a four-year honours degree, the Postgraduate Certificate of Education, and specialist certificates — notably the part-time, in-service further education certificate.[10] The way was far from smooth, and some colleges were to find the path of validation for their BEd proposals — and then for their diversified courses — through the universities.

Until 1978 the Committee for Education operated through panels and working parties, with the core membership of visiting parties to institutions drawn from the Committee, and from other subject boards. Four boards were created in 1978 — for in-service, undergraduate initial training, postgraduate initial training, and further education, together with a range of specific panels for areas such as educational technology.[11] By the end of the 1970s, with Norman Lindop having taken over the chairmanship from 1974, the Committee had established itself as a unit which functioned in parallel with those for science and technology, arts and sciences, and research. From the mid-1970s the Committee and its officers were engaged in a process of sponsoring debate and planning, including through such conferences as one on school experience and the assessment of practical teaching, held in York in October 1976 — a pioneer conference from which emerged a CNAA-funded research project which reported three years later.[12] From the mid-1970s, indeed, comments one of the officers, 'the teacher education area of the Council was very active as a focus and sponsor of discussion concerning course development for some seven or eight years'.[13] The Committee was not laying down patterns of teacher education to be followed, but was contributing, at a time of considerable difficulty and change in the system, to debate about future directions. In 1975 the Council agreed to the award of the degree of Master of Education, on condition that it was not taken as a precedent for a variety of other masters' degree titles.[14] Two years later a new Diploma in Professional Studies in Education was approved, for the first of which — in health education — guidelines were approved in December 1977.[15]

The developments in teacher education were inseparable from those relating to the Diploma of Higher Education (DipHE) and to the diversification of the colleges. The intake to initial teacher training in the colleges was 30,000 in 1975. In 1976 the figure was set at 20,000, and it was expected in that year that the figure would not exceed 15,000 in the following and subsequent years. The DES was suggesting that 30,000 places could be used for diversification.[16] The DipHE, recommended by the James Committee as a first stage in teacher education, was interpreted more broadly by the 1972 White Paper. It was to fill a gap in the provision of two-year courses, was to be offered as 'a genuine and useful addition to those forms of higher education already available', would have the same entry qualifications as for degrees, and could be either a terminal qualification with which to enter appropriate forms of employment, or provide a foundation 'for further study and be designed, where appropriate, in such a way as to earn credit towards other qualifications, including degrees and the requirements of professional bodies'. The objectives would be achieved more readily 'if courses were developed on a unit basis'.[17] The CNAA was to interpret this to mean that most DipHE programmes would be designed to have 'two distinct outlets for their successful Diplomates. These may be into existing degree schemes in the same college or another, into specially planned third-year academic or professional courses, or into employment'.[18] The CNAA committed itself to the Diploma. The universities did not. The CNAA made 'a tacit political bargain with the DES . . . for the CNAA to have had a dagger in its hand and kill off the government scheme would not have done'.[19]

Whether the colleges saw the DipHE as a genuine alternative to existing provision, or as a structural device for redesigning their curriculum, is open to doubt. It was problematic for those institutions committed to 'concurrent' teacher education, where a Diploma might mean devoting the first two years to 'academic study' without related professional work and school experience. The modular possibilities, on the other hand, were attractive. As the meeting convened by Edwin Kerr and Sir Kenneth Berrill in January 1973 discovered, much discussion of the DipHE revolved around such questions as when students on college DipHE courses would be able to make their decisions about training for teaching, and differences for the training of primary and secondary teachers. At the same time there were anxieties about such matters as uniformity of standards and transferability between institutions.[20] When the CNAA consulted its related institutions and others about the future guidelines for the DipHE many of the polytechnics pointed out that the emphasis on an 'interlock' between the Diploma and degree programmes prevented the Diploma from being seen as an award in its own right, and devalued it: it appeared to be a failed degree.[21]

Following the work of the joint UGC/CNAA DipHE Study Group which was chaired by Walter (the following year to become Sir Walter) Perry, Vice-Chancellor of the Open University, the CNAA set up a DipHE Group, chaired by James Porter, Principal of the Berkshire College, with half of its membership from the universities and half from colleges or polytechnics with an interest in teacher education. It was to act as a subject board, consider and where appropriate approve proposals which fitted the CNAA-university guidelines. The Group would review all proposals with an eye to determining issues of policy.[22] The Group met for the first time in March 1974 with several proposals already before it. It decided to visit North East London Polytechnic, for example, but declared a Huddersfield proposal to be unacceptable in its present form. It had reservations about a proposal from Crewe and Alsager, and in the case of the Berkshire College recognized that the proposed DipHE linked with a BEd proposal undergoing revisions for a 1974 start, and with a BA that had not yet been submitted. It decided to join the team visiting Berkshire to discuss the BEd revisions. At its next meeting the Group received a paper from Joyce Skinner on 'A possible college of education model' — one of several 'models', including a university model by Professor John Ziman. Skinner thought that the Diploma might have particularly useful currency outside teaching for young women. There was a rapid increase in the number of proposals before the Group in 1975, and James Porter recalls taking part in two-day visits roughly every other week.[23] The first proposals to be approved were Berkshire's own scheme and a more radical one from North East London Polytechnic within the framework of its School for Independent Study.

The DipHE did not become a major feature of the higher education landscape. Given the commitment to its having the same entry qualifications as the degree, it did not become a clear alternative for large numbers of students. The universities ignored it. The difficulty from the outset was that the Treasury would only give approval for mandatory awards for DipHE students if it had a two 'A' level entry. With the DES having to settle for this, and with the Diploma being seen in higher education as merely equivalent to the first two years of a degree programme, it became not an alternative track in higher education, but an ambiguous poor relation to the degree. For the colleges and polytechnics attempting to implement it the DipHE raised problems of 'interlock' with other programmes, and transferability to other institutions — with a need for considerable attention to student counselling. The number of students nationally obtaining the CNAA's Diploma of Higher Education in 1977 was only 293, of whom approximately half transferred to 'linked' or 'top-up' courses in the same institution. Only thirty diplomates transferred to other institutions.[24] At a conference on academic diversification in higher education in 1977 William Gutteridge suggested that the main questions regarding the DipHE now included: its purpose within higher education; the problem of the coherence of a two-year programme and modular structures; possibilities for outlets and transfer, and the feasibility of a one-year 'top-up' course of study to produce a degree. In discussion which followed 'many members remained sceptical as to the feasibility of the Dip.H.E. and commented on the ephemeral interest in existing Dip.H.E.s . . . enrolment for future courses would depend on the flexibility exercised in allowing entrants with qualifications other than two 'A' levels to enrol, and members regretted the intransigence of the DES in this matter'.[25] Later the same year James Porter presented a document on the Dip.H.E., on behalf of the Group, to the Council, suggesting, among other things, that a national 'transfer agency' was needed to deal with the problems of students wishing to move from a DipHE in one institution to a degree course in another.[26]

In the small number of institutions where the DipHE was established and survived there was both strong commitment and, at least initially, interest by schools, further education colleges and the press. It never satisfied the White Paper's interest in another, shorter, flexible model of higher education. It did, however, form an important element in the thinking of the new generation of 'colleges of higher education' which emerged out of the cross-currents of the early and mid-1970s. It was one element in the search, on occasion the scramble, for diversification. Even less than with the designation of the polytechnics was the CNAA in the 1970s confronting a policy-driven situation. The polytechnic developments had at least been the outcome of clear-cut decisions, however weakly the intentions were defined and followed through with sustained resources. The position with the colleges after 1972 was simply one of confusion in which the only clarity was the haste to cut teacher education by whatever means. The colleges or institutes of higher education, as the diversified colleges became known, were not 'designated'. They were shuffled, whether they were local authority or voluntary colleges, into an uncertain status with an increasing sense of urgency in reshaping themselves if they were to survive. The overriding mission of the mid- and late 1970s was in fact to survive, to engage in the politics of remaining 'free-standing', of amalgamation or extinction. If the DES had any policy beyond the contraction of the system it was not declared. No sooner were the colleges given the signal to diversify than limits were placed on diversification. Colleges only recently opened were closed. The colleges grappled with widespread early retirements of staff in teacher education, permissions to prepare courses from the DES in the case of teacher education, and from the Inspectorate and the Regional Advisory Councils for other courses. They had entered the new world of changed qualifications for teacher education, and the negotation of validation by a university which they knew or the CNAA which they did not. There were constant announcements of further cuts and closures, an unending stream of private message and public ambiguity. The number of colleges was reduced from 159 in 1972 to 52 in 1982, either by closure, mergers between colleges, amalgamation with polytechnics or, in a small number of cases, with universities. For the CNAA there was the problem of ascertaining standards and realistic intentions in institutions besieged daily with signals of instability.

In the three years to 1975 the CNAA's workload more than doubled, and that of the Combined Studies (Humanities) Board increased even faster.[27] As the colleges sought to establish degree courses other than in teacher education it was naturally towards the humanities that they mainly turned, and attempts to use their existing strengths in those areas, together with opportunities for combined and modularized courses, resulted in often extremely complex proposals. One senior officer's reflection on the processes that took place in the colleges and in the CNAA was:

> It has been my experience that Boards, with depressing regularity, have received submissions which on a first reading look structurally ingenious but on close analysis are found to be padded out with individual syllabuses that are academically lightweight and have little or no functional relation to the structure they are supposed to illuminate ... something is disastrously wrong with planning procedures when staff only partially understand or accept the rationale of a course and a visiting party finds a farrago of assorted bits and pieces behind a facade occasionally breathtaking in its baroque audacity.[28]

Fortunately not all the colleges were as over-enthusiastic, though most were entering uncharted territory, and the CNAA recognized and confronted the difficulties, particularly in 1976 and 1977. It did so not only through the stringent processing of applications and the guidance it offered individual institutions, but also through more general analysis of the problems faced by institutions making the transition from 'monotechnic' to diversified colleges. At two meetings in January and May 1976 the Council discussed a paper presented by the Chief Officer on 'Diversification in the former colleges of education'.

The essential message of the paper was that of multiple difficulties. The problems of diversification had been enormously increased 'because the interdependent conditions have not been fulfilled'. There had been a shortfall in applicants and in funds:

> Teacher training places have been slashed and in-service plans postponed. The diversified courses that have started are limited in number and, in competition with existing courses, are not all recruiting well. The DipHE, perhaps the key to diversification, has likewise suffered from the contracting situation.

Colleges had closed. Others were 'in jeopardy'. The DES had laid down that diversified courses should be 'wholly or mainly constituted of elements common to existing or proposed courses of teacher education or to other advanced courses already approved and ... no additional staff is required'.

The structure of many BEd courses, however, made this impossible. The paper went on to describe the difficulties encountered by the CNAA's boards. The quality of staff for the type of work proposed 'often leaves much to be desired'. Some of the departments were small and without sufficient staff with relevant expertise in areas it was proposed to teach. Schemes were over ambitious, the majority of them being for BA (Hons), when it would have been more realistic to start with something less demanding. Colleges were inexperienced in designing BA courses, had under-resourced libraries in many cases, and were trying to 'do too much too quickly'.[29] The Combined Studies (Humanities) Board had found it difficult to ensure comparability of standards across different boards and panels, given the complex arrangement of joint validation with the Committee for Education.[30] Norman Lindop, as Chairman of the Committee for Education at this stage, considered that the Council had been placed in an impossible position by the sudden introduction of a new range of institutions 'and the need for urgent action to solve problems externally created'.[31] The Council had already, the previous year, requested a meeting with the DES, and the Chief Officer, the Chairman of the Combined Studies (Humanities) Board (Gutteridge), the Chairman of the DipHE group (Porter) and the Senior Assistant Registrar responsible for Arts and Humanities subject boards, Ann Ridler, met with a group of six DES representatives. In response to an outline of the CNAA's difficulties the DES officers expressed the view that the difficulty lay with the Committee for Education, 'which appeared to take a divergent and insufficiently flexible view' on the question of devising course units in common between the BEd and other courses. Gutteridge pointed out that the Combined Studies Board was not opposed to common teaching for the two degrees, but underlined the difficulties in practice.[32]

The CNAA took other steps. Following its discussion of the Chief Officer's paper the Council held a conference for the colleges on 'Planning for academic diversification'[33]. The Committee for Education gave special attention to the question of college libraries and set up a working party in 1974 to advise on provision in colleges proposing to diversify their courses, and over the next three years it offered guidance on ways of assessing the quality of provision, emphasized the importance of the standing of the head of the library service or resource centre, of consultation with the library in course development, and of initiating students into making effective use of the library and learning resources.[34] The rate of approvals continued, however, to be slow, provoking press comment, notably in 1976, on the differences between the CNAA and the universities in their approval rates. In *The Times Higher Education Supplement* David Hencke reported that many college and polytechnic directors believed that universities 'are relaxing their validation standards to enable former colleges of education to start new arts and science degrees', and quoted Edwin Kerr as being confident that colleges succeeding with CNAA validation would consider it to have been worthwhile. A leading article described the CNAA process as 'sticky and demanding' and believed that when the Council finally approved diversified courses in the colleges they would find the efforts to have been beneficial. An article in *The Times Educational Supplement* on the same day talked of bitterness among college principals at CNAA treatment, and their turning to universities for approval.[35] Whatever the problems for the CNAA and for the institutions, and however irritating it was for DES officers or some college principals, the CNAA was working methodically to ensure that complex questions of comparability of standards were resolved to the satisfaction of the various parts of the validating machinery. The very existence of this new and substantial element of 'public sector higher education' was politically sensitive in various ways. For the polytechnics, still struggling to establish their place in the pattern of higher education, the advent of this group of diverse institutions could be seen as 'jeopardizing'[36] their position, given what the CDP considered an ill-defined interpretation by the DES of 'advanced further education'. The CDP presented an image, not only to the colleges of higher education, but also to many people in the CNAA, of a privileged club, not wanting the colleges to come under the CNAA, and bent on ensuring that the colleges had a secondary role in the public sector of higher education. Conservative MP Keith Hampson expressed the view in 1977 that the new institutions had not been planned as part of an integrated post-school system, but by default. He thought it scandalous that a new type of higher education had emerged 'as a result of piecemeal decisions, often ill-prepared, and taken in conditions of near total secrecy, and which is simply not geared to meeting the country's most pressing requirements'.[37] Whether or not the criticism was justified, British higher education had now been extended by a considerable addition to its 'advanced further' and 'public' sector. The 'piecemeal' entry of the former colleges of education and some other colleges which had not previously secured polytechnic status was not quite along lines that the Robbins Committee had proposed, but the picture of higher education that had been developing from the early 1960s was now broader and more complex. So were the CNAA's commitments.

At the same time as teacher education and the new colleges of higher education were becoming a major component of the CNAA's repertoire of subjects and institutions, the Council and the NCDAD were coming closer together. Stewart Mason, the new Chairman of the NCDAD, was — as we have seen — convinced by the early 1970s that a merger was both inevitable and desirable. Through informal contacts in 1971 and 1972[38] and formally in 1972 agreement was reached in principle to amalgamate. The final stages of the negotiations coincided with the presence of Michael Clapham as Chairman of the Council, and Edwin Kerr as Chief Officer, both of whom played influential parts in the process. Clapham was a committed negotiator, and Kerr did a great deal to assuage the anxieties that existed in the NCDAD and its institutions. The major traumas of the merger of many colleges of art into polytechnics were now past. Goodwill had been encouraged by reciprocal representation on validation visits,[39] but there was still strong opposition when Kerr accepted an invitation to meet the NCDAD at its premises at Park Crescent — having been warned by some polytechnic directors that he was going into the lion's den and would be devoured.[40] In the event the NCDAD accepted Kerr's and the Council's assurances. In January 1973 the NCDAD wrote agreeing the merger 'in principal' (sic!),[41] on the grounds of the incorporation of many colleges of art in polytechnics, the parallel validation processes, and the growing interest in cross-disciplinary and joint subject courses at degree level. The merger was to take effect in September 1974.[42] A further statement in April 1974 indicated that the CNAA's necessary Charter changes had been completed, and that other titles for the combined organization had been considered but that the CNAA's title would be retained. A fifth CNAA Committee would be set up for Art and Design, and pending a reconstitution of the Council's committees and boards in 1975 the present NCDAD members were being asked to serve as as nucleus of the future committee. From September 1974 the Diploma would become a BA with Honours, and students on existing courses or with a DipAD awarded between 1966 and 1974 could convert it to a BA if they wished. There would be no retrospective recognition of the Higher Diploma as an MA.[43] The NCDAD's Chief Officer was retiring, and his deputy, Robert Strand, and an Assistant Officer, Frank Hatt, transferred to the CNAA. At its meeting in May 1974 the Council agreed that when the respective premises of the NCDAD and the CNAA had been disposed of, the newly-combined organization would move into premises in Gray's Inn Road. The CNAA was not aware that the new premises were on part of the site of what was once the Home and Colonial Infant School Society, which from 1836 had been one of the country's first teacher training organizations, and had occupied 334–54 Gray's Inn Road in 1839.[44]

To allow more time for new procedures to come into effect, the reapproval of the DipAD courses due to take place in the autumn of 1975 was postponed for a year. The new Committee for Art and Design was then faced with a major review of 127 first degree courses. One hundred and forty committee and board members took part, and the colleges and departments had to face a different kind and volume of documentation. Twenty-one of the 127 courses received renewal for less than five years.[45] At the same time as negotiating this amalgamation and setting the new machinery in place, the NCDAD and the CNAA were dealing with what Strand calls the 'large and prickly subject' of the validation of the major art colleges in Scotland.[46] In January 1973 the Scottish Education Department, on behalf of the four Central (Art) Institutions, formally approached the CNAA with a proposal for their Associateship and Diploma courses to be recognized for a classified degree in art and design. The CNAA's provisional Committee for Art and Design was willing only to accept the Honours Associateship for a classified honours degree, and the Associateship for an unclassified degree. This was to be the major stumbling block in difficult and often angry negotiations, in which Stewart Mason played a key part — anxious to avoid a precedent for unclassified degrees in other parts of the United Kingdom. Long battles ensued, with an intensification of the controversy when the CNAA approved a BSc sandwich course in Industrial Design (Technology) at Napier College, Edinburgh — not one of the Central Institutions. For this and other reasons Edinburgh College of Art withdrew from negotiations with the CNAA and obtained university validation. The other three — Glasgow, Dundee and Aberdeen — together with the Scottish College of Textiles, Galashiels, achieved recognition for their courses in stages.[47]

The developments in art and design coincided with one phase of the CNAA's involvement with teacher education and the colleges of education. Developments in the creative and performing arts coincided with only a slightly later phase. Whereas in art and design the CNAA was negotiating with an established, parallel validating body and with institutions operating courses accepted as being of degree standard, in the creative and performing arts it was moving further into complicated and confused territory. The arts were represented in the CNAA both as elements in some combined humanities courses, and increasingly in teacher education courses. There was also mounting interest, however, in the early 1970s in the possibility of CNAA validation of 'professional' courses in the areas of drama, music and dance. The Gulbenkian Foundation was exploring training for the performing arts, and by the middle of the decade the CNAA found itself confronting the complex range of elements of the creative and performing arts in its existing courses, and expressions of interest by institutions proposing specialist courses — notably in drama and in dance and movement. In this whole area the initiative for development came from the CNAA itself, which acted, in the phrase of one key participant in the developments, as 'a watering can',[48] with one of the officers, Ann Ridler, very much involved. A drama panel was set up in 1974, in order to consider schemes which avoided the polarization of practical courses on the one hand, and the literary aspects of dramatic art on the other hand, and attempted to integrate the two.[49] In June 1975 a meeting of all those who chaired humanities and arts boards and panels discussed the validation of theatre courses and a range of arts courses. A Creative and Performing Arts Panel, meeting for the first time in February of that year, became a Board, and from the outset was looking at proposals such as that from Middlesex Polytechnic for a BA and BA(Hons) in Performance Arts, an ambitious proposal which was greeted with reservations but encouragement, as was a proposal for such a degree in Creative Arts at Trent Polytechnic. The panel was initially established under the chairmanship of the late John Holden, Deputy Director of Manchester Polytechnic, to assist the Combined Studies (Humanities) Board in the consideration of 'creative and performing arts components of combined studies or arts and humanities schemes', and combined courses in the creative and performing arts, to act as a focus for discussion of interdisciplinary matters in the field, and to promote research.[50] When it became the Combined Studies (Creative and Performing Arts) Board it set up its own panels, including, in November 1975, a Movement and Dance Panel under the chairmanship of Peter Brinson. The complex and intensive developments in this general field in the 1970s can be seen by taking this panel as an illustration.[51]

Brinson, before taking over the Gulbenkian Foundation in London in 1972 had chaired an arts committee of the Foundation, set up to discuss and provide financial help to the performing arts, and particularly to dance, which had had, in his words 'a raw deal'. It was logical, when he took over the Foundation, to concentrate on dance, and Gulbenkian in Lisbon approved. From early 1973 some £250,000 a year was awarded to choreographers, designers, dancers and others, beginning with travel scholarships. The sums increased, and funding was provided for a choreography department at the London School of Contemporary Dance and at the Royal Ballet School. Brinson had by this stage, therefore, acquired a reputation of not being committed to any one institution, and enquiries pointed to him as a neutral Chairman of the new panel, which he was asked to chair, and by virtue of his chairmanship he also became a member of the Creative and Performing Arts Panel, and then Board. The purpose of the dance panel was to assess applications for degrees in dance, and as Brinson emphasizes, 1975–76 was still a period when it was possible to envisage the development of subjects and the availability of resources. The panel therefore looked at proposals from such institutions as the West Sussex Institute of Higher Education, Dartington College of Arts, the Laban Centre for Movement and Dance, Worcester College of Higher Education, and Ilkley College of Higher Education. The Ilkley proposal did not get far, and the Worcester course, having been approved, later had validation withdrawn. The Movement and Dance Board, as the Panel became, was responding to a movement in higher education to develop the performing arts. A Standing Conference on Dance in Higher Education began with a wide membership, but contraction by the end of the 1970s left the organization with a much depleted membership.

From the outset the work of the Panel and Board was intensely time consuming. The institutions did not know what the criteria or standards were, and the process of validation normally meant two or three visits to the institution — with the first visit being a learning process for the institution, to hear what the process was all about. The Combined Studies Board was also time consuming: the CNAA was 'greedy for time'. Brinson could cope with the work only because he was at the Foundation, where people could see him, which had concerns close to those of the CNAA, and which allowed him time to take part. Others were not so fortunate, and the Director of the Laban Centre had to give up membership because of the pressure of time. The validation process depended, in Brinson's account, on Ann Ridler's well-prepared prior documentation, and the ability of himself and members to pay the two or three visits needed in each case. There is no doubt that the CNAA's concern with the assurance of standards was understood in the approval process of a new area such as this. Experienced and 'honoured' teachers of dance had to be told that their courses could not be approved. Dartington had to change its course considerably in order to gain approval. The Laban Centre, which finally gained approval for the country's first BA in Dance, failed to obtain approval when initially submitted.

Wherever the initiatives for these developments came from — and John Holden at Manchester played a significant part — Brinson is emphatic that:

> . . . once the CNAA even began to lend its support to this development, there literally was a kind of explosion, and plainly institutions had been looking and waiting for validation in this field . . . John Holden took a most catholic attitude towards the arts . . . The CNAA was a marvellous learning process which . . . drove me into intimate contact with a wide range of higher education courses, in dance primarily, which taught me the criteria for judging dance as a higher education subject . . . I would say that the CNAA was responsible for establishing the arts in higher education, first as subjects valid for higher education, and second as subjects valuable to the country, in other words it helped to establish a national reputation for the arts at this level, which had never existed before. Previously they had been assumed to be something that belonged to the Royal College of Art, the Slade School, the Royal Ballet School, and so on.

In doing so, the CNAA 'made its most valuable contribution'. In establishing them as higher education subjects it expanded 'the notion of the nature of knowledge'. Before all these developments it was widely accepted that knowledge was something that was 'transmitted by words and absorbed by words', and suddenly when faced with 'establishing the criteria for the arts as higher education subjects . . . we were forced to look at these subjects . . . and at what way they contributed to the role of higher education . . . The whole area of non-verbal knowledge was opened up . . . That may be the major contribution of the CNAA in this field'.

By 1980, when the network of institutions offering courses in the creative and performing arts included other colleges and polytechnics, there were difficulties. The Combined Studies Board in October of that year set up a special working party to discuss a variety of difficulties being encountered, including resource constraints facing the BA in Music at Huddersfield Polytechnic, acute accommodation difficulties facing the creative arts course at Newcastle Polytechnic, and poor recruitment and various kinds of dissatisfaction at some other institutions. The opportunities of the mid-1970s were struggling to survive — and the role of the CNAA, having established its commitment to the arts — was to continue to encourage and promote, but also to be critical, to investigate, and when necessary to withdraw approval.[52]

The fourth major indication of the increasing scale and complexity of the CNAA's validation role was its acquisition of responsibility for the Diploma in Management Studies. This diploma had, since the beginning of the 1960s, been under the control of a Committee for the Diploma in Management Studies, for England, Wales and Northern Ireland, and a Scottish Joint Committee for Diplomas in Management Studies. A proposal emerged in 1974 that the work of the two committees should be transferred to the CNAA, a working party of the three bodies was set up, and in November 1975 the CNAA's Management Studies Board considered a statement of intent. The working party had foreseen 'a growing potential overlap of courses and qualifications'. To avoid confusion for polytechnics and colleges, students and employers, a single range of management awards under the CNAA was envisaged. The Management Studies Board was to be reconstituted appropriately, and was 'to report to the Council and the two Committees upon the machinery which may be necessary to ensure a continuity of standard and of provision of courses at diploma level'. It was not intended that colleges should have to resubmit or revise their current schemes at the point of transfer.[53] The transfer took place in September 1976, before which the Standing Conference of Heads of Management Departments had held a two-day conference on 'The DMS and the CNAA'.[54] Unlike the arrangements for the transfer of the Diploma in Art and Design, which involved a change to a degree award, there was no immediate programme of revalidation in this case, and a five-year review programme was introduced, with the intention of integrating the DMS into the work of the Council as much as considering the courses themselves. Direct responsibility for DMS policy in England and Wales was initially that of a panel (a panel for Scotland remained separate for several years) and this became a Board after the Committee for Arts and Social Studies was split in 1978 and a Committee for Business and Management Studies created — a decision which produced some controversy. Professor MacRae, retiring Chairman of CASS, thought the move would isolate business and management studies from the human dimension of social studies. The CNAA, he and others believed, had made great progress in improving the standards of business studies, and had begun to do the same for management studies, but 'the job of improving management studies has hardly begun. To improve standards it should remain within the arts and social studies committee'. Others, including Edwin Kerr and the Reverend Dr George Tolley, Principal of Sheffield City Polytechnic and Chairman of the new Committee, believed that the split would enable greater attention to be given to business and management courses, and make it possible to involve the business and management community more in the work of the Committee.[55] From 1976 the Panel or Board, and its parent Committee, were concerned with discussions about the future of management studies, providing advice to external examiners drawn from business and industry, extending CNAA influence in the field, and holding meetings for members who were involved in visits. In its guidelines on the DMS and other 'courses for managers' issued in 1979 the Council defined access to the Diploma — which had been seen from the outset as a postgraduate award — in terms of flexible entry: in addition to the broad treatment of management studies and its supporting disciplines it incorporated

> opportunities for applied studies in an area of activity appropriate to candidates' interests and experience. The standard of a course is reflected in the pace and the treatment of the material, which makes it appropriate for graduates, but other managers of equivalent ability but who are not graduates are also eligible for selection. All DMS candidates must have had work experience of a kind which will enable them to benefit from and contribute to the course.[56]

When the CNAA took over the DMS there were nationally some 6600 students enrolled on courses, and that was to be the order of magnitude of enrolments through the late 1970s and 1980s. While business studies had become a major component of CNAA-validated undergraduate courses, the DMS was the stepping stone into concern for part-time continuing education in the management field.

What the acquisition of responsibility for the DMS illustrates is the way an area of study could rapidly 'come of age' in the CNAA. In 1971 Cynthia Iliffe succeeded Jean Rossiter as Senior Assistant Registrar for Arts and Social Studies, and when, six months after her appointment the responsibilities were divided she took charge of business and social studies.[57] At that point the CNAA was still primarily concerned with the validation of new degree courses in business studies, with few at the stage of application for renewal of approval. The Business Studies Board was primarily concerned with matters relating to the curriculum and to adequate resourcing, and as Cynthia Iliffe describes it:

> We'd be saying things like 'you need three extra staff . . .'. We were concerned with the start-up and whether people had the right idea about business studies . . . They were very much discipline-based degrees in those days, there was very little functional expertise . . . I think we really forced the institutions to be much more thorough with the disciplinary underpinning to the degree.

Maurice Pocock, Head of the School of Business and Social Studies at Ealing College of Technology, who had by then taken over the chair of the Board from W.F. Crick ('who kind of invented the business studies degree'), was very concerned that 'the degrees should be for business and not about business, that they should be integrated, that the sandwich placement should be fully worked out . . .' For the Registrar:

> it was a straightforward job. It sounds like an enormous amount, but what one actually did was: documents came in, documents went

to boards (of which there were a number in the business and social studies area), boards commented on them, you sent a minute off to the institution, you went on a visit, you wrote a report, and that was that. There was very little interchange with staff in institutions.

There was little or no overt resistance to the development of business studies degrees, for two sets of reasons. The Board Chairman and members were enthusiasts and adopted a 'proselytizing' role:

My recall of those early days is that there was tremendous enthusiasm to get the degree courses off the ground. There was a lot of stress on resources, and by resources I don't just mean books in libraries, I mean staffing resources primarily . . . and we used to be very fierce about the quality of course leadership, for example.

In the institutions themselves the position was that the degree proposals were being put together by people in different discipline-based departments, and the development of departments of business studies or business and management studies came later —

so you would actually be talking to economists, lawyers and accountants, and very often you had a feeling that the first time they had come together to talk to each other was when the CNAA arrived.

Cynthia Iliffe shared with the Board a feeling that it could be rather 'a hybrid sort of degree course at first', but Pocock and the Board really believed in it, understood that the Crick model of a discipline-based degree had provided it with an academic foundation, but even then 'we talked a lot about integration'.

It is against that background that the DES approach to the CNAA to take over responsibility for the DMS has to be seen. A major development of the area had taken place, the CNAA was being seen to be 'fierce' in its approach, and institutions were being obliged to be 'thorough'. The negotiations over the DMS brought the CNAA members and officers into closer contact with people from various professional bodies, and the national profile of the CNAA in the field of business studies was therefore high by the mid-1970s. With enthusiastic Board members, an experienced Registrar and a small staff, and the accumulated validation experience of the late 1960s and early 1970s, the scene was set for the acquisition of a major award in the field, and the continued development of business and management studies that we have seen. The basis in this case was the CNAA's own confident development of the field from the outset — unlike the other cases of amalgamation, or responses to different kind of initiative or pressure.

These illustrations give some idea of the range of CNAA validation work and subject development in the 1970s. There are other significant examples. Computer technology was giving rise to a variety of innovative developments, and the field was in general pioneered by the CNAA and its institutions before the universities took up the challenge. The Hatfield

Polytechnic was moving towards computer instruction for all students because, said Norman Lindop in 1971, 'the computer is a part of modern culture', and in 1970 *Computer Weekly* was drawing attention to the CNAA's contribution to computer availability in Scotland.[58] By the mid-1970s the CNAA and its institutions were making a major contribution to legal education: a survey in 1976/77 showed that there were then thirty-two university law schools and twenty-two polytechnics and other colleges offering undergraduate law degree courses, the most recent being at the Polytechnics of North East London and Preston in 1975, and the Polytechnic of Wales in 1977. The transfer of courses from London external to CNAA was by then complete, but there had also been a growth of CNAA part-time law degree courses — at Ealing, Leicester, Liverpool, Manchester, Newcastle and Wolverhampton — with others in the pipeline.[59] By the end of the 1970s the CNAA had established a Diploma in Professional Studies in Nursing, joining the twenty courses now in existence for the Diploma in Professional Studies in Education. Science and technology still accounted for the largest group of students, though recruitment for technology was encountering difficulties in Britain generally. The increasing diversity of studies in this area was reflected by the creation in the 1970s of new CNAA boards to cover such fields as Combined Studies (Science), Computing and Informatics, Environmental Studies, Health and Medical Services, and Transport. Food Science became Food, Accommodation and Related Sciences. The growing diversity in the structure of degrees was reflected in the creation of an Interfaculty Studies Board (there was some argument about whether it should be a full committee) in 1977, reporting to all the committees that had an interest in its activities. The relevant work of the DipHE Group transferred to this Board, whose existence indicated the extent of the thinking taking place about broad ranging degrees in and between science, technology and the arts and humanities — as well as in education.

None of these new and developing areas of study was without its problems, and the committees and boards had to be constantly confronting difficulties of either a general and continuing or a highly specific kind. Bryan Overy, who joined the CNAA as one of two Senior Assistant Registrars in Science and Technology in 1968, underlines the kinds of difficulties that had to be faced.[60] First, the boards and the Committee for Science and Technology had the problem of deciding 'how far a subject was "degree worthy", because new subjects started springing up like grass in a corn field':

> I remember housing studies, for example, was one of the crunch points as to whether you could actually make a degree out of something of that kind. And then people would point to odd things like paper technology that some of the universities had had for years, and said — 'Well, what's odd about housing studies?'

At a more specific level there were matters like the involvement with the Military College at Shrivenham, where students were military employees and where the College wished the students to handle security classified material in their courses and possibly even to examine them on classified material. One corner of the Instrumentation and Control Board activities was concerned for weeks or months with grappling with the problem. And thirdly there was the long problem of the changeover from the NCTA honours degree equivalent to a system in which there were honours and unclassified degrees. Different areas of the CNAA wrested with this 'in radically different ways':

> The technologists, in handling any new, slightly practically oriented subject, like quantity surveying and estate management, tended to adopt a 'walk before they can run approach' in approving unclassified degrees fairly extensively, until they found that arts and pure sciences were, for whatever reason, not going down that road to any extent. We appeared to have students of the same native wit coming to courses in the arts and the sciences and the technologies, and the technologies were requiring quite a lot of these colleges to kick off with unclassified degrees, and finally began to weaken a little, I think, when they found that business studies and art and design were doing no such thing. And this remained a very difficult area for a long time.

There were conceivably differences in the quality of the students entering the courses, but there seemed to be 'different appraisals of the market, and what an honours degree was all about'.

The making and implementing of CNAA policy for the introduction of new subject areas and the extension of established ones were therefore constantly faced with a range of problems which had to be faced at officer and board levels, and in debate in committee and Council. The CNAA was constantly having to negotiate on uncertain frontiers, and interpret and define forms of higher education for which there were no clear precedents or guidelines. An integral part of the 'new frontier' activities — and therefore of the diversification of higher education — was the widespread development of academic and professional networks, not only through the validation machinery, but also through conferences and meetings devoted to curriculum and subject development. From the mid-1970s in particular the CNAA became increasingly involved in organizing and participating in conferences directly or indirectly related to its role in broadening access, widening curricula and enhancing standards. In 1976, for example, the Combined Studies (Science) Board held a conference on the problems of designing, validating and operating combined studies courses in science (with addresses and seminar discussions on such topics as modular degree schemes, interdisciplinarity, project-orientated courses, course management and science, industry and the professions). The CNAA conference on School Experience and the Assessment of Teaching had been held the previous month.[61] In 1977 the Council arranged the conference on Planning for

Academic Diversification in Higher Education, a meeting to discuss the need for and design of undergraduate courses in transport studies, a seminar to discuss the problems of including art and design in courses which contained other subjects, and a conference on mathematical education — including particularly mathematics and computer studies at the postgraduate level.[62] A meeting on sports and recreational studies was held at the end of 1977, at a time when there was no formal CNAA organization to consider courses in this area. A Recreation and Sports Studies Board was set up in 1978, and in the same year a further conference was held on human movement studies — with support from the Gulbenkian Foundation. By the time the conference was held in September approval had already been given for undergraduate and postgraduate courses at six colleges and polytechnics in England, Ulster Polytechnic and Dunfermline College of Physical Education.[63] Also in 1978 was a conference — held at Stratford-upon-Avon, and again with Gulbenkian support — on the possible impact on the arts and education of the seven recently-approved CNAA degree courses in the creative and performing arts.[64] Some of these activities related to institutional developments (for example, on diversification), others to new ways of approaching familiar ground (for example, on school experience), others to new approaches to the packaging of knowledge and its applications (for example, a conference on communication studies held in 1978[65]), others to the representation of existing activities for the first time in higher education (for example, in the creative and performing arts), and yet others on the mechanics of the CNAA's own work in validating courses and seeking to assure standards (for example, a conference on the role of external examiners held in October 1978).[66]

Over the space of a decade the CNAA had become a different organization. It was capable, in Edwin Kerr's words, of dealing with large and small.[67] It had followed the logic of its foundation by expanding its subject and institutional frontiers, embracing studies it believed important for access to and provision of higher education, and for routes into diverse employments in industry, commerce and the professions. In doing so it also extended and sharpened the tools by which it assured standards across the growing territory of higher education, but at the same time it struggled with the problem of those institutions which increasingly felt that they had served a long enough apprenticeship. The logic of the CNAA was not simple and uni-directional. The next chapter considers the specific question of the CNAA's relationships with its associated institutions, and the policy pressures operating from and towards the Council, and carries that account through to the 1980s. Before doing so it is important to underline the fact that the Council's preoccupations in the 1970s extended beyond the essentially curricular ones considered so far.

The CNAA was becoming increasingly involved, for example, with validation in Scotland. In 1976, in response to a White Paper on devolution to Scotland and Wales, the CNAA commented that it had always been sensitive to the specific conditions and needs of Scotland, and that it might be appropriate for the CNAA to set up a Scottish Committee. It considered, however, that 'there is no academic case for making special arrangements for Wales', given the similarity of the educational system in Wales to that in England. At the point, in July 1978, when the Council agreed in principle to create a Committee for Scotland, the CNAA was validating courses with a total enrolment of approaching 9000 students at thirteen Scottish institutions. The Committee met for the first time in Edinburgh in October 1979.[68]

The Council continued to be concerned with a range of general issues, including research. A working party under Professor Rochester produced a report which was published in 1974 on *Resources for Research in Polytechnics and other Colleges*. The Report emphasized what had been the Council's interpretation of its Charter and Statutes from the outset — if the Council's degrees were to be of comparable standard to those awarded by universities then:

> colleges must provide facilities for staff to further their knowledge by advanced study, research, consultative work or secondment to other fields of employment. Hence the Council expects a significant proportion of staff involved in teaching of courses leading to its awards to be engaged in research; moreover, colleges are expected to provide a high standard of specialized accommodation, library provision, academic, technical and administrative staff and good working conditions generally. As a result, it is widely accepted that the Council has assisted significantly in the improvement of all these factors in colleges offering courses leading to its degrees.

The Council sought to encourage 'a broad range' of research and related activities, including fundamental and applied research, consultancy and curricular development, private study and creative work in the arts. A central conclusion of the report was that colleges should assume that all academic staff teaching for the Council's degrees would 'undertake some definite activity falling within the various categories of research' that it had outlined. There was 'value in avoiding a rigid division between those who "do research" and those who "carry the teaching load"'.[69] The strength and breadth of these definitions and emphases were to prove encouraging to many institutions, and people in institutions, struggling to establish their own research policies and activities. The Council considered papers and had discussions on the design of modular courses and issues affecting sandwich courses, responded to policy documents on sixth forms and engineering, surveyed its own past work and considered its future roles, discussed resource constraints and perceptions of its institutional visits and the work of the subject boards.

The CNAA at the same time agreed a 'reciprocal transfer' of credit with the Open University, and related to, and negotiated with, a variety of other bodies in higher education. Most of the debate between the CNAA and the CDP concerned 'self-validation', the CNAA's role, progress towards autonomy or some particular aspect of the relationship between the CNAA and the polytechnics — and the discussions were on an ad hoc basis. Not until 1980 was there a proposal to establish a permanent liaison committee between the two organizations. CDP participation in the 1970s discussions of this relationship, and notably of moves towards 'partnership in validation', will feature in the next chapter, but it is important to note that the CDP, with an established office and secretariat, and the authority of the first in the field, was never matched by the Standing Conference of Principals and Directors of Colleges and Institutes in Higher Education. The polytechnic directors were often deeply divided over policies, but the CDP was able to take part in higher education debate as the putative rival to the CVCP. It lobbied the Secretary of State, gave evidence to Parliamentary Select Committees, debated everything from student wastage rates to student militancy, from application forms to computer provision. It met with HMIs and DES officers, set up its own committee machinery, and by 1978 could present a view of 'the polytechnics' fulfilment of the purposes for which they were created'. A decade after the White Paper had defined their purposes, they had successfully recruited students; provided sandwich courses; established themselves in science and technology, administrative, business and social studies, and other subjects; focussed on vocationally-oriented courses; sustained a commitment to part-time courses, and secured a firm basis for further growth. In the document which outlines this progress, and elsewhere, the CDP was anxious to distance itself from other institutions in the public sector.[70] Almost all of its meetings discussed relations with the CNAA.

A Committee for Academic Policy (CAP) was created by the CNAA in 1978, with the aim of advising the Council on policy issues of general concern and to coordinate activities which spread across subject areas. A parallel Committee for Institutions was created the following year. From July 1972 a Committee of Officers met at regular intervals. At its inception only seven senior officers were involved, to assist the Chief Officer who had been delegated particular functions by the Council, and to act as a senior management team. It would provide an opportunity to discuss drafts of papers for committees and consider policy issues for which boards and others might need guidance.[71] Given the rapid expansion of the CNAA's activities the Committee had a membership of eighteen officers by September 1974, twenty-five by March 1977, and thirty-three by the beginning of 1979. Given also the considerable reliance of the Council and its committees and boards on the officers to prepare discussion papers, and the contributions of the officers to conferences and elsewhere, these meetings served both as a staff development exercise and as a forum in which ideas and formulations could be clarified. It looked at the problems of the validation machinery itself, for example in conditions of the expansion of teacher education and the array of complex diversified courses which raised logistical and other problems for the CNAA. It was an opportunity to raise concerns about everything from external examiners to the assessment of modular courses, from a pamphlet on mature students to course regulations. It occasionally spent a whole day on 'policy review' discussions, and by the end of the 1970s was itself devolving more discussion to the individual operational units.[72]

A sense of the role of individual officers in the Council's policy formulation and implementation processes at this stage of its history can be derived from a single indicative case.[73] Ann Ridler joined the CNAA in 1969 as an assistant to Jean Rossiter, Senior Assistant Registrar for Arts and Social Studies, and became Assistant Registrar (the first appointment with that title in the CNAA) in that area in 1971, and Senior Assistant Registrar in 1973 — a title commuted for all its holders to Registrar in 1976. She was responsible for the CNAA's response to the James Report, and acted as Secretary to the joint CNAA-NCDAD group in 1972–73. With the diversification of the colleges the workload increased substantially in the arts and humanities particularly, and the rapid growth of the CNAA's work in arts and social studies was fuelled by the transfer of courses from London external degrees. Her responsibilities extended to cover the creative and performing arts, communication and cultural studies, and recreation and sports studies. There were meetings with HMIs on diversification, meetings of committees and working parties, and what she describes as 'the massive amount of advisory work we undertook with staff from institutions as part of their preparation for validation. It could be two or three substantial consultations a week in parallel with two or three visits or Board meetings a week'. The 'atmosphere of the job' changed from about 1974, as new fields of study were validated and the CNAA organization became more complex:

> The horror year in my memory was 1975–76. I had three-quarters of an Assistant Registrar and spent sixty-five nights away from home on Council visits. The work of planning visits to massive multi-subject degrees from colleges of education largely new to CNAA work, the huge amount of advisory work involved and the sheer quantity of report writing was horrendous.

From the start, however, visits took place in 'a campaigning spirit' — campaigning for better facilities, higher standards, improved staff workloads in the institutions. Local authorities listened and were generally responsive. What was particularly at stake, and what made the job particularly attractive, was that the outcome was educational opportunities for the under-privileged, increased chances to study for degrees.

In both its policies and practices the CNAA was revealing the promises and the tensions of the system. In the specific cases discussed — especially the rapidly changing colleges of education and new subject areas — the Council's machinery, standards and purposes were often being put to the test, giving rise to frustration and controversy. The University College at Buckingham was one such case. Established as a privately-financed institution by a Planning Board which first met in January 1969, UCB had at an early stage to consider what awards it might offer in advance of the Charter it hoped to obtain. It first approached the CNAA in 1971, and after some initial doubts on the part of the Council, it was told the following year that the CNAA might be able to consider a formal approach on condition that the new institution was not called a 'university' — since the CNAA was precluded by its Charter from the validation of universities. Detailed discussions took place in 1973. Professor Max Beloff, Principal of the College, wrote in June welcoming assurances that there were no legal impediments to applying for the 'accreditation' of courses, and in November the CNAA considered that the College had agreed various conditions, and the Council approved a statement of principles to be communicated to Buckingham. To the chagrin of Buckingham, however, because it meant the postponement of the opening of the College, the CNAA declined in 1974 to approve Buckingham courses in general and a law degree in particular. There was a hostile reaction at the CNAA's General Committee — its 'inner cabinet' — in April to Buckingham's proposal to operate on the basis of an eighty-week, two-year degree programme. The CNAA's Charter required the degrees it approved to be 'comparable' with those of universities, and the General Committee — and Council itself — thought that two-year degrees would stretch the interpretation too far: students would be under too much strain, and British degree courses were in any case already shorter than in most other countries. Further discussion with Buckingham resulted in a report to the Council commenting that the College representatives had presented 'a low level of academic argument'. The CNAA visitors, led by a university vice-chancellor, considered that the resources, accommodation, library and staffing were inadequate, but it was the two-year proposal — strongly defended by Buckingham — that proved the sticking point, and following the protracted negotiations the College decided to withdraw.[74] The issue of two-year degrees had led to long discussions on the Council. The UGC had been asked for and supplied a list of existing two-year courses, of which there were few, and all required more than two 'A' levels as an entry qualification (most were, in fact, conversion or second-degree courses). The majority of the Council considered that the proposal would conflict with its Charter obligations. It responded therefore on the basis of a principle and judgment of quality, and was accused of political prejudice.[75] The new frontiers were not without their hazards.

By any measure the contribution of the CNAA and its associated institutions in the 1970s was considerable. The decade had begun with the consolidation of the polytechnics and the transfer to the CNAA, with varying degrees of difficulty,[76] of the external degrees of the University of London. Edwin Kerr came to the Council early in the decade committed both to reforming validation procedures, and to rethinking the balance between the CNAA and the institutions:

No one can deny that the Council has done a great deal to improve the quality of education. I still believe that even for the most senior colleges, there is value in an external incentive — provided that the Council does not continue for ever its inspectoral function, and becomes instead more of an advisory body in partnership with the colleges.[77]

In an early paper for the Council he adumbrated what he was later to name 'partnership in validation': final authority should remain in the hands of the Council, but academic boards in 'experienced institutions' could be authorized 'to reach decisions in defined areas', decisions to be reported to the Council and normally accepted by it as 'acts of the Council'. Responsibility delegated to institutions could include the registration of PhD degree candidates.[78] Throughout the 1970s all of these elements were to feature in the Council's attempts to find the appropriate balances under its Charter, and to handle the increasingly complex range of subjects and institutions. With what degree of innovation this entire process took place it may be difficult to judge in retrospect, but it is important to note that to many observers at the time the very act of establishing the CNAA and its institutions firmly in the picture of higher education was a major innovation, apart from any judgments about the specifics of the CNAA's activities. There was comment throughout the period on the innovative aspect of the rapid development of the CNAA and public sector higher education. Sir Alex Smith, Director of Manchester Polytechnic and Chairman of the CDP, addressing a conference of principals of Colleges of Advanced Education in Australia in 1975, underlined the strengths of the polytechnics — and of the binary system — in overcoming, among other things, 'the anaemic state of our economy'. He saw himself as one of a 'new strain of educators', a 'polytechnician', in a sector that was concerned not only with scholarship but with something more: 'it is design, it is action, it is synthesis, it is professionalism, it is the application of knowledge'. Of importance in all of this was the CNAA, and it 'is steadily being recognized how significant an innovation this was in education'.[79] In the same year Peter Chambers, at West Midlands College, from amidst the 'encirling gloom' of the colleges of education, and recognizing the CNAA's own 'in-built conservative practices', felt that 'the overall impact of the CNAA has been beneficial for the colleges and that its commitment to innovation is a major factor in curriculum innovation within the colleges of education. It would seem no coincidence that the colleges with perhaps the greatest reputation for innovation are moving towards the Council's fold'.[80] In the following year, Maurice Peston told a committee of the House of Commons that 'those who doubt the innovatory possibilities of British education and the capacity of the DES and the LEAs to help things forward should study the CNAA and the polytechnics over the past decade. There have been remarkable achievements here which must not be blurred by the fact that there remains a long way to go'.[81]

One of the crucial questions emerging for the CNAA during the 1970s was in fact the extent to which it could take initiatives as well as being responsive. The Council's Charter did not formally require it to initiate, to enter policy arenas, to sponsor development, and in fact it prescribed the CNAA's role in the 'diffusion and extension of the arts, sciences and technologies' as being through the approval of courses of study and the granting of awards. The CNAA was finding, however, that to 'determine the conditions governing the grant of such awards' meant to see courses in broad institutional, academic and professional contexts. It meant taking initiatives which would ensure the maintenance and enhancement of standards through subject and curriculum development, and opportunities for the improvement of teaching and assessment, and for the consideration of new approaches to course structures and management, interdisciplinary, vocational and other issues in the development of public sector higher education. While the major policy-making and orientation roles rested with the members of the Council and its multiplicity of committees, the search for promotional roles in association with the institutions was inevitably a key part of the activities we have seen the CNAA's officers playing. The Council was in the 1970s recruiting a large number of relatively young staff, who saw the job, in the words of one of them, as 'a creative experience',[82] engaging in curriculum development, relating to senior academics on the Council's committees and working with peers in the polytechnics and colleges, generating ideas, disseminating good practice, advising on the planning and monitoring of courses, and in general developing an identity for the CNAA which combined the validation role with access to professional networks, research and advice on evaluation and other processes contingent on the validation relationship.

The Duke of Edinburgh retired from the Presidency of the CNAA in January 1976, to be succeeded by the Prince of Wales. Prince Philip had stipulated a maximum of ten years for his period in office, and had extended it by a year to enable Prince Charles, who was serving in the Royal Navy, to take over at an appropriate moment. The Council's first President had taken the position extremely seriously, and in addition to his ceremonial duties had invited the Chairman and Chief Officer at regular intervals, often twice a year, to meet with him, to discuss matters of interest to him, and to bring him up to date on the Council's activities. Sir Michael Clapham described the process as subjecting them to 'regular *viva voce* examination'.[83] On leaving the office of President, Prince Philip wrote:

> I am delighted that the CNAA has developed into such a sturdy institution in such a relatively short time. It has definitely become an accepted and essential part of the whole structure of higher education.[84]

Prince Charles was installed as President at a degree congregation in Edinburgh in 1976, and Sir Michael took the opportunity to underline to him that whatever 'the tribulations of our staff, who deal with the paper work of over 80,000 students and over 1000 courses, the Council itself and its committees and subject boards are concerned with one thing only, and that is quality'. The Prince of Wales would be presiding over what was now by far the largest degree awarding body in the United Kingdom.[85]

Sir Michael Clapham himself retired as Chairman at the end of 1977 having served on the Council from its beginning in 1964 (and he was at this point the only remaining member from the original Council), and been its Chairman for seven years. The CNAA, he had thought at the outset, was something that 'ought to happen'. He had seen the CNAA establish itself in the eyes of many — though employers in the more conventional industries had been slow to recognize the public sector and adapt their recruitment policies. He had 'believed passionately' in innovation, as had many of the polytechnics. He had strongly espoused the idea of contrasting and complementary studies whereby arts students would have some basic science and science students complementary studies of some kind. The notion had not been popular with many of the arts people in the Council, and he recalls one lady saying in a meeting that she would 'not give up one page of Beowulf for all the science in the world'. That, said Clapham, 'was the sort of trouble one had in Council'.[86]

Sir Denis Rooke, Chairman of the British Gas Corporation, became Chairman of the Council at the end of 1977, with its student numbers still rising by anything from 6 to 13 per cent a year. Its total numbers on taught courses reached almost 140,000 by the end of the decade. Of the 1703 courses in operation in 1980–81, 1201 were first degree courses. The students on first degree courses numbered 45,759 in science and technology, 33,274 in arts and social studies, 15,361 in art and design, 12,911 in education, 12,782 in business and management, and 3142 on inter-disciplinary courses. Over 35,000 of them were on sandwich courses and over 13,000 were part-time. The Prince of Wales was presiding over, and Sir Denis Rooke was chairing, what was indeed by far the largest degree granting body in the United Kingdom.

Notes

1 Francis, HS interview.
2 Edwin Kerr (1976) 'Principles and practice of validation' in Michael M. Raggett, and M. Clarkson, (Eds) *Changing Patterns of Teacher Education*, Falmer Press.
3 DES (1972) *Teacher Education and Training* (The James Report), HMSO, chapter 5.
4 CN, Report of the Lord James Committee of Enquiry into Teacher Education and Training, July 1972.
5 UGC/CNAA (1973) *A New BEd Degree*, December; CN Committee for Education minutes, 25 January 1973; Cmin, 23 February 1973.
6 Cmin, 23 February 1973.
7 Sir Derman Christopherson, MD interview.

8 CEdmin, 25 January, 4 May and 12 July 1973. 'Major schemes' from Didsbury and Berkshire was the Committee's description.

9 Committee for Education, Certificate BEd Overlap, 16 May 1974.

10 CEdmin, 15 October 1974.

11 A.G. Nokes (1985) 'The CNAA and teacher education', CN mimeo.

12 Myra McCulloch (1979) *School Experience in Initial BEd/BEd Hons Degrees Validated by the Council for National Academic Awards*, CNAA.

13 David Francis, private communication.

14 Cmin, 20 May 1975.

15 David Françis (1984/85) 'An award for teachers: An evaluation of the Diploma in Professional Studies in Education (of the CNAA)', mimeo.

16 Chief Officer's paper to Council, May 1976.

17 *Education: A Framework for Expansion*, London, HMSO, 1972, pp. 32–3.

18 CN (1977) *The Diploma of Higher Education of the Council for National Academic Awards*.

19 Sir Derman Christopherson, HS interview.

20 CN, Notes of a meeting held at the Polytechnic of Central London 24 January 1973 to discuss the academic problems of the Diploma of Higher Education and the BEd degree.

21 CN, Diploma of Higher Education Study Group minute, 1 May 1973; Guidelines for Diplomas of Higher Education: comments made to the Council for contribution to the Transbinary Conference on 15 June 1973.

22 CN, The Validation of Proposed Diplomas of Higher Education, n.d.

23 DipHE Group, minutes, 27 February, 12 and 26 March 1973; 14 March 1974; 7 January and 10 June 1975; Porter, HS interview.

24 DipHE Group (1977) 'Analysis of transfer of diplomates', autumn, 10 April 1978. See also Alex Bruce *et al.* (1989) *The DipHE Experience*, CNAA.

25 M. Gaskell (1977) 'Conference on planning for academic diversification in higher education', memo on group discussion on the place of the DipHE, 14 January.

26 Cmin, 24 May 1977.

27 Cmin, 22 July 1975.

28 R.G. Murray (1978) 'Planning for diversification', *Journal of Further and Higher Education*, 2, 1, pp. 59–60 (paper first given at the CNAA conference on 'Planning for Academic Diversification in Higher Education', 1977).

29 CN (1976) 'Diversification in the former colleges of education', May. The DES requirement was in *Circular 6/74*.

30 Report of Combined Studies (Humanities) Board conference, 7–9 February 1975.

31 Cmin, 17 February 1976.

32 CN, Report of a meeting with DES representatives, 12 March 1975.

33 Cmin, 15 February 1977.

34 College of Education Libraries Working Party, minute 26 April 1974; Final Report of Working Party on Libraries and Learning Resources (1977).

35 David Hencke (1976a) 'University validation standards easier than CNAA, say polys', *Times Higher Education Supplement*, 7 May; (1976b) 'Degrees of hope', 7 May; *Times Higher Education Supplement*; Stephen Cohen (1976) 'Colleges get cold shoulder in bid for degree courses', *Times Higher Education Supplement*, 7 May. Copies of these items were circulated to Council members for the meeting on 25 May 1976.

36 CDP minute, 11 July 1973.

37 Keith Hampson (1977) 'Murder, he says', *The Guardian*, 19 July.

38 Robert Strand (1987) *A Good Deal of Freedom*, CNAA, pp. 139–40.

39 Hanrott, HS interview.

40 Kerr, HS interview.

41 Cmin, 4 January 1973.

42 CNAA and NCDAD (1973) 'Amalagamation of CNAA and NCDAD: Statement to all interested parties', 26 February.
43 CNAA and NCDAD (1974) 'Amalgamation of CNAA and NCDAD', April.
44 Information from J.A. Brown, PhD candidate, University of Wales, Bangor.
45 CN, Committee for Art and Design (1979) *Report on the Review of BA Hons Degree Courses in Art and Design, 1975–76*, CNAA.
46 Strand, *A Good Deal of Freedom*, p. 146.
47 For the position in Scotland I am grateful to Strand, *A Good Deal of Freedom*, pp. 166–78.
48 Brinson, HS interview.
49 Drama Panel minute, 8 November 1974. For the CNAA and drama generally see Martial Rose (1979) *The Development of Drama in Higher Education, 1946–79*, King Alfred's College, Winchester, particularly pp. 29–37.
50 CN (1975) Report on an Informal Consultation between Committee and Board Chairmen and Officers concerned with Creative and Performing Arts, 24 June.
51 Information which follows on the Dance and Movement Panel from Brinson, HS interview.
52 Letter of 11 August 1980 concerning a working party meeting on 22 October 1980, together with a Survey of Problems, prior to a meeting the same afternoon of CASS, which was to receive a report.
53 CN, Management Studies Board minutes, 19 November 1975.
54 Management Studies Board minutes, 29 June 1976.
55 Judith Judd (1978) 'CNAA split over new management studies committee', *Times Higher Education Supplement*, 22 September.
56 *Courses for Managers*, CNAA, 1979, 3.
57 Information which follows from Iliffe, HS interview.
58 Richard Bourne (1971) 'More than technology', *The Guardian*, 18 January, quoting Lindop; Gerald Cox (1970) 'Careers in Scotland', *Computer Weekly*, 17 September.
59 J.F. Wilson and S.B. Marsh (1978) 'A second survey of legal education in the United Kingdom: Supplement No. 1', University of London, Institute of Advanced Legal Studies, pp. 1–2.
60 Information which follows from Overy, HS interview.
61 *CNAA Commentary*, no. 7, December 1976, p. 4.
62 *ibid.*, p. 3; *CNAA Commentary*, no. 8, November 1977, p. 2; *CNAA Commentary*, no. 9, April 1978, p. 3.
63 *CNAA Commentary*, no. 9, p. 3; *Human Movement Studies: Conference Report*, CNAA, 1980, p. 80.
64 *CNAA Commentary*, no. 11, March 1979, p. 4.
65 *CNAA Commentary*, no. 9, p. 4.
66 *CNAA Commentary*, no. 11, p. 4.
67 Kerr, HS interview.
68 Cmin, 17 February 1976 and 25 July 1978; Committee for Scotland minute, 8 October 1979.
69 CN (1974) Committee for Research Degrees, Report of the Working Party on Resources for Research Degrees in Polytechnics and other Colleges, April, pp. 3 and 8.
70 CDP minutes 1970–80, CDP correspondence files 1969–74.
71 Committee of Officers minute of second meeting, 7 September 1972.
72 Committee of Officers minutes passim 1972–8; Bryn Jones (1978) Review of Operation of Committee of Officers 1977/78: paper to Committee of Officers, 17 July.
73 Ridler, HS interview; Ridler paper, Not Only . . . But Also . . . , for limited internal CNAA circulation, 20 August 1987.

74 Cmin, 23 February, 19 July and 18 November 1973, and 21 May and 23 July 1974; Report on a Meeting between Professor Max Beloff, the Chief Officer and the Secretary on Friday 26 April 1974 (Committee of Officers papers, 6 May 1974); Joyce and Jonn Pemberton (1979) *The University College at Buckingham*, Buckingham Press, pp. 63–6.
75 Sir Michael Clapham, HS interview.
76 Outlined in the CNAA's Evidence to Committee of Enquiry into Governance of the University of London (Murray Committee), November 1970.
77 Quoted in Peter Scott (1972) 'CNAA's new pastures: Where does it go from here?', *Times Educational Supplement*, 1 December.
78 Edwin Kerr (1973) The Changing Nature of the Council's Work, draft paper for the General Committee, 13 December.
79 Alex Smith (1975) 'A philosophy for the polytechnics', *Times Higher Education Supplement*, 5 September.
80 Peter Chambers (1975) 'Course validation and curriculum innovation: A critique of the influence of the Council for National Academic Awards on the Colleges of Education', *Education for Teaching*, 97, p. 4.
81 *Tenth Report from the Expenditure Committee: Policy Making in the Department of Education and Science*, HMSO, 1976, p. 196.
82 Gaskell, HS interview.
83 Sir Michael Clapham, Address to CNAA Degree Congregation, June 1975. Other information about the Duke of Edinburgh as President from Clapham, HS interview.
84 CN Chairman's file, vol. 2, letter to Sir Michael Clapham, copied to Dr Kerr, 7 January 1976.
85 Sir Michael Clapham, Address to CNAA Degree Congregation, October 1976.
86 Sir Michael Clapham, HS interview.
87 CN, *Annual Report 1980*, pp. 19 and 24–5.

Chapter 7

Interpreting Partnership

Partnership, self-validation, academic independence, delegation, greater responsibility, sharing of responsibility, academic freedoms . . . this is some of the pervasive vocabulary within the CNAA and between the CNAA and its institutions in the 1970s. We have already noted that the polytechnic directors were seeking a larger measure of academic independence almost from the moment of designation — most publicly through the CDP press statement in July 1971 expressing a wish for the polytechnics to secure charters. The CNAA's annual report for 1970–71 recognized the search for greater independence.[1] In fact, within months of the creation of the CDP in December 1969 it was agreeing that the obtaining of charters was a 'legitimate aim'.[2] The CDP's 1971 statement suggested five years as the period within which some of the polytechnics could realistically hope to obtain a charter. From the outset the polytechnic directors were divided on matters of strategy, on the nature of future relationships with the CNAA, on the precise nature of the aims. Some were more impatient than others. In July 1971 the Chairman of the CDP wrote to three polytechnic directors who were apparently intending to make a direct approach to Mrs Thatcher, as Secretary of State, 'in relation to the possible granting of degree awarding powers to your polytechnic': individual initiatives, he considered, were premature.[3] The decade had begun with the CNAA not only on the brink of some of the expansive changes we have discussed, but also in increasingly strong cross-currents of debate about validation and relationships.

The CNAA, with the uncertainties born of divided interests and aims within the Council and between different levels of the CNAA's own expanding machinery, was looking for ways to pursue the goal of greater academic independence for the institutions. In practice this aim meant some form of relaxation or simplification of the validation procedure in cases where college development justified it. In November 1971 the Council set up a committee to consider its future relationships with the colleges — 'to consider what changes are desirable to afford greater independence to polytechnics and colleges in planning and operating courses leading to the Council's degrees'. In an interim report in July 1972 the Committee recommended that the main aims should be: '(a) easier approval or re-approval when this is justified by the strength of a college; (b) the development of a partnership between Council and colleges based on a reduction in the inspectoral function and a development in the advisory role of the Council; (c) less documentation from colleges'. On this basis the Council issued a statement the following year on *Procedure for Validation of Courses of Study*, the kernel of which was the CNAA's wish to respond differently to institutions which themselves differed widely in range of work and in experience: 'an application from a college where the staff for the proposed course is of known academic quality and experience may not require the same scrutiny of detail by the Council as in other cases'. The document ranked in order of importance the factors it wished to take into account in a new procedure: its knowledge of the institution 'as a whole', the quality and experience of the staff, and the papers submitted for the proposed course (the last justified by the fact that 'the discipline involved in preparing and documenting a proposal for the approval or re-approval of a course of study is extremely valuable to the College submitting it'). The procedure focussed essentially on the work of the subject boards and their mode of operation, and a range of approaches was envisaged:

> At one end the Council may approve a proposed course on the basis of the documents submitted by the College and without a visit to it, while at the other end the Council may consider a proposed course in full detail as at present. In between these two bounds there can be a series of different approaches to meet each case on its merits. It is hoped that more and more of the applications for renewal of approval will be such that they can be granted without any extensive dialogue on them being necessary, and indeed that many of them can be granted without any visit being made to the College by representatives of the Council or vice versa and without any special conditions being attached to the approval.[4]

The general principles of the document were spelled out in some detail. The CNAA's focus at this point was on building up a picture of institutions that would enable it to relax the rules in some cases: the focus was smoother course approval as a reward for experience.

This could clearly, however, not be sufficient in the long run. Assuming that the Council would continue to retain 'final authority', Edwin Kerr nevertheless pointed out, at the end of 1973, the logic of the decisions the Council had made. One path to go down might begin from the priority the Council had given to its knowledge of the particular institutions: 'it seems that we should now begin to build even more positively on this and consider a move in which certain institutions were granted particular responsibilities . . . the academic board in an experienced institution engaging in work of high quality should be authorized by the Council to reach decisions in defined areas', and within understood frameworks of report and action.[5]

On the very day his paper went to the General Committee the polytechnic directors were meeting in conference at Coombe Lodge, together with Toby Weaver and others from the DES. Some of the directors present were opposed to pressing for charters at that stage. Weaver talked of 'gradual disengagement from more detailed control by CNAA'.[6] Those discussions were fitted into a regular CDP meeting which itself discussed 'polytechnic autonomy', and in which a variety of views were recorded — the institutions were at different stages of development; the CNAA had established national status and its degrees were accepted currency; the CNAA was known to be giving serious attention to ways and means of giving greater freedoms to experienced colleges; emphasis should not be placed on charters as such. . . . The only conclusion the meeting was able to reach was 'that guidance be sought from officers of DES as to ways in which greater academic autonomy might be achieved'.[7]

For the next two or three years the directions, possibilities and practicalities continued to be discussed, with those polytechnic directors on the Council and its committees having a particularly difficult part to play in formulating policy. The CDP explored ways of countering what many of its members considered the continuing, excessive domination of the relationship by the subject boards, which were often — in spite of the tensions involved — seen in a more positive light by academic staff, appreciative of the peer contacts they entailed. One proposal emanating from the CDP Academic Affairs Standing Committee was that 'self-validation' might be achieved by instituting polytechnic Academic Advisory Committees, on the model of those for the CATs and the new universities — such AACs 'initially involving representatives of the CNAA'.[8] The majority feeling in the CDP was moving towards support for development within the CNAA. A 1974 CDP paper talked of 'a transitional process' from dependence on a validating body to self-validation 'within a relationship with CNAA'. It talked, as Kerr had done, of responsibility for individual course validation being delegated to Academic Councils or Boards: 'the Boards would become agents of CNAA' — what the paper described as a 'process of accreditation'. Such a change 'need not mean the conclusion of our relationship with CNAA. On the contrary, we believe it offers the prospect of evolving a new and useful relationship'.[9] The Council was not, however, willing to accept a form of accreditation of this kind. In 1974/75 the CDP pursued the ideas of self-validation and delegated authority in the form of accreditation as a first stage towards the autonomy they were seeking. It welcomed the direction CNAA discussions were going, held a joint meeting to discuss the CDP's ideas, but the Committee learned at a meeting in June 1975 that the CNAA had not supported a CDP paper on 'accreditation'.[10]

The CNAA's ideas were taking a different shape in 1975, showing an unwillingness to go as far as delegating authority for the approval of courses, but pursuing the idea of 'internal validation'. Several drafts of a paper on

'Extensions of Validation Procedure' were debated amongst officers and in Council meetings in the first half of 1975, and in July at Kerr's suggestion its title was changed to 'Partnership in Validation'. Early drafts referred to the Council's feeling that the 'time is ripe' or 'now is an appropriate time' to 'grant a greater degree of responsibility' to institutions which were ready to 'receive' or 'assume' it.[11] At its July meeting the Council heard some members complain that the proposals did not go far enough and would not lead to greater freedoms for institutions, and heard others wonder if the long-term aim was in fact 'complete autonomy'.[12] *Partnership in Validation* was immediately published, and institutions and the Council's committees and boards were asked to submit comments by January 1976. The Council proposed to produce a revised document by July 1976 and receive applications from institutions in the following academic year — a timetable that in the event was overshot by some three years. *Partnership in Validation* envisaged a dynamic relationship with institutions, the prospect of a closer partnership in which 'the procedures leading to validation are progressively transferred to them'. Particular institutions were to be authorized to carry out the 'main validation procedures' leading to the *Council's* approval of courses in their 'well established subject areas', with their freedom to organize their affairs in this way being subject to a quinquennial review:

> The system would bring about a close association between the Council itself and the institutions in which academic strength would be recognized and aspirations for academic freedom met in a way different from the traditional one of creating wholly autonomous chartered institutions.

The Council would consider seeking modifications to its Charter to allow it to delegate added powers. The time was ripe, in this formulation, not to 'grant', but to 'move towards granting', more responsibility for the validation of courses. The Council recognized

> the existence within a number of institutions of high quality academic work, experience, maturity, constructive self-criticism, and effective and thorough academic decision-making processes.

The emphasis was therefore on the internal procedures of the institutions — a way of sharing the Council's procedures. The Council intended to specify subject areas in which responsibility could be delegated to an institution, to authorize institutions to modify existing courses and introduce new ones in subject areas for which the Council had given prior agreement, and to determine the criteria and methods for specifying subject areas and conducting quinquennial reviews. Crucial to the operation of the scheme was the CNAA's recognition that some institutions had established successful 'internal validating committees' as sub-committees of Academic Boards, 'responsible for considering schemes on their behalf before they are submitted to the Council', and others had developed faculty or school machinery to do the same. Adopting this model, the CNAA decided that institutions using the proposed new procedures 'would be expected to have a particularly effective internal procedure: the Council would require the formation of an Institution Validating Committee'.[13] Whatever the ultimate aim might be, for the moment the CNAA was going as far only as delegating or sharing aspects of the validation process — which meant accepting the limitations of the CNAA's existing Charter.

One step that the CNAA had taken, and one that many polytechnic directors and others considered a basis on which to build, was to promote the development of college research degrees committees. From 1972, where an institution had sufficient experience of conducting and supervising research work, and had an established committee geared to the vetting of research proposals, it could be authorized to register candidates for the CNAA's degree of MPhil, without going through the CNAA's own degree registration machinery. Registrations for the degree of PhD were still to be through the CNAA. In 1972 eleven colleges were granted delegated authority for MPhil registrations. In the discussions of the mid-1970s it was hoped in some institutions that this step might be the forerunner of others involving greater delegation of powers.

The CDP had welcomed the broad direction in which the CNAA's discussions had been going in 1975, but liked little or nothing in the *Partnership in Validation* document. Its Academic Affairs Committee began its draft response — 'Since the document is generally at variance with CDP policy, the Academic Affairs Committee felt unable to recommend its acceptance by CDP'. That Committee, and the CDP itself, took issue with the proposal to authorize internal validation related to specific subject areas and not to institutions as a whole. The Committee complained that no real freedom was being offered, and indeed that more constricting mechanisms were involved. The CDP considered the paper from its Academic Affairs Committee, and agreed that 'the CNAA should be informed that the CDP did not wish to accept the form of partnership proposed in the discussion document': the notion of a different approach leading to a better form of partnership should be explored.[14] Although the CDP continued to be critical of the partnership proposals and of other aspects of CNAA's operations — including perfunctory and over-large visits and 'undue attention . . . being accorded to criticisms of the management of polytechnics'[15] — it was unable to agree on the policy direction in which to go. At a CDP conference there was 'a divergence of opinion' amongst directors on the issue of self-validation. Some felt the present arrangements to be satisfactory, believing that 'there had been a marked change for the better in the CNAA system over the years and felt that subject boards fulfilled a useful role'. Others thought the CDP 'should not back down from accreditation as this would seem to suggest that CDP were not a body to be taken seriously'. It was difficult to reach an agreed policy and the CDP was now waiting for the CNAA to make the next move'.[16]

The criticisms from the CDP, and from a meeting of heads of institutions recently visited, together with some Council members, focussed on the quality and unclear roles of visits, over-concern with resources, the reporting process, and other issues, and the Council decided to review the position in these respects under the continuing discussion of the partnership scheme.[17] The comments received on *Partnership in Validation* from institutions and the Council's committees and boards were summarized, presented to the Council, published and circulated. It was concluded from the responses that the majority 'considered that the benefits which the present system had provided should not be discarded in favour of a far less obviously secure form of validation'. The Chairman thought two main 'extreme counter-arguments' had emerged and the remainder lay somewhere between:

1 The view that rested on the belief that the only true and ultimate test of academic responsibility lay in an institution validating and awarding its own degrees. Many polytechnics were now as large as many of the universities and in a similar, if not better, condition than the CATs were at the time they became universities. To keep them in tutelage to the CNAA was both humiliating and unfair.

2 The belief that self-validation was not an ideal system and that it prevailed in universities for historical reasons only. The system offered by the CNAA had the advantage that it drew upon much wider academic expertise than any single institution could offer.

Broadly speaking the responses were taken as a reaffirmation of the existing partnership at two levels — between the Council and institutions, and between subject boards and academic staff: 'the mechanisms proposed in the paper for modifying the partnership had clearly been rejected', but the rejection of the proposals did not mean that the matter could there rest. The number of responses opposed to the proposals on the grounds that they did not go far enough towards independence was very small — only a few academic boards of institutions had expressed that view.[18] There had been general endorsement of the broad aims of *Partnership in Validation* to respond to increasing maturity on the part of associated institutions, but dislike of the detailed machinery. The Council could not in these circumstances follow the schedule it had outlined. It asked the officers to reflect on the discussions which led up to, and followed the issue of, *Partnership in Validation*, and subsequently accepted the advice offered in an officers' paper to set up a working party to pursue the discussion further and report back in May 1978, after consulting the Council's committees and boards. The CNAA, like the CDP, had momentarily achieved stalemate.

The Working Party on Partnership in Validation met seven times between November 1977 and May 1979, and submitted an interim report as expected in 1978 — only to find its proposals rejected by the Council. The working party reviewed the existing system, roles, alternatives and the range of views being expressed — from allowing institutions to stand alone to preserving the CNAA's role in maintaining standards. It explored the meanings of 'independence' and confronted the argument that the Council was itself a myth and the reality was the powerful and almost autonomous subject boards. A good deal of discussion focussed, in the early meetings, on whether and how to reduce the 'all-pervading' influence of the subject boards, and at its second meeting discussed an officers' draft paper which sought to undermine the boards and considered the pros and cons of the CNAA relating primarily to institutions as a whole.[19] In the later meetings, and after the rebuff by the Council, opinion moved towards the creation of a CNAA 'Committee for Institutions', as Hugh Glanville, Registrar for Institutional Reviews, proposed it in January 1979 — a Committee to have oversight of review visits, to coordinate institutional reviews and course validation, to give priority to consideration of the reports of visits, and to monitor the 'interplay between the internal procedures of the institutions and the Council's procedures for the approval of courses'.[20] A proposal canvassed in the CDP by David Bethel, Director of Leicester Polytechnic and a member of the CNAA's working party, was for an individual 'Institutional Committee' for each institution designated as having achieved 'mature status', to act on behalf of the CNAA, to consult with the institution and to replace institutional visits[21] — another CDP proposal which did not gain CNAA support. The working party adopted the proposal for a Committee of Institutions — as did the Council, and in due course it was established.[22] As a counterweight to this strengthening of relationships at the CNAA-institutions level the move to weaken the role of subject boards was reversed and the proposals adopted provided for greater integration of the boards than at first suggested.[23] It also placed greater emphasis on what it termed 'interdependence' rather than autonomy — the need for public sector institutions to relate to one another — perhaps through regional groupings — within the system.

The Council considered the report of the Working Party in detail in February 1979. Some polytechnic directors on the Council — including Geoffrey Hall from Brighton and Norman Lindop from Hatfield — found the report to be 'depressing' and lacking in any radical solutions. Hall considered that any development that could meet the expectations of the institutions should have the aim of assisting them 'in achieving full maturity'. The CNAA was acting as a deterrent by preventing difficult decisions from being taken internally. It was important to reduce the CNAA's workload, establish an 'alternative means for maintaining standards', and provide institutions with a basis 'from which independence might be achieved'. Bethel explained that the Working Party had not felt that the Council would be prepared to support such radical views, and other Council members supported the report. It was an 'evolutionary' model that was being proposed, and it was endorsed by the Council,[24] which asked for further work to be done on some details, and for the proposals to be published. A model for further development of the concept of partnership had been agreed, and *Developments in Partnership in Validation* — the 'blue book' as it was nicknamed from its cover — was in circulation by September.

Before this phase of the process was brought to a conclusion, however, an event occurred — in September 1978 — which heightened the sensitivities involved in some of the debates. Teesside Polytechnic began life as Constantine College and in 1978 merged with the Teesside College of Education. It was a small Polytechnic, had a history of poor local authority support, and the CNAA had had occasion to be critical of it as an academic community. An institutional review visit was scheduled for May 1978, and Hugh Glanville, newly-appointed from within the CNAA as Registrar for Institutional Reviews, had the job of making the arrangements.[25] He was already aware of the possibility of situations in which approval would not be the automatic outcome of such visits, and indeed the CNAA had already, as a result of institutional visits, imposed stern conditions to be met in some instances if approval was to be continued. The CNAA was soon to face the situation in an even more dramatic way.

Before the visit to Teesside took place Glanville went up to the Polytechnic to discuss plans for the visit, and returned to London after what he describes as 'a bizarre day'. The Polytechnic was in the process of amalgamating with the College, and in a discussion in the Director's office the College Principal was obviously shocked to hear things said by the Director that had not been previously shared with him. The Director seemed to know nothing about the College. The papers prepared by the Polytechnic for the visit were 'abysmal'. Glanville indicated in a memo to Kerr that he thought there were problems ahead. On the two-day visit things in fact 'got progressively worse'. Each member of the visiting party, which was chaired by Edwin Kerr, reported back to the group on separate initial discussions with the faculties these were in some disarray. In general meetings the Director attracted all problems to himself and found himself in difficulties. The visiting party, including an HMI in attendance, was horrified, dropped their agenda for the second day and went through the problems as they had perceived them with the management group and the Academic Board:

> hoping that someone would tell us we were wrong — nobody would. Not even the Director would say we were wrong. We finally debated at great length whether it would be possible to avoid making explicit reference to the Director. It was finally agreed while still in Teesside that it would have to be done, and the only way was by explicit reference to the role of the Director, quoting the Articles of Government.

At the final meeting between Kerr, Glanville and the Director, Kerr told him what would be in the report, and it was a brief meeting because the Director said 'he had nothing to say'.

Kerr reported on the visit at the July meeting of the Council, drawing attention to 'the adverse criticisms contained in this report', emphasizing that it had been a strong visiting party, and that it had reached its conclusions unanimously. He summarized:

> The Polytechnic was beset with resource problems but the cause of the Visiting Party's overriding concern was the poor quality of the leadership and the lack of initiative being taken by the Academic Board. There was no real Academic plan and there were no grounds for confidence that the resource levels necessary to support the standards of the courses leading to the Council's awards would be maintained. Despite these serious reservations it was recognized that there was some good academic work being done.

A Council member who had been on the visiting party supported the statement and endorsed the Chief Officer's leadership on the occasion of the visit. The Academic Board

> had been given ample opportunity to respond constructively but had palpably failed to do so. Neither had they demonstrated an adequate awareness of the essential problems which they had to resolve.

There was some concern expressed at the Director being singled out for criticism, but the Chief Officer considered that the criticism was necessary 'since it was the leadership which was stifling academic development and progress'. The Council accepted the report, amending one sentence to read: 'For reasons which are apparent from the rest of this report the Visiting Party could not feel assured that the Director was fully and properly exercising his responsibility for the "internal organisation and management and discipline of the Polytechnic", in accordance with the Articles of Government'.[26] The final version of the report was sent to the Polytechnic and — with Kerr assuring the Council that the responsibility could not have lain with the CNAA itself — was leaked to the *Times Higher Education Supplement* and appeared in its issue of 8 September, under the headline: 'Closure threat to poly in CNAA's toughest-ever report'. Copies of the report, it indicated, had been 'circulated confidentially to Cleveland County Council and members of the Governing Body and the Academic Board':

> It describes the Polytechnic as dispirited, poorly led and understaffed. The computer unit is on the verge of 'complete collapse', the library is inadequate and the relationship with the local authority is bad. 'On visiting the departments and faculties members found a polytechnic which still contains some academic work of a high standard, but which in general is dispirited, confused and without confidence', the report says.

The Council was understood to have taken legal advice before inserting the section on the Director, Dr John Houghton. Because of poor management the Polytechnic had not had the same 'close and supportive relationship with the authority that the College of Education had enjoyed'. The *THES* added in an editorial that the withdrawal of CNAA recognition could result in the grave consequence of the closure of an institution in the largest conurbation in Europe without a university:

> The real failure of the Polytechnic is that it has not established a community of academics with a corporate identity and with sound machinery for democratic decision making.

Over the next few days the CNAA report was national news. For the *TES* 'Poly faces closure after report', for the *Daily Mail* 'Chaos college faces collapse', for *The Daily Telegraph* 'Degree threat to polytechnic over low standards', for *The Guardian* 'Poly may be left out on academic limb'. *The Sunday Times* ran a feature on 'The college where key books are on four-hour loan', reporting that:

> members of the academic staff last week agreed vehemently with many of the Council's criticisms and expressed relief that the polytechnic's problems were being brought into the open at last. 'The management system is the most atrocious I have experienced', said one. 'Nobody lays down priorities. There is no strategy, no vision, no policy, no sense of direction'.[27]

The Council issued a statement on 13 September, correcting some points in the press reports, emphasizing that the visiting party had indicated that it believed the Polytechnic had 'the potential to rectify the grave situation in which it finds itself', and stressing that the visiting party had not suggested that courses as currently taught were below an acceptable standard. If, after a further review, the Council decided that students should not be admitted to any courses leading to its awards, the position of existing students would be safeguarded.

The CNAA had clearly discovered an unhappy situation inside the Polytechnic, and between it and the local authority. As *The Sunday Times* pointed out, there were staff who more than welcomed the CNAA's judgments on the long-standing problems of the Polytechnic. One article by a member of staff, while critical of some aspects of CNAA's procedures, stated clearly that

> many of the CNAA's diagnoses of Teesside Polytechnic's ills had already long been articulated by staff within the college, and to a great extent the CNAA report was welcomed by the teaching body. Although people feared for their jobs in the wake of the CNAA threat to withdraw blanket validation from the Polytechnic in 1980, there was also a sense of relief that the problems had now been stated

in a form and in a language which our masters would find difficult to ignore.[28]

The visiting party had concluded that the management problems were a threat to the academic standards of the institution, and most faculties were affected. In one of them the visitors faced the problem of the relationship between the staff and a head of department being the subject of a libel action, and a refusal by the staff to meet the visitors in the presence of the head of the department (resolved by the visiting party member who chaired the meeting allowing the head of department to stay until he had to leave 'for another meeting').[29] On 12 September the Polytechnic's Academic Board called for the 'immediate resignation, retirement or removal' of the Director.[30] The governors in fact accepted the Director's offer to go on 'indefinite leave', a move which angered the staff, but one which gave rise to a four-man team of senior executives to manage the Polytechnic — in fact until a new Director was appointed.[31] The CNAA's procedures, its concern with the total academic environment in which its courses were offered, had led it — at a time when its relationships with the institutions were under intensive discussion — to a position in which it could directly influence the management and operation of an institution where it perceived weaknesses, as well as the institution's own relationships with governors and the local authority. It was visibly true that the CNAA, as one education correspondent put it, was 'busy about the job it was set up to do — to award degrees and to make sure that the standards of them are at least up to university level'.[32] The implications of Teesside were not, however, lost on the other polytechnic directors, who went into a flurry of activity in October.

At the beginning of October the Chairman of the CDP, wrote to the Secretary of State complaining essentially of two things. Since CNAA reports were always likely to reach a wide readership they 'must be based on conclusive evidence and should not identify individuals for serious criticism in a manner which cannot allow them to defend themselves in accordance with the established rule of law'. In the Teesside case the evidence was 'not reasoned and substantial in a manner to command confidence in the CNAA'. Secondly, if the polytechnic in question had deteriorated in resource provision and management to the point suggested, this pointed to the lack of an early warning system through the Inspectorate, who had a responsibility for the monitoring of standards in non-university institutions.[33] The CDP also issued a statement expressing its increasing concern over recent years at the way the CNAA conducted quinquennial reviews. It considered the Teesside report as 'the culmination of this process and finds aspects of the report distasteful and unacceptable'.[34] The CDP also expressed its concern at the fact that no polytechnic director had been on the visiting party (in fact, when the visiting party was first put together, it did include a polytechnic director, who withdrew at the last moment).

One CDP paper suggested the Council visit to Teesside exemplified the aspects of CNAA activity which were giving rise to concern: 'while not adducing any evidence which indicates an objective failure of student or employer satisfaction or of academic standards, the report makes serious criticisms of the management of the Polytechnic, based on a cursory inspection and conversations with members of staff'.[35] The CDP recorded its concern about CNAA quinquennial visits and reports, and while considering it proper for the CNAA to judge whether an institution was a 'satisfactory environment for advanced work' thought it was not competent to adopt a 'judicial role'. The CDP called for a moratorium on institutional reviews.[36] An exchange of letters with Sir Denis Rooke then followed, and in December the Council basically affirmed the importance of institutional visits as the means by which the CNAA built up a picture of institutions and enabled it to exercise its responsibilities, and asked the Working Party on Partnership in Validation to give consideration to the form such visits should take.[37]

A return visit to Teesside was planned for 1979. In October 1978 Cleveland County Council earmarked substantial additional funding for the Polytechnic,[38] the post of Director was advertised but first time round was not filled when interviews took place in April 1979 (with Lord Boyle, Vice-Chancellor of Leeds University, and Professor Maurice Kogan of Brunel University among the advisers for the appointment[39]). A confident graduation ceremony at which the Chairman of Governors spoke optimistically took place in February 1979,[40] and at its meeting in May 1979 the Council received a report of a preliminary visit by a small group of members and officers the previous month to the Polytechnic. They reported on discussions with the Directorate, heads of departments and central services, the Academic Board, the governors and members of the local education authority: 'the visiting party believed that the Polytechnic had made real and substantial progress and had felt that there was a different atmosphere from that encountered by the visiting party' the previous year. The Council agreed to postpone the next full visit from the summer of 1979 until later in the year, and to release a press statement that had been agreed by the visiting party with the Polytechnic and the Teesside Education Authority.[41] The local press announced a 'Poly comeback', and when the CNAA reapproved the Polytechnic's BSc in Mechanical Engineering later in the month it announced — 'Poly wins a tribute from CNAA'.[42] When the full institutional visit took place in December the Council found that the expectations of the preliminary visit were being fulfilled.[43] The Teesside events were crucially important at this stage of the development both of the CNAA and of its associated institutions, but the outcomes were ambiguous. On the one hand they strengthened the polytechnics' resistance to the institutional review element in the CNAA's procedures, but on the other hand they confirmed for the CNAA the value of gaining intelligence about the overall health of the institutions. Into the discussions of partnership in validation, the 'blue book' and the possibility of new validation arrangements with 'mature' institutions were fed the varied attempts to draw lessons from and conduct dialogue around the specific difficulties encountered over the Teesside visit.

By the time the CNAA published *Developments in Partnership in Validation* the CDP was voicing increasingly strong criticisms of CNAA practice. It was talking of a 'gulf' between the two bodies, seeing the partnership discussions as revealing that the CNAA was not prepared to go very far towards new relationships, and criticizing validation visits in particular: they were 'more often than not' unsatisfactory in meeting the assumed objectives.[44] The *Developments* publication was hardly likely in this situation to satisfy the strongest of the CNAA's critics. *Developments* in fact was what it described as 'an evolutionary development of the Council's present procedures, which will also allow experimentation with more radical variations'. The six-part model it presented comprised:

  (i) Improvement of the procedures for the initial approval of courses.

 (ii) Introduction of indefinite periods of approval, subject to regular progress reviews.

(iii) Replacement of the process of the renewal of approval of courses by progress review visits.

(iv) Extension of the limits within which institutions can change approved courses.

 (v) Provision for institutions to propose variations from the normal validation methods.

(vi) Improvement of the procedures for linking course validation and institutional reviews.

The Council was proposing, therefore, a variety of amendments to existing validation procedures, lengthening the reins in various ways, and — in item (v) of the model — offering institutions a way to go beyond what was proposed. Its implementation proposals included the creation of the Committee for Institutions and an immediate start on considering 'possible longer-term models'. In spelling out its arguments for the proposed pattern, the Council was once again reinterpreting the balance that had been at the centre of its concerns from the beginning: there was nothing in the Charter and Statutes 'which prevented greater recognition from being given to an institution's own internal procedures where these could be shown to be rigorous and effective. Council was doubtful, however, if a system of internal validation could ever be a complete substitute for a system of external validation'. It emphasized that many people considered that direct contact between boards and course teams was 'one of the most valued aspects of the Council's operation', and the Council concurred with this view as long as boards worked within the policies laid down by the committees. Some models of development had been proposed which would require changes in the Charter and Statutes, but since there was no evidence that the government wished to see any change in the basic role 'of the Council or in the status of institutions in the maintained sector', the Council had given priority in the shorter term to developments within the existing Charter and Statutes. Such developments, however, 'should not preclude further changes in the foreseeable future'.[45] In the letter accompanying the document to the Council's institutions the Chief Officer underlined that 'the Council is already engaged in examining possible longer term models'.[46]

There were problems, old and new. The emphasis in *Developments* on boards being required to work within committee policies, and the changes of procedure envisaged in the first four items of the new model, did not mean automatic changes in the 'inspectoral' functions of the boards. Amongst officers and boards there were some who could not, or would not, relinquish old attitudes: 'never mind what the blue book said, this is what we are going to do'.[47] Some CNAA members were aware of opposition to the concept of partnership in validation among the Council's officers, particularly some whose main responsibility was to subject boards. At a meeting of the Committee for Education in October 1979, 'there was a feeling that the boards were beginning to develop "identities" of their own, separate to that of the Committee'.[48] In 1980 the CDP was talking of CNAA 'dogmatism', and in suggesting the establishment of a liaison body with the CNAA it looked for the establishment of a 'special relationship'. In early 1980, however, there were differing views in the CDP and the polytechnics. In the polytechnics themselves, as one CDP document on reactions to *Developments* indicated, 'in general, the proposals are welcomed, although with some reservations'. There were already favourable comments on changes in institutional and review visits. One polytechnic had expressed its fears to the Council that not all boards would operate the new arrangements, and had received an assurance from the Chief Officer that 'corrective action would be taken as soon as possible where any Board was seen not acting in the spirit of the new arrangements'.[49] There were, therefore, problems that *Developments* sought to solve, and in doing so had to contend with entrenched positions. There were also new problems within the institutions, as some commentators were quick to point out. Increased partnership of the kinds intended both made greater demands on the senior staff of institutions, and increased their authority within the overall procedure. It also, as was pointed out from Scotland, affected the committee structure, its purpose and value, within institutions:

> Working through committees may provide opportunities for a form
> of participation in decision-making in an institution (a cynical view
> would be that at least it may give the illusion of this), but by their

nature committees can be introspective and restricted in their outlook. Generally they evolve as comfortable structures in the establishment being more effective in maintaining the 'status quo' than in encouraging change, and rarely do they encourage innovation.[50]

It was suggested that the new arrangements would also weaken the roles of course teams in institutions, to the benefit of heads of departments and central administrations, and another commentator talked of the danger of increased internal conflict between management and 'the grassroots'.[51] Alternatively, there continued to be 'grassroots' feelings that in spite of the hazards of peer review through external validation, the process was more palatable in some subject areas than the hazards within institutions. Discussing the implementation of partnership in validation, the Sociological Studies Board, for example, heard concern about the 'apparent lack of sympathy which may exist in institutions' internal monitoring and validation procedures to academic developments in sociology, in that the views expressed may be harsher and more inhibiting than those expressed by the Board'.[52] It is important to emphasize that the policy statements of the CDP disguised serious conflicts of opinion at crucial moments amongst the polytechnic directors, but also were frequently at variance with the views of the principals of the colleges of higher education and other institutions, and with the sentiments of the academic boards or staff of the polytechnics. The strengths and weaknesses of the CNAA's procedures, old and new, contained what the CDP considered to be 'dogmatism', but what other constituencies often regarded differently.

Within the CNAA what the partnership debates and their outcomes indicated was the crystallization of opinion around a modest but significant liberalization of the validation base of the CNAA's roles. The move was far enough to suggest the future transfer of greater validation responsibility to institutions, but not far enough to suggest the degree of autonomy that many of the polytechnic directors had sought. The difficulty in reaching agreement about this, or any greater measure of development, had lain partly in the fact that neither the CNAA nor any of its internal structures or external partners or constituencies was homogeneous, and the evolution of 'partnership' was therefore through a constant, complex and difficult process of negotiation. The frustrations and criticisms arose from clear enough aspirations on the part of institutions for the maximum attainable independence — but far from agreed as a concept within institutions and organizations. The difficulty lay also in what had been interpreted by the late 1970s, inside and outside the CNAA, as a valuable tradition. Validation, wrote one active university participant in the CNAA's affairs in 1977, 'has been hailed as the most important single educational innovation since 1945'. The CNAA was by then 'on the move not only to the greater degree of independence in validation implied by the debate on *Partnership in*

Validation but also towards different forms of validation, more in tune with the situation of higher education in the late seventies'. The whole process was the 'institutionalization of academic common sense'.[53] Another university member of a CNAA Committee commented that the CNAA 'does a meticulous job as far as I can see and the overall standard of CNAA courses which gain approval is probably much higher than in most universities'.[54] The standards of CNAA courses were therefore so well established that major shifts in, or the removal of, the validation tradition through peer review might imperil what had been achieved. The tendency in the Council therefore was to seek a sufficient measure of 'self-validation' to enable institutional progress to be made, but to marry it with the protection of the external validation system which appeared to be the best defence of hard-won standards.

The CNAA's concern for the defence of standards throughout this period was a concern for institutional and course considerations and student access and outcomes. In registering those concerns it was paying some of the penalties of the pioneer, anxious to ensure adequate monitoring of both traditional and novel courses — single subject and multidisciplinary, full-time, part-time and mixed mode, organized by year or in modules. Many of these structures were both challenging and, in British education, relatively new. The CNAA gave its first approval to a modular course, for example, in 1972 — the logic of which was ultimately to bring the Council strongly into the field of credit accumulation and transfer. From the early 1970s it was validating courses structured in macro-modules and micro-modules at colleges and polytechnics.[55] By 1976 officers were producing papers reviewing the design, aims, differences and validation problems of modular courses, and the modular structures being validated were — in validation and management terms — complicated. In 1973 the City of London Polytechnic obtained CNAA approval for its modular degree, beginning with fifteen subjects and a first year in which students reappraised their objectives and had guidance and counselling available. Oxford Polytechnic began its modular course in 1973 with seven fields of study, all in science. In 1974–75 the CNAA approved arts and humanities fields at Oxford, the following year education, catering and food science, and in the following two years languages, law and a range of social science fields were added or assimilated. By 1983 almost all the major areas of the Polytechnic were represented in the modular programme, and the number of students on the modular programme was by now greater than the total numbers of students in some colleges.[56] While the discussions of partnership in validation were taking place in the late 1970s, therefore, the CNAA had had some decade and a half of validation experience, but the rapid expansion of subject areas and such relatively recent developments as the DipHE and modular courses, and the uncertainties surrounding public sector higher education in a swiftly changing economic climate, all helped to strengthen the view that the Council should not move too rapidly into a higher gear of change. At a

Leverhulme seminar on higher education in 1981, Gerry Fowler commented that the CNAA's 'Partnership in validation' might be held to point the way forward to a national system of awards whose standards were assured by the institutions offering the courses, and periodically scrutinized from outside. Unfortunately, however, 'no one, least of all the CNAA itself, seems certain of the precise meaning and intention of "Partnership in validation" '.[57] Good intentions and uncertainty are a not infrequent outcome of compromise.

The ways forward for the CNAA in its relationships with the institutions were articulated in various forms in the 1970s, and a perspective on the complexities may be helped by taking two of them. As Chairman of the CNAA and strongly committed to its activities, Sir Michael Clapham was a consistent advocate of increasing the responsibilities of the institutions it validated. He resisted, however, the notion that the polytechnics were merely a new breed of university. At an awards ceremony at the Polytechnic of the South Bank in 1974 he castigated those people 'who would like to make polytechnics exactly like universities', and who ignored the fact that the polytechnics had the distinctive feature of not only pursuing knowledge for its own sake, but also treating the acquisition of knowledge as 'never far removed from its application' — and constructing courses of study accordingly.[58] The following year, at a CNAA awards ceremony, he emphasized that it was planning, for academic reasons, a 'major shift in the work of validating courses from the Council to the Polytechnics and Colleges running them'. Departments, with some external advice, could now be capable of evaluating their own courses. The CNAA hoped 'to move with reasonable speed to a situation in which first departments with established academic reputations, and later whole institutions, can undertake the scrutiny of new courses internally, looking to the Council for almost automatic approval'. The outcome would be to 'enhance the academic responsibility of the institutions of higher education', as well as diminishing the administrative pressure on the CNAA.[59] In 1976 he went a stage further in his address to the CNAA's degree congregation, by discussing the position at both sides of the relationship with institutions. The CNAA's own system, he concluded, was thorough, but also 'cumbrous and laborious':

> It generates paper in sickening profusion; it makes unconscionable demands on the heroes of the piece, the thirteen or fourteen hundred volunteers drawn mainly from 'that two-handed engine' we pompously call the binary system of higher education . . . but with all its faults the system works. At its best it works well, clarifying objectives, improving ideas, through dialogue between academic equals working to a common end. At its worst the procedure leads to irritation, the dialogue to acerbity.

The Council was not content with the system, and was working to improving the partnership — in a dialogue with partners that the Council needed to continue as its 'most urgent agendum'. But that was perhaps not enough, and he went on to explain to the congregation and to the Prince of Wales as the new President that there was a 'more searching question' to be asked about validation:

> should this be done at all? Should we advise Her Majesty under whose Charter we operate, that the time has come to devolve our responsibilities gradually to the institutions who are our partners? . . . Would it be a proper recognition of the quality of their teaching and administrative staff to accept their judgment of academic standards absolutely and make them mature degree awarding bodies? Or would it be a sign of still greater maturity for their staff to go on contributing to a national system, a system in which the collaboration of the entire academic community could raise standards higher and judge quality more surely?

Having asked the question, he offered no personal answer: 'Like jesting Pilate, I stay not for an answer: though the question awaits our collective resolution'.[60]

Sir Michael Clapham had what he later described as 'wild hopes' that the process of delegation would be achieved within two or three years of his vacating the chairmanship in 1977. It was certainly his 'personal aspiration' that this would be the case, though he was aware that this was not a view that was universally shared.[61] When he retired from the chair Frank Hornby sent in a note about Clapham's contribution to the CNAA in the early years. In 1971, as Chairman-to-be he found himself in 'a maze of important policy items', including 'how best to give appropriate independence to colleges experienced in courses leading to CNAA degrees and/or the DipAD'.[62] Placing quality and independence in combination in such questioning, he reflected the problems and pressed for them to be treated with urgency to achieve a 'collective resolution'. Neither urgency nor unanimity were easy to achieve, and the 'blue book' of 1979 clearly went only one step, though a significant step, in the direction to which Sir Michael Clapham pointed. While *Developments* was being finalized there were, as Edwin Kerr pointed out to the institutions, other longer-term models being discussed. A second perspective on the partnership issue is offered by a contribution made to the seventh meeting of the Working Party on Developments in Partnership in Validation in May 1979.

The Working Party had been instructed by the Council to begin a consideration of longer-term developments, and possible models of development was an agenda item for this meeting. Chairing the Working Party, Edwin Kerr called on David Bethel to present his views. Bethel spoke as a member of the Working Party, not as Chairman of the CDP, though he underlined that Sir Denis Rooke had recently given an undertaking that the CDP would be consulted. Bethel indicated that all institutions conducting courses at degree level in all countries except the United Kingdom conferred their own awards. Should the position of the polytechnics be maintained 'in perpetuity'? Could standards be preserved at the same time as giving institutions greater autonomy? The power to make their own awards was in the interests not only of the polytechnics, but also of higher education as a whole. His preferred model for accomplishing this was one of 'accreditation', and he described a process by which this could be accomplished:

> Institutions could be granted charters or licences to confer their own awards but it would be in the interests of higher education if the C.N.A.A. maintained a role in the validation of the courses leading to those awards. Thus institutions thus granted these charters or licences would be required to 'accredit' their courses with the C.N.A.A. every five years. It might even be possible to extend this process more broadly across higher education so that there was a national system of accreditation. In sum, the power to award their own degrees would be conferred only to those institutions which had been accredited by the C.N.A.A. for this purpose. The advantage of this approach would be that it would enable a mixed economy to be operated i.e. some institutions be validated in the present way; others who were 'chartered' would not necessarily be accredited for all their courses in that their courses would be validated in the present ways.[63]

The discussion that followed indicated difficulties but 'found attractions in the proposal'.

Accreditation was not a concept that had gained currency in Britain at this time, and in developments over the next few years it was to receive a variety of interpretations in British further and higher education. The version that Bethel was working towards in this statement was not precisely the road that the CNAA was to take in the mid-1980s but it was an outline model of development at the end of the 1970s which attempted to go beyond the decisions contained in the CNAA's 1979 document. It looked afresh at the elements in the established balance between the CNAA and its institutions, retaining standards at the centre of debate, defining a continuing role for the CNAA, justifying and describing the process towards greater institutional autonomy, conceding the need to take account of different stages of development, and looking towards possible implications for the whole of higher education. It was to take several years and unexpected pressures before general progress in this direction was achieved, but it is important to remember that there were views being canvassed in the CNAA and more widely that pointed towards a possible further 'collective resolution'.

Notes

1 CN, *Annual Report 1970-71*, p. 7.
2 CDP, minutes, 13 July 1970.
3 Letters to the Directors of Portsmouth Polytechnic, of North East London Polytechnic, and of City of London Polytechnic (CDP Corres General, File 1, May 1970–July 1971).
4 Letter from Kerr to Lindop, 2 August 1972, Committee of Officers papers 7 September 1972. CN, *Procedure for Validation of Courses of Study*, 1973, Preface, pp. 1-2.
5 Kerr, draft paper for General Committee, 13 December 1973.
6 CDP, Notes of meetings held at Coombe Lodge with Mr T.R. Weaver, Mr D.E. Lloyd Jones and Dr H.W. French, 13 and 14 December 1971, CDP Corres General, File 1.
7 CDP minutes, 13-15 December 1971.
8 CDP minutes, 13 January 1973.
9 A Policy for the Development of Validation of Courses (1974), CDP paper, 74-37.
10 CDP minutes 16 July 1974; Accreditation of Polytechnics for the Validation of CNAA Awards, 2 January 1975, CDP paper AA-74-37; Report on a Meeting between CNAA and CDP representatives, 16 April 1975, CDP paper 75-40.
11 Changes in Validation Procedures, Committee of Officers paper 3 March 1975; Cmin 20 May 1975.
12 Cmin, 22 July 1975.
13 CN (1975) *Partnership in Validation*, July.
14 CDP Academic Affairs Committee, Draft Letter in Response to CNAA Paper 'Partnership in Validation', CDP paper 75-117; CDP min, 17 December 1975.
15 Report on a CDP meeting held . . . with the Chairman and Chief Officer of the CNAA, 29 April 1976, CDP paper 76-57c.
16 Report on the CDP discussion at Danbury Park on Self Validation and Accreditation (1976), CDP paper 76-57d.
17 Cmin, 20 July 1976.
18 CN (1976) *Partnership in Validation. A Summary of the Comments Received on the Council's Discussion Paper* [autumn], pp. i. 1-2 and 10.
19 Working Party on Partnership in Validation min, 11 November 1977 and 18 January 1978.
20 Hugh Glanville (1979) Proposal for a Committee connected with Institutional Reviews and Related Matters, 16 January.
21 CDP (1977) Partnership in Validation, 27 June, CDP paper 77-84.
22 Working Party minutes, 30 May 1978.
23 Working Party minutes, 14 April 1975.
24 Cmin, 27 February 1978.
25 Description of the visit is from Glanville, HS interview.
26 Cmin, 25 July 1978.
27 *Times Higher Education Supplement*, 8 September 1978; *Times Educational Supplement*, 8 September 1978; *Daily Mail*, 9 September 1978; *The Daily Telegraph*, 9 September 1978; *The Guardian*, 9 September 1978; *The Sunday Times*, 10 September 1978 (article by Peter Wilby).
28 Alan Bradshaw (1979) 'Secret attack on "problem" poly', *The Social Science Teacher*, 9, 1.
29 Private communication from former member of the department concerned.
30 *The Guardian*, 'Poly chief asked to resign', 13 September 1978.
31 *Times Higher Education Supplement*, 'Teesside action fails to satisfy', 22 September 1978.

32 John Fairhall (1978) 'One degree under', *The Guardian*, 14 September.
33 CDP paper 78-151.
34 Peter David (1978) 'Polytechnic directors put pressure on CNAA', *Times Higher Education Supplement*, 6 October.
35 CDP paper 78-163.
36 CDP minutes, 19 October 1978.
37 Cmin, 5 December 1978. See also paper by Glanville (1978) The Council's Interest in Institutions, November.
38 *Times Higher Education Supplement*, 'County earmarks £1m for Teesside', 13 October 1978.
39 *Mail* (West Hartlepool), 10 January 1979; *Northern Echo*, 10 January 1979; *Evening Gazette*, 13 March, 21 and 23 April 1979; *Northern Echo*, 27 April 1979.
40 *Evening Gazette*, 7 February 1979.
41 Cmin, 8 May 1979.
42 *Evening Gazette*, 9 and 30 May 1979.
43 Cmin, 11 December 1979.
44 CDP minutes, 25 April and 30 May 1979; The views of Polytechnic Directors on Specific Aspects of CNAA Practice, CDP paper 79-115.
45 CN (1979) *Developments in Partnership in Validation*, June, pp. 3-7.
46 Kerr to heads of institutions, 5 June 1979.
47 As reported by former CNAA officer, private communication.
48 Committee for Education minutes, 12 October 1979.
49 Report of a meeting between Officers and Chairmen of CDP and Officers of CNAA, 14 March 1980; Notes on some Preliminary Reactions among Polytechnics to 'Developments in Partnership in Validation', 8 April 1980, CDP paper 80-89.
50 B.J. McGettrick (1980) 'CNAA validation as a contract: Some influences on evaluation', *Evaluation Newsletter*, 4, 2.
51 Judith Hargreaves (1982) 'A valediction for validation: "Partnership" and power in the current education climate', *Journal of Further and Higher Education*, 6, 2; Harry Webster (1980) in symposium on 'CNAA validation and course evaluation: Implications of the "Partnership in validation proposals" ', *Evaluation Newsletter*, 4, 1.
52 CN Sociological Studies Board, Implementation of Partnership in Validation, Meeting with Sociology Course Leaders and Heads of Departments in which Sociology Degrees are located, 3 June 1980.
53 Clive Church (1977) 'Validation systems' in Report of a Conference on Planning for Academic Diversification, Cmin, 7 January.
54 John Rex (1978) 'The purposes of sociology teaching', *New Society*, 25 May, p. 415.
55 Clive Church (1976) 'Modular courses in British higher education: A critical assessment', *Higher Education Bulletin*, 3, 3. An extended version is with Committee of Officers papers, 26 April 1976.
56 *Times Higher Education Supplement*, 'Polytechnic's modular degree plan wins CNAA approval', 2 March 1973; David Watson, (1985) 'The Oxford Polytechnic modular course 1973-83: A case study', *Journal of Further and Higher Education*, 9, 1, pp. 14-15. See also David Watson (1989) *Managing the Modular Course: Perspectives from Oxford Polytechnic*, Society for Research into Higher Education.
57 Gerald Fowler (1982) 'Past failure and the imperative for change' in Leslie Wagner (Ed.) *Agenda for Institutional Change in Higher Education*, Society for Research into Higher Education, p. 88.
58 Sir Michael Clapham, Address to Polytechnic of the South Bank Presentation Ceremony, 25 February 1974.
59 Sir Michael Clapham, Address to CNAA Degree Congregation, 3 June 1975.

60 Sir Michael Clapham, Address to CNAA Degree Congregation, Edinburgh, 1976.
61 Sir Michael Clapham, HS interview.
62 Hornby, Brief Note on Sir Michael Clapham's Contribution to the Work of the CNAA in the First Eight Years of its Life, 11 January 1978, accompanying letter to Kerr of same date, Chairman's file, vol. 2.
63 Working Party on Developments in Partnership in Validation minutes, 18 May 1979.

Chapter 8

Experiencing the CNAA

In the previous two chapters we have seen, first, some of the ways in which the CNAA and its institutions extended the subject range available to students in public sector higher education and new institutions came into the CNAA's ambit, and secondly, steps towards and perceptions of greater partnership with all associated institutions and some measure of greater independence for the more experienced and 'mature'. It is impossible to document extensively how the institutions themselves experienced the CNAA in the 1970s, but glimpses of some aspects of that experience in a small number of institutions will fix the debates, policies and processes of the last two chapters more firmly in the institutional realities of the decade. The ideal range of experience and insights would include those of course teams and the various participants' views of institutional review visits, college members of CNAA committees and their perception of their roles, and the experience of academic registrars and others of the sustained relationships with the CNAA's officers. The most that we can do here is give some hints of these fuller profiles of institutions' experience.[1]

Brighton and the Meaning of a Polytechnic

At the first meeting of Brighton Polytechnic's Academic Board in July 1970 it was reported that the CNAA had reapproved the honours course in Computer Studies, but had restricted the intake to one year. The ordinary degree had not been approved at this stage. Limited approval was because of the serious staffing and accommodation problems of the department. Similar limitations were imposed on courses in electrical and electronic engineering, and the total student intake had had to be reduced from 100 to 80 on CNAA insistence. The Academic Board recorded its grave concern at the staffing and accommodation situation that had been criticized by the CNAA. Although, the following year, a visiting pharmacy panel approved honours and ordinary courses for five years, it expressed concern about the Polytechnic's library facilities. The Academic Board at the same time congratulated one of its members on being invited to be Chairman of the CNAA's Physics Board. In 1972 the Academic Board agreed that future student/research assistants would register for higher degrees with the CNAA.[2]

In September 1972 the Board received a letter from the CNAA indicating that the Council was anxious to find ways of devolving greater independence to the colleges, and that in that spirit documentation for the reapproval of courses need not be as extensive as hitherto: 'there was general agreement (in the Academic Board) that any move by CNAA to widen the degree of academic freedom given to colleges should be welcomed'. The Polytechnic's faculties were invited to comment on the CNAA's proposals, but at the following meeting in December it was reported that no comments had been received, and the Board agreed to write to the CNAA expressing 'general acceptance'. At two meetings early in 1973 the Board commented on the proposed merger of the CNAA and the NCDAD. In March it drew attention to the fact that the name of the CNAA was just becoming recognized, and it was therefore desirable to retain the name of 'CNAA' for the new body. In June it welcomed the merger 'as a step of historic significance not only for art and design but for the whole field of higher education'. In 1973 the Board also received an interim report from a '1980 Committee', set up two years' earlier at the suggestion of the Director, Geoffrey Hall, with the terms of reference of considering the role of the Polytechnic in the 1980s. The Committee had surveyed widely the nature of 'a polytechnic', the specific characteristics of Brighton Polytechnic, and the contexts in which it operated — including the CNAA. It was concerned with philosophy and with planning, attempting to be both far-sighted and realistic. In relation to validation it emphasized the creative role of the polytechnics themselves within the validation structure, given the increase in polytechnic members relative to university members on CNAA boards. It looked carefully at the constraints and limitations imposed by numerous external bodies — including the DES, the LEAs, the RAC, the CNAA and many professional institutions — and it concluded that 'the initiative for course proposals and the generation of academic innovation lies almost entirely with the Polytechnic itself. We believe that even greater initiative from Polytechnics is likely to be welcomed in future by the various bodies which at present "oversee" our activities, in particular the CNAA'. The report did not see the CNAA as unduly restrictive — and in fact felt that in many ways the professional bodies 'had been more restrictive than the CNAA in their demand for inclusion of curricula detail'. On the question of institutional autonomy the report commented in general terms that 'no polytechnic is uniformly developed across all the degree courses and the CNAA etc may have a role to play in monitoring the less strong areas. Premature independence may be harmful to the standing of a degree. It should be remembered that it took time for the CNAA degree to gain credence'. The 1980 Committee had invited the CNAA's Chief Officer to spend an afternoon with them discussing informally the future role of the CNAA, and it received the 'general impression that the CNAA was reducing its "inspectorial" role and replacing it by a "partnership" role'. On the future of the polytechnics the Committee believed they had an opportunity to define themselves, not in relation to some 'imagined deal' in the university sector, but in terms of 'the broader aims of HE and of the community as a whole':

> If polytechnics are to become more than second-chance, third-rate, last-choice institutions of HE striving to pull themselves up by their academic bootstraps to quasi-University status, they must demonstrate to their prospective students, to staff and to society at large that they have aims and objectives independent of the University sector.

There was overlap of purpose with the universities, but the polytechnics needed to demonstrate their own educational philosophy. Course content needed to be scrutinized in order to ensure they met the need for men and women:

> who possess, in addition to the specific skills and basic knowledge relevant to their profession, an ability to communicate effectively in various modes in the immediate job situation and outside it, preferably in at least one foreign language; who understand and accept responsibility for the broader, scientific, technological, economic and social implications of their own professional activities and plans; who accept the need for and actively pursue their continuing education, and re-education.

This was 'a formidable ideal', but the opportunity for change in this direction was provided by the CNAA: 'much of this is however implicit in the requirements of the CNAA revised conditions, for course approval'.[3]

Interestingly, in the context of the growing discussion about partnership in validation, the Polytechnic Director put to its Policy and Resources Committee in November 1974 a paper on 'Consideration of self-validation'. It explained the CDP policy that polytechnics should eventually validate all their own degree courses and have full academic control of their courses, but given the practical and political difficulties the CDP would be supporting a move by the CNAA to 'find a formula whereby individual Polytechnics are given delegated authority . . . to take complete charge of arrangements for degree courses, subject only to a quinquennial review'. The Director set out for discussion the criteria he thought might be invoked in the selection of colleges to receive such delegated authority, and made a precise proposal for Brighton Polytechnic:

> I suggest that if this Polytechnic wishes to be in a position to validate its courses, which I certainly hope it will, we shall need to take an urgent look at our present procedures for examining the proposals

prior to their being sent to CNAA. A small but experienced group
of academics should, in my view, receive final proposals from
Faculty Boards and review these proposals . . .

The Committee did not agree. It discussed the proposals at length, and
members 'expressed various reservations upon self-validation as far as
Brighton Polytechnic would be concerned'. The meeting recorded four of
these reservations:

— The Polytechnic perhaps had not yet matured sufficiently in order
to assume the added responsibility.
— Problems could arise due to the difference in standards and in
expertise between the various departments: that is, it might be
desirable to have self-validation in certain areas but not in others.
— The Professional Institutions may not be willing to accept so readily
any qualifications obtained under a self-validation system.
— The idea of having a separate validating committee which would
report to the Academic Board was not generally supported . . . a
suitable faculty system could do the necessary work.[4]

Two months later, at the beginning of 1975, the first quinquennial
review of the Polytechnic took place, and in its documentation to the CNAA
it emphasized, among other things, its continued strong commitment to
sandwich courses — in spite of recruitment and validation difficulties, and
it outlined the philosophy underlying its approach to 'contrasting studies'.
It no longer believed that the interests of general education could be served
by adding 'general' or 'liberal' or 'complementary' studies to the students'
main courses. It sought, therefore, to meet the requirements of the CNAA's
1971 regulations by integrating communication, contextual and 'broadening'
elements into the main course work, and it had revised its course and
departmental structures accordingly.[5] Five years later the Polytechnic was
to admit that at the time of the 1975 review it 'was at a somewhat early
stage in achieving academic unity', had had great difficulty over resource
provision, and 'much of the CNAA criticism at that time was concerned with
this'. Transfer to the new East Sussex County Council improved the position,
despite the difficult economic situation, and the Polytechnic merged, in 1976
and 1979 respectively with Brighton College of Education and the East
Sussex College of Higher Education.[6] By the end of the decade the
Polytechnic was a more complex but more confident place. In April 1980
the Polytechnic held a conference on 'The implications of partnership in
validation'. The conference discussed the Kingston, Sheffield, Newcastle
and other possible models of partnership, and much of the experience of
members of the conference from other institutions was harnessed to the
particular position of Brighton. The tone was set at the beginning when the
Polytechnic Director responded to opening comments by Edwin Kerr:

Both the Polytechnic and the Director personally welcomed the new proposals contained in the policy statement for *Partnership in Validation* . . . The institution had taken the opportunity to rethink its internal procedures, and one of the major tasks to be completed prior to an institutional response . . . was the full development and implementation of sophisticated validation, monitoring and evaluation systems . . . the principles and process contained in this were not totally new to the institution, and their development had been part of the evolution of the Polytechnic.[7]

Berkshire College of Education/Bulmershe College of Higher Education: Lessons in Orienteering

In April 1972 the Principal of Berkshire College of Education, James Porter, received a document from the North East London Polytechnic entitled 'The organization of CNAA visits and similar events'. Passing it to his secretary he wrote on it: 'Open CNAA file please'.[8] A connection with the CNAA had been symbolically established. Porter had finished his stint as a member of the James Committee on Teacher Education at the end of the previous year, and he was anxious to explore the possibilities of the CNAA. Porter was aware from the James Committee that there were demographic problems ahead, and it was important for the College to become well-established quickly. It needed to expand, in and beyond teacher education, and as he was later to comment: 'expansion meant the CNAA'.[9] In February he had been to see Francis Hanrott at the CNAA, and he circulated a report of the meeting. The College had in mind a fairly ambitious scheme for a BEd and a BA, and since the proposal was for a unit-based scheme Hanrott's advice to the College was to consult other institutions with experience — including the City of London Polytechnic, Enfield College of Technology and Notre Dame College of Education, Glasgow. Hanrott thought it would be difficult for the College to cover the whole range of courses it was considering. Porter recommended that visits should be made to the three institutions, and also to Milton Keynes College of Education, which was proposing a unit-based arrangement with the Open University. Having clarified CNAA procedures and possibilities, Porter's particular proposal was to consult the local authority and the Chairman of the Governing Body 'to ascertain their reaction to the major development in the growth of the College', in terms of undergraduate studies in education and other fields — including the DipHE. Amalgamation with the University of Reading, as a School or Faculty of Education, was also a possibility, but, he felt, unlikely.[10]

Future policies were now debated in the Academic Board and Academic Council, and a Development Committee and development groups were the focal point of planning. Francis Hanrott and Ann Ridler visited the College, held discussions with heads of department and the development groups, and attended a meeting of the Academic Council.[11] Porter wrote in December to say the Academic Board had decided to make a formal approach to the Council.[12] Early in 1973 the University considered the College's proposal for amalgamation, and turned it down. The College was now planning for a considerable expansion to 2000 students, and members of staff visited other colleges to discuss their progress with CNAA validation. One of them brought back from Didsbury College one of a new generation of CNAA jokes, and it appeared in a staff bulletin:

> C.N.A.A. is an anagram for Mt. CANA and it took them a bloody long time there to turn water into wine.[13]

In March the Governors and the Authority approved the approach to the CNAA to validate academic and professional awards, and in April the Principal told the staff that they had only until June to prepare the BEd submission if the CNAA was to visit the College in the autumn term and students were to be admitted to the course in 1974. From now on, and throughout the decade, the demands on the staff for the planning of new courses, revising of submissions, responding to CNAA conditions, dealing with the entirely new style and magnitude of detailed documentation, were to be considerable — taken together with the other crises and vicissitudes of cuts in teacher education, financial and other pressures, and the constant threat of obliteration as teacher education institutions were closed before their attempts to diversify had taken hold.

The CNAA visit to consider the proposed BEd took place in November, two weeks after a similar visit to Didsbury College had approved its proposals. The Principal of Didsbury wrote to James Porter to say that one of his Principal friends and colleagues had prayed for them during their CNAA visit, but he could not be sure for $(n + 1)$ years if prayers had been responsible for the College's success. He sent, not prayers, but good wishes for the event: 'if our experience is typical you will have a most demanding but very pleasant time'.[14] The Berkshire letter submitting the BEd proposals to the CNAA described them as the outcome of 'a fundamental reconsideration of the College's approach to the personal and professional education of the student'.[15] It was, in fact, a wide-ranging, unit-based degree proposal, covering a large number of education strands and subject areas, and the visiting party contained thirty-five members, from the Committee for Education and fourteen panels, groups or boards — accompanied by the Chief Officer, Registrar and Assistant Registrar for Education. The College's preparations — and rehearsals — had been intensive.[16] The Honours BEd degree was approved. The College was then successful in obtaining validation for a DipHE, with units linked to the BEd, but the Diploma students — like the College itself — needed a BA option also. In 1974 the proposed BA was rejected as not being of a sufficiently academic standard. It took the College two years to recover from this dampening of an earlier euphoria, and to obtain CNAA approval for a more modest and conventional major/minor degree structure than had been originally proposed.[17]

In 1975 Berkshire College of Education became, following an Academic Board proposal, Bulmershe College of Higher Education, and the target of 2000 students was reduced to 1600. An officers' visit to the College took place in March 1976 and was heavily critical of its academic structure and course planning. The visiting party expressed 'grave concern' about arrangements for planning and internal validation. The planning group for the BA was inadequate: 'at no time was a course programme subjected to rigorous academic criticism'. The visiting party knew that the College itself was unhappy about its course planning procedures, and recommended that 'urgent action should be taken to set up a validation group of the Academic Board'. This weakness had no doubt contributed to the failure of BA submissions, and the visitors hoped that a strong internal validation structure 'would encourage the development of a capacity for self-criticism which was under developed in the College at present'.[18] The Principal wrote to Edwin Kerr, who had chaired the visiting party, to explain an important moment of change in the College that had been highlighted by the visit. The internal academic structure had in the past been 'highly personalized and dispersed'. Major responsibility had been lodged with individual teachers, 'and this devolution of academic and professional responsibility has worked well, and is, of course, typical of much university practice':

> As I am sure you noted, however, the College is now increasingly aware of the problems which this more organic structure gives rise to, and your visit coincided with the point at which such issues are being fully debated but have yet to be resolved.

Porter also indicated that while he and his colleagues understood the Council's need to be 'even-handed in its treatment of all the institutions with which it deals', it ought to be possible for the CNAA to take account of the level of resources and academic potential. Where it was satisfied about these it ought to be willing to maintain a 'continuing dialogue':

> This should enable problems to be solved in a way that maintains the integrity of the insitution but at the same time brings to bear the experience and expertise that are represented by the C.N.A.A. The College has already benefited greatly from its formal and informal contacts with the Council and its officers. Together we have identified a number of central questions, and we are anxious to share in the task of finding answers . . . in spite of your excellent chairmanship, I am conscious of the fact that the College does least well in the kind of 'set piece' debate that inevitably characterizes your formal visits, and I write in the hope that we shall be judged more on the evidence of what we achieve through our continuing relationship with the Council.[19]

For the rest of the 1970s the College was involved not only with the growing problems facing the public sector, and the particularly difficult ones associated with teacher education, but also with the details of a changed academic structure, new internal validation procedures, and a development plan which would satisfy the College's need for limited growth and respond adequately to the 1976 criticisms by the CNAA.

King Alfred's College: A 'Crushing Moment', Before and After

In May 1973 the Academic Board of King Alfred's College, Winchester, a Church of England college, adopted a paper outlining the College's policy proposals for the next three years. The College's future had been debated in the Board and at other College meetings, and various options had been actively considered — including mergers with the University of Southampton and other institutions close at hand and farther afield, none of which seemed likely. A merger with the University had been more or less ruled out by Southampton in February, and at that point opinion in the College was in favour of retaining its existing independent status, and of seeking validation for its future teacher training and diversified courses from the University. In the May paper on the future of the College, as in previous documentation, no consideration was given to the possibility of validation by the CNAA. The College was planning substantial developments in teacher education, a DipHE in General Studies, and a BSc (Technical), all of which it was intended to put to the University.

Within weeks, however, there were doubts. The University of Newcastle was known to have refused validation for new Courses from its associated colleges, and it was not clear that Southampton would be any more willing to validate degrees in subjects other than in teacher education, or to do so as degrees equivalent in status and title to those of the University. Was there, the Vice-Principal asked in a memorandum in June on 'Our present position', 'a case for seeking free-standing status with CNAA validation' rather than in a relationship with the University — which was clearly what the College would prefer.[21] 'Between the lines' of the government's policy, as deduced from its responses to a Select Committee and other sources might be read a government preference for validation by the CNAA.[22] The College continued to consider the various possibilities of amalgamation — including with Winchester School of Art, which was itself about to begin a CNAA BA degree — but nothing came of these. In December the College decided, with much heart searching, to go to the CNAA for validation. The Principal had to reassure members of the Governing Body that the CNAA was a 'reputable organization', had to obtain the approval of the Bishop for an approach to the CNAA, and satisfy himself and the College as to the CNAA's procedures for initiating a consultation with Didsbury College in November 1973.[23] All the correspondence with the University indicated how much the College regretted having to turn to the CNAA, and there were warm expressions of appreciation and goodwill on both sides. Geoffrey Nokes, the Registrar for Education, met with the Academic Board in January 1974, and a visiting party chaired by Sir Derman Christopherson came to the College in May. It was a successful visit in that the visiting party encouraged the College to go ahead with a submission.

The College was by this time already considering a range of proposals to put to the CNAA — five professional awards and one 'non-professional award', a BA Ordinary and Honours in Humane Studies, the main subjects to be English and history initially, with a number of complementary studies. It was hoped that all the courses would be approved for a start in September 1974.[24] In fact, by July it was a three-year Certificate, a three-year BEd, a four-year Honours BEd and a PGCE that were submitted, and in October a full-scale visit by the Committee for Education took place. On the first day, in addition to the two officers, there were eight representatives of the Committee and the Education Studies Panel present, and on the second day five of these plus twenty-seven representatives of seventeen CNAA boards and panels. The visiting party declared itself impressed by 'the very considerable progress made by the College in a limited period to redesign and extend its pattern of courses'. It applauded the College's environment and facilities, its well qualified and cooperative staff, its community spirit and other aspects of the College's life. It did not, however, believe that the proposals were coherent and well-developed enough, or that the College's course control machinery was adequate.[25] The Principal describes what happened:

> The C.N.A.A. representatives were taken to catch their various trains and the Principal was left to enter a packed senior common room which went deathly quiet on his entry and stayed that way until he had given the main gist of what he had just been told, promising a full written report in the morning. It was a crushing moment for the college.[26]

The Principal wrote to the Southampton Vice-Chancellor to tell him what had happened. The College had met with an 'initial rebuff', primarily for reasons of coherence and course control. Preparations for the visit had put 'enormous pressure on the total institution; the two day visitation itself is to say the least, harrowing; and at the end of the day to be met with a rejection can be devastating to the morale of a college'. There were now fresh papers to be prepared and further procedures to be gone through, but by the time the Principal came to write this letter, more than three weeks after the visit, he felt obliged to comment: 'on the whole the initial rebuff is proving salutary and it is certainly bringing coherence to the College and I hope this, in turn, will have some spin-off in our courses'. The Vice-Chancellor replied that he was sorry that the College was having 'a little trouble' with the CNAA, but 'I don't suppose it surprises you since they are known to be pretty strict in their scrutiny.[27] King Alfred's was not the only college to find, after the initial 'rebuff', that the experience had its 'salutary' side.

The CNAA urged the College to resubmit for a 1976 start, but it was confident enough to press for, and obtain, approval to try again for 1975 in limited main subjects, postponing other subjects and professional courses until the way forward with the BEd was clear. The BEd did, in fact, gain approval to begin in 1975. A proposal for a BA, beginning with English as the main subject and drama and history as complementary components, was turned down by the relevant CNAA boards for a 1975 start, but got off the ground based on history as the main subject in 1976. The College was now planning separate degree courses in order to meet the CNAA's demands for coherence and progression, and a second BA honours course based on English as the main subject was approved the following year. Drama was available as an associated subject of both degrees, and a degree in drama, theatre and television followed in 1980. Approval for a DipHE in social and environmental problems was obtained in 1977, by which time other professional courses had also been approved, including a diploma in special education in 1975. In February 1976 a CNAA officers' visit took place to the College to judge its suitability as an environment for the Council's awards. In approving the institution, the visiting party noted the congenial atmosphere, and the 'lively attitude and general enthusiasm of the staff', as well as the difficulties the College was facing in widening its horizons and adjusting to the requirements of a new validating body. Some members of the College had expressed their frustration over 'the delays involved in course validation', but the visitors reminded the College 'that the Council could not apply to the colleges of education standards and attitudes which differed in any way from those applied to other colleges and polytechnics'.[28] The visiting party approved the College as a centre for CNAA work for five years.

The College formally welcomed the CNAA's moves towards partnership in validation in 1975, emphasizing the importance both of a significant measure of independence for institutions, but also of 'a relationship with a central body, such as the C.N.A.A. . . . enabling issues to be seen and planning to be effected in a broader sense than might otherwise be the case'. The College was actively preparing a validation panel as a major sub-committee of the College Council.[29] Its approval for a PGCE in 1975 was renewed in 1979, and although there were criticisms of some structural aspects of the course the working party that considered it commended 'its attempt to be innovative'.[30] By late 1979 the College was considering a proposal to simplify revalidation procedures along 'partnership in validation' lines, by including representatives from other institutions teaching similar courses, and from the CNAA, making it 'a competent validating body with powers to validate, or refuse to validate, or to validate with conditions'.[31] An institutional review visit in 1980 confirmed the College as a centre for CNAA awards, and considered that its evolution and its development of new courses 'has been a significant achievement'.[32] When the Principal, Martial

Rose, came to write a history of the College he did so partly in terms of its 'steady course' in association with the Church of England and with inputs from various directions. The period of the 1970s included a new scheme of government for it as a college of higher education, no longer concerned exclusively with teacher education. The 'steadiness' of the College in this period was helped by the association with the CNAA:

> In 1973 an anxiety expressed about the CNAA was that it was faceless, impersonal. It has not proved so. Through continuing contact with its officers, its Committee and Board members, and in particular external examiners, the validation exercise and subsequent running of courses have been as personalised as that experienced at the university.[33]

Five years separated the 'crushing moment' from the institutional review of 1980 and the recognition of a 'significant achievement'.

Newcastle Polytechnic: Course Review to Joint Validation

In 1974 Newcastle-upon-Tyne Polytechnic created a Course Coordination Sub-Committee of its Academic Planning and Development Committee. A preamble to the minutes of the Sub-Committee, when it met in December of that year, began: 'It is possible that certain polytechnics will receive a measure of self-validation from the CNAA in the foreseeable future', and therefore this coordinating sub-committee had been established. The Polytechnic already possessed an 'Academic Validation Group' which was reviewing the structure of courses. In February 1975 that Group recorded that consultations had been taking place between the CNAA and the CDP on the possibility of self-validation, and the Assistant Director (Academic) of the Polytechnic had prepared a document for the CDP in that context, recommending that the CNAA should retain a quinquennial 'watching brief', and outlining a range of criteria for the introduction of self-validation, including 'gradual introduction of self-validation by applying it first to areas in the Polytechnic which have successful experience of initiating and running CNAA degree courses and comparable advanced courses'. The Academic Board recognized the strength of the CDP view that 'accreditation should be of an institution as a whole, rather than being initially restricted to particular subject areas within the institution'. The two views were reconciled by underlining the institution's responsibility to seek expert external advice as appropriate.[34] As a result of the internal discussions around these issues the Academic Board agreed in October to replace the Validation Group with a Course Review Sub-Committee — also relating to the Academic Planning and Development Committee.[35] This new Sub-committee reflected both the extensive discussions and developments taking place within the Polytechnic and its reactions to the CNAA's proposals on partnership in validation, which the Polytechnic did not entirely accept, but which it saw as a means of opening up further dialogue. The Academic Registrar suggested to the Academic Board that it should welcome the intention to devolve increased responsibility to institutions, and recognize that the CNAA would have a continuing and important role for the foreseeable future. He indicated, however, three main weaknesses in the CNAA document: it intended to recognize an institution only in respect of 'certain defined subject areas'; the paper was 'insufficiently adventurous, and is too constrained by the traditional relationship between the Colleges and the CNAA'; the CNAA would itself be involved more than in the past with a range of matters regarding the 'general running of the institution, which it is difficult to see as being its proper concern'. This paper by the Academic Registrar was part of what was intended, in February 1976, to be a 'free ranging discussion' of partnership in validation by the Academic Board.[36]

By this stage in the Polytechnic's development it was in its seventh year since three Newcastle colleges had been amalgamated to form the new institution. The three original institutions — the Municipal College of Commerce, the College of Art and Industrial Design, and the Rutherford College of Technology — were joined in 1974 by the City College of Education, and a merger with Northern Counties College of Education took place in 1976. Given the size of the Polytechnic the CNAA decided in 1975 — as it did also at Liverpool Polytechnic — to experiment with 'faculty visits', which preceded the main Council visits and the reports of which were available to the quinquennial visiting party. This procedure was continued in 1976, and the visiting party on that occasion welcomed the fact that the Academic Board 'regarded academic planning as a key activity', and welcomed the innovation in setting up the Course Review Sub-Committee — though it pointed out that the Sub-committee would find it difficult to scrutinize effectively reports on some 176 courses.[37]

John Clark became Assistant Director (Academic) of the Polytechnic in 1975, having been a head of department there for the previous five years.[38] From the mid-1970s he saw what he considered to be signs of a 'less than satisfactory situation'. That was the time 'when the system itself ought to have been changing and recognising that there was a growing maturity within the polytechnics, but we were still bound by a seemingly unchanging system'. Newcastle had achieved coherence in the academic planning and development process, and realized that it 'ought to take responsibility for the quality of education provided . . . not simply find out every five years whether a course was judged to be satisfactory or not'. Newcastle was the first to develop the concept of the course review: 'others were making their own moves and that type of system caught on fairly quickly but unevenly'. Polytechnic confidence in the CNAA system was being shaken, and the CNAA was coming under the pressures that resulted in the blue book. Newcastle's record in terms of submitting degree courses successfully to the CNAA was uneven — as was the case across the polytechnics. The Polytechnic Directorate came to the conclusion that 'we needed to establish our own internal system of making sure submissions which left the Polytechnic were in the view of the Academic Board of high quality'. Prior to this period around 1975 'lip service had been paid by the decision-making part of the Newcastle system'. Clark was asked to develop an internal system and he and the heads of faculties decided that 'we needed to produce an internal system that applied to all our courses, degrees and non-degrees, and it needed to be an annual process — which was unheard of in those days':

> I searched in the literature, certainly in the UK and as best I could elsewhere, for help with what to do and I found nothing that was of help. Stuff was published in the United States but it didn't seem applicable to our system. So amongst the decisions that were taken early on was first of all that we would start with a *central* system rather than a dispersed one, to try to bring uniformity in interpretation of standards, and I do believe that that was one of the best decisions we made, because we were able to develop an internal system of validation and review which we were later able to devolve to faculties.

At that time the CNAA was very little interested, and for the first year or so in fact it did not occur to Clark that he might inform the CNAA on the existence of the internal system. In the first year the Course Review Sub-Committee reviewed more than 150 courses, requiring documentation as part of the process, and seeing the course leader and members of every course team: 'I am bound to say that we uncovered some awful practices. We found, for example, that not every course had a properly constituted course leader, that there was no minimum standards approach adopted in terms of what the functions of a course team were . . .' The Polytechnic was to be 'stung' in the process by a couple of bad experiences. In one case, that of a professional course, the first indication of trouble was the declared intention of the professional body to withdraw recognition. There had been pressure from the clinical staff not to have 'interference' from an internal body, problems were therefore being kept within the course, and not being picked up within the Polytechnic. It was decided that full institutional responsibility would be established, and this situation would not happen again. On another occasion, where the internal system felt that a humanities degree course was operating satisfactorily, a CNAA subject board considered withdrawing approval, on the grounds that there had been no development in the main subject that contributed to the course, as suggested by the lack of research and other indicators. The Polytechnic decided as a result of this experience that it needed to develop a system of *subject* review as well as *course* review, and the Polytechnic moved in fact in that direction.

After a couple of years of the new internal procedures a turn-around in attitudes within the Polytechnic was taking place, and in the second half of the 1970s it ascertained that there was a good correlation between the internal findings and those of the CNAA. Courses were being approved without serious conditions being attached. Interest in the Polytechnic's procedures was being expressed elsewhere. Edwin Kerr himself was interested and put people in touch with Newcastle to find out what was happening. It was the early 1980s, however, before internal validation and review machineries became the norm. Newcastle's own conclusion was that given the degree of correlation between the Polytechnic's findings and those of the CNAA, the latter was 'adding very very little, if anything, to our own conclusions'.

By the late 1970s, therefore, Newcastle Polytechnic was a confident institution looking for ways to change its relationship with the CNAA in the direction of placing greater responsibility on the Polytechnic's internal course review machinery. Like Brighton and other polytechnics, Newcastle also felt the need to define its roles as a polytechnic, and early in 1979 it described itself as being 'above all concerned with the teaching and learning processes of students, and to this end is engaged with other colleges in providing a diversified and coordinated system of FE and HE in the sub region'. As a large and comprehensive institution it was difficult for it to have 'a highly distinctive academic programme', but:

> distinctiveness can be approached through the quality of certain areas of excellence. The strength of the Polytechnic should lie in the ability to conform to the Polytechnic ethos of practical creativity by emphasising such factors as design, action, synthesis, professionalism and application of knowledge; and to react swiftly to anticipate the demands for both specialist and interdisciplinary courses. The majority of courses should include a more general element of education for life in society, as well as providing broad based and specialised/vocational education. Courses should be designed to meet the rapidly changing needs of employers in industry, commerce and the professions.

To achieve such ends, the Polytechnic needed to develop research in a variety of applied forms, and serve the community in a variety of ways.[39] It also looked at the *Developments in Partnership in Validation* document in 1979, saw reflected in it approaches to validation and course review which had been Newcastle's own emphases, and decided to exploit the CNAA's willingness to explore other models.[40] It submitted a 'mid-term report' to the CNAA on the operation of Newcastle's internal validation and review procedures (in June 1979), and hoped the CNAA would accept the account as 'an indication that the Polytechnic has, over a number of years, evolved policies and procedures in these areas of the highest standards required to meet the strict CNAA requirements for significant transfer of responsibility in academic matters'. The Polytechnic therefore looked forward to 'a period of constructive discussion with the Council leading to a negotiation of appropriate terms of partnership, carrying with it the prospect of a future overall system simplified in nature, and giving greater responsibility and freedom to the Polytechnic'.[41] A working party chaired by John Clark surveyed the Polytechnic's system of academic planning (including the operation of some recent changes which had led to course coordination becoming the responsibility of the parent Academic Planning and Development Committee and not of a separate sub-committee) and drafted a response to *Developments* which would lead to the development of a system of 'joint validation'.[42] The time was ripe, the Polytechnic suggested, for a 'substantial change' in the relationship between the Polytechnic and the CNAA. It invited the newly-established CNAA Committee for Institutions to conduct a formal assessment of the Polytechnic's validation and review procedures, and if the outcome was satisfactory to agree that all future course proposals and the reapproval of courses should be carried out by Joint Validation Panels, comprising representatives of the Polytechnic's Academic Board, representatives of the appropriate CNAA subject board or boards, and external academic or professional persons.[43] The Committee for Institutions visited Newcastle in July 1980 — various informal contacts between the Polytechnic and the CNAA having taken place.[44] In November 1980 the Committee for Institutions and the Polytechnic Academic Board approved a draft agreement between the CNAA and the Polytechnic, which, the Director indicated, 'will when finally approved, give the Polytechnic the substance of what it is seeking'. The opening paragraph of the proposed agreement read:

> The Council for National Academic Awards, and the Academic Board of Newcastle upon Tyne Polytechnic agree that from 1 September 1981 the validation and review of courses at the Polytechnic which lead to the Council's awards shall be undertaken jointly. This agreement results from the wish of both parties that their respective processes and procedures for course validation and review be combined in a spirit of collaboration and partnership, and from a common commitment to the maintenance of academic standards.

The finalization of the agreement was to be subject to a successful outcome to the institutional review visit scheduled for June 1981, and in the meantime a pilot scheme of joint validation would cover a number of courses coming forward for validation or review in 1980–81.[45] What had been agreed, and was in fact to be implemented at Newcastle following the 1981 visit, was a procedure which would eliminate one stage in the validation process by combining what up to that point had been the final stage of internal validation with the external one.

The CNAA held discussions and reached agreements in 1980 with Sheffield City Polytechnic and Kingston Polytechnic also, the intention being to explore in various ways the options open to the CNAA and to the institutions in pushing back further the boundaries of validation. The experiments which followed from the blue book suggestion that the CNAA would consider other proposals for partnership in validation were therefore to be few in number, and while other polytechnics and colleges watched with considerable interest from 1980 how these schemes developed, some — like Bulmershe and King Alfred's — did not have the experience and strength, or in many cases the aspiration, to go in the same direction. Some of the other polytechnics, and the CDP in particular, were suspicious of schemes which might divert energy and interest away from the aim of some form of independence, rather than being steps towards it. Newcastle, however, had read the messages in the blue book and in the system, was aware of what John Clark described as the 'seemingly unchanging system' of the recent past, and saw its proposals for joint validation as being, in the words of the Director, Laing Barden, 'the substance of what it was seeking' — and as a step in a direction.

The Experiences

None of the institutions whose experience we have glimpsed was 'typical' in its relationships with, and perceptions of, the CNAA in the 1970s. There were polytechnics holding aloof from changes arising from the *Developments* 'blue book' in the hope of more substantial or different ones ahead. There were colleges of higher education with different experiences of the validation of their teacher education and 'diversified' courses. There were specialist institutions succeeding and failing in their aspirations to grow and to consolidate. There were institutions of all kinds being shaped differently by their financial and political relationships with their controlling local authorities or other bodies in the case of the voluntary colleges. There were institutions whose staff were playing greater or lesser parts in the work of the CNAA itself, and whose messages and forecasts were being received in different college structures and climates. There were visible across the system different institutional policies based on different histories of status attainment or frustration. There were institutions with very different proportions and profiles of advanced work, and very different patterns of validation by the CNAA and other validating bodies — including the universities, the Business Education Council, the Technician Education Council (and when these amalgamated Business and Technician Education Council (BTEC)).

The CNAA had acquired in the 1970s not just a wider network of 'partners', but also a complex pattern of relationships with institutions whose academic and administrative shapes were vastly different, and whose political, financial and planning relationships with other bodies were equally different. Perceptions of the CNAA were inevitably diverse, both amongst and within institutions.

Notes

1 The only systematic attempt to review perceptions of the CNAA in this period was a dissertation by David Francis, at the time Assistant Registrar in Education at the CNAA. His 1985 University of Sussex MA dissertation was entitled 'Partners in validation: An exploration of the perceptions of their validating body held in five colleges of higher education associated with the CNAA'.
2 All information in this section on Brighton Polytechnic is from the minutes of the Polytechnic's Academic Board unless otherwise stated.
3 BPoly, 1980 Committee, Interim Report, 1973, pp. 6, 10–12 and 39–41.
4 G.R. Hall (1974) Consideration of Self Validation, 14 November; Policy and Resources Committee minutes, 18 November.
5 CN, Quinquennial Review Brighton Polytechnic, January 1975.
6 CN, Quinquennial Review 1980, Brighton Polytechnic.
7 BPoly (1980) *Report of a One-Day Conference on 'The Implications of Partnership in Validation'*, 26 April, p. 4.
8 Bulmershe file C5a CNAA.
9 Porter, HS interview.
10 Porter (1972) 'Notes on Meeting at the Council for National Academic Awards held on Tuesday 8 February, 15 February, File C5.
11 Academic Council, 3 July 1972, report on informal visit of representatives of the CNAA. All references to Academic Council and Academic Board in this section on Bulmershe are to the College's (now University of Reading's) Council and board files.
12 Porter to Hanrott, 22 December 1972, file C5a.
13 *Staff Bulletin*, summer 1973.
14 Frank Gorner to Porter, 31 October 1973, file C5a.
15 Letter with Academic Board papers, n.d.
16 CNAA visitation for discussion of a proposed BEd (Hons) degree, 1–2 November 1973 (for membership, programme and planning).
17 Clem Adelman and Harold Silver (1984) 'Bulmershe: Diversification in a free-standing institution' in Alexander, Robin J. *et al.* (Eds) *Change in Teacher Education*, Holt, Rinehart and Winston, pp. 254–6.
18 Report of Visiting Party, 4 March 1976, CNAA General Corres. 1 June 1975–28 February 1976.
19 Porter to Kerr, 10 March 1976.
20 King Alfred's College, Winchester, 'The future of the College: Policy proposals for the period 1973–1976', 23 May 1973; The future of the College: Staff/student conference' (26 February 1973), Box no. 2 (Princ) University of Southampton (references in this section are to files at King Alfred's College).
21 RWB (Vice-Principal), 'Our present position', 25 June 1973, Box no. 2 (Princ).
22 Martial Rose (1983) *A History of King Alfred's College, Winchester 1840*–1980, Phillimore, pp. 118.
23 Correspondence Principal and K.B. Kettle and the Bishop, December 1973 and February 1974; The Didsbury CNAA course for BEd, conversations with Mr C.D. Rogers, Assistant Course Development Tutor, 19 and 20 November 1973, Box no. 2 (Princ).
24 Principal to Mrs Ridler, 19 March 1974, Box no. 2 (Princ).
25 CN, Committee for Education, Visit to King Alfred's College, 22 and 23 October.
26 Rose, *A History*, p. 123.
27 Rose to Professor Gower, 13 November 1974; Gower to Rose, 21 November 1974, Box no. 2 (Princ).
28 CN, Officers' Visit to King Alfred's College, Winchester, 4 February 1976.

29 King Alfred's College, CNAA Document 'Partnership in Validation' (July 1975) College Response, 28 January 1976, Box no. 2.

30 CN, Committee for Education, Postgraduate Initial Training Board, Report of a Meeting to Discuss the Renewal of the PGCE, 4 June 1979.

31 Rose to CNAA, 15 October 1979, enclosing proposals for renewal of approval procedures in connection with the BEd/BEd Hons course; M. Sweetman to Rose, 26 October 1979.

32 CN, Report of a Visit, 6 November 1980.

33 Rose, *A History*, pp. 126–6.

34 Newcastle Polytechnic, Academic Board minutes 19 February 1975 and attached paper on self validation (references in this section are to the minutes and other files at the Polytechnic).

35 Academic Board minutes, 15 October 1975.

36 Academic Board minutes, 18 February 1976; memo by Academic Board Secretary (Academic Registrar), 13 February 1976 convening the meeting; Peter Torode, Partnership in Validation, paper for the Board.

37 CN, Council visit to Newcastle upon Tyne Polytechnic, 18 June 1976.

38 The following is from John Clark, HS interview.

39 NPoly, Role and Purpose, Academic Board paper 17 January 1979.

40 P.F. Torode and J.L. Clark (1979) 'Developments in partnership in validation', memo, 21 August.

41 NPoly, 'Mid Term' Report to the Council for National Academic Awards on the Operation of the Polytechnic's Internal Validation and Review Procedures through the work of the Course Coordinating and Course Review Committees, June 1979.

42 NPoly, Report of the Working Party on Partnership in Validation, Pt I: Academic Planning under Re-organisation; Developments in Partnership in Validation. The Response from Newcastle-upon-Tyne Polytechnic (1979–80).

43 NPoly, Partnership in Validation: Summary of Proposals from Newcastle-upon-Tyne Polytechnic (1979–80).

44 For example, NPoly, Notes of an Informal Meeting between the Director and Assistant Director of Newcastle-upon-Tyne Polytechnic and Council Officers, 11 September 1979.

45 Professor L. Barden, Director, memo to Heads of School, 10 December 1980.

Chapter 9

Making Judgments and Being Judged

The CNAA entered the 1980s with over 120 associated institutions offering some 1700 courses leading to its awards. Nearly 130,000 students were registered on these courses — about a third of all degree students in the United Kingdom. Over 2800 students were registered for its research degrees, and its subject boards contained some 2200 members, drawn from the universities and the public sector, commerce and the professions.[1] The Parliamentary Select Committee to which that information was communicated early in 1980 itself reported later in the year and made a recommendation which linked the CNAA with the Open University, although in doing so it commented that they had both 'proved remarkably successful institutions and we hesitate to suggest that they be disturbed'. The recommendation was for the Secretary of State to initiate a dialogue between the two bodies, with a view to the CNAA helping the OU to have links with all non-university higher education, and accelerating the expansion of continuing education, using the OU's techniques and coordinated from the colleges and polytechnics.[2] As early as 1973, in fact, the OU and the CNAA had issued a joint statement outlining various ways in which they could work together, widening the use of OU materials, allowing CNAA students credit for OU courses, and other possibilities.[3] The important point is that the CNAA was entering the 1980s with the possibility of encountering judgments of its role which saw it as successful and not to be disturbed, and capable of important extensions of its activities. It saw itself, when it described its place in British higher education in 1979, as having created, 'in concert with the non-university institutions of higher education . . . a firmly established and recognized system of higher education outside the university sector'.[4]

The CNAA also entered the 1980s with the recent history of having failed fully to settle the issues of relationships with the polytechnics and colleges, and it had a Committee on Longer Term Developments, following on from the debates which produced the 'blue book'. It was not only the polytechnic directors who had anxieties about the propriety of the CNAA's emphasis on the importance of its 'institutional review visits'. In 1981

Christopher Ball, after being involved in CNAA boards and committees for some fourteen years — and having become Warden of Keble College, Oxford, the previous year — expressed his doubts in a much publicized public lecture at Thames Polytechnic. Referring to quinquennial review visits — of which he had personal experience — he confessed to 'an ineradicable scepticism about the appropriateness and value of this part of the Council's work'. He did not believe that the Charter and Statutes had been intended to enable the CNAA to approve institutions, as distinct from courses. For reasons which he discussed, he thought the system of institutional reviews was 'impractical, unreal, impertinent and unprofessional'. Set against that judgment was his 'main thesis' — if in its short life the Council 'had made any contribution to "the advancement of education, learning, knowledge and the arts" it is primarily through the work of the subject boards', the outcome being 'an astonishing range of pioneering courses exploring new ground in syllabus content . . . course design . . . examination arrangements, and in many other aspects'.[5] This view of the CNAA's subject board work was widely held both within the boards and within the institutions, though it would be difficult to say how much support it might have had at academic board level or amongst academic and administrative staff. The CNAA had at this point considerable experience in promoting or encouraging the kinds of curriculum development to which Ball was drawing attention, but it had also underpinned its judgment of the standard of courses by setting them in their wider contexts, including by emphasizing academic board responsibility in sustaining standards and guaranteeing appropriate student experience. Although the CNAA had come under increasing pressure in the 1970s, particularly from the CDP, to relax its control, from the end of the 1970s the ambiguities in judging the CNAA's role in this respect increased. In a changing economic situation and fragile funding, and with increasingly ambivalent or hostile political and public opinion towards higher education in general, the CNAA as a 'system' appeared to offer a measure of protection in a cold climate. CNAA 'conservatism' was as much a product of the anxieties throughout higher education as of any built-in resistance to change.

The expansionist phase of higher education, and expectations of expansion, came to an end from the mid-1970s. Under a Labour government expenditure was reduced by policy decision and by inflation. The going, in Lord Annan's words, was 'tough' for education, and 'tougher' for higher education, in 1976.[6] After the implementation of the binary policy, as we have seen, the events of the mid-1970s reflected little that could be called policy, particularly with regard to teacher education and the transformation of the colleges of education. When Lord Crowther-Hunt became Minister of State for Higher Education after the election of the Labour government in 1974 he found to his surprise that:

> the Prime Minister gave me no general guidance about the government's higher education policy nor any indication of what he hoped I might achieve in the department when he offered me

the job. Nor did the Secretary of State for Education, Reg Prentice, when I reported to him during my first day with the Department's higher education policies which I then inherited.[7]

The Conservative government of Margaret Thatcher came into office in 1979 with no clearer policy for higher education. What intentions there may have been were subsumed in the determination to reduce public expenditure, to 'change the philosophy of life in dealing with public affairs', and to respond to worldwide recession by cutting budgets all round.[8] When the new Conservative Secretary of State, Mark Carlisle, addressed a conference on 'The future development of higher education' he began with a statement about finance:

> The ever-increasing investment of resources in higher education has now come to an end. This sector must compete with other education sectors and other services for what our government intends should become a diminishing public expenditure cake. Our last White Paper indicated a slightly diminishing level of funding for higher education, and while I cannot give you the exact details, I am afraid that this is likely to continue to be the pattern over the next few years.[9]

The 'diminishing cake' was the major policy context within which the CNAA and the institutions were now to operate. Demographic change was another, as the DES and others tried to grapple with the likely future trend of student numbers following a fall in the birthrate since 1964. A major debate had been initiated under the Labour government in 1978, with the publication of a discussion document on *Higher Education into the 1990s*, which did no more than set out five possible projection models on which policy might be based.[10] Mark Carlisle, having started with cake, went on to the number of 18–21-year-olds, which would peak in the mid-1990s, then decline rapidly.

Of central and immediate importance for the CNAA in its concern for standards was the effect of economic pressures on the resources of the institutions it validated, an issue which straddled its interest both in institutions and in courses. The Chief Officer wrote to the polytechnics and colleges in July 1979 reminding them that the Council had always been sensitive to resource issues as related to the standards of courses, and pointing out that in 1978–79 institutional reviews had revealed that some institutions were experiencing difficulties. It seemed likely from further public expenditure cuts already announced that the difficulties would become greater and more widespread, and the Council wished to be alerted to any 'exceptional difficulties', so that it could discuss them with the institution concerned and, if appropriate, with the funding authority.[11] Early in 1980 the Council repeated this statement to the Select Committee on Education, Science and Arts.[12] From 1979 higher education in general was the target for regular, substantial and often dramatic government cuts in funding. In 1979, for example, there was talk of university bankruptcies and closures.[13] It was clear, as Mark Carlisle emphasized to the conference in 1980, that higher education was expected to take its share of continuing public expenditure cuts. In 1980 and 1981 the cuts continued and deepened in education generally, and cuts in local authority spending meant considerable reductions in college and polytechnic staffs. The particularly serious university cuts in 1981 meant an overall reduction of 17 per cent over three years, and a reduction of 20,000 in student places.[14] The *THES* headed its survey of the year: '1981: Year of the cut'.[15] Polytechnics and colleges faced another round of cuts in 1982. The effects on provision and standards were constantly on the agenda of the Council and its committees. Discussion of responsibilities for the guardianship of standards was taking place in a rapidly changing economic and political environment.

The economy and demography were two of the themes of direct importance to higher education that surfaced particularly in the latter part of the Labour government's period of office and continued under the Conservative government from 1979 — with what differences from the financial outcomes that might have resulted from a continued Labour government is an interesting but difficult speculation. A third theme inherited by the Thatcher government was the national management of higher education in the 'maintained' or 'local authority' sector. There was a view, shared by government, the local authorities, the CDP, the CNAA and others, that some form of greater coherence or coordination in the funding of public sector higher education was necessary, though how this might be achieved and who would control the coordinating machinery were inevitably matters of major disagreement. The job of exploring possibilities was given to a Working Group set up by the Secretary of State in 1977 (chaired by Gordon Oakes, Minister of State for Education and Science, and containing among its thirty members Sir Michael Clapham, and a number of polytechnic directors and college principals — and Edwin Kerr as one of the 'alternates'). The Working Group made recommendations — which in some quarters were seen as over-complicated — for a national system of funding deriving largely from revenue collected from local authorities through a pool — and with maintaining authorities providing 15 per cent of the cost of providing public sector higher education. The system would be controlled — and this was the Working Group's core recommendation — by a new National Body with terms of reference on the following lines:

> To collect, analyse and present, where appropriate in conjunction with the Department of Education and Science and the University Grants Committee, information affecting the demand for and supply of higher education in the maintained sector; to advise the Secretary of State and the local authority associations on the total provision which should be made for it; to consider and issue guidance on the programmes and estimates submitted to it by authorities and, where appropriate, institutions; to allocate funds for recurrent expenditure and to advise on the allocation of capital expenditure; and to have

general oversight of the development of maintained higher education and its cost-effectiveness.[16]

The Bill which followed from this report was shelved with the announcement of a General Election, and though the new government was to make different proposals about a new system and its control what the Oakes group had done was set out the agenda and all its components — local authority responsibility for the institutions, centrally dispensed funds, forecasting of demand and supply, the relationship between financial allocations and programmes, and general financial oversight. By 1979 the outlines, though not some of the most significant content, of a new funding and controlling system were in place, and the question would ultimately be: what relationship would it have with the CNAA?

The question of giving advice to the new national body was crucial for the CNAA. Its 'peer review' relationship with the institutions had been carefully constructed as a means of making judgments specific to the institution concerned, without any 'ranking' of one institution or course against another. The CNAA was not choosing where courses should be run or selecting which institutions should develop or contract. It was making judgments about the standards of courses and of the means of their delivery to students. The new body would be deciding on resources and making decisions on whether to allow courses to start or to continue. Its decisions could result in the closure of courses or even institutions, and by offering advice the CNAA could therefore by implication be helping to decide on such closures, or expressing preferences between institutions. It was a new situation for the CNAA. Another aspect of the divided responsibilities between the CNAA and funding and approving mechanisms did not surface clearly in the Council, but it was discussed in various contexts. This related to the very logic of such a division. From his appointment as Chairman of the Council in January 1978 Sir Denis Rooke, for example, was concerned about the CNAA's inability to pass judgment on the wisdom of developing particular courses or subject areas. The institutions obtained initial approval to plan a course from their Regional Advisory Councils, and although HMI through that procedure could judge the need for particular courses, the CNAA had no such option when faced with a course submitted for approval on grounds of academic quality. There were some, and Sir Denis Rooke was one, who felt that the two processes should be merged so as to enable the CNAA to have some control over subject and course provision as well as over standards. He discovered in discussions with Ministers and senior officials of the DES that there were insurmountable political difficulties to ending this separation of powers.[17] The CNAA itself never formally broached such a policy discussion.

In setting up a new national body, the local authorities were largely in favour of a machinery that would essentially be a way for local authorities individually to negotiate on behalf of their institutions with a body which represented them collectively.[18] By 1981, however, the government was moving towards a solution which included central funding through a body which would be responsible for the polytechnics and only a proportion of the colleges, excluding many with advanced work validated by the CNAA. Central funding was to be a mechanism for defining and planning a sector of higher education more closely paralleling that funded through the UGC. The government's consultative document and speculation in the press aroused concern about government 'takeovers' and 'centralization',[19] and an Under Secretary at the DES gave a reassurance in 1980:

> What about the prospect of removing polytechnics for financial and administrative purposes from the local sector into direct grant relationship with central government? Again, we see no such prospect. The local authority associations have gone on record many times as saying it is their view that polytechnics should stay where they are. Government Ministers have endorsed that view.[20]

Central government was, however, on the brink of changing grant relationships in more ways than one, and before the decade was out the polytechnics had ceased to stay where they were. For the CNAA, however, the immediate issue was different. It underlined in response to the government's consultative document on higher education outside the universities that national planning and funding could not be carried out satisfactorily 'without taking matters of academic quality fully into account'. Planning and funding meant making 'academic judgments about what is being or can be offered with the resources available'. In this extremely detailed document the Council set out the arguments against and for the CNAA becoming closely involved with the National Body — one crucial one being that:

> the traditional function of CNAA has been to judge whether courses are of at least the minimum acceptable standard. For CNAA to become involved in the comparative ranking of courses would imply a change in its methodology and in its relationships with institutions.

The dangers suggested there were to prove very real, and the comment prophetic. The arguments in favour of involvement, however, were strong — including the avoidance of a National Body sub-structure to parallel that of the CNAA, and the difficulty of avoiding calling on the CNAA's considerable experience of peer group evaluation if any ranking judgments were to be made. The document even discussed the possibility of the CNAA's functions being 'recast and incorporated into the National Body'. The Council concluded that it was 'willing in principle to give academic advice', conditional upon the CNAA being adequately represented in the structure of the new body, in order 'to ensure that the CNAA's advice was properly understood and interpreted'.[21] From this point on there were divided views in the CNAA about the principle of giving advice, and the kinds of advice that could or should be given.

The National Advisory Body for Local Authority Higher Education (NAB) (the latter phrase replaced by Public Sector Higher Education when its powers were extended to cover the voluntary colleges) was established in February 1982,[22] and for the next two years the work of the CNAA was largely dominated by the question of relationships with the NAB, and with the implications of its decisions and an ensuing crisis for relationships with the CNAA's institutions. Late in 1982 the Council consulted the institutions on its possible role in relation to the NAB. In doing so it underlined that 'there is a strong body of opinion within Council and its committees that CNAA should take care, in collaborating with any national planning and funding body, not to prejudice its traditional role as an independent validating body or to undermine the further development of partnership with its associated institutions'. What, therefore, were the kinds of advice that the CNAA should give, and by what means should it be given? The Council emphasized three points: it would probably 'be wisest for CNAA not to attempt to rank courses or institutions but simply to give objective appraisals'; The CNAA's advice should be formulated through 'full and open discussion with the institution'; it would become increasingly important to rely on institutions themselves 'to conduct rigorous and regular evaluations of the quality and viability of what they offer and to propose realistic academic development plans based on their evaluations and such guidance as the national body can give them'.[23] The Council uneasily adopted the view, when the responses had been received, that it 'was not in the public interest, or in the interest of the PSHE system, for it to decide against giving "quality" advice to NAB', while recognizing the concerns that had been expressed by institutions and other bodies.[24] Communicating its decision to the NAB the Council continued to tread a tightrope: it wished to develop an 'appropriate and effective' relationship with the NAB, in a way that would 'retain and enhance the confidence of the institutions'. The CNAA would be willing to transmit 'factual information provided it is neutral', and no information would be supplied 'which includes or could imply a quality judgment on courses or on institutions'.[25] In general, this proved to be a viable strategy, and the CNAA was able for several years to influence NAB decisions on particular institutions and courses, in the difficult conditions of financial stringency. It based its advice to the NAB on the known strengths of courses and institutions, as part of the planning of the distribution of national resources, but the long-term positive contribution that the CNAA could make in this direction was at a very early stage seen to be fragile, and the confidence of the institutions was undermined.

From the early autumn of 1983 the Council was aware that the initial plans developed by the NAB 'showed a lack of qualitative discrimination', but some Council members doubted the wisdom of attempting to offer advice that would appear to discriminate between institutions, but it was decided to go as far as possible to indicate to the NAB 'where the main strengths of the system were to be found'.[26] The sensitivities involved, and the short time-scales within which the CNAA could respond, meant that there were bound to be dangers in the procedure. The NAB's first major task was a planning exercise for 1984–85, to be conducted under fourteen 'programme' headings. The Achilles heel of the process for the CNAA was to be Town and Country Planning. When the CNAA was consulted the NAB had in mind to close four centres offering full-time degree courses in this area — at Chelmer-Essex Institute of Higher Education, Coventry (Lanchester) Polytechnic, Gloucester College of Arts and Technology, and the Polytechnic of Central London (PCL). In the CNAA's response to the proposed plans for course closures — a response agreed by the Council's Town Planning Board, a working group of the Council and the Council itself — a variety of phraseologies was used. The Coventry courses were described as being 'of high quality as judged by a wide range of criteria'; in the case of PCL the Council stressed 'the unique urban/metropolitan policy emphasis of the course'; the Council was 'unable to make a case that the courses at Chelmer and Gloucester were of "particular quality"'. It argued for the retention of the two former courses, but pointed out the value of the rural planning emphasis of the latter two. The CNAA was already aware that the NAB was making a special case for the retention of courses at Oxford Polytechnic as being of 'particular quality', and in confirming that view the Council did not wish to imply that it considered Oxford to 'enjoy a special pre-eminence'. In arguing for the retention of the Coventry and PCL courses the Council was 'aware that the consideration of the above advice could lead to further proposals for closures from the NAB. The Council is prepared to offer further advice if necessary'.[27] The Council had now placed itself in a position of being seen to be a party to whatever closures the NAB decided — the closures being seen to be related to CNAA judgments of quality. The ensuing controversy was intense and acrimonious. If Teesside had been a crunch issue for many of the polytechnic directors, town and country planning did the same for the CNAA's institutions in general. The trust between the Council and its institutions now appeared to be in jeopardy. Information collected in the validation process and in specific and understood conditions now seemed to be available to another body for quite different purposes. Validation itself seemed to be in question.

Following often tense debates inside the CNAA, the Council explained its position and took further action. It reviewed the procedures, agreed that advice should continue to be given, but decided on measures to consult more closely with the institutions, and to present its future advice with more care and within the longer time frame that the NAB's future programmes of planning should allow. It reasserted the basic principles on which it intended to continue to act, emphasizing

(i) that the traditional function of validating and reviewing courses and institutions will be kept separate from the function of providing advice to NAB, unless and until Council decides otherwise;

(ii) that the purpose of validation and review visits remains that of judging whether courses are of the required standard to receive approval or to continue in approval . . .;

(iii) that Council is anxious to ensure that the process of external peer group evaluation is not adversely affected by its involvement with the NAB and is further developed on a partnership basis.[28]

The Council established a Working Group on Relationships with the NAB, consisting of the chairmen of the Council's five committees and four other members of the Council, two of whom were directors of polytechnics, and two were principals of colleges of higher education. The task of the Group was to oversee, on behalf of the Council, the processes of consultation in the CNAA's boards and committees and with the institutions, and at its first meeting it issued a statement of intention to consult.[29] It was clear to all concerned, in the CNAA and the NAB, that in the context of government policy for higher education there would be more difficult decisions to make about contraction and course closures, and the CNAA — while not itself being a party to closures — could not distance itself totally from the process. The NAB would, with or without the CNAA's advice, be making decisions, and the CNAA had a general concern to ensure as best it could the protection of quality in its associated institutions. In 1984, when the government decided to make the NAB — established initially for a three-year period — permanent, the CNAA welcomed the government's decision, and emphasized the importance of continuing independence for the validating bodies, but also that 'a constructive relationship between the NAB and the validating bodies will be crucial if the quality of provision in the public sector of higher education is to be maintained and enhanced in the difficult years ahead'.[30]

The town and country planning episode, and the general early unease about the CNAA's relationship with the NAB, sharpened the Council's understanding of its need to be aware of the delicacy of its relationships with its institutions, and its interest in going ahead with developments arising out of the partnership in validation exercise. Within the institutions the damage done in the autumn of 1982 was repaired quickly in spite of the hazards to the system and to the individual colleges and polytechnics that obviously lay ahead. The repairs resulted to a substantial degree from the openness of the NAB itself in the way it conducted its own relationships with other bodies and with the institutions. It had a difficult operation to conduct and in spite of the harsh decisions it became the target for remarkably little criticism and complaint. By establishing a framework of system-wide understanding of the tasks to be performed and the open, consultative way it intended to operate, the NAB provided an underlying level of reassurance that was important to the institutions in the middle of the 1980s. The procedures adopted by the CNAA and the principles it reasserted also restored a large measure of the confidence that had been abruptly shaken.

In all the documentation and discussion in the CNAA, and between the CNAA and others, in the period when a national body was being planned and established, there is emphasis on the need for the new body to work closely with the UGC. Within the public sector attention was being constantly drawn to the financial differentials between the two sectors, with a lower unit cost per student in the public sector, and less support for research. Even if there was no end in sight for the binary system, it was felt in the CNAA and in the institutions that there would be gain from having some coordination between two national bodies responsible for the financing of higher education. This was a view held to some extent by government also. In 1983 the Parliamentary Under Secretary of State, William Waldegrave, considered that with the establishment of the NAB the government:

> now has two formidable bodies with which to engage in dialogue about the development of higher education as a whole — an objective which has been seen as desirable for many years . . . for the first time real progress is being made towards providing for explicit and open debate on higher education policy, followed by action through properly constituted decision taking bodies.

Among the jobs to be done was also the removal of 'various nonsensical binary line snobbisms'.[31] The creation of the NAB was in fact only a limited step as far as prospects of eroding the status differences between the two sectors were concerned. When the UGC consulted the universities in 1984 about, among other things, differences with the public sector, *The Economist* described the response as a mixture of arrogance and 'a pinched sniff of hauteur: universities do research; polytechnics are meant to be vocational, but have forsaken their role to play at jobs only traditional dons can do'.[32] Polytechnics, as the *New Statesman* commented a year later, still had a very poor public image:

> A national opinion poll commissioned by worried polytechnic governors last year showed many misconceptions among MPs, industrialists, and the public about their work. Thus 36 per cent thought they taught O levels (wrong), 44 per cent thought they taught A levels (wrong), and 34 per cent thought they awarded degrees (almost right). As Roger Adams of Plymouth Polytechnic, who chairs the polytechnic committee of the lecturers' union, NATFHE, says: 'It may take 1000 years at this rate before people recognise the difficult job we do'.

It was hardly surprising, therefore, that some polytechnics, including Middlesex, Portsmouth and North East London, were considering changing their names to include the word 'university'.[33] If the polytechnics were facing continuing problems in having their identities recognized, and in some cases wished to be universities or 'polytechnic universities' — a move resisted by the government and the NAB — the colleges and institutes of higher education had even greater difficulties, still being thought of in many cases as 'teacher training colleges' or 'technical colleges' or some other label that neither described their real identity nor indicated their presence in the landscape of 'higher education'. It was hardly surprising in this case that some of the colleges which had at an earlier stage missed out on the polytechnic designation should now actively seek it.

The polytechnics and colleges remained strongly committed to the labour market, as one research study on a polytechnic suggested, in at least two ways: 'a commitment to responding to student demand and particular student constituencies, and a commitment to designing courses in relation to the labour market'. There were still, however, tremendously varied employer perceptions of the quality and employability of polytechnic graduates.[34] The colleges were finding that their student populations differed in some respects from those of both universities and polytechnics, with many of their students coming from families with no previous experience of higher education and preferring what most of the colleges were — 'small, congenial, and not too far from home'. About two-thirds of their students, as Adelman and Gibbs found in the late 1970s, had chosen to enter a college of higher education in preference to other institutions of higher education: 'this is especially so for B.Ed. students but less so for B.A.s, where just under half of them would have preferred a university place'.[35] Five years later Gibbs and Harland discovered that differences between college and university student constituencies were being reduced as a result of the widening of access by the universities — threatening areas of recruitment for the colleges which had 'traditionally been their preserve' — including working-class and older students. They also found, in the conditions prevailing at the time, that college students were facing serious employment problems,[36] as these diversifying institutions struggled to establish themselves in the market place in areas other than teacher education, and to provide adequate careers guidance services. The polytechnics and colleges in their sometimes quite different ways were facing the difficulty, together with the CNAA, of coupling assurance of the standard of their degrees with their credibility with the schools, the parents and the employers.

At a national policy level the CNAA in the early 1980s was responding in many directions other than those linked directly to validation or public sector planning, and much of its discussion and activity related in a variety of ways to establishing a presence for the public sector in areas affecting the position of the institutions, their subjects, their courses, their recruitment. At one meeting of the Committee for Academic Policy in 1980, for example, the agenda contained responses to four official documents (a report of the Select Committee on Education, Science and Arts; recommendations from a group reviewing higher education in Northern Ireland: a DES consultative paper on *Examinations 16–18*; a DES discussion paper on *Continuing Education: Post Experience Vocational Provision for Those in Employment*), as well as CNAA policy papers on *Higher Education into the 1990s*, and microelectronics and information technology (IT). The Council and its committees were considering issues relating to multicultural education, the financing of the arts, sandwich courses and much else. Edwin Kerr told a conference in 1980:

> in recent months we have expressed views directly to the Secretaries of State for Education and Science, Industry, Scotland and Wales. We have met with other Ministers to discuss Finniston, capping the pool, course planning, college government and a national body. We have also met the Higher Education Enquiry for Northern Ireland and the Parliamentary Select Committee. We are also involved with many official and professional bodies.[37]

The Council also undertook a study which resulted in a two-day seminar in the autumn of 1982 and a consultative paper on the *Future Development of CNAA's Academic Policies at Undergraduate Level*. The seminar, the publication and the wider discussion set some goals for the CNAA and its associated institutions in the framework of national developments — diminishing resources, the NAB, the OU, the low age-participation rate and the impending demographic decline, a feasibility study on credit transfer (the Toyne Report) and a range of other contextual features of higher education. Some of the most central areas emphasized in this discussion were access by mature, non-standard entry and ethnic minority students, issues relating to curricula and assessment, and credit accumulation and credit transfer.[38]

One of the Council's most active concerns in this period, however, was its evidence and response to the Finniston Committee of Inquiry into the Engineering Profession, which produced the report on *Engineering Our Future* in 1980. This influential report made recommendations relating to the initial and continuing training of engineers, schools and higher education, qualifications, registration and licensing of engineers and national arrangements for promoting and strengthening what it described as 'the engineering dimension' in the British economy.[39] The CNAA in response welcomed the emphasis in the report on design, problem solving and the creation of bridges between the formation of engineers and engineering practice in the proposed new degree of BEng (though the CNAA thought the report should have said more about management and marketing, including interpersonal skills and managerial finance).[40] From this point and for several years, the Council, its Committee for Science and Technology, and the Committee for Academic and Institutional Policy devoted considerable energy to new developments in the formation of engineers. A policy statement in 1982 included as one of the Council's purposes: 'to encourage the adoption of an emphatic engineering applications emphasis in CNAA's approved engineering degree courses and to accord due recognition to such courses'. It expressed the view that the Finniston Report had, as was widely recognized, created an opportunity 'which is unlikely to recur in the foreseeable future, to improve the profession of engineering', and it set out the framework in which the CNAA would validate BSc(Eng) and BEng courses — with a strong emphasis, as in the Finniston Report, on engineering applications.[41] The following year it explained why it now proposed to drop the BSc(Eng). Engineering, as the Finniston Report itself had strongly underlined, was not — as was commonly and mistakenly assumed — a subordinate branch of science: in the CNAA's terms it was 'a discipline distinct from science'. The presence of both terms in the title had been a source of confusion and it needed to be replaced. The Council spelled out its understanding of the future shape of engineering education in terms of the development of the student's intellectual and imaginative skills and powers:

> The direction of a student's engineering studies must be towards greater understanding and competence, and effective communication. He must be encouraged to develop the ability to see relationships, to synthesise and to appreciate modes of thought, attitudes and practices other than those of his main discipline . . . Because of the nature of the engineering profession, an engineering degree course should provide a technologically broad education, particularly in its early stages . . . Engineering degree courses should give due consideration to the place and importance of money, manpower and marketing on the work of an engineer, i.e. they should treat engineering in its business environment.[42]

The CNAA rarely came as close as this to formulating curriculum content, but the circumstances were exceptional. A national opportunity was being taken to point in a new and necessary direction, and the CNAA's own institutions were in the forefront of the development of the BEng, of 'engineering applications' and the bridging of courses and industrial experience. It co-funded research based at Leicester Polytechnic on 'The goals of engineering education' and in 1985 it was one of the sponsors of a conference on 'What makes a BEng course?'[43] It consulted with the Business and Technician Education Council and the Engineering Council on the variety and level of engineering awards. In the early 1980s nothing indicated more clearly than this process the capacity of the CNAA and its associated institutions to respond to, and lead in, significant areas of the curriculum of higher education. Business studies, teacher education or the creative and performing arts would offer other examples across the same period.

One of the Council's constant preoccupations was also the question of access by 'non-standard' students. The public sector in general had a tradition of catering for 'mature' or 'second-chance' students. In 1976 about a third of the 35,000 students admitted to undergraduate courses validated by the

CNAA were aged 21 or over,[44] and throughout the 1980s the Council was concerned with improving access for these and other students with or without the usual formal qualifications. In 1984 it compiled data on access or preparatory courses which provided an alternative to 'A' levels, and it supported research aimed at describing and appraising the policies of CNAA-associated institutions 'concerning the admission to first degree and DipHE programmes of applicants not holding standard entry qualifications', as well as research on the assessment of 'prior experential learning' which might count for admission to courses of higher education'.[45] The Council's underlying philosophy in this respect was outlined in a statement which drew attention to the flexibility in its 1979 Principles and Regulations 'in relation to the admission of students and to encourage institutions to take greater advantage of the Regulations to extend access to higher education to a wider range of students',[46] and while the responsibility for widening access lay with the institutions the CNAA was constantly alert to the possibilities of encouraging further development in this direction.

In some respects the CNAA was operating as what Maurice Kogan, as we have seen, described as 'a super-Senate for non-university insti-tutions'.[47] Its Committee for Academic Policy covered the wide range of issues and areas we have indicated, and in 1983, for example, found itself reviewing the Council's criteria for 'general education', last formulated in 1979, when Principle 3 defined the general education aims that needed to underlie all programmes of studies validated by the CNAA. Since that time there had throughout the CNAA been, as the Committee noted, 'a wide divergence, not merely of interpretation of the Principle, but also of willing-ness to subscribe to such a statement of Council's general educational aims'. Some of the Committees had found Principle 3 in places 'nebulous and obscure' (in the case of Arts and Social Studies, which preferred not to review it — perhaps for that very reason), some reaffirmed their support for it, and the Interfaculty Studies Board reported that it had on occasion 'found considerable discrepancy in the views of different Boards about the centrality of Principle 3, and ways in which it might be operationalized in relation to particular courses'.[48] The CNAA's Committee for Institutions was responsible for implementing the intricacies of the Council's changing processes of institutional approval — having in 1980 issued a set of 'Notes for the guidance of institutions' on the reviews, setting out the expectations which the Council considered the institutions would share in operating their periodic self-reviews. The paper reflects the continuing concern not just to find forms of partnership, but also to define the criteria against which to judge standards — a balance of institutional goals and the values of higher education in general: 'each institution should be considered in its own terms, although against the common objectives of institutions engaged in higher education'[49] — a form of judgment-making difficult to arrive at in practice, as the American system of accreditation was finding at the same time. Reports of institutional visits continued to reflect a considerable range of detailed judgments by visiting parties on all aspects of institutional life and organization — from student welfare to secretarial provision, from the composition of faculty boards to computer services, from expertise in internal validation to college morale. In both of these cases the CNAA's machineries were looking for short-term and longer-term policies. From 1981 the Council's Development Services considered how the CNAA's own office systems could be adapted 'to offer appropriate support for the implementation of the Council's *Developments in Partnership in Validation* policy', and in response produced a scheme of Files on Courses in Institutions (FOCII) which would be an information system accessible to both the CNAA and each institution, to be regularly updated with available data and material and simplifying the preparation of CNAA visits for both parties.[50]

The Committee for Scotland had become a regular and active component of the CNAA's machinery, holding meetings of institutions validated by the CNAA, concerning itself with the improvement of relations between the Council and Scotland, research, the outcomes of institutional reviews, and government moves to establish a new Scottish Tertiary Education Council (STEAC), which was set up after consultations in June 1984. Of the Committee's other involvements one of the most crucial was to be the process of reviewing teacher education in Scotland. When the Secretary of State for Scotland announced in 1983 that primary teaching in Scotland was to become an all-graduate profession, with Diploma courses being replaced by four-year BEd courses, he expressed the view that he hoped the new courses would be validated by the CNAA. At the same time a Scottish Council for the Validation of Courses for Teachers (SCOVACT) was established, and in the event the Secretary of State left it that courses might be validated by the CNAA, SCOVACT or individual universities. The convenor of SCOVACT was invited to become a member of the Committee for Scotland, and a CNAA observer attended meetings of SCOVACT. Of the six colleges which put forward proposals in 1983–84, half submitted them to SCOVACT and the other half to the CNAA.[51]

From 1979 the CNAA extended its work to Hong Kong. Other countries — including Ireland and Australia — had shown interest in the CNAA's form of operation, but in the case of Hong Kong there was to be a sustained and direct relationship. The approach from Hong Kong invited the CNAA to advise the University and Polytechnic Grants Committee on the validation of degree courses. This applied initially to Hong Kong Polytechnic, but the advisory role was quickly extended to cover two polytechnics, a college and an Open Learning Institute. The CNAA advisory role was intended to assure the UPGC that courses in non-university institutions in Hong Kong 'attained and continued to attain an academic level at least comparable to that of courses approved by the CNAA in the United Kingdom'. The Chief Officer, supporting the proposal at a Council meeting in December 1979, met with some opposition to the extension of the CNAA's role outside the UK — though the DES assessor made it clear that the government was likely to support the Council in developing such an advisory role. From that meeting, through a first review by the CNAA in Hong Kong in 1981, and regular review and advisory activities in the 1980s the CNAA developed — under the guidance of a sub-committee reporting to the Committee for Academic Policy (from 1984 the Committee for Academic and Institutional Policy) — a capacity to offer advice on academic standards to a third party. Sir Denis Rooke, commenting on experience of discussing the CNAA with people in other countries who had in any way interacted with it, underlines how complimentary they invariably were about the CNAA and its operations. The Hong Kong connection was the most sustained form of such interaction.[52]

The central mission of the CNAA remained, however, the work of validation and the maintenance and enhancement of standards in its associated UK institutions. Following the publication of the 'blue book', *Partnership in Validation*, and the commitment to review longer-term possibilities, the Council created a Working Party on Longer Term Developments, knowing that the partnership arrangements so far adopted did not preclude more radical changes. The Working Party solicited opinions on the work of the Council and in 1982 received comments from Her Majesty's Inspectorate. The Chief Inspector for Further Education in England acknowledged the 'outstanding contribution' the CNAA had made to non-university education, thought the subject boards were the most important part of the Council's work, though they sometimes 'behave irregularly', and suggested that the validation process had 'created a considerable bureaucracy given to excessively theoretical consideration of curriculum and structure. Much less appears to be known about actual standards of academic performance'. Institutional reviews were 'the most widely and seriously criticized aspect of the Council's work ... We suggest that this procedure is subject to a fundamental examination with regard to its necessity and particularly in relation to the large number of now well managed institutions in existence'. Rather less forthrightly, Scottish HMI — while considering the work of the Council to have been 'one of the major developments in higher education in the past twenty years' — thought some of the Council's 'sector' committees seemed to be 'Committees in search of a function', and the institutional review, from Scottish experience, 'has still to prove itself'. Given the brevity of institutional visits 'we are sceptical about the ability of the visiting party to make some of the judgments they offer'.[53] The CDP welcomed the creation of the Working Party, outlined the achievements of the CNAA at some length, indicated its 'failures' — that is, its 'sins of omission and commission' — and suggested 'changes to increase effectiveness'. These related largely to specific issues such as subject board procedures. It wanted to see an adequate computerized data base linked to quality analysis and enhancing the CNAA's role 'as the public guarantor of standards by using its privileged position to use its data for research into principles and models for the maintenance of standards whilst progressively withdrawing from the paternal role it has developed during the developmental period'. It looked towards 'a change in style in the CNAA operation whilst recognising the present transitional period in developing the partnership in validation policy', and towards an ultimate review of the CNAA's Charter, which had been written at the time 'when no-one could have envisaged the present development of HE'.[54] The CDP's aspirations for the polytechnics remained unchanged, but the mood at this time was distinctly subdued. The Council, responding to the first report from its Working Party, acknowledged a consensus that the CNAA needed to look more fully at fundamental questions 'relating to the overall context and general conceptual framework within which the relationship between the CNAA and its associated institutions needed to be considered'.[55] In July 1983 the Council endorsed the general lines on which the Working Party was working, and in December received its second report. By now the Working Party was reviewing all the changing circumstances affecting the CNAA's work — the NAB, the Welsh Advisory Board, cuts in public funding, increasing demand for more industrially relevant courses and cost effectiveness, a possible fall in the size of the 18 + cohort, and developments in the CNAA itself and in the institutions. The Working Party and the Council were struggling with ways of adopting less detailed review and validation procedures, devolving more responsibilities, achieving more emphasis by the boards on the teaching, experience and outcomes of courses, and the impact on all of its procedures of the creation of the NAB.[56] Partnership in validation had led to changes, but four years after *Developments* the Council was still making difficult progress.

One of the reasons for the difficulties was the growth of the CNAA itself as a bureaucratic machine, having expanded to keep pace with the considerable increase in its activities. By the beginning of the 1980s it had over forty 'senior staff', including registrars and assistant registrars. With Edwin Kerr substantially involved as a member of other national bodies, including the Advisory Council on the Supply and Education of Teachers, and from 1982 the National Advisory Body, and given the scale of the organization, a number of Assistant Chief Officers were appointed from 1978. The CNAA was servicing committees and boards with approaching 2500 members, assessors and specialist advisers, and was dealing with over 130 associated institutions. Within this machinery CNAA officers often performed quite different roles. Those involved in subject board validation were the link between the voluntary membership and the institutions, essentially, as one former officer put it, as 'go-betweens and oilers of the works'. In institutional reviews, chaired by the Chief Officer or an Assistant Chief Officer, the relationship could be different, particularly at a time when institutional reviews were in some cases being met with a degree of hostility. One of the sensitivities involved in the growth of the CNAA as an organization was therefore the different degrees to which *officers* exercised influence and control, as distinct from the exercise of the authority of the

CNAA as such. There were widely differing perceptions.

While seeking to modify its review procedures the CNAA was at the same time working with what had become an increasingly complex set of procedures as embodied in regulations which had in many cases become more and more cumbersome as they had been revised and re-revised. Given the scale of the operation and the range of subjects and courses with which it was dealing, the CNAA had acquired many of the characteristics of a classic bureaucracy, and one of the obstacles to any major change of policy was the embeddedness of the regulatory procedures. They had been set up and expanded for particular purposes, and could be judged to be effective. Disturbing such established patterns in order to meet new pressures and circumstances is one of the problems bureaucracies constantly have to face. Working within the context of a charter, and responding to multiple constituencies, make the problem even more acute.

In April 1984 the Secretary of State for Education and Science appointed a Committee of Enquiry, chaired by Sir Norman Lindop, who had been Director of The Hatfield Polytechnic until 1982. The Committee's remit was to 'identify and examine key issues for the effective and efficient maintenance and improvement of academic standards in the way those responsible for the academic validation of first and higher degree level courses in the public sector in Great Britain discharge their responsibilities'.[57] By that date, when the CNAA itself came under scrutiny, five years had elapsed since *Developments in Partnership in Validation*, and the Council had agreed only limited moves towards the greater relaxation of validation foreshadowed in 1979. We shall return to some consideration of reasons for the pace and nature of change in this period, given its importance to an understanding of the establishment and impact of the Lindop Committee, the political background against which it deliberated, and the abrupt changes which took place from 1984 in the operation and direction of the CNAA.

The developments in partnership in validation generally from 1979 were seen as minimal by many of the institutions and CNAA officers: 'Partnership in validation didn't amount to much' was the verdict of one of the latter. Validation seemed to have continued with only minor modifications, as the CDP constantly maintained. The Working Party on Longer Term Developments seemed to reach a series of stalemates by considering various validation models unlikely, in the CDP's view, 'to initiate a dramatic departure from the peer group evaluation process'.[58] Models of accreditation received little attention or support in the Committee for Institutions and elsewhere. From 1981 Newcastle Polytechnic offered a way forward, but one that was also perceived as a way of prolonging the stalemate. Only a small number of polytechnics considered taking advantage of the 'blue book' offer to negotiate alternative forms of validation, and Newcastle proved to be the most important to do so. It suggested, as we have seen, a form of 'joint validation' that would capitalize on the

Polytechnic's experience of internal course review, making the final stage of its internal validation procedure a joint exercise with the CNAA, thus eliminating one stage in the process and giving the Polytechnic a real partnership role in the final decisions. The CNAA agreed to an experimental period of joint validation for one year, later extended to two, and Newcastle produced an evaluation of the experiment in the summer of 1983. In the first year the procedure had positive results, but there were problems in that year in persuading subject boards and their visiting teams to cooperate. At the end of the first year the Council had to ask the committees to 'encourage' the boards to collaborate fully in the joint validation approach, or communicate their reasons for not complying to the Council. Almost all the boards had in the first year in fact failed to understand or to respect the joint approach, and there was at least one chairman of a visiting party who did not realize that the Polytechnic members present were not merely 'in attendance'.[59] The process ran more smoothly in the second year and the experiment was judged a success by both the Polytechnic and the Committee for Institutions.

The Council had seen the agreement as a way of gaining experience of a model of joint validation, and clearly in doing so was building on its knowledge of the Polytechnic's experience since the mid-1970s of an internal process of course validation and review, and of subject review. The Council reviewed the operation of the guidelines for the experiment that it had laid down in 1981, and received a statement from its Committee for Institutions at the end of 1983 indicating that

> During the 1981–82 and 1982–83 academic years, twenty-two courses were validated in the experimental mode and, by means of questionnaires to CNAA members and officers and Polytechnic staff participating in the joint validation events, an extensive analysis was conducted by the CNAA into the effectiveness of the joint validation model relative to conventional procedures. The evidence collected demonstrated unequivocally that the experiment had shown that joint validation is at least as effective as conventional subject Board validation.

The Committee recommended that the experiment should be regarded as concluded, and that 'joint validation should be adopted as the normal and established form of relationship between the Council's subject Boards and the Polytechnic for the purpose of course validation and review', subject to the 'reserved powers' of both parties as laid down in the earlier guidelines.[60] The Polytechnic's Academic Board also concluded that the joint validation experiment had been 'successfully carried out and joint validation has been demonstrated to be an acceptable and workable mode of operation'. The process had been 'at least as rigorous and effective as "traditional" CNAA validations, and at best the quality of the validation is enhanced by the joint mode'. Joint validation should now be 'the established mode of operation between CNAA and this Polytechnic', and it should no longer be necessary to negotiate with individual subject boards as to whether the joint mode should operate. It urged that the joint validation model should become available to other institutions.[61] The Council in fact agreed that joint validation should be the basis of future relationships with Newcastle Polytechnic. The Polytechnic's Academic Board, however, was looking beyond joint validation to the possibility of further and progressive delegation of responsibility from the CNAA. It began to formulate a model of 'institutional accreditation' and this was submitted to the CNAA in June 1984. The proposals were designed to retain the principle of external peer group review, build on the strengths of the joint model, but continue the process of 'progressive delegation of responsibility for academic standards to the Academic Board, as appropriate to a major and mature institution'. The proposal was basically for a process of periodic reaccreditation, and in the intervals between institutional review visits the Polytechnic's Academic Board would be empowered 'to validate, approve and introduce new courses, to validate and reapprove established courses, to conduct progress reviews of established courses and to make modifications to courses'.[62] By the middle of 1984, however, the context of the discussion had changed.

From late 1980 the Council had realized that under the terms of *Partnership in Validation* a variety of possible models and developments for partnership might emerge and was anxious to ensure that its resources were not overstretched in the short term. Other institutions began discussions about possible ways ahead, but apart from Newcastle only Kingston and Sheffield Polytechnics made attempts to reach agreements which could be considered as experimental in the same sense as that with Newcastle, and neither made much progress at the formal level. Kingston produced a model of 'complementary' course validation, which, by the end of 1983, was deemed to be still 'evolving and developing', but the Committee for Institutions expressed its 'disappointment at the lack of progress, in practical terms'.[63] Within the CDP, and at meetings of the Committee for Institutions, there were expressions of 'misgivings' about the Newcastle model and whether it went far enough to meet the aspirations of other polytechnics or their directors: it was said to emphasize 'individual institutions' relationships with Council' rather than regional or wider collaboration amongst institutions in their relationships with the Council.[64] From June 1981 the Council's moratorium on other agreements with institutions meant that on the one side the CNAA was awaiting the outcome of an experimental period mainly with Newcastle, and on the other were those institutions and the CDP eager to see a bolder step towards accreditation. Portsmouth Polytechnic was one which explored a set of long-term objectives without going the Newcastle route. There was the possibility it might seek to acquire its own Charter, and given its long history of degree level work, the number of its courses and students, and its record in research and scholarship, such an aspiration 'could hardly be thought implausible'. At this time, however, the Polytechnic was seeking to define what might be possible while under the umbrella of the CNAA. By 1984, the Polytechnic's President explained, although the CNAA had been aware for a number of years of the need:

> to devolve more responsibility to institutions for the approval of courses, the Council has found singular difficulty in moving in this direction. The partnership in validation paper produced in 1979 offered the prospect of a limited loosening of the reins but, in the event, progress under this policy has been strictly limited. Relatively few institutions made proposals under the partnership in validation arrangements, but even so, the Council was quickly moved to discourage further applications for special relationships.

In drafting proposals the Polytechnic expressed its scepticism about whether the Newcastle scheme could provide adequate scope for the further development needed by Portsmouth, and the Newcastle scheme would indeed 'prolong the apprenticeship of the institution beyond that which could be considered reasonable'. What it wished to propose, therefore, was that the CNAA should approve the Polytechnic's procedures for the oversight and validation of courses, receive external examiners' and other reports from the Polytechnic, delegate to the Polytechnic the power to validate and operate courses and determine degree results 'without further reference to the CNAA', and conduct an institutional review after five years to evaluate the experience.[65] The Polytechnic expressed to the CNAA its dissatisfaction with the operation of the subject boards, and was uninterested in a model of joint validation which implied the continued involvement of the boards. The Portsmouth propositions were discussed during an institutional review visit in 1984, when the Chief Officer indicated that the Council would not be able to accept the handing over of course validation entirely to the institution, but he suggested an arrangement whereby the boards might intervene at any time and the CNAA would retain the right to withdraw the arrangement at any time.[66]

Across the polytechnics, but only in a small number of cases in the colleges and institutes of higher education, discussions were taking place to explore the pace and type of changes they wished to see. At an institutional review at Leicester Polytechnic it argued against the Newcastle model as demanding in time and other resources, and expressed a wish to negotiate a relationship similar to that being proposed by Portsmouth. In June 1984 the Academic Board of Manchester Polytechnic was expected, also at an institutional visit, to make proposals 'similar to those of Portsmouth and Leicester polytechnics'.[67] The essential tension for the CNAA was with the major institutions, and it reflected what Norman Lindop called an 'asymmetry of power — one side can cast the other into outer darkness'.[68] It was these institutions which questioned whether CNAA validation was still necessary for the maintenance of standards. The CNAA had encouraged and was already responding in limited ways to the development of internal validation machineries which were now experienced and reliable and need be subjected only to regular institutional accreditation. Coupled with its anxieties about CNAA advice to the NAB in 1983 was the CDP's critique of the CNAA's 'slow progress towards developing a simple and effective (for the CNAA as well as for institutions) approach to the accreditation of institutions and their academic boards'.[69] The colleges, most of which had shorter experience and less interest in delegated responsibility than the polytechnics, were nevertheless restive at some of the vagaries of the subject boards and visiting parties. A study of five colleges of higher education in 1982–83 found much support for external validation and the partnership in validation policy, but also criticism of the maverick views of some visiting party members, problems caused by discontinuities of membership of parties from visit to visit, and the tendency of a visiting party 'to develop a "mentality", "momentum" or "chemistry" of its own, which might not necessarily reflect the views of its parent board'. As these colleges developed their internal validation machineries they often had ambivalent views about the CNAA's procedures. David Francis explains:

> The major impression I derived from my visits and interviews was of the growing confidence of course leaders and senior staff in the abilities of their colleagues and themselves to maintain and develop successful degree courses. This was combined with an appreciation of the value of the external quality control procedure provided by the Council that was not uncritical, but was aware of the room that existed for improvement of these procedures. Explicitly those interviewed may have argued that 'partnership in validation' was a myth or, as one course leader put it, 'the Brave New World looks very similar to the Old World', but their descriptions of their perceptions and practices indicated such a partnership existed.[70]

The CNAA's stalemate had to do not only with this diversity of institutions and developments, but also with reluctances to explore new approaches beyond the status quo of the framework established by the Charter. As Chairman of the Working Party on Longer Term Developments, Edwin Kerr responded, in June 1984, to discussion about the responsibilities of subject boards and whether these could under the Charter be transferred to institutions: 'the Chairman stated that he did not believe Council had power to delegate responsibility for validation'.[71] Sir Denis Rooke, as Chairman of the Council, was known to consider that accreditation was not an option for the CNAA in the foreseeable future. In early, informal discussions with senior civil servants and Ministers he had discussed the question of institutions being allowed to award their own degrees, and:

> the government certainly made it absolutely and thoroughly and abundantly clear from top to bottom that the answer to that was

'no', they were not going to allow, under any circumstances, the Statutes of CNAA to be changed so that individual polytechnics could award their own degrees, no matter how mature they were . . . In terms of giving more responsibility to institutions, they were quite happy to do that as long as it was only the major ones, and as long as there was no question about it that the CNAA was in the end the arbiter of everything. I think they were very keen to see the continuation of peer review . . . without I think actually understanding how demanding that is of resources.

They had initially thought it was expensive for administrative reasons that could be put right, and only slowly came to understand that the scale of the consultation that was going on all the time made it very slow to change and very expensive.[72] The context set for the Council by its Chairman, therefore, was one that had itself been set out by the government, which was eventually to change its mind, under the pressure of new events and different understandings.

The Council and its committees were at this stage, therefore, hearing muted messages about possible policy directions, alongside other and stronger messages of hoped-for changes in validation and progress towards accreditation or some other form of greater institutional autonomy. From the polytechnic directors and college principals, however, they were hearing anything but a unified voice, and were often aware that the firm demands for independence from the polytechnic directors were not always matched by the views of their academic staff. There were always, in Professor Gutteridge's experience, 'two strands' in the polytechnics themselves, and additionally some of the directors moved towards and others away from the notion of complete autonomy.[73] Reflecting on this period from 1979 to 1984 both Norman Lindop and George Tolley, as former polytechnic directors, described the CNAA's position in terms of its 'dirigiste' and 'centralist' tendencies, its posture in a blind alley while surrounded with increasing polytechnic disenchantment.[74] In the polytechnics and amongst other CNAA officers there was a view that the CNAA had failed to grasp the opportunity in 1979–81 that was to become central to the Lindop Committee's proposals in 1985. The Council's 1981 moratorium on new agreements with institutions was seen by many as symptomatic of the CNAA's lack of understanding and urgency.

Apart from these considerations, it is important to look at other factors affecting the internal life of the CNAA in this period, and a significant one already alluded to was the role of the subject boards. There are two opposing, but possibly compatible, views of the subject boards in this period. Expressed strongly at the time by many people in many ways was the conviction articulated by Christopher Ball — himself a former board chairman — that the boards were the 'real' work of the CNAA, encouraging and enabling diversity, innovation and access. This was a view widely held also in terms of the professional networks or scholarly community which resulted from the peer review process. The contribution of the boards to such developments, the extensive involvement of members from academic institutions, the professions, industry and commerce, the creative and promotional role of the CNAA officers primarily concerned with the work of the boards, and the role of the boards in incorporating crucial new discipline areas into the CNAA's range of work — all of these have been underlined and exemplified. In the late 1970s and 1980s, however, there was an increasingly strong view that the boards were also one of the principal obstacles to progress.

Within the Council itself there were moves to ensure that boards operated in line with its policies. In 1982 it set out its revised *Procedures for the Validation of Courses*, which among other things drew attention to the importance of the institutions' own internal mechanisms and 'increasing harmonisation between institutions' procedures and the operation of subject Boards'.[75] Two years later the Committee for Academic Policy was discussing how to develop 'genuine dialogue' between subject boards and course teams, and ensure that officers serving the boards acted 'within the framework of Committee policy'.[76] Norman Lindop, like other polytechnic directors, describes the subject boards as having grown 'out of control' of the main committees.[77] There is no doubt that visiting parties, and in some cases their parent boards, were neither aware of nor willing to implement more relaxed policies in course validation. David Billing, at the time a CNAA officer on secondment as Associate Director of the West London Institute of Higher Education, talked in 1983 of the composition of the boards as 'one source of conservatism'. As 'peer groups' reflecting the balances in higher education, it was 'perhaps inevitable that they should have the built-in caution expected of a cross-section of people from established departments'. The CNAA did not *intend* to be conservative, and its policy responses demonstrated the fact: 'what is less clear is that the CNAA Subject Boards have assimilated the philosophies of the Committee for Academic Policy.'[78] Some CNAA senior officers past and present talk of the 'powerful' Subject Boards having 'gone their own way', officers having often seen themselves as 'working for subject boards' rather than the CNAA, and all the Council's major strategic aims having been 'scuppered by subject boards' defending their own neck of the woods, 'reflecting disciplinary cultures'. These views of the boards are compatible with those which are strongly supportive of their work in that they reflect different stages of the CNAA's development, and diverse interpretations of the way the CNAA needed to go. For a decade from its foundation the CNAA's subject boards played the crucial role in determining what constituted standards in the newly-developing institutions and in establishing the credibility of their courses. From the late 1970s, as the CNAA struggled to respond to the pressures of particularly its major institutions, as the Committee for Institutions and related CNAA policies became an increasing focus of CNAA activity, and as institutions set their sights on the reduction of detailed and laborious course validation, the strength and subject-defensiveness of the boards could be seen as in opposition to moves towards more relaxed validation procedures, and towards accreditation. Those polytechnic directors who chaired subject boards often found themselves in an ambiguous position.

The subject boards, therefore, are one element in any explanation of the slow pace of change in the CNAA's policies and practices between *Developments in Partnership in Validation* in 1979 and the Secretary of State's establishment of the Lindop Committee in 1984. Other elements would need to be considered. The Council had taken what the majority of its members probably considered a major step forward with the *Developments* policy and saw the need for a period of caution. Moves towards the establishment of a national body for the public sector, and the creation of the NAB in 1982, absorbed a considerable amount of CNAA attention during this period. The Council and its committees were to some extent paralyzed by the diversity of perspectives on ways forward, and Edwin Kerr came to see as a tactical error the presentation to Council by the Committee on Longer Term Developments of a variety of possible models, when a single model might have overcome the Council's hesitations.[79] Whatever the reasons, the Council took an entrenched position against accreditation, and once it had done so the Chief Officer was unable to press further for any advance in that direction.

At the same time the CDP failed to develop a unified, coherent policy and operational strategy aimed at securing greater institutional autonomy. The CDP, the Standing Conference of Principals, and other bodies representing the polytechnics and colleges, also failed to communicate effectively with one another and to see themselves as partners in a policy exercise — the colleges, in fact, with the exception of a small group of proto-polytechnics, were too preoccupied with other issues to have much interest in this policy area. In general, however, at the level of the Council there was a hesitation to see, for instance, the agreement with Newcastle Polytechnic as a step towards a fuller design for self-validation or accreditation, and a hesitation to see discussion and action in that direction as important and urgent. That there had been a failure of some kind became clearly apparent once the CNAA understood the implications of the appointment of the Lindop Committee, and began to move both of its own accord and under external pressure towards a system of greater delegation of responsibility, and then accreditation. The CNAA's relative policy inertia between 1979 and 1984 contributed in a major way to the pressures and problems it encountered in the mid-1980s.

In February 1983 a former member of staff at the Polytechnic of North London wrote to the Chairman of the CNAA and to Sir Keith Joseph, the Secretary of State, alleging political bias and malpractice in the assessment of students in sociology and applied social studies at the Polytechnic. The letter arrived at the CNAA just before a visit to PNL, on 23 February 1983, to review the degree courses in the two subjects. In the absence of the Chief Officer in Australia, the letter was not communicated to the visiting party, which conducted its review in the normal way. The BSc (Hons) Sociology had been first approved by the CNAA in 1972, and the BA (Hons) Applied Social Studies in 1977. The visiting party agreed that both courses should continue in approval. A number of concerns were expressed, relating for example to course objectives and structures and library resources, but any reservations were in the context of awareness of the staff's 'genuine attempt to confront academic and structural problems' on the sociology course, and 'an imaginative attempt to deal with problems' on the Applied Social Studies course. The visiting party of five members from the Social Studies Board and six from the Public and Social Administration Board (accompanied by an observer from the Central Council for Education and Training in Social Work and four CNAA officers) had not found anything untoward.[80] Sir Keith, meanwhile, was confronted with allegations regarding one of his bêtes noires — PNL.

Keith Joseph had, while the Conservative Party was in opposition, been disturbed by the campus activities of student radicals, including prolonged and highly public events at PNL — discussed in a book entitled *The Rape of Reason*, one of the authors of which was to become increasingly one of his political associates. He had misgivings both about PNL and about sociology, and the new allegations touched off a train of events in which the CNAA was implicated. The Council itself had in the past been anxious about the problems at PNL, including earlier allegations about political bias in sociology. The Council's Chairman reported in 1975 that two major visits had been made to PNL in two years — an 'unusual step' — and the more recent one had recorded a 'marked improvement in the atmosphere and work of the Polytechnic'. CASS was consulting external examiners' reports and pursuing other investigations, and the course was shortly due for renewal of approval.[81] Following the accusations the Social Studies Board 'welcomed the reassurances contained in all the (external examiners') reports, and was satisfied that high academic standards were being maintained'. Over the next three years the Board continued to monitor the course, and though it made criticisms these were unrelated to bias, which was not detected. In 1978 a visit by Professor Cotgrove of the University of Bath, Professor Gould of the University of Nottingham, and Michael Young of the University of London, reported being encouraged by developments, and impressed by the thoroughness of newly-instituted course monitoring procedures.[82] Following an institutional review visit in March 1983 the report was critical of some aspects of the Polytechnic's Directorate and the Academic Board, and the lack of a sufficiently self-critical spirit in the Polytechnic, but the particular question of the allegations was not part of the review.

At very short notice Keith Joseph arranged for an HMI inspection to take place at the end of April/beginning of May 1983, and — in the Inspectors' own words — it 'came close to the period of examinations for some of the students. Teaching programmes were virtually finished on some of the courses, and some students were either engaged on personal revision or were concentrating on completion of their written assignments. The May Day Bank Holiday affected the time available for first-hand observation of classes, but the consistency of the evidence from the work seen makes it unlikely that additional observation of teaching would have fundamentally altered the main findings of this report'. The HMI arrived, in fact, at some firm conclusions, some of them supportive, some critical. It was critical mainly of student spoon-feeding, casualness in student attendance and inattention in lectures, 'academically bizarre' references in course booklets, and the narrow — that is, extreme left — viewpoints of some lecturers. The crucial sections of the report read:

> It appeared to HMI that in both teaching and marking, tutors had over-compensated because of their concern to allay the natural anxieties felt by non-traditional students about assessment procedures and examinations. They were too preoccupied by the difficulties students might face in completing projects and dissertations and, as a result, had built into the courses elaborate procedures to allow for extenuating circumstances should students fail to hand in work for assessment. For similar reasons tutors circulated quite defined revision topics well in advance of the examinations . . . Coupled with the previous references made to the air of casualness that pervaded much of the tutor/student classroom interaction, together with the narrow perspective of much of the suggested reading, it comes as no surprise that so few students 'fail'. The fail-safe procedures virtually make this an impossibility.

Academic rigour, and by implication the validation procedures of the CNAA, were impugned.[83]

The popular press had a field day when the report was available at the beginning of October, and it became known that Sir Keith Joseph intended to order an official investigation. *The Standard's* headline was 'Degree that no one could possibly fail', *The Mirror's* was 'College where nobody fails', *The Mail's*, 'A college where no one can fail'. The emphasis was different in other headlines: '"Marxist" poly faces probe', said *The Express*; 'Marxist-bias poly courses condemned', said *The Daily Telegraph*, following it with an editorial entitled 'An academic nightmare', suggesting that the polytechnics, being under local authority control were even less exposed than universities to 'proper public scrutiny'.[84] The CNAA had in the meantime conducted its own enquiry into the allegations. The Chairman of the Council asked Dr Jack Earls, a member of the Council, an engineer and Principal of Humberside College of Higher Education, together with

Dr Arnold Goldman, an Assistant Chief Officer of the CNAA, to investigate and report. They scrutinized the relevant CNAA and Polytechnic papers, met the Directorate of the Polytechnic, its own enquiry team and senior members of staff in sociology. Dr Earls reported to the Council in July that 'he and Dr Goldman had come to the conclusion that the allegations could not be substantiated'.[85] Their report was considered by the Chairmen of the CNAA's Committees, and they concurred that 'there was no evidence to support the allegations concerning the courses and the Secretary of State was informed accordingly'. At the same meeting where this was reported the Council also considered a request from the DES to comment on the HMI report.[86] The Council conceded that HMI had more evidence of what actually happened in classrooms, but emphasized that the CNAA was concerned in its validation procedures with a wider range of components and evidence of the students' experience of learning and its outcomes. It expressed its confidence in the members who took part in the CNAA's validation procedures, and in the work of the external examiners. The CNAA's boards and committees, the response indicated, were critical of much of the evidence and perspectives in the HMI report, and the Council expressed its disagreement with the report principally in the following terms:

> CNAA, on the basis of the wide range of specialist advice available to it, has found no academic 'bias' or 'unacceptable narrowing' of the courses and does not, for example, see the provision of 'hand-outs' in that light. Informality — though not slackness or discourtesy — is rightly regarded as a positive teaching technique . . . That a high proportion of non-standard entry students, whether unqualified or equivalently qualified, graduate with Second or First Class degrees testifies to the adaptation of teaching methods to this clientele . . . The popular press response to HM Inspectors' report as saying that 'no student can fail' on one or other of these courses is rejected.[87]

The CNAA was not alone in criticizing the Inspectors' report. A leading article in the *THES* castigated it for its 'ignorance of the standards that can reasonably be expected . . . and the Inspectorate's well known obsession with appearances — are the students taking proper notes/too many notes? Have they had their hair cut?'. The *TES* began its comments by saying that the report raised 'more questions than it answers'. *The Guardian* detailed a catalogue of suspicious circumstances, beginning with the Inspectorate being 'wheeled into action at short notice', looking at courses already being remodelled to remove faults already acknowledged, and producing a report which the HMI were ill-equipped to write, on the basis of a rushed and cursory inspection.[88] It was Sir Denis Rooke's view, expressed to the Secretary of State, that HMI were responsible, on a continuing basis, for knowing what went on in teaching situations. If there was indeed something wrong at PNL the HMI should have picked it up and reported on it at an earlier stage, and were themselves to blame for having been remiss. The view at PNL was clearly that whatever weaknesses there might have been in the courses as approved in the 1970s, these had been taken into account in the revised courses now soon to begin.

Sir Keith Joseph waited until April 1984 to announce his next step. Although the specific events had been triggered by a single letter of complaint, there were other problems to face at the same time. The vexed but recurring question of polytechnic status was one. The government's policy of abolishing 'quangos' and reducing levels of public expenditure and bureaucracy was another (including the disbanding of the Schools Council and cuts in the Civil Service). Although the Lindop Committee's remit was to cover *all* validation at degree level, including that of colleges by universities, it was clearly the role of the CNAA that was central to the decision to appoint the Committee. The CNAA was in the dock, and was not invited to be in any way a party to the enquiry. The establishment of the enquiry itself meant that the Secretary of State — and his advisers — were not convinced that the CNAA was of its own volition able fully to respond to the concerns of the Secretary of State, civil servants or HMI. Sir Norman Lindop, familiar with the public sector as former Director of Hatfield Polytechnic, was appointed to chair the small Committee. It comprised Mr D. Leighton Davies, former Deputy Managing Director of Racal Electronics, and five members from the academic world — Dr Joseph Dunning, former Principal of Napier College, Edinburgh; Professor Geoffrey Elton, Professor of Modern History at the University of Cambridge; Professor Elie Kedourie, Professor of Politics at the University of London; Sir Alec Merrison, former Vice-Chancellor of the University of Bristol; and Lady Warnock, Mistress of Girton College, Cambridge. It reported at the end of twelve months.

While the Committee was sitting the CNAA issued a consultative paper on future relationships with the institutions and considered the responses, particularly with regard to a proposal to introduce two modes of relationship with the CNAA. One of these, Mode B, would enable the Academic Board of an institution to have authority to validate and review all courses leading to CNAA awards, a development to which we shall return in the next chapter. In supplying evidence to the Lindop Committee, therefore, the CNAA — mainly through a recently created Chairman's Study Group — was able to underline a process already taking place inside the organization. On the one occasion that the CNAA was invited to meet with the Committee Edwin Kerr spoke of the work of 'self-analysis in which Council had been engaged for some time. The Lindop enquiry had accelerated the process'. Sir Alastair Pilkington, who had become Chairman of the CNAA barely four months before the Lindop Committee was appointed, emphasized that the Council's new proposals would involve major changes. The CNAA members present at the meeting were pressed to explain how the CNAA could 'guarantee the quality of the product', and to comment on whether it made excessive demands on institutions, to the detriment of their teaching.

The members of the Chairman's Study Group recognized the existence of the problem, and thought the new proposals would alleviate it, particularly in offering a substantial measure of autonomy to Mode B institutions. The CNAA, it was emphasized, could not — under its Charter — accept autonomy for institutions as an objective. Other issues discussed included relations with the NAB. Edwin Kerr indicated that 'with hindsight CNAA realized that the question of advice on town planning had not been well handled', but that the subsequent development of a policy of responding to NAB requests with descriptive and not comparative information had been supported by the overwhelming majority of the institutions.[89] The Lindop Committee also approached the CNAA for information at various times. Written information was provided on methods of initial validation and subsequent review of courses, methods of giving due recognition to differences between institutions, external examiners, and courses and institutions from which the CNAA had threatened to withdraw approval. The Committee also received the papers of the Working Party on Longer Term Developments, and were informed of the meeting dates of the CNAA's committees, boards, panels and visits to institutions, in order that the Lindop Committee members could attend (and advantage was in fact taken of these opportunities).[90] Other evidence to the Committee included a statement from the CDP expressing the belief that the process of validation could be simplified, that little progress had been achieved in taking account of the maturity of institutions, that 'external peer group evaluation at the institutional level' was an acceptable principle (together with the role of external examiners), that the CNAA's subject boards were an important transitional device whose value had now diminished, and that there were no 'valid academic reasons why some public sector institutions should not be self-validating'.[91] Discussion about possible forms of accreditation and its implications was taking place in the journals,[92] and the CNAA was receiving responses to its consultative document expressing a variety of attitudes towards extended partnership in validation, new and divided modes of validation, and accreditation — which was what a significant proportion of the polytechnics and major colleges of technology or higher education wanted.

The Lindop Committee reported in April 1985. It drew attention to the existence of two views of the enormous growth of public sector higher education as compared with that of the universities, one of which saw validation as a major, continuing contribution to the institutions and to the system, and the other of which saw it as an 'interruption of the historical pattern of development which brought academic autonomy to institutions as and when their circumstances and public needs justified it'. There were conflicting views, similarly, about the CNAA, on the one hand enthusiastically welcoming its detailed examination of course proposals, and on the other hand criticizing its focus on course intentions rather than delivery or outcomes, and the heavy-handedness of its procedures. This had resulted, in the Committee's view in the growth of 'a ponderous and inflexible system in which form is disproportionate to substance'. In presenting its criticisms of the CNAA's procedures the Committee was equally, but differently, critical of the validating universities, whose validation procedures were not demanding enough, and in some cases applied 'double standards, requiring less of college students . . . than they require of their own students'. The Committee's proposals for the future rested on three principles:

(i) institutions should be expected and encouraged to take responsibility for the maintenance and improvement of their own academic standards, insofar as they can and wish;

(ii) the validation system should recognize and accommodate the differences that exist between institutions in the extent to which they can appropriately take this responsibility;

(iii) the prominence given to validation in the public sector should be no more than proportionate to its significance.

At the centre of future intentions should be the safeguarding of standards, not by external validation or other forms of external control, but by the more reliable 'growth of the teaching institution as a self-critical academic community'. Present validation procedures were therefore unsatisfactory, and the CNAA's proposed new 'Mode B' was not an acceptable solution to the problems — it involved too many controls to be appropriate for some institutions. The Committee therefore considered three options. Option 1 was to keep validation in some form for all the institutions, but provide for a broader range of delegated powers and responsibilities; option 2 was to bring the CNAA system of validation to an end, allowing those institutions which wished to have external validation to obtain it from a university or public sector institution, and to give degree-awarding powers to any institution teaching at degree level that wanted them; and the third — the Committee's preferred option — was:

as an intermediate position, to make provision allowing any institution that so wished to apply to the Secretary of State for power to award its own degrees and thus to become self-validating. Those that did not wish to apply, or whose applications were unsuccessful, would continue to be externally validated, although there would again be a broader range of delegated powers, including accreditation, available to institutions judged suitable.

The report discussed in detail the implications of accreditation (under which formal responsibility for degrees would rest with the CNAA, and which would enable the CNAA to withdraw accreditation if it saw fit), and full 'autonomy in validation' (under which institutions would award their own degrees, without this carrying any 'necessary implications for their title, status or funding, or for the types of educational provision they make'). The Committee believed that both forms of greater institutional independence should be available, but also responded to the criticisms it had heard of the

CNAA's validation procedures — including excessive paperwork, lack of consistency and coordination between the constituent parts of the CNAA (for example across the boards, and between course reviews and institutional reviews), and insufficient emphasis on 'the delivery and outcome of courses'. It was with the transfer of attention and resources from the scrutiny and discussion of documents to the more difficult task of assessing delivery and outcomes that the Committee was ultimately most concerned. In respect of many of the criticisms the Committee acknowledged that the CNAA was already taking steps to tackle the problems. The Committee concluded:

> The importance of the contribution made by the CNAA to higher education is beyond question; without it the public sector could not have developed so far and so fast over the past twenty years.. The very speed of that development, however, makes it imperative that the CNAA should shake off its apparent tendency to rigidity if it is to be able to continue to foster rather than stifle the achievement of high standards in institutions.

It believed that the majority of institutions would wish to continue to be associated with the CNAA in some way, and that the CNAA would continue to have an important role as 'a central focus for the public sector, uniquely placed to take initiatives to foster academic developments.[93]

By this point in 1985 the Lindop Committee had presented a challenging set of options, the CNAA was moving quickly to consult and plan in advance of, and beyond, the Lindop Report, and Sir Keith Joseph's decisions were awaited following on the enquiry he had ordered.

Notes

1 CN (1980) Funding and Organization of Courses in Higher Education: memorandum from the Council to the Select Committee on Education, Science and Arts, 24 March.
2 House of Commons (1980) *Fifth Report from the Education, Science and Arts Committee, The Funding and Organization of Courses in Higher Education, I*, pp. 1xxxviii-1xxxix.
3 Open University and Council for National Academic Awards (1973) A Joint Statement, July.
4 *The Council: Its Place in British Higher Education*, CNAA, 1979, p. 17.
5 Christopher Ball (1985) 'The advancement of education' in Dorma Urwin (Ed.) *Fitness for Purpose: Essays in higher education by Christopher Ball*, Society for Research into Higher Education and NFER-Nelson, pp. 10–12.
6 Lord Annan (1976) 'University challenge', *The Guardian*, 25 March.
7 Lord Crowther-Hunt (1983) 'Policy making and accountability in higher education' in Michael Shattock (Ed.) *The Structure and Governance of Higher Education*, Society for Research into Higher Education, pp. 47–8.
8 Lord Annan (1982) 'British higher education 1960–80: A personal retrospect', *Minerva*, 20, pp. 1–2.
9 Mark Carlisle (1980) 'The future development of higher education', *Coombe Lodge Report*, 13, 13: *Polytechnics in the 1980s*, p. 533.

10 DES and SED (1978) *Higher Education into the 1990s: A Discussion Document*, 1978; Peter David (1978) 'Ups and downs of finding a way over the hump', *Times Higher Education Supplement*, 19 May. See also E.G. Edwards *et al.* (1978) 'Into the 1990s — Projection or policy?', *Times Higher Education Supplement*, 27 October.

11 Kerr to directors and principals, 12 July 1979.

12 CN (1980) Memorandum to the Select Committee, 24 March.

13 'Cuts "may close some universities"', *The Guardian*, 19 October 1979.

14 '20,000 fewer places for students by 1985', and editorial, 'Universities under the knife', *The Times*, 3 July 1981.

15 *Times Higher Education Supplement*, 1 January 1982.

16 *Report of the Working Group on the Management of Higher Education in the Maintained Sector*, HMSO, 1978, 13, pp. 56–7.

17 Sir Denis Rooke, HS interview.

18 Council of Local Educational Authorities (1981) *The Future of Higher Education in the Maintained Sector: A Consultative Paper*, CLEA, pp. 11.

19 Bidy Pasmore (1981a) 'National body to run polytechnics and colleges', *Times Education Supplement*, 30 January 1981; and (1981b) 'The great takeover bid', *Times Education Supplement*, 20 February.

20 David Lloyd Jones (1980) 'The future of higher education in the public sector', *Coombe Lodge Report*, 13, 2: *Where Do We Go from Here?*, p. 41.

21 CN (1981) Response to the Government's Consultative Document on Higher Education in England Outside the Universities, 20 November.

22 For a study of the NAB see Nigel Robin Stinton (1985) 'The National Advisory Body for Public Sector Higher Education: An account of past development and present practice', MSc in Educational Studies dissertation, University of Oxford.

23 CN (1982) Possible Role of CNAA in Relation to Interim National Advisory Board for Local Authority Higher Education in England: A Discussion Document, 28 September, circulated 4 October.

24 Kerr to all CNAA members, 23 January 1983.

25 CN (1983) Relations between the Council for National Academic Awards and the National Advisory Body, 13 August.

26 Cmin, 19 September 1983.

27 CN (1983) Response to the NAB Secretariat Proposals for Courses in Town and Country Planning (30 August), September.

28 CN (1984) Relationship between the CNAA and the NAB: Statement of CNAA's present position and notice of intention to consult further with institutions, 19 March. See also Cmin, 14 December 1983 and Kerr to directors and principals, 20 January 1984.

29 CN (1984) Relationship between the CNAA and the NAB, 19 March.

30 CN (1984) Response to the Government's Consultative Document concerning its review of the National Advisory Body for Local Authority Higher Education in England.

31 Speech to the AUT/NATFHE/NUS lobby, 1 March 1983.

32 *The Economist*, 21 April 1984, p. 26.

33 Paul Flather (1985) 'Tories squash life out of the polys', *New Statesman*, 19 July, p. 89.

34 C.J. Boys (1984) *Inside a Polytechnic* (Expectations of Higher Education: Institutional Case Study No. 2), Brunel University, p. 3. See also Department of Industry (1977) *Education and Management: A discussion Paper*, p. 6; C. Bacon *et al.* (1979) 'Employers' opinions of university and polytechnic graduates', *The Vocational Aspect of Education*, 31, 8; Judith Roizen and Mark Jepson (1985) *Degrees for Jobs: Employer Expectations of Higher Education*, Society for Research into Higher Education and NFER-Nelson.

35 Clem Adelman and Ian Gibbs (1979) *A Study of Student Choice in the Context of Institutional Change: Synoptic Report*, p. 32.

36 Ian Gibbs and John Harland (1984) *The Diversified Colleges: Student and Graduate Experience. Short Report*, July, pp. 19 and 25.

37 Edwin Kerr (1980) 'A CNAA view on the future of higher education', *Coombe Lodge Report*, 13, 13: *Polytechnics in the 1980s*, p. 537.

38 *Future Development of CNAA's Academic Policies at Undergraduate Level*, CNAA, 1983. See also R.A. Barnett (1984) 'Innovation and consultation', *Times Higher Education Supplement*, 10 August.

39 Committee of Inquiry into the Engineering Profession (1980) *Engineering Our Future*, HMSO.

40 CN (1980) Council's Response to the Report of the Committee of Inquiry into the Engineering Profession, July.

41 CN (1982) Development and Validation of Engineering Degree Courses, December.

42 *Engineering Our Future*, p. 24; CN (1983) Engineering First Degree Courses, 26 October, policy statement and Attachment C.

43 S.A. Reid and R.A. Farrar (1985) *What Makes a BEng Course: A Report on a Symposium*, CNAA.

44 CN (n.d.) *Opportunities in Higher Education for Mature Students*.

45 Norman Evans (1984) *Access to Higher Education: non-standard entry to CNAA first degree and DipHE courses'*, CNAA; Norman Evans (1988) *The Assessment of Prior Learning*, CNAA.

46 Quoted in (1984) *Access/Preparatory Courses*, CNAA, p. 3.

47 Maurice Kogan (1986) *Education Accountability*, Hutchinson, p. 78.

48 CN (1983) Committee for Academic Policy, Principle 3 — the Council's general education criteria, 4 November.

49 CN (1980) Committee for Institutions, Institutional Reviews: notes for the guidance of institutions, July.

50 *Files on Courses in Institutions (FOCII): Policy and Operation*, CNAA, October 1984.

51 CN (1983) Committee for Scotland, Report to Council on the ninth and tenth meetings . . . 22 June; CN, *Annual Report 1983–84*, pp. 11–12.

52 Cmin, 11 December 1979; CAP (1981) Report of the CNAA to the Director of Education, Hong Kong, March; CN, *Annual Reports*, 1980, pp. 11–12; 1981, pp. 12–13; 1985–86, p. 12; Rooke, HS interview.

53 HMCI Norris (1982) Initial Comments Submitted by HMCI England, 18 June; The Work of the Council in Retrospect: The Views of HM Inspectorate in Scotland, n.d. Both with Working Party on Longer Term Developments, Specific Suggestions contained in Submissions from Interested Parties, 10 September 1982.

54 CNAA (1982) Working Party on Longer Term Developments: A Response, CDP paper 82–47, 5 March.

55 Cmin, 5 July 1982.

56 Working Party on Longer Term Developments, Draft Second Report to Council, 7 December 1983.

57 Committee of Enquiry (1985) *Academic Validation in Public Sector Higher Education*, (The Lindop Report) HMSO, p. 1.

58 CDP minutes, 16 November 1983.

59 CN, Revised Guidelines for Joint Validation and Review of Courses at Newcastle-upon-Tyne Polytechnic (1982/83 session); CN, Developments in Validation, n.d. (Newcastle Polytechnic File 41.2, Joint Validation (1) Areas of work); Clark, HS interview.

60 Committee for Institutions minutes, 15 November 1983.

61 Summary of Conclusions and Proposals from the Academic Board of Newcastle

upon Tyne Polytechnic, arising from Consideration of a Report of the Two Year Experimental Period of Joint Validation, P.F. Torode (Academic Registrar), 14 October 1983 (File 41.2).

62 The Future Relationship between Newcastle upon Tyne Polytechnic and the CNAA (a paper from Newcastle upon Tyne Polytechnic dated June 1984).

63 CI minutes, 15 November 1983.

64 CI minutes, 13 June 1984.

65 Portsmouth Polytechnic, Academic Council, Validation: a discussion paper designed to assist in the formulation of policy and the definition of long term objects (with a paper on monitoring and validation) [1984] (Newcastle Polytechnic File 41.2).

66 Working Party on Longer Term Developments minutes, 11 June 1984; An Alternative to the Newcastle Model (paper with Working Party min).

67 CI minutes, 13 June 1984.

68 Norman Lindop (1985) 'Validation revisited', *Times Higher Education Supplement*, 29 November, p. 15.

69 CDP Chairman to E. Kerr, 16 November 1983, CDP paper 83–217.

70 David Francis (1983) 'Partners in validation: An exploration of the perceptions of their validating body held in five colleges of higher education associated with the CNAA', University of Sussex MA project, p. 30 and passim; David Francis (1985) 'Validation: Perceptions of partnership, *Journal of Further and Higher Education*, 9, 2, p. 29.

71 Committee on Longer Term Developments minutes, 11 June 1984.

72 Sir Denis Rooke, HS interview.

73 Gutteridge, HS interview.

74 Sir Norman Lindop and Tolley, HS interviews.

75 *Procedures for the Validation of Courses 1982*, CNAA, p. 1.

76 CAP minutes, 14 June 1984.

77 Sir Norman Lindop, HS interview.

78 David Billing (1983) 'Practice and criteria in validation under the CNAA' in Clive H. Church (Ed.) *Practice and Perspective in Validation*, Society for Research into Higher Education.

79 Kerr, HS interview.

80 CASS, Social Studies Board and Public and Social Administration Board, Polytechnic of North London, Report of a Visit on 23 February 1983 . . .

81 Cmin, 4 November 1975.

82 CN, Summary of the Validation History of the BSc (Hons) Sociology and the BA (Hons) Applied Social Studies at the Polytechnic of North London, with Cmin, 13 December 1983.

83 DES (1983) Report by HM Inspectors on the Polytechnic of North London: BSc Sociology, BA Applied Social Studies Courses, pp. 3–4, 14–15 and passim.

84 *The Evening Standard*, 4 October 1983; *The Daily Mirror*, 5 October 1983; *The Daily Mail*, 5 October 1983; *The Daily Express*, 5 October 1983; *The Telegraph*, 5 and 6 October 1983.

85 Cmin, 5 July 1983.

86 *ibid*.

87 CN, The Publication of Reports by HM Inspectors: with particular reference to the publication of HM Inspectors' report on the Polytechnic of North London . . ., with Cmin, 13 December 1983.

88 *Times Higher Education Supplement*, 7 October 1983; *Times Education Supplement*, 7 October 1983; *The Guardian*, 7 October 1983.

89 Report of a Meeting . . . between the Chairman and Members of the Chairman's Study Group and the Lindop Committee of Enquiry . . . 23 January 1984, with CAIP minutes, 14 February 1985.

90 Report on Interrelations to Date between Council and the Committee of Enquiry . . ., with CAIP minutes, 15 January 1984.
91 Academic Validation in Public Sector Higher Education: evidence submitted by the CDP to the Committee of Enquiry, CDP paper 84–111.
92 For example Roger Adams (1984) 'From validation to accreditation', *NATFHE Journal*, December.
93 Committee of Enquiry (1985) *Academic Validation in Public Sector Higher Education*, pp. 6–7, 12–13, 19–22, 32–9, 40–7 and 48–60.

Chapter 10

Making Responses

When Sir Keith Joseph and his fellow Secretaries of State for Scotland, Wales and Northern Ireland issued a Green Paper on *The Development of Higher Education into the 1990s* in May 1985, the Lindop Committee had already reported. The Green Paper recognized that the Lindop Report had proposed major changes 'designed both to secure more responsible and effective control of standards and to meet the aspirations of institutions for greater autonomy', and the government was considering the recommendations.[1] Other advice was to be forthcoming on the future shape of higher education — notably through the Scottish Tertiary Education Advisory Council — but the Green Paper set out to address policy questions applicable generally to the United Kingdom. The contexts in which the CNAA operated were changing yet again, this time with government policy moving toward the establishment of new directions for higher education as a whole.

The starting point, and dominant theme of the Green Paper, was Britain's poor economic performance, with its implications for manpower, standards, subject priorities, research and the promotion of what it called 'the entrepreneurial spirit'. There were clear messages of stronger government intervention to give direction to higher education, including through a policy of 'selectivity and concentration' in research, and the slimming down of the system in response to an expected decline in student numbers in the 1990s: some institutions might need to be closed or merged, and other 'large changes' might be required.[2] The message for subject balance was equally clear. The government believed it to be right to maintain 'a distinct emphasis on technological and directly vocational courses at all levels, leading to a switch in output in favour of graduates and diplomates with corresponding qualifications'. While considering that for many occupations a 'rigorous arts course provides an excellent preparation', the Green Paper made it clear in the section on subject balance that 'the main thrust . . . is towards technological and vocational courses'. Arts provision should 'to some extent be concentrated in the interests of cost-effectiveness', and consideration for quality argued 'that for the most part it should be within the university sector':

It will be subject to rationalisation, and admission to the arts in the universities will continue to be highly competitive ... Those responsible for counselling intending students (and, perhaps, particularly girls) about their subject choices should be aware that the proportion of arts places in higher education as a whole can be expected to shrink.[3]

The government believed that a decline in student numbers of some 14 per cent would take place between 1990 and 1996, and offered planning and funding predictions against that background. All the discussion in the Green Paper, however, was geared directly to improving the 'work orientation' of higher education, bringing higher education closer to industry, commerce and the public services, and improving the output of higher education not by increasing but by concentrating resources. In the section on research, for instance, there was reference to academics needing to 'keep up with relevant scholarship', but there was 'no evidence that all academic staff must engage in research'. Greater concentration and selectivity in this area might mean that 'some departments or even whole universities will lose research funding from the UGC'. A modest level of research 'almost wholly of applied character' would continue to take place in public sector institutions.[4] The government agreed that the polytechnics needed to improve their public image, and that other colleges were looking for a change of status, but whether 'polytechnics or other principal colleges' should award degrees in their own names was being considered in the light of the Lindop Report.[5]

The UGC and the NAB had offered substantial advice to the government regarding the future of higher education, and though both had recognized the centrality of the demographic and accountability questions being addressed by the government, neither had carried the argument as far as the Green Paper. Former HMI Clive Booth, Director of Oxford Polytechnic, reflected on the Green Paper a year after its publication and asked whether the government in fact had a higher education policy at all. The Green Paper had not yet led either to a White Paper or to a comprehensive statement of government policy. There were, however, enough clues from the Green Paper and government action to make an 'informed guess'. The main policy planks seemed to be:

Reduce public funding in real terms.

Tailor the number of places broadly to demographic trends.

Discourage entry by squeezing financial support for students.

Cut the social sciences and expand technology.

Government policies were expenditure-led, based on Treasury views of what the country could afford: 'one beauty of this approach to determining expenditure is that ministers feel relieved of any great need to debate policies on their own merits'.[6] The UGC produced what was described as 'one of its most critical statements ever',[7] in response to the Green Paper. Whatever the demographic predictions the country would continue to want at least as many graduates. The Green Paper had 'displayed little understanding of the problems and cost of restructuring the university system to meet the government's various objectives'. The UGC was 'disappointed' and 'concerned', and drew attention to a range of 'unrealistic assumptions' and 'inconsistencies' in the Green Paper. Sir Keith Joseph had spoken to the CVCP in an attempt to reassure the universities about the future of the humanities, and the UGC welcomed the clarification:

> it is unfortunate that it was possible to interpret the Green Paper as suggesting that there were particular problems in the humanities which were not shared by the sciences. As you said, the training of the mind provided by an arts course is highly valued by industry in its own right . . . Vocational relevance is not confined to courses preparing students for a limited number of specific kinds of employment.[8]

The problems at this point, as the UGC and higher education generally recognized, was not only how to respond to the government's intention to restrain spending and restructure the system, but also how to debate the government's heavy emphasis on vocational courses. Public sector higher education had traditionally defined its role in terms of a strong vocational commitment, and the universities were now having to reinterpret or re-present their roles in response to critical and mounting pressures.

When, in 1984, the NAB was seeking responses to its own draft of advice to the government, the CNAA emphasized the successes and further potential of the public sector, and the characteristics of the public sector that needed to be strengthened. It underlined the virtues of the peer review system, the increasingly complex demands on higher education that had to be met, and the problems of 'parity of esteem' for the public sector.[9] Like other bodies, the CNAA was anxious about the resource base for the maintenance of standards, and like other bodies this issue was prominent in its response to the Green Paper itself. The CNAA's Committee for Academic and Institutional Policy (CAIP) took a first step towards formulating a response in June 1985, when it agreed to urge the CNAA to make 'a robust response to the Green Paper, challenging its assumptions, putting forward positive alternatives to the government's plans, and highlighting the centrality of the issues of resources'. In preparing the response it asked for the following to be emphasized:

(i) the Green Paper rested on fundamentally unsound assumptions — about the relationship between higher education and the economy, about demand for higher education, and about the resource implications of government proposals;

(ii) the paper showed a lack of any real policy on research in the public sector;

(iii) the quality and value of humanities, fine art, combined studies and sandwich education must be defended;

(iv) DES's proposed performance indicators should be scrutinised.[10]

The CNAA's consultations on the Green Paper included a conference organized by CAIP, and after much deliberation the Council responded with as positive a statement as it could muster. It underlined the contribution the CNAA had made to the development of the public sector, indicated that the Green Paper categories of arts and science, liberal and vocational, pure and applied, did not fit many of the courses validated by the CNAA, and suggested that it was the duty of higher education not simply to respond to society's perceived needs, but 'to help to shape the expression of those needs through critical discussion'. Even a modest move towards science and technology could cause 'irreversible damage to arts and social studies without achieving the desired objectives for science and engineering' — for which it was not possible to find enough qualified candidates. The Council strongly defended arts, humanities and social studies for the general and specific skills they developed, and questioned the assumption in the Green Paper that arts provision should be concentrated in the university sector. The equal part that the public sector played in these areas related, among other things, to the opportunities they provided for mature students. The CNAA believed that the public sector also needed to be congratulated on the level of research activity it had achieved, and believed that there were no grounds on which to distinguish between the two sectors 'in their concern for research'. With regard to resources, the CNAA pointed out that higher education had in general reacted negatively and defensively to the Green Paper 'because they feel under attack'. Institutions would not welcome changes if they feared they would be worse off at the end of the day, and the Council therefore advised the government in its White Paper to provide incentives to both institutions and students 'to adopt a more flexible approach to higher education'.[11]

In its comments on the Green Paper, and simultaneously on the review of higher education in Scotland by STEAC, the CNAA was making a strong defence of the public sector, its courses, its standards, its range of students, its research and its record in, and potential for, responsiveness to the constituencies with which it worked. Although the CNAA's own position was uncertain it continued to represent the views of the public sector and to explore the possibilities of development for its institutions and processes. In its response to the Green Paper, for example, it emphasized both the research the CNAA itself was conducting on public sector students and their careers, and new opportunities for students being developed by the CNAA.

In the latter case the reference was to a Credit Accumulation and Transfer Scheme (CATS) to be launched in the spring of 1986. Under this scheme students would be able to register direct with the Council:

> to be given credit for existing qualifications or experience, select an individual package of courses chosen from those offered by HE institutions and other bodies, and ultimately achieve a CNAA award. It has been particularly interesting to see, even before the public launch of this scheme, how many employers are interested in CNAA accreditation of their own training courses.[12]

This scheme was in fact launched in March 1986 with the support of the Minister for Higher Education, George Walden, and a new Registrar, Derek Pollard, was appointed to direct it. It was initially intended to begin as a pilot scheme in the London area — a proposal which proved to be impractical, and it admitted any intending student who could get to the CNAA office or to any of the participating UK institutions. By the end of September of that year some thirty-five universities and sixty-five public sector institutions had expressed their support for the scheme, and in the session 1985–86 over 600 individual students sought the service of the CAT scheme, with some 200 being placed in courses by the end of September. Local consortia of institutions were being established, and by 1986 more than sixty industrial and commercial concerns had approached CATS with a view to their in-house training courses being recognized for CNAA awards — and two such schemes were approved on a pilot basis. Twenty-four professional bodies had at the same time sought agreement for programmes of continuing professional development to be recognized within the scheme.[13]

The main stimulus for the development of the country's first such scheme of credit accumulation and transfer had been the 1979 report of a project funded by the DES and directed by Peter Toyne. The Toyne feasibility study of 'educational credit transfer' itself followed a decade of discussion of the possibility of awarding and transferring credit, and the Toyne report acknowledged both previous proposals and such developments as the growth of modular courses and the agreement between the CNAA and the Open University to enable students 'to transfer between them with credit for past studies'. Gordon Oakes, as Minister of State, had held a consultative meeting in 1977, a Steering Committee met for the first time later that year (including Edwin Kerr from the CNAA and Ray Rickett from the CDP), and Toyne was appointed Project Director from the University of Exeter.[14] No national scheme was launched as a result of the Toyne Report, but the CNAA began to take a direct interest in the possibilities of credit transfer, and not only within the United Kingdom. One of the Assistant Chief Officers, John Salmon, suggested in 1981, for example, that 'there is an urgent need to consider some system of credit transfer extending beyond the bounds of one country'.[15] The CNAA's 1983 conference on the future of courses at the undergraduate level provoked further interest, as did the work of Norman Evans, supported by the CNAA, on the assessment of prior experience for advanced standing in higher education. Evans, together with two polytechnic directors, suggested to the CNAA that it should take an initiative in expanding student opportunities through a credit accumulation system, under which the CNAA would validate courses and register students, and develop reliable procedures for crediting students with assessed 'experiental learning'. Edwin Kerr convened a Working Party on Credit Transfer and Accumulation in October 1983 and it began the process of considering a pilot scheme, which would include a central registry and data bank, take account of differences in existing courses and the possible need to promote new ones 'along the line of modular schemes for the purpose of an inter-institutional scheme', allow students to choose their own path through available courses — with an effective counselling service, and identify the problems of funding, course levels, the involvement of other bodies, and so on.[16]

In 1984, given that the CNAA was under scrutiny, with the appointment of the Lindop Committee and the known background of suspicion or hostility at ministerial and senior civil servant levels, it was surprising and reassuring to the CNAA to receive a letter about 'professional updating and credit transfer' at the end of July. The letter, from Peter Brooke, Parliamentary Under-Secretary of State at the DES, came some four months after the appointment of the Lindop Committee and invited the CNAA to play an initiating role in achieving collaboration to develop a credit transfer scheme. The aim was to enable professionals to undertake part-time or full-time study after having entered the labour market, to build on their first degrees, add to their qualifications, and increase their mobility. This suggested some kind of modular structure of a coherent whole, which should enable professionals changing their place of employment to study at 'major centres around the country' and 'continue to add to their collection of successfully completed modules leading towards a qualification'. The role of the CNAA was seen as central:

> To achieve this goal requires some catalysis of collaboration between a number of further and higher education institutions around the country. It seems to me that the CNAA as a common validating body in the public sector is in a unique position to initiate this process of collaboration. I should like to suggest therefore that the CNAA takes the lead in getting together an appropriate group of further and higher education institutions, between them covering as much of the country as possible and including universities if this is feasible. It would be particularly helpful, I believe, to involve the Open University . . .[17]

This was welcome endorsement both of the CNAA's interest in credit transfer, and of the kind of continuing role Ministers might be expecting the CNAA to continue to play. It went ahead with the planning of a scheme which would enable students to transfer in this way, and also to take advantage of the learning experience at their places of employment. The Council adopted the CAT scheme, intended to be transbinary, and to enable students to pursue a flexible course with maximum possible exemption for their existing qualifications and learning.[18] It established an Advisory Board, charged particularly with continuing the exploration of the potential for recognizing industrial training and prior learning and its assessment.

The scheme developed rapidly, particularly by bringing into existence consortia — either regional or covering particular subject areas — of educational institutions and associated industrial or other organizations. In October 1986 some thirty consortia were believed to exist — the speed of growth made it difficult to know exactly how many — in various parts of the country and in subject areas such as education, art and design, and building. There was a strong movement to integrate in-house industrial and professional training into the scheme, and there were difficulties in establishing a proper financial base for the scheme and for the consortia.[19] Peter Toyne was chairing the Advisory Board, which by late 1986 had discussed regulations, a pattern of awards 'providing a network of bridges and ladders', a student handbook and other features of the scheme. Progress was being made towards setting up an advisory service for students, a seminar had been held on the accreditation of non-traditional programmes of study and the assessment of prior experiential learning, and the central registry was promoting a flow of information and contacts amongst consortia and institutions. The scheme was seeing itself as an 'academic broker' in relation to the educational and training needs of industry.[20] The CNAA was offering a perspective on the future for educational institutions and employers, for professional bodies and for students, and it was supporting research into such areas as the assessment of experiential learning and the applicability of a system of credit transfer to in-service education for teachers in Scotland.[21] The scheme was based on a credit points system, leading to a Certificate of Higher Education, a Diploma of Higher Education, a degree or honours degree, a postgraduate diploma or a master's degree, with up to half the credit for the qualification (and exceptionally more) being allowable for prior learning.[22] The CAT scheme had rapidly become one of the major new landmarks in higher education in the 1980s.

The fact that, in its response to the Green Paper, the CNAA could point to research it was supporting on the careers of public sector graduates indicated that the Council had established a capacity for undertaking or supporting such activities. Interest, particularly at officer level, in establishing some kind of research and development unit surfaced strongly in 1977, when proposals for such a unit emerged for discussion. The proposals were in fact an adjunct of those for what became the Committee for Academic Policy (CAP), and initially there was some confusion amongst the Council's committees and boards about what was being suggested, and some mixed reactions to the suggestions. In a paper in March 1977 on the creation of such a unit the concept of a research and development unit gave place to one of a Development Services Unit, the concept that was to become adopted.[23] Discussions were still taking place hesitantly in 1978 when the Council complained of the lack of evidence supporting a draft Council response to the government's *Higher Education into the 1990s*. Edwin Kerr, responding, acknowledged that the Council 'did not have the machinery to undertake the necessary research', and commented that 'if a Research and Development Unit were established within the Council at some future date then such work could be undertaken'.[24] By the beginning of 1979 CAP was making specific proposals to the Council for the formation of a Development Services Unit (DSU), and the final decision was taken a year later when the General Committee approved the resources for the establishment of the Unit.[25] The Unit was initially to be directed by Bryan Overy, Registrar for Technology, but he became Secretary to the Council on the death of Barrie Bleach, and the DSU was established in 1981 with Rita Austin as Registrar for Development Services. By mid-1982 the DSU Steering Group had given priority to funding two projects on courses with supervised work experience, work on the CNAA's own information services, and projects on the profiling of institutions, the teaching of design management, and access to higher education by students without standard qualifications.[26] For the next four years, therefore, the DSU serviced some of the CNAA's own needs for research and data — including for the CATS development — and supported work elsewhere that related to the development of strategic areas of curriculum development in public sector higher education. The new service was responding in part to long-standing criticism in the public sector of the lack of both adequate data and sufficient research.

In 1984 a new proposal emanated from the General Committee, initiated by the Council's Chairman, Sir Alastair Pilkington, for a major extension of work in this field, at least for an initial period. The proposal was for a Development Fund. Sir Denis Rooke had sought to strengthen the finances of the CNAA, at a time when an unexpected influx of students into public sector institutions had also resulted in a very substantial surplus from the increased fees paid to the CNAA. There were Council members who pressed for the money to be fed back into the local authorities by a further reduction in student fees (one had already been implemented). The proposal pressed strongly by Sir Alastair Pilkington was for a sum of £540,000 a year (the interest on £6 million) to be used for a three-year period to support development projects. There were other Council members who opposed the proposal on the grounds that such development initiatives would be unlikely to bring actual improvements to the system. Opposition to the proposed fund, as expressed by HMI assessors and others, did not, however, carry the day, and the Development Fund was agreed:

The majority of members took the view that research and development work in higher education was an area which had been seriously underfunded in the past and expressed strong support for the establishment of the Development Fund as a means of enabling institutions, and also CNAA itself, to undertake developmental initiatives which would not otherwise be possible.[27]

A third of the budget for the new Fund was to cover 'applied research and research-and-development projects' of the kind already supported by the DSU, and the remainder was for new developmental initiatives.[28] A Development Fund Sub-Committee (of the Committee for Academic and Institutional Policy) was established to oversee the Fund 'initially for three years', to be deployed 'primarily for educational development initiatives and innovations in polytechnics and colleges which are aimed at securing improvements in the quality of course delivery'. Projects with possible outcomes applicable across more than one institution would be particularly favoured. The delivery of intended outcomes was to be monitored, and results were to be disseminated as widely as possible.[29] Under a new Registrar, Alan Crispin, the DSU undertook, together with the Sub-Committee, to establish priorities and procedures, and launch and administer the Development Fund. An invitation to apply for the funding of projects resulted in the receipt of over 600 outline proposals. From then on the Sub-Committee and the officers played an active role in approving, negotiating, managing and monitoring projects. The project areas which emerged initially as priorities and indicated both the interests of the institutions and their readiness to explore and improve their own practices, were — procedures for internal validation and evaluation; assessment and external examiners; experiential learning; improving the supply of skilled graduates in engineering; the use of Open University materials in public sector institutions; distance learning; and access to higher education.[30] Once substantial grants for developmental work in these areas had been allocated a small grants scheme was agreed, with the aim of ensuring that 'an impact can be made more quickly across a wider spread of institutions'.[31]

In 1987, when the Sub-Committee was conducting an interim review of the working of the Fund, it recorded the processing of over 800 applications, a 1:10 approval rate, and a set of priorities which reflected both the needs and interests of institutions and those of the CNAA and its perspectives on developments in higher education: access; open learning; teaching, learning and curriculum development; credit accumulation and transfer; assessment and external examiners; databases on students in higher education; internal validation and evaluation; higher education and work. Project committees had been established to cover clusters of cognate projects, the officers were working closely with prospective researchers and with projects, and a major dissemination effort was under way.[32] Development Fund grants went both to polytechnics and colleges with track records of work in the research and development field, but also to other institutions anxious to make progress in research directions — in both cases related to professional concerns and institutional development. Grants were also directed towards work on system-relevant issues —for instance, the vocational nature of higher education, and CNAA-validated courses in particular; the relationship of institutions and the labour market; access courses, and external examiners. It was clear from the response that public sector institutions had felt themselves starved of resources to examine their own procedures, problems and potential. In addition to the project committees the DSU ran workshops on areas of potential interest — notably where there were multiple proposals emerging in a particular area of potential importance, and in general cross-institution collaboration was encouraged. Bids were also invited for work in areas identified as of general interest to the system, and work was supported that would have relevance for the CNAA itself and higher education more widely. This was the case, for example, with the work on CNAA graduates, their employment and experience after leaving college, on vocationalism, and on databases on students in higher education.[33]

At the end of three years, given other developments affecting the CNAA, the Fund was not continued, though the work of the Development Services Unit was continued at approximately its resource level before the Fund was created, and with objectives adjusted to the changing circumstances of the CNAA and public sector higher education. Through both CATS and the Development Fund, and in other ways, the CNAA had, however, initiated and supported developments designed to enhance opportunities for students, improve the flow of data into the CNAA, the institutions and higher education generally, and develop essential processes of self-validation and evaluation. It had been directing attention to such curriculum areas as design management, and sponsoring development work in a range of topics related to teaching and learning, and to the enhancement of standards in the planning and delivery of courses. Increasingly the process had become one of responsibility for development work of these kinds with other funding bodies — including the Manpower Services Commission and then the Training Agency, the Design Council and others. All of these developments towards widening access and improving performance had been taking place in the conditions of a harsh economic climate.

While peforming these functions for public sector higher education the CNAA remained within the tensions concerning its future relations with institutions, and possibly concerning its own future. There was to be a year's hiatus from the publication of the Lindop Report in April 1985 to the response by the Secretary of the State in March 1986. In the meantime the Council's consultative process was aimed at exploring further developments in the validation and review process, including through the establishment of a Chairman's Study Group in July 1984. What was involved at this point was the pursuit of the promise and the expectations generated by debates leading up to the blue book and by that document itself, together with the sense of threat that had accompanied events leading up to the Secretary of State's decision to inaugurate the Lindop enquiry. The Council's interest in 1984 was to continue a process, and to anticipate events.

In December 1984 the Council adopted as a basis for consultation a set of proposals from the Chairman's Study Group aimed at preserving a nationally-based system of external peer review and at providing 'a major incentive to all institutions associated with the Council progressively to exercise greater authority . . . for the maintenance and enhancement of academic standards in partnership with the Council'. Other objectives were to recognize the 'complementary and mutually supportive role' of the CNAA and the institutions, and to ensure that validation was conducted in ways which would maintain and improve standards but also be cost-effective. This was the basis for the proposal for two types of institution — Mode A, which would involve a 'positive and deliberate development of the relationship between institutions and Council', and Mode B which would go further and involve a new form of relationship 'whereby the Academic Board of an institution exercises authority for the validation and review of all taught courses leading to CNAA awards'. In the latter case institutions would have to satisfy the Council as to their 'proven record of experience and achievement', their objectivity in the evaluation of proposed and existing courses, and their record of acting 'decisively thereafter'.[34] Responses from the institutions to these proposals ranged from disquiet to hostility — though not always for the same reasons. Initial responses from the CNAA's own committees were to say the least lukewarm — mainly on the grounds that nothing much would be changed, and the proposal was divisive — a view also strongly argued by the diversified former colleges of education. The larger established institutions tended to emphasize that the proposals did not meet their aspirations, that the proposal for two modes fell short of accreditation proposals already under discussion, that the advantages of the two modes and transition from one to the other were unclear, and that it was 'inappropriate, artificial, divisive and invidious'. The Committee of Officers was reported as expressing disquiet at the haste with which the proposals had been developed, and 'at CNAA's move away from a validating role'.[35]

The Chairman's Study Group reported to the Council in March 1985, before the Lindop Report was published, on its consideration of the responses to the consultative document. The Group had accepted the force of the arguments against the two modes, and the majority of the Council concurred, taking the view that it was preferable to regard institutions as being 'on a single continuum, albeit a continuum which in practice had various distinct points along it'. The Council Chairman expressed the view that pending the publication of the Lindop Report it was important to continue to develop the Council's thinking about future forms of relationships, and to be prepared to implement changes more quickly than in the past. The majority of the Council's members also agreed with the view of the Study Group that 'the arguments advanced by a number of institutions in favour of the grant to institutions of even greater authority than that envisaged under Mode B deserved serious consideration'. It was generally accepted that this would include ways by which the CNAA might delegate 'not only powers to validate courses but also powers to approve courses and to award degrees, subject to periodic review'. It was also underlined that since institutions were generally not corporate bodies the CNAA had to be sure that academic boards were sufficiently free of local authority control to be able to exercise appropriate control over their own affairs. The benefits of external peer review should also, it was emphasized, not be lost. The Chairman's Study Group was asked to explore further how 'further powers might be delegated by Council to institutions, including powers to approve courses and award degrees'. It was also asked to consider not only what was possible under the existing Charter, but also what changes might be necessary, and to have appropriate discussions with officials and Ministers.[36] The boundaries of the CNAA's definition of the problem of relationships with institutions were beginning to be redrawn.

A special meeting of the Council was held at the beginning of June 1985 to consider a response to the Lindop Report. The Council's committees had met promptly and their discussions were reported to the Council together with a draft response from the Chairman's Study Group. The DES had indicated some of the issues arising from the Report on which comments were particularly invited, including the principles and options, continued validation and institutional and/or subject accreditation, the CNAA's validating and institutional review procedures and the possibility of bringing the CNAA's finances under Ministerial control.[37] (It was known that Sir Keith Joseph had been perturbed at the CNAA's freedom to accumulate a multi-million pound surplus, and the use of that surplus for the Development Fund had been achieved, as we have seen, against resistance from HMI assessors on the Council.) The resounding common message from the Council's committees, whatever the differences, had to do with the CNAA's system of peer review. The Committee for Art and Design, anxious about fragmentation and varying standards if, under Option 3, some institutions were to lie outside the CNAA, also expressed 'wholehearted support for its belief in the value of peer group evaluation and the need for its continuation'. Arts and Social Studies emphasized the CNAA's role in establishing and maintaining national standards, formulating national policy, and encouraging innovation and disseminating 'best practice', and felt that 'the main thrust of the response should be the necessity of retaining a nationally-organised and centrally-operated system of peer group review'. Business and Management agreed that 'the most important and valuable function of the CNAA had been to provide a unique national external peer review system', and recorded that 'many of the university members within the CNAA system felt that the CNAA process could with advantage be extended to the universities'. Education believed that 'the evidence of quality and health in public sector higher education owes much to peer review and to the operation of this through the CNAA. The contraction of peer review is seen as potentially impoverishing higher education'. The Committee for Scotland wished to see the maintenance of 'a nationally organised system of external peer group review. This could be available to autonomous institutions as well as to those whose courses were externally validated'. It was generally recognized, most explicitly by the Reviews Coordinating Sub-Committee, that a nationally organized system of peer review 'need not necessarily be one of control but rather a means of ensuring quality across the whole of higher education'.[38]

In its reponse the Council welcomed 'in general terms' the principles proposed by the Committee of Enquiry, and immediately went on to affirm its conviction of the need for institutions 'to be externally accountable for the quality of their courses, and for the comparability of standards to be assured nationally'. Fundamental to the operation of the Council under its Charter and Statutes were the concepts of a national system of quality assurance, a system of peer review involving members from the universities, colleges, industry and the professions, and the means of providing such quality assurance to funding and other bodies. While the CNAA had carried out its obligations under the Charter, the very success of the development of public sector higher education had convinced the CNAA that 'major changes to the Council's Charter and Statutes are now necessary', in order to be able to delegate the power of course approval to institutions 'through accreditation', and to empower them to award degrees in their own name. The Council intended to petition the Privy Council to this end. This would enable the Council's two roles to be distinguished more clearly:

(i) as a validating body concerned with the approval of new courses and the conferment of awards;

(ii) as a review body reponsible for a national system of external peer review throughout the United Kingdom.

Experience has convinced us that the best way of achieving the maintenance and enhancement of standards, external accountability and national comparability is through a national and independent system of peer group review.

The Council enunciated its own four principles — ones which were in fact to be the basis of its further consultation with institutions: the quality of courses across the public sector needed to be maintained and enhanced and national comparability of standards preserved; a nationally-organized system of review was required; each institution had to be entrusted with the fullest possible responsibility for the quality of its programmes; and the process of validation and review needed to be simple and effective. The Council's response indicated that a framework for streamlining validation and review had been under discussion since October 1984, and outlined the basis of its suggested future relationships with institutions, acknowledging the unique character of each one, developing a 'spectrum of individual relationships' on the basis of consultation, allowing them to confer their own awards, subject to periodic review jointly by the CNAA and the institutions. For some institutions continued CNAA approval of course proposals would still be necessary, for others powers to approve and review all or some courses could be devolved under a system of accreditation. Criteria for determining which institutions could be accredited would need further study. The Council indicated the extent to which it was already slimming down its procedures, agreed that the legal provisions governing the relationship between local authorities and their institutions needed to be reviewed, and rejected the proposal to bring the finances of the CNAA under Ministerial control as 'not befitting a chartered body'.

The Council also resisted the idea in Lindop's 'Option 3', by which any institution so wishing could apply to the Secretary of State 'for power to award its own degrees and thus to become self-validating'.[39] Sir Alastair Pilkington expressed to the Secretary of State his own strong personal rejection of Option 3, on the grounds that public sector institutions were in many ways different from universities, and should not be turned into universities. Pilkington saw the proposal as totally illogical. Implementing it would be saying that:

> because the CNAA has been successful in lifting standards, and in maintaining standards in the polytechnics, then the polytechnics should become like universities, which haven't looked after quality consistently. It would be the ultimate irrational decision. And I merely can tell you that when that original team was put together under Lindop I did say — they will find in favour of the polytechnics being treated like universities. How can they do otherwise? — I said, because when the university representatives go and have a look at good polytechnics, they'll say: 'Good heavens, I'd no idea they looked after quality so well as this. They look after quality better than most universities, therefore how can we do anything except give them the status of a university?' . . . And when the findings came out like that, I had to say — this is the ultimate irrational decision — because you succeed, do away with it'.[40]

The territory of 'autonomy', 'self-validation', 'university status', 'degree awarding powers', 'charter', 'accreditation', had always been a complex one, and some kind of clarification was now necessary and imminent. Accreditation had as a principle been considered by Frank Hornby and Sir Michael Clapham, had been pressed on Council Chairmen in the late 1970s and early 1980s by Edwin Kerr. It had been debated in Council committees and working parties, and had been strongly urged on the CNAA by the CDP. Pressures on the CNAA, internal and external, had now led the CNAA to take a significant step, particularly in conceding the need for Charter changes which would enable an accreditation system to be introduced. It had, at the same time, listened to voices — including that of the Lindop Committee itself — which asserted the quality and importance of its past procedures and their contribution to standards across public sector higher education. The National Advisory Body made a similar kind of response in underlining the variety of ways in which the CNAA had contributed to standards, access and innovation in the public sector, but also in agreeing that 'a uniform policy (ie in relation to validation arrangements) may no longer be appropriate, and more specifically, that (in many institutions) a greater measure of freedom from detailed academic controls may be both warranted and desirable'.[41] The position of the CNAA was now not a simple one. It had to await the Secretary of State's decisions. It had already been consulting about its future relationships with institutions. The revision of charters was not a quick or an automatic process. What accreditation and freedom to award degrees in their own name meant in detailed terms for non-university institutions needed to be considered with care. Any new models of relationships would be in some form of competition with existing models that had reached an advanced stage of development — notably in the cases of Newcastle and Sheffield polytechnics. Work on all of these issues had to take place alongside the continuing responsibilities of the Council, and plans to streamline existing review and validation procedures. In this last case, the Reviews Co-ordinating Sub-Committee indicated in May 1985 that it and the Chairman's Study Group had been focussing on the principle that the Council should rely more than in the past 'on the entrusting of responsibility to institutions which merit that trust, and that it should take more positive action to regulate the extent of its contacts with institutions as a demonstration of its confidence in them'. The Sub-Committee now set about considering the meaning of 'streamlining' in the context of the four principles that the Council was enunciating in response to the Lindop Report.[42] In July the Chief Officer wrote to all institutions associated with the CNAA inviting each academic board to make proposals for 'the development of its relationship with CNAA in the immediate future', with the aim of introducing as quickly as possible such changes as could be effected under the Council's existing Charter and Statutes. The letter set out the four principles, enclosed a set of suggestions for streamlining validation and review procedures, and stated the intention of reaching 'individual agreements with all institutions as quickly as possible'.[43]

June and July 1985 were crucial months for the CNAA. In addition to its response to the Lindop Report, the Council was effectively lifting its earlier embargo on new agreements with institutions, inviting all its institutions to state their choices for the immediate future, negotiating further developments with Sheffield and Newcastle polytechnics, and beginning the process of exploring new directions. New institutional agreements with the two polytechnics, to be finalized by the Reviews Co-ordinating Sub-

Committee towards the end of July, were seen as major steps — the most far-reaching that could be achieved under the existing Charter. At a meeting of the Council in mid-July Sir Alistair Pilkington emphasized 'the importance and historic signficance of the proposed changes, which would represent the first stage in the development of an entirely new form of relationship between the CNAA and institutions'.[44] The Council now knew that it would be the autumn at the earliest before the Secretary of State's decisions were announced.

The new agreements with Sheffield and Newcastle began to take shape when an institutional review of Sheffield City Polytechnic took place on 11-12 June. The Council had already decided on the need to streamline validation and review, and given the visiting party's confidence in the Polytechnic it was decided to recommend that an agreement be reached with Sheffield to take effect from the 1985/86 session. The release of this information in the *THES* caused some consternation at Newcastle, whose previous relationship with the CNAA under partnership in validation had been the most extensive and pioneering. Newcastle had been discussing with the CNAA progress towards an accreditation model, including during a visit to Newcastle by Sir Alastair Pilkington and Edwin Kerr in November 1984. The Polytechnic therefore protested to the CNAA that there had clearly been a prior intention on the part of the CNAA before visiting Sheffield to reach an agreement along the lines already proposed by Newcastle, and the announcement had been made without informing Newcastle of either the intention or the outcome.[45] The CNAA moved quickly to bring Newcastle into the negotiations on special institutional agreements. The Newcastle proposals had not been formally considered, but they had indeed, as one CNAA document indicated, been discussed within the CNAA and 'had had an important formative influence on the thinking of the Chairman's Study Group'.[46]

The proposal that emerged from the Sheffield visit was for the transfer to the Academic Board of 'the conduct of all course reviews, and the validation of new courses, subject to the involvement of members and officers from the Council's committees and boards in the internal review and validation processes and a full exchange of information including, where appropriate, papers between the Polytechnic and the relevant subject board of the Council on the review and its outcome'.[47] The proposal was for a one-year arrangement pending the decisions of the Secretary of State. Both agreements were finalized in October. The one with Newcastle acknowledged the experience of the Polytechnic during the experimental and joint validation phases, and involved 'full delegation of CNAA's authority so far as is permitted by its present Charter'. It acknowledged the recent history of the Polytechnic's attempts to move the CNAA towards a new model, and it expressed the Council's agreement to delegate to the Academic Board the validation of all proposed new courses and the progress review of all established courses leading to CNAA awards. Proposals by the

Polytechnic for the approval of new courses would normally be accepted by the Council. Each of the Polytechnic's validation/progress review panels would contain at least two members drawn from the appropriate CNAA subject boards. The Sheffield agreement contained similar clauses.[48] The Council saw these two agreements as pointers towards the relationships that would follow future Charter and other changes if the Secretary of State endorsed what the CNAA had proposed. At the same time as pursuing its explorations about the Charter and related matters, the CNAA was receiving responses and proposals for the negotiating of agreements from many of its institutions. By the end of October sixteen polytechnics, three colleges of higher education and Napier College and Robert Gordon's Institute of Technology in Scotland had all indicated their wish to negotiate a delegation of authority for course validation and review. The Council was working out in detail the criteria and procedures to be involved in negotiating these proposals, and relating them to the programme of institutional review visits.[49]

At this point the Chairman of the CDP wrote to Sir Keith Joseph to express the concerns of its Officers' and Chairmen's Committee. Noting that Sir Keith's decisions on the Lindop Committee's recommendations were still pending, the letter was concerned primarily to express opposition to the recent CNAA developments:

> Some polytechnics are now in negotiation with the CNAA over specific developments of CNAA validation modes which appear to offer substantial delegated powers to the polytechnics. Given the pressure which CNAA has exerted to attempt to make as many of these agreements as possible, it is not surprising that individual institutions, sensing perhaps that their bargaining position is very good at this stage, have decided to enter into negotiations even though your decisions about the Lindop Committee's recommendations remain unknown. In fact, when we met you, we predicted that this would happen.
>
> The Officers' and Chairmen's Group wants you to know that the negotiations which are taking place with the CNAA are meant to be without prejudice to the outcome of your considerations. Some institutions have indeed decided to take no action on the CNAA's overtures until your decisions are known.

The letter went on to emphasize that this was a moment for 'far-reaching changes in validation procedures', and it believed that 'a simple revamping of CNAA validation, however great the apparent simplifications', would have a 'demotivating' effect on the polytechnics which had developed their own effective internal procedures over recent years, 'in the anticipation that the polytechnics would eventually become responsible for their own awards'. It saw the Lindop proposals as the way towards maintaining and improving standards, and 'preservation of the status quo, whilst appearing to offer more explicit guarantees, is likely to have the opposite effect'.[50] As on previous occasions, the polytechnics had not been able to present a united front in relation to future policy, and some of the institutions' directors were rejecting the CNAA's immediate steps in the hope that the longer-term would bring more substantial ones. At a meeting of the Council the previous month the Chairman had in the meantime reported on a meeting which he, the Chief Officer and three members of the Council (including two polytechnic directors) had had with the Secretary of State and some of his advisers:

> It was clear that one of Sir Keith's main concerns was whether, under the Council's proposed arrangements for delegating greater authority to institutions, the Council would still be sufficiently aware of what was happening in institutions to be able to intervene if necessary.

Under such an arrangement would the CNAA have the means and the will to withdraw accreditation? The CNAA representatives had reassured him on these points. It would receive regular reports from the institutions, and would continue to have the responsibility and the power to act on evidence.[51]

Prospects for the CNAA were far from clear. Throughout this period in 1984–86 there had been clear signals that some senior figures in the DES and the Inspectorate were hostile to the CNAA and were advising the Lindop Committee and the Secretary of State accordingly, but by the end of 1985 there were glimpses of a softening of attitude. Peter Brooke's letter on credit transfer in mid-1984 had been something of a straw in the wind. The Secretary of State's questions at this meeting did not appear to be going in the direction of the maximum autonomy proposed in the Lindop Committee's Option 3. To only a few people in the CNAA were these subdued signals available. For most, the recent past suggested the slow working out of a post-PNL vendetta.

The CNAA received the Secretary of State's statement on 17 March 1986, at the same time as Sir Keith made a statement to the House of Commons. His Parliamentary statement was brief, and underlined the government's agreement with the Lindop Committee that the most effective safeguard of an institution's academic standards was 'the existence within it of a strong, cohesive and self-critical academic community'. The government was not persuaded that 'certain polytechnics or colleges need to be granted full autonomy in validation with powers to award their own degrees'. It welcomed the changes that the CNAA was already making along the lines of the Lindop Committee's Option 1: 'institutions will be able to seek substantially greater responsibility for validation and review of their courses and, subject to amendment of the CNAA's Charter, authority in certain cases to award degrees in their own names'. Existing arrangements had 'rightly, been criticised for their bureaucracy and excessive reliance on course documents', and the government welcomed the CNAA commitment to the simplification of its procedures. In a more detailed document released at the same time the government accepted the view that there should be 'a range of arrangements, including accreditation of whole institutions or areas of work within institutions, which would reflect differences between institutions'. The government agreed that what the CNAA had already initiated was consistent with Lindop's Option 1, though with an amendment to its Charter the CNAA was intending to go beyond it with proposals for accreditation. The government expected institutions to collaborate with the CNAA in developing accreditation. The government would review the position in due course in the light of experience by the CNAA and the institutions. All of these changes would, it was underlined, 'reduce the amount and alter the character of CNAA's work'. The government's assessors would help to bring about the improvements in the CNAA's validation procedures. The CNAA needed to find ways of developing responsibility 'while at the same time being able to satisfy itself that an institution's internal management and course review arrangements and the academic standards actually achieved are satisfactory'. Validation as currently practised would continue to apply in some cases, and in others institutions would acquire accredited status. The government's statement noted with approval that CNAA's current 'experimental agreements with institutions leave the latter free to determine the size and composition of course approval and review panels subject to a minority being drawn from CNAA committees and boards'. It accepted the CNAA's view rather than the Lindop Committee's view that institutional reviews should be discontinued in the case of accredited institutions, but it did accept the Committee's view that the CNAA needed to clarify and reduce to a minimum its documentation requirements: 'with no sacrifice of rigour, the CNAA now can and should adopt a more collaborative and less formal style of operation'. A 'significant reduction' could take place in the resources required by the CNAA, and it needed to effect savings and set fees at a level that would avoid accumulating or maintaining a surplus.[52]

Sending copies of these statements to Sir Alastair Pilkington, the Secretary of State suggested that, subject to a number of reservations of detail, the government had 'broadly endorsed' the Council's response to the Lindop Report, and expected the Council now to implement as quickly as possible the broad principles it had enunciated. The DES would be consulting with the CNAA on specific targets for the proposed reductions in staffing, recurrent expenditure and financial reserves. Sir Keith Joseph expressed the view that under Sir Alastair's leadership improvements in the Council's management and structure and organization had already been introduced, and he hoped that the Council would 'feel able to welcome the proposals in this letter as a constructive contribution to the work on which you have already embarked'.[53] The Council's position was now clear. It had begun the process of changing its relationships with the institutions, and in April 1986, following receipt of the Secretary of State's letter, it authorized the Chairman to set up a group of Council members to recommend a broad strategy framework for the future, covering all aspects of the CNAA's work, and including the search for a Chief Officer to replace Edwin Kerr, who had announced his resignation from the position. The nature of institutional agreements, validation procedures, accreditation, finance and staffing, and a range of related issues were all now on the Council's agenda against a background of Ministerial decision, the expectation of rapid implementation of directions already determined, and the knowledge that the slimming down of the CNAA was an option that had been chosen over the possibility that the CNAA might have been disbanded altogether. Both Sir Keith Joseph and his successor as Secretary of State, Kenneth Baker, clearly considered that the CNAA had a continuing role to play even in relation to accredited institutions — at least pending some future review of the position and the desirability of going towards the fuller autonomy of the Lindop Committee's Option 3. Sir Norman Lindop's reflection was that the Secretary of State's decision not to dispense with the CNAA was significant — 'one day it might be useful'.[54]

The uncertainties in the CNAA were now of a new order, relating to reorganization, jobs, future roles, the timetable of change. As further evidence on which to base its future planning the Council also commissioned evaluations of the Newcastle and Sheffield agreements, and Janet Powney and Clem Adelman respectively reported on the detailed working and implications of the two agreements. By the middle of 1986 the CNAA had at its disposal evaluations of the thoroughness, fairness, openness and rigour of the processes of self-validation and review.[55] While the further steps in redesigning relationships were being pursued, the procedures for initiating institutional agreements were being agreed, and the Council adopted a common format for proposed agreements with institutions involving delegated authority for course validation and review.[56] A number of discussions were now taking place simultaneously. A working party was set up to review validation procedures — an officers' working party having already considered changes in documentation requirements. A working party was convened on the information needs of validating committees, given the view that the Council's existing information systems might not be providing adequately for the needs of validation. A working party on the Council's Charter and Statutes, chaired by Edwin Kerr, had met twice before the Secretary of State's response to the Lindop Report, and then began to meet with representatives of the DES and the SED in order to present initial proposals for amendments to the Charter in July. Edwin Kerr, who had now left the CNAA, returned to present the changes to the Council meeting. The Strategy Group had met three times by mid-June and intended holding further meetings before the July meeting, its focus being the development of a model for the accreditation of institutions, including the future role of external examiners, on which the Lindop Committee and the Secretary of State had commented. The Strategy Group was also beginning to look at the future committee structure of the CNAA.[57] The Council was now entering the difficult waters of reaching agreement on broad strategies and detailed matters of implementation.

The July 1986 meeting of the Council, which received an interim report from the Strategy Group, considered its recommendations for a broad framework of an accreditation model. Controversy was engendered around the continued operation of peer group review nationally administered, the precise nature of the CNAA's continuing responsibilities for academic standards, other aspects of the retention by the CNAA of past roles, and differences that were perceived between the Strategy Group's stated objectives and principles, and the model itself. By October the Council had an agreed consultative document on *Quality and Validation: Future Relationships with Institutions*. It proposed to move beyond the present category of agreements with institutions to negotiate accreditation and other forms of relationship as soon as possible once the Charter and Statutes had been amended (and institutions which had not previously sought special agreements would not be disadvantaged). The document spelled out the CNAA's continuing responsibilities, including for the promotion and dissemination of good practice in public sector higher education, the development of a national system of peer review, and the improvement and strengthening of the system of external examiners. Against that background it proposed a system of accreditation which meant 'the granting by the Council of a licence to an institution to start and to modify courses designed to lead to the qualifications of Council'. Accreditation would mean that institutions would have full responsibility for the approval and review of taught courses, with research degrees continuing on the existing basis. To be accredited an institution would have to demonstrate that its academic board had effective arrangements in place for validation and the monitoring and periodic review of courses. It would have a minimum of two CNAA nominees in the validation and review machinery, would conduct reviews at intervals of not more than five years, would bring any serious problems promptly to the attention of the CNAA, would appoint its own external examiners once its nominations had been approved by the CNAA, and would conduct jointly with the CNAA a review of the institution at intervals of between five and seven years. 'Non-accredited' institutions would continue to submit courses for validation by the CNAA, which would seek to work jointly with institutions. In these institutions the CNAA would encourage 'sound procedures for the internal validation and review of courses of areas of work', and the development of these procedures to a point where they could meet accreditation requirements. They could apply for delegated authority of various kinds, and they would be subject to institutional reviews at intervals of five to seven years, or in 'planned stages'. All institutions would be able to confer awards in their own names, on the Council's behalf, clearly indicating the name of the institution on the certificate, but also indicating that the award was 'in respect of a course offered within the terms of the Council's Charter and Statutes'. The document outlined a new, simplified committee structure for the CNAA, involving a smaller number of wider-ranging 'subject committees' with ad hoc panels.[58] The old-style subject boards would now disappear.

A summary of the replies from institutions, student unions, professional bodies, CNAA committees and members, was presented to the Council in February 1987. Most of the 160 replies received supported the Council's proposals in broad terms, but there were reservations — often expressing opposing views: the larger institutions, for example, resisted the idea of two CNAA nominees being included in institutions' approval and review process (as possible CNAA 'policemen'), while some other respondents considered two not to be enough to enable the CNAA to exercise effective control over standards. Smaller institutions often saw the proposals as divisive — as did student unions, industrial members of the CNAA and the CNAA committees — and leading to public misunderstanding of the quality of courses offered by accredited and non-accredited institutions. The larger institutions tended to argue that the presence of two CNAA nominees was inconsistent with the principle of full responsibility for approval and review of courses, and argued that research degrees should be the responsibility of institutions on the same footing as taught courses. Most of the smaller and specialized institutions considered that they would not be applying for accreditation, at least not in the shorter term. There was widespread concern at the loss of subject boards without their replacement by a credible means 'for gathering and disseminating national intelligence about good practice and innovations in curriculum and course design and in teaching and learning strategies, in particular fields of study'. Larger institutions suggested extending the interval between review visits to between seven and ten years, and there was general concern about the resource implications for institutions in taking over work previously done by the CNAA.[59] The Council considered the responses, summarized them for the benefit of the institutions and all CNAA members, amended the consultative document and in February 1987 adopted and circulated *Future Strategy: Principles and Operation*.

It had altered the vocabulary to distinguish between 'accredited' and 'associated' institutions, the standard required for awards in both cases being the same. All institutions currently offering courses leading to CNAA awards were automatically approved as associated institutions, and any of them could apply to be accredited. All relationships with the Council would be periodically reviewed. The definition of accreditation and of the responsibilities of accredited institutions was reaffirmed, and in the case of associated institutions the role of the CNAA in working in close partnership with them (complementary to, and where possible jointly with them) was made clear. The proposal that institutions should review all their courses every five to seven years was retained — the review process to include 'persons from outside the institution', including from industry, commerce or the relevant professions. CNAA members could act as external participants, 'but this is not mandatory'. The CNAA had retreated from its insistence on two members to be included in peer review panels, but expressed its commitment to the continuation of the peer review system in the following form:

> In order to contribute to the maintenance of the peer review system, it is anticipated that accredited institutions will invite CNAA members and officers to participate in a number of their course validation and review exercises.

Accredited institutions would lodge copies of validation or review reports with the CNAA, and also copies of other records and a brief annual report. The Council set out its own obligations, including the provision of appropriate information as a basis for validation and review, and advice to all institutions on 'good practice in validation, monitoring and review'. It would act as a 'national centre and focus for information and intelligence on curriculum development, course design, learning strategies, student assessment, performance criteria, credit transfer and other matters of common concern'. The Council's own new structure would involve the creation of a Committee for Academic Affairs, an Accreditation Committee which would be a temporary body whose duties would then be absorbed by the CNAA, and twelve subject committees which would be responsible for the validation, review and approval of courses at associated institutions. A register of specialist advisers to be available as necessary would be drawn up, and the roles of subject officers in relation to validation and to the gathering of intelligence were defined. Procedures for the appointment of external examiners, and their roles, were laid down, and in a set of appendices the Council indicated in detail the requirements for accreditation, the application procedures to be followed, and the terms of reference for the subject committees in advising the Council, preparing policy and disseminating information, validating and reviewing courses in associated institutions, and working with institutions in improving those processes.[60]

In March 1987 the Council finalized its structure by agreeing that there would be two main committees, the CAA and a General Committee, and three other committees reporting directly to the Council — the Committee for Scotland, the Committee for Higher Doctorates and the Committee for Honorary Degrees.[61] Later that year it was also agreed that 'institutions with experience of running College Research Degrees Committees (CRDCs) with extended powers, normally for a minimum of two years, should be eligible to apply for accreditation of research degree work'.[62] The Council had in these ways, not without opposition and hesitations, withdrawn from its main last positions in reserving powers over course validation and review in accredited institutions through a mechanism of CNAA representation or presence. It had brought research degrees into the accreditation process. Both had been demands from some of the polytechnics in response to the CNAA's consultative document in October 1986. The accountability process had been moved further into the institutions' machineries than initially suggested by the CNAA. In 1987 the new decisions were moving rapidly towards implementation. The necessary Charter changes to permit particularly what was intended under the scheme of accreditation were agreed by the Privy Council, and the supplemental Charter was received by the Council in February 1987. Article 3(c) of the Charter now gave the Council the power:

> to permit such bodies as the Council may from time to time determine . . . to approve either courses of study or programmes of supervised research to be pursued by candidates to qualify for awards under this Our Charter.[63]

Under this provision the CNAA adopted an 'Instrument of Accreditation' under which an institution would be permitted to approve courses leading to the award of CNAA's degrees, certificates and diplomas, subject to a number of conditions, including: the arrangement by the institution for each of its approved taught courses to be reviewed at intervals of not more than seven years; a review at intervals of not more than seven years by the CNAA of the 'effectiveness of the Institution in maintaining the standards of taught courses leading to CNAA awards'; the involvement of people from inside and outside the institution in the process of approval and review; the provision of the CNAA with reports and documents as specified; the powers of the CNAA to 'require further information . . . and to act as necessary if it judges the standards of CNAA awards may be at risk', and to withdraw accreditation if it judges the institution to be failing to maintain the standards of its courses or to comply with the conditions laid down.[64] Accreditation was now in place, the procedures whereby institutions could apply were in place, and the institutions unable to meet the conditions for accreditation would also be able to seek 'substantial delegation of authority to make changes to approved courses and to undertake the planning and organization of course validation and review exercises'.[65] The CNAA had reached a turning point in its history, and the pattern of higher education had undergone another major change.

The proposed 'Instrument of Accreditation' was sent to all CNAA-related institutions in June 1987, with a letter in which Malcolm Frazer, the Chief Executive, invited them to apply.[66] Some had already begun their discussions of accreditation, particularly where special agreements had previously been in operation and where preparations were being made for review visits. In April Newcastle upon Tyne Polytechnic, for example, had already submitted its recent record and future intentions with regard to quality and standards. It welcomed the CNAA's view that 'a significant part of its future role will be to act as a national centre for the exchange of intelligence and good practice . . . The Polytechnic regards an important part of its present and anticipated future relationship with the CNAA as being a process of mutual learning from experience'. It noted that the inclusion of CNAA members in validation and review panels was not to be mandatory, expressed its commitment to a nationally-organized system of peer review, and indicated its intention to continue to invite CNAA members to participate in its panel 'as appropriate and to seek advice in this regard from CNAA officers'.[67] The formal invitation to submit applications had given 30 August 1987 as the deadline for the first round for consideration. Between the Council's agreement of policy and the closing date for the first round of applications there had been only six months. Twenty-six applications had been received, from twenty-one polytechnics, two colleges or institutes of higher education, and three Scottish Central Institutions. It was decided that the consideration of application would in all cases include a visit to the institution concerned, and that the Chief Executive would chair all visits, and Malcom Frazer chaired the first of these — at Manchester Polytechnic — in November. Not all the institutions which applied achieved accreditation at the first attempt, and two years into the process some had still not secured approval. After the first round of applications other rounds followed. Twenty-nine institutions obtained accreditation for taught courses by September 1988 — all but three of them (Dundee College of Technology, Napier College, Edinburgh, and Ealing College of Higher Education) polytechnics. From the same date eight of the polytechnics were also accredited for research degree programmes. A year later the tally of institutions accredited for taught courses was thirty-eight, and for research degrees twelve. In a year-and-a-half the relationships between the CNAA and its major institutions had been fundamentally transformed. The long process of debate and controversy had ended, at least for the moment, in an agreed role for the CNAA and an acceptable model of advance for its related institutions.

From *Developments in Partnership in Validation* in 1979 to the appointment of the Lindop Committee in 1984 the CNAA, often preoccupied with other issues, had moved laboriously on questions of relationships with institutions. The complexities surrounding events at the Polytechnic of North London, questions of the CNAA's organization and finance, and government policy in general, sharpened the issues and helped to establish a momentum of change. The CNAA acted quickly and decisively enough from 1984 to persuade the Secretary of State that it had a viable and useful future. By the time of the *Future Strategy* document and the implementation of the scheme of accreditation and association it had gone through major difficulties and major changes, and more lay ahead. Taking over the chairmanship of the CNAA, by Sir Denis Rooke in 1978 and by Sir Alastair Pilkington at the beginning of 1984, in both cases meant something different from what they expected. Sir Denis Rooke discovered that the question of partnership in validation was not as settled as his predecessor, Sir Michael Clapham, had hoped it was after a decade of debate — 'it's all plain sailing from now'. Rooke discovered that in the Council and the system it was far from plain sailing in fact, that the Council's 'form of words' belied a lack of thought and agreement. There was additionally a 'tremendous administrative task required', without the Chairman being directly involved in the administration. When he became Chairman he looked at the finances and:

> concluded that if the Council was going to have freedom to develop in the future to meet the changing demands of an ever expanding polytechnic sector, it was necessary to get away from a budget in precarious balance year on year. I was afraid that some unexpected occurrence could tip the Council over into the position that it just ran out of money.

For a variety of reasons, therefore, 'it turned out to be a totally different and much more demanding task than I expected'.[68]

When Sir Alastair Pilkington, President of the Pilkington Company, was invited to become Chairman he had no conception of the problems lying immediately ahead. Before taking over the chair he accompanied Sir Denis Rooke and Edwin Kerr to see the Secretary of State and 'came out reeling' from the confrontation over PNL — and Sir Keith Joseph's preoccupation with it surfaced whenever he was with people from the CNAA. Once in the chair Pilkington's 'hazy picture' of an organization that was 'well respected' and constituted a 'happy family' was further shattered, when he attended a 'horrifying' dinner with the CDP. He had to confront not only 'the reality of the CNAA but also the perception of the CNAA':

> That is what surprised me . . . the perceptions at that time that the CNAA was struggling to hold on to a position of acting as a sort of heavy father, or even nanny.

The Newcastle experiment was clearly not enough to satisfy the aspirations of many of the polytechnics. Lindop 'had to happen'. The CNAA was 'in the dock', and its own response to the report indicated 'a new future' for the organization.[69] Chairing the Council through the problems of Lindop, consultation, the Strategy Group, the detailed consideration of Charter revisions, accreditation and association — and the outer perimeter of contacts with the CDP, the DES, Ministers and others — was not quite the 'interesting and comfortable job' he had at first expected it to be.

An additional problem that the CNAA had had to face in the 1980s, as we have seen Sir Denis Rooke underline, was that of its internal organization and financial controls — an issue which arose acutely in relation to the sudden accumulation of a considerable surplus in the early 1980s. Rooke had become Chairman at a time when the CNAA's finances were 'teetering' on the brink of the red and the black.[70] Since the CNAA was self-financing through the receipt of student registration fees, and did not have direct grant income, it had to control its own levels of income and expenditure. Sir Denis Rooke made a dedicated attempt to improve the CNAA's finances in order to guard against the difficulties of constantly existing on the borderline of deficit. Fee levels had to be determined well in advance, and an increase in fees was fixed with the expectation that student numbers in the public sector in the coming period would probably fall. Government financial constraints on the universities in fact contributed to a substantial influx of students into the polytechnics and colleges. Interest rates, also expected to fall, did not do so. The CNAA found itself with an increasing surplus and considerable reserves. The Council was faced with questions of investment with which it had not previously had to deal, and for which its personnel were ill-equipped. Immediate responsibility for managing the finances was that of the new Secretary of the Council, Bryan Overy, who was at the same time responsible for a wide range of the CNAA's other activities — including establishment, conferments, membership, visits and meetings. In the new situation, however, it was no longer, in Overy's words, 'good enough to know something about book-keeping'. Over-reliance on promises of suitable computer financial packages led to other problems. The packages turned out to be unreliable — and the auditors involved were also 'learning the computer game' at the same time. The Chairman was giving guidance on ways forward, and a Price Waterhouse report on how to improve the CNAA's accounting was helpful and implemented.[71] Some of these and related difficulties had by this stage, however, undermined some confidence — notably in the DES — in the CNAA's financial management[72] — which was ultimately to surface as one factor in the discussion around the Lindop Committee's proposal that the CNAA's finances should be brought 'under Ministerial control'.[73]

In November 1985, after the Lindop Committee had reported and while Sir Keith Joseph's response was still awaited, and against a background of known hostility to the CNAA in some influential circles, *The Economist* published a vicious attack on the CNAA, based on leaked information about its finances, reserves and procedures. The article described the work of the CNAA as a shambles, morale as low, its validation of courses inadequate, and the organization as 'overmanned, over-financed and badly damaged'. Standards of courses were too low. The best option available to Sir Keith Joseph would be 'that preferred by Sir Keith Joseph's advisers: scrap the CNAA altogether'.[74] Price Waterhouse had in fact produced a second report for the CNAA on its management and organization, as they were in October 1984. The report indicated that it believed that Council members and the Chief Officer were not being adequately served by existing procedures for monitoring and controlling the organization of staff, and members were not adequately aware of issues regarding organization, systems and management. There were differences of interpretation of the CNAA's role between members and officers, and the management information available to members was insufficient to allow them to carry out their responsibilities. The existing staffing structure was complex and difficult to manage, there was duplication of effort, high levels of staffing and internal communications difficulties. Responsibility and accountability for resources management was inadequately defined, and none of the computer systems assigned high priority in 1980 had been successfully implemented. Some problems were being caused by an absence of defined responsibilities and staff inexperience, there was scope for improved management training, and there were serious problems arising from congested office space, insufficient meeting rooms, and the need for better space planning.[75] The Chairman, the General Committee, the Council, the Chief Officer, were from this point engaged in a series of sharp decisions about all of these issues, and the decisions taken were undoubtedly as important to the DES and the Secretary of State in responding to the Lindop Report as were the CNAA's initiatives with regard to its relationships with institutions. This was the force of the comment in Sir Keith Joseph's letter to Sir Alastair Pilkington in March 1986, acknowledging that under the Chairman's leadership the CNAA had made improvements in the Council's management, structure and organization.

The particular internal difficulties that these events indicate relate directly to the account of the CNAA as an organization expanding rapidly to cover new institutions and new areas of work in the 1970s. The CNAA had assumed responsibility for a rapidly growing population of students and institutions, and priority attention was being devoted in the early 1980s to issues of the national organization of public sector higher education, the maintenance of an enormously varied pattern of course and institutional approval and review, and the nature of future relationships with the related institutions. Some of the underlying problems of management and organization were not brought into the centre of the Council's attention until the problems intensified. Experience of this kind is not uncommon as organizations expand on the kind of scale we have seen in the case of the CNAA.

It was at the point at which the CNAA's future strategy was agreed, and issues of organization and administration were being resolved, that Edwin Kerr left the CNAA. He had been Chief Officer for nearly fifteen years and his period of office not only coincided with the major expansion of the Council's range of activities, it was a formative element in that expansion. Frank Hornby, as we have seen, could only have dimly foreseen the explosion of institutions and subject areas with which the CNAA was to be concerned. Edwin Kerr's interpretation of the Chief Officer's role involved what one of the officers working with him described as 'making an enormous amount out of the role', and another as encompassing and taking advantage of opportunities 'in an extraordinary way'. He contributed directly and often decisively to the development of teacher education, art and design, management studies and other areas in public sector institutions, and chaired many of the Council's key committees and working parties. He played an important and often a strategic part in the work of other bodies — most notably the National Advisory Body. He had the difficult job over a long period of time of managing an operation which often involved as many as sixty to seventy subject boards, and a system of complex accountabilities for standards in what was rapidly becoming the sector with the largest number of students. His role combined that of executive officer with that of vice-chancellor, and the other difficult job over a long period of time was balancing the CNAA's system of controls with the pressures to delegate responsibility to institutions. Some polytechnic directors saw him, in this respect, as an obstacle or, in the word of one of them, a 'blockage' to the more rapid delegation of responsibility which they sought. Sporadically, and then more consistently after the Teesside visit which he chaired, some polytechnic directors and on occasion the CDP as such — in the words of one participant in the events — 'gunned for him'. One polytechnic director, reflecting on the twenty-year history of the polytechnics in 1988, commented on the fact that both Hornby and Kerr were themselves from the public sector, and 'their contribution to British higher education has been greatly underestimated. Kerr has played a major role in shaping the polytechnics'.[76] The *THES* reflected in 1986 on the past and present of the CNAA, and the new roles that would need to be developed as Malcolm Frazer took over as Chief Executive. In doing so, it linked the role that Edwin Kerr had played with the changes in higher education itself. He was the person who 'more than any other made the CNAA'. His retirement had been greeted with 'a sense of relief in some quarters' (and one can only guess that the *THES* was referring to the CDP and the DES), and there were those who thought he had been 'too inflexible, and that he had been too slow to share the formidable power of the CNAA with its aspirant institutions'. It was perhaps too soon to judge the justice or injustice of such charges, but it was essential:

> to give him public credit for his great service to the polytechnics and colleges over almost 15 years . . . it may be worth recording that the high academic standing of the public owes far more than many of its leaders are prepared to acknowledge to the 'inflexibility' of the CNAA. If the binary policy has succeeded in its best intention to broaden our once wretchedly narrow vision of higher education in Britain without sacrificing genuine excellence, Dr Kerr is among those entitled to much of the credit. If the polytechnics and some colleges are now ready for a new and freer relationship with the CNAA, that too is another consequence of his success. The new role of a reshaped CNAA should be regarded as a culmination, not as a repudiation, of its — and his — past achievement.[77]

The pace of change had quickened in the CNAA and in public sector higher education from the middle of the 1980s, and further changes had become imminent once the government had published its White Paper on higher education in April 1987. Change had become almost a constant in the affairs of the CNAA. Dr Malcolm Frazer was appointed to replace Edwin Kerr in 1986. Frazer had been a professor and Pro-Vice-Chancellor at the University of East Anglia, and had a long association with the CNAA. He took up his appointment at a time when sea-changes were taking place in higher education, when the CNAA's newe strategy had to be implemented, and when the organization of the CNAA itself was about to change radically. One of Malcolm Frazer's immediate roles was, in fact, to oversee the restructuring of the CNAA as part of the implementation of the new strategy. The CNAA's staff was reduced from 165 to 110, the number of Council members from thirty-five to twenty-five and the number of committees and boards from seventy-five to twenty-five. Sir Ron Dearing became Chairman of the CNAA but the following year resigned to become Chairman of the newly formed Polytechnics and Colleges Funding Council forecast in the White Paper to replace the NAB. He was in turn succeeded in 1988 by Sir Bryan Nicholson, Chairman of the Post Office, as had been Sir Ron Dearing. The change-over took place half-way through a year in which, in Sir Bryan Nicholson's words, 'many far-reaching changes were being carried through', the greatest of which was accreditation, and others included 'the new streamlined committee structure and the reduction in the number of staff at Gray's Inn Road'. The outgoing and incoming Chairmen recognized 1987–88 'to have been a most important year in CNAA's history', and what lay ahead was a 'new, clear and important role for the Council in British higher education'.[78]

At the end of 1988 Her Royal Highness The Princess Royal accepted an invitation to become President of the CNAA, and she officiated for the first time at a CNAA ceremony the following year. The Duke of Edinburgh had, as we have seen, taken an interest as President in the work of the CNAA as a new contributor to the expansion of higher education, and Prince Charles had been active as President. He had taken a particular interest in engineering and design, and had on one occasion invited Sir Denis Rooke to bring a group of engineers for a discussion with him (and Bryan Overy from the CNAA had taken part). He had spoken at CNAA conferences, and though he had been briefed for the awards ceremonies at which he had officiated, his speeches were his own.

It is important to remember that at the same time as these changes of leadership, scale, direction and procedures the CNAA was continuing in the second half of the 1980s to perform established functions. For example, it was continuing to give advice to the NAB in partnership with the institutions and as a result of continuing consultation with them,[79] normally a great deal more amicably that at the outset — though memories of the town planning episode died hard. Trent Polytechnic, for example, refused in 1984/85 to receive a visit from the Town Planning Board, as CNAA advice had resulted in the NAB's withdrawal of approval for its course, and the Polytechnic explained that it therefore no longer had confidence in the Board or its officers, 'and a visit was thus not welcomed'. The dispute continued under the Council's new Committee for the Built Environment in 1986.[80] In general, however, the CNAA's institutions were now expressing approval of the way in which the CNAA was 'arguing their cases with the NAB and ensuring that the NAB was fully aware of the implications of its proposals'.[81]

The CNAA was at the same time continuing to press for developments in research in the public sector, particularly following the welcome given to its 1984 policy statement on *Research and Related Activities*. The Council's policy on information technology continued to percolate through the work of the boards and committees. In 1986, for example, the Committee for Arts and Humanities reviewed the effects of the Council's 1982 policy statement on IT in undergraduate courses, and planned for a further discussion of the use of IT through interaction with course teams.[82] Support for, and the promotion of, sandwich courses remained a preoccupation of the CNAA. Following its concern in the early 1980s over problems of student placements and related matters, and its support for research on supervised work experience, the CNAA expressed disappointment at the lack of government commitment to sandwich education. The DES published a report in 1985 on the costs and benefits of sandwich education (the RISE Report), and although the Report accepted that there had been general support over time for sandwich courses, the CNAA's committees 'generally concurred with the view that they regret the fact that the RISE Report has not provided a clear commitment in the future to sandwich education'. The committees also commented on the fact that the 1985 Green Paper, 'although more supportive than the RISE Report itself, again seems not to place a higher priority on the further development of sandwich education'.[83] The Committee for Education was continuing to grapple with the problems of a continually changing field of professional preparation. Validation had to take account of a context that had changed as a result of the government's establishment of the Council for the Accreditation of Teacher Education. The Initial Teacher Education Board expressed its commitment in 1986 to validation through a system of peer interaction, but recognized that responses to CATE and its accreditation criteria were inevitable. Course developments were under new external constraints, and CNAA visiting parties had to avoid making recommendations that ran counter to 'imperatives under which an institution is operating'.[84] The Committee was issuing discussion papers and notes on multicultural education (which led to considerable controversy through to meetings of the Council itself), the relationship between access courses and the BEd, language and literacy in teacher education, IT, mathematics and science in teacher education courses, special educational needs, modular schemes in in-service teacher education, teacher education and the school system in Scotland, and a variety of other topics. The Committee for Engineering had seen through the conversion of the majority of the CNAA's engineering courses to BEng, and in 1987–88 adopted revised guidelines for first degrees in engineering, including the provision of a 'double award' of BEng/MEng for students following MEng programmes. The Committee was constantly confronting the issue of a declining pool of 'traditionally' qualified entrants to engineering courses and more flexible approaches to engineering education, and responded to proposals by the Engineering Council for new approaches to engineering degree programmes. It was approving an increasing number of engineering degree courses, particularly in electrical and manufacturing engineering. Under the CNAA's new structure in 1987–88 the Committee for Engineering found itself responsible for more courses than any other subject committee (computing having become part of its remit).[85]

'Managing design' continued to be a major interest of the CNAA, with work being supported on teaching the use of design in management, and the value of professional and business awareness in art, craft and design degree courses.[86] In these and other respects business was 'as usual', and this kind of continuous commitment was not diminished by other events. In the session 1987–88 almost a quarter of a million students were registered for CNAA awards, over 220,000 of them on taught courses, 4190 for research degrees. Of nearly 2300 courses in operation for all types of first degree, master's degree, diploma and certificate awards, 1446 were full-time first degree, and 325 were part-time, first degree courses. The largest numbers of such part-time courses were in engineering and science. In that session 140 courses were newly-validated, half of them being postgraduate or post-experience courses. Approximately 42 per cent of the students on CNAA degree courses were in science and technology, 25 per cent in arts and social studies (including consumer and leisure studies), 15 per cent in art and design, and smaller percentages in business and management, teacher education and interdisciplinary studies. Twenty-nine per cent of the students were on sandwich courses, and 11 per cent were part-time.[87] The CNAA and its related institutions were continuing to expand provision and access, against the background of continued financial constraint and the intense scrutiny that had taken place of the CNAA and its operations in particular, and — since the 1985 Green Paper — of the system of higher education in general.

That wider scrutiny was eventually encapsulated in the White Paper, *Higher Education: Meeting the Challenge*, in 1987, and in the Education Reform Act of the following year. The turbulence in higher education resulting from the government's continuing programme of financial cutbacks had not diminished by this period. Straws in the wind about possible increases in government funding were not enough to allay fears that perhaps even more difficult changes lay ahead. The Secretary for Education, Kenneth Baker, gave a commitment to the expansion of higher education in September, but at that stage no costing was involved, and he dismissed talk of the possible closure of one of the universities only to add: 'That does not mean to say that there will not have to be change, but closure — no'.[88] Only the day before one of the popular newspapers had run a feature entitled: 'If our universities were animals, they'd be pandas'. That quotation, from the producer of a Channel 4 documentary on the University of Newcastle, accompanied his comment that the universities were an 'endangered species'. The paper described the current cuts in higher education as being 'more than a sign of the financial times. They could spell disaster as every university in Britain tries desperately to strip 2½ per cent from its spending every year for the next five years'.[89] The expectations of the universities were profoundly confused, trying to see the realities amidst the vocabularies of cuts, expansion and change, and the public sector was at the same time being promised increased funding, without the nature and purposes of the funding being too clear. A great deal now hinged on the forthcoming government White Paper and its reactions to the views taken of its precursor, the Green Paper of 1985. In the event what the White Paper did was remove some of the blunter crudities of the Green Paper, propose major changes in the management and funding of higher education, and confirm the underlying message if not the vocabulary of the Green Paper. The White Paper made no attempt, for example, to continue the discussion about 'balance' in the curriculum in the discrete and forthright way that the Green Paper had done, and by doing so sought to present the new proposals without arousing the kind of hostilities that the previous formulations had generated. It accepted the range of purposes for higher education enunciated almost a quarter of a century earlier by the Robbins Committee, adding on the first page — no doubt with the memory of Green paper conflicts in mind — that 'the encouragement of a high level of scholarship in the arts, humanities and social sciences is an essential feature of a civilised and cultured country'. It did so alongside reference to the value of research, and especially basic research, 'together with those areas of learning and scholarship which have at most an indirect relationship to the world of work'. Meeting the needs of the economy was 'not the sole purpose of higher education', but there was continued emphasis in the White Paper on the importance of greater commercial and industrial relevance, and the fostering of 'positive attitudes to enterprise which are crucial for both institutions and their students'. The government intended to do all it could to encourage and reward approaches which brought higher education closer to the world of business.

The White Paper expressed the government's commitment to increasing student numbers, one of the means of improving access being by credit transfer schemes, including the CNAA's Credit Accumulation and Transfer Scheme. The emphasis in this connection was not on increased funding but on 'better value for the very large sums of public money made available for higher education'. It recognized that 'hard and sometimes painful decisions are involved but is committed to achieving the further gains in value for money that will be needed, particularly if access to higher education is to be widened in future. This means pursuing both quality and efficiency'. On academic standards the White Paper welcomed progress made by the CVCP and the universities in developing codes of practice for maintaining and monitoring standards, but believed that universities, 'individually or collectively, should do more to reassure the public about the ways in which they control standards'. With regard to 'the polytechnics and colleges sector'

— the term which, it was argued, more appropriately fitted the reality than did 'public sector', since universities also received public funds — the White Paper had asked the CNAA to accredit institutions judged ready for it, to increase delegation to other institutions as far as practicable, and to pay more attention to the quality of teaching and learning and to student outcomes 'in both academic and employment terms'. The CNAA had agreed a strategy for its future relations with institutions, resulting in 'virtual self-validation' for many of them:

> This is consistent with the Government's wishes. The Council is reviewing its own structure and working practices in the light of this new approach. It is also strengthening the external examiner system as a further safeguard of academic standards. These changes should enable the CNAA to maintain, indeed even enhance, its role as the main guardian of standards in polytechnics and colleges, while reducing its own operating costs and encouraging greater self-reliance amongst institutions. The Government welcomes the CNAA's change of direction and now looks to its early implementation and to agreement on targets for reducing the Council's staffing and expenditure.

Other strategies for increased efficiency in higher education were outlined, including further 'selectivity' in the distribution of resources for research.

The most radical departures in the White Paper were in relation to changes in the structure and national planning of higher education. One feature of the proposals was for polytechnics and some other institutions 'of substantial size engaged predominantly in higher education' to be transferred out of local authority control (the criteria for the second group of institutions were to be a minimum of 350 full-time equivalent students and more than 55 per cent of their activity in higher education). Although the reasons given for this move included the polytechnics' national profile, their well-established position catering on average for more students than universities, and their high-quality contribution to higher education, part of the background to the development was the government's general interest in reducing the overall powers of the local authorities. This aspect of government policy was reflected in the discussion of planning: for purposes of funding it was neither desirable nor appropriate 'for each local authority to plan and fund its institutions in isolation'; more progress needed to be made in 'rationalizing scattered provision and concentrating effort on strong institutions and departments'; progress in planning was necessary if the polytechnics and colleges were to meet the changing needs of industry and commerce in the 1990s and provide in new ways for a wider range of students; this called 'for a more effective lead from the centre and the reward of success and enterprise in meeting new national needs, in place of a system giving undue weight to local interests'. Local authority and voluntary colleges meeting the criteria would be given corporate status. The institutions transferred from the local authorities would have governing bodies with strong representation from local and regional industry, commerce and the professions 'and on which dominance by local authority representatives is no longer possible', though it was not intended to weaken the local and regional links and roles of the institutions concerned, 'on the contrary, these should remain a distinctive feature'. The government was proposing to develop a system of funding 'contracts' to replace grants. The planning and funding of this sector would be the responsibility of a new Polytechnics and Colleges Funding Council, which would replace the National Advisory Body. The PCFC was to be an 'independent non-departmental body appointed by the Secretary of State for Education and Science'. It would have a small membership 'with a strong industrial and commercial element, as well as members from higher education institutions'. The Secretary of State would provide 'general guidance' to the PCFC and would have 'reserve powers of direction'. At the same time the University Grants Committee would be replaced by a Universities Funding Council, which would be responsible for the allocation to universities of the funding whose level would be decided on by the government. The government would be particularly concerned to see that the UFC's arrangements for making funds available to universities 'properly reward success in developing co-operation with and meeting the needs of industry and commerce'. The funding of the Scottish universities was to remain an integral part of the UFC rather than the responsibility of a new body to cover university and non-universities in Scotland, as had been recommended by the Scottish Tertiary Education Advisory Council.[90]

There were mixed responses to the White Paper. The polytechnics generally welcomed the proposal to give them corporate status, and the release from local authority control was viewed by most — but by no means all — directors and principals of polytechnics and colleges as a further step towards real equivalence with the universities, and therefore as bolstering their institutional strengths and statuses. There was widespread alarm on the other hand at the prospect of increased central control over both sectors of higher education. Local authorities were no longer to be allowed, for example, to make a contribution — known as 'topping up' — to institutions for whose finances they had been responsible — and it was estimated that this would mean a loss of £40m to the polytechnics and colleges.[91] Both the universities and the polytechnics and colleges were deeply concerned about future funding, and the CNAA's response to the White Paper, while broadly welcoming, drew attention to the resources issue as a matter of concern:

> Council considers it vitally important that the admission of additional students to higher education should be accompanied by proper access to additional resources. CNAA's validating experience in recent years suggests that any further diminution in levels of

resourcing would in many cases place the quality of courses in jeopardy.[92]

In all of these respects the government had made what amounted not only to firm recommendations, but also to decisions which were not intended to be negotiable. Without any major alterations the White Paper proposals were carried into effect, either through the 1988 Education Act or through other regulations. Although the White Paper itself was more circumspect in most respects than its Green Paper progenitor, papers issued by the DES at the same time as the White Paper made the underlying intention of the proposed transfer of the twenty-nine polytechnics and twenty-eight 'other institutions' (with eleven others given the opportunity to opt in) to PCFC control and corporate status extremely clear. In a paragraph entitled 'objectives' the DES indicated that:

> The institutions will provide higher education and training in line with the objective set out in chapter 1 of the White Paper, and in response to local, regional and national needs. The Government will, in particular, expect institutions to concentrate on equipping students for working life, on encouraging entrepreneurial attitudes among students and staff and, where appropriate, on carrying out applied research.[93]

The Council's response to the DES's consultative document on the changes in national planning for higher education was concerned primarily with the nature of the relationships to be established between the new PCFC and the CNAA.[94]

Given their corporate status and the pressures on them to sell their services — including for research — in the market place, the polytechnics and former local authority and voluntary colleges were from 1989 to some extent in competition with one another and with the universities. Higher education in general was being driven towards a new relationship with 'clients' and 'consumers', and the image of American universities, both public and private, was not far from the model of planning embodied in the White Paper. The majority of funding for higher education remained, however, government-provided, though the government's expressed intention was to diminish the proportion of public moneys in higher education funding. The British Conservative government was not alone in moving in such a direction for higher education generally — as various European governments of different political profiles, as well as the Labour government in Australia, followed suit. The ambiguity for British higher education lay in the uncertain balance between government funding and what could be earned by selling services to industry, local authorities and others. For the polytechnics and colleges the additional ambiguity was that between strong government steerage and the relative freedoms of incorporation and accreditation. The level of fees for full-time courses remained a government decision, competition for overseas students became real, and forms of strategic planning, publicity and public relations — for many of which advice and expertise had to be purchased — became a new feature of the day-to-day lives of the institutions.

The polytechnics, local education and voluntary colleges designated in the White Paper acquired corporate status on 1 April 1989 (Bulmershe College of Higher Education, losing a significant amount of 'topping up' from its local authority, negotiated a merger with the University of Reading, which itself was having financial difficulties). For the institutions the transition to corporate status meant major, often anguished, internal changes in time for the handover. While the PCFC was to negotiate and distribute funds, it planned to do so with a looser rein than had the NAB, leaving institutions free to plan their own courses and expenditure. The institutions submitted overall Strategic Plans by the end of June 1989, and on that basis the process of allocating the central resources available was undertaken, though at that stage the principles on which the PCFC was to allocate them had not been finalized. The CNAA was also involved in discussing with the PCFC what advice on quality it might be appropriate for the Council to give.

At all points in its history from 1964 the CNAA was part of a constant process of change in higher education. From the mid-1980s the CNAA itself underwent radical changes, as did higher education as a whole. Through the 1970s and early 1980s the CNAA had been responding to expectations of, and within, the system, though with some internal resistance to the more substantial changes that some institutions and some people were anxious to take place. It had been constantly faced with the problem of how best, at any given time, to define the difficult balance inherent in the dual role it had been set in helping its related institutions to develop, at the same time as retaining responsibility for standards. From 1984 it made its responses regarding new relationships with its institutions, following a long history of attempts at compromise and progress. *Future Strategy*, a changed Charter, accreditation and restructuring were outcomes both of that long history and of changed circumstances. The CNAA had at the same time established its reputation as being able to take initiatives, promote development, offer intelligence and advice, and participate actively and effectively in the formulation of policy and the improvement of practice in higher education. It had survived to make its mark in both familiar and new ways in yet another landscape of higher education.

Notes

1 Secretary of State for Education and Science, *et al.* (1985) *The Development of Higher Education into the 1990s*, HMSO, p. 28.
2 *ibid.*, pp. 3–5.
3 *ibid.*, pp. 8–9.
4 *ibid.*, pp. 20–1.

5 *ibid.*, p. 37.
6 Clive Booth (1986) 'Is there a policy at all?', *Times Higher Education Supplement*, 16 May.
7 Ngaio Crequer in *Times Higher Education Supplement*, 22 November 1985.
8 UGC response to the Green Paper on higher education, as a letter from Sir Peter Swinnerton-Dyer to Sir Keith Joseph, 11 November 1985.
9 CN (1984) National Advisory Body for Local Authority Higher Education, 'Towards a Strategy for Local Authority Higher Education in the late 1980s and Beyond' — Response by the Council for National Academic Awards.
10 CAIP minutes, 13 June 1985.
11 CN (1986) 'The Development of Higher Education into the 1990s': CNAA's Response to the Government Green Paper.
12 *ibid.*
13 CN, *Annual Report 1985–86*, pp. 9–10.
14 Peter Toyne (1979) Project Director, Educational Credit Transfer: Feasibility Study, Final Report, Vol. I: Text, n.p.
15 J.E. Salmon (1981) 'Credit worthiness and credit transfer' in Standing Conference on Higher Education, *Proceedings of the Third Annual Conference 1981: The Development and Operation of International Higher Education Programs*, p. 34.
16 CN (1983) Working Party on Credit Transfer and Accumulation minutes, 18 October 1983.
17 Peter Brooke to Edwin Kerr, 31 July 1984 (with CAIP papers 84/20).
18 CN (1984) Pilot Credit Transfer and Accumulation Scheme in the London Area, October.
19 CN (1986) Credit Transfer: current developments and future needs: report of a CNAA workshop . . . 26 June.
20 CN (1986) Credit Accumulation and Transfer Scheme: a summary of progress, September.
21 CN (1988) *Development Services Briefing 7: Curriculum Analysis and Credit Transfer* (report on 1987 project by B.J. McGettrick and M.J. Hanlon at St Andrew's College of Education, Glasgow).
22 CN (1988) Registry for Credit Accumulation and Transfer.
23 Rita Austin (1977) The Creation of a Research and Development Unit, 17 March.
24 Cmin, 2 May 1978.
25 Cmin, 14 February 1979; General Committee minutes, 4 February 1980.
26 CN (1982) The Role of the Development Services Unit, 14 June.
27 Cmin, 11 December 1984.
28 The CNAA Development Fund (report to CAIP), 25 October 1985.
29 Development Fund Sub-Committee, Constitution, with CAIP papers, 13 June 1985.
30 Development Fund Sub-Committee, Report of the Second and Third Meetings (report to CAIP, 25 October 1985).
31 Development Fund Sub-Committee, Report of Meetings held on 22 November 1985 and 7 February 1986 (report to CAIP, 21 February 1986).
32 CN (1987) The Development Fund: an interim report, November.
33 Cf John Brennan and Philip McGeevor (1988) *Graduates at Work: Degree Courses and the Labour Market*, Jessica Kingsley; Harold Silver and John Brennan (1988) *A Liberal Vocationalism*, Methuen; Tom Bourner and Mahmoud Hamed (1987) *Entry Qualifications and Degree Performance*, CNAA, Development Services, and various Development Services publications on first degree classification, students on part-time first degree courses . . .
34 Consultative Paper on the Development of Council's Relationship with Institutions, 28 November 1984, sent to Principals and Directors by the Chief Officer, 11 December 1984.

35 Chairman's Study Group, Analysis of Responses to the Consultative Document on the Development of Council's Relationship with Institutions, 18 February 1985.

36 Cmin, 12 March 1985.

37 DES, List of Issues on which Comments are Invited, with Council agenda, 4 June 1985.

38 Minutes of Committees, with Council agenda 4 June 1985.

39 Response of the Council for National Academic Awards to a Report of the Comittee of Enquiry into the Academic Validation of Degree Courses in Public Sector Higher Education, 6 June 1985.

40 Sir Alastair Pilkington, HS interview.

41 'NAB's response to the Lindop report', *NAB Bulletin*, summer 1985, pp. 14–15.

42 Reviews Co-ordinating Sub-Committee, A Framework for the Streamlining of Validation and Review, 9 May 1985, received by CAIP, 3 June 1985.

43 Kerr to Directors and Principals, 12 July 1985.

44 Cmin, 16 July 1985.

45 Newcastle Polytechnic, 'Institutional Accreditation', n.d.

46 Council's Relationships with Institutions: a report on developments since 4 June 1985, with Council papers, 16 July 1985.

47 *ibid*.

48 Newcastle-upon-Tyne Polytechnic and CNAA, Agreement between the Polytechnic and the Council, 4 October 1985; Sheffield City Polytechnic and CNAA, Agreement between the Polytechnic and the Council, 4 October 1985; CAIP, The Development of the Council's Relationships with Institutions: a report on the present position, 5 November 1985 (with CAIP papers, 14 November 1985).

49 Institutions which have notified the Council of their Wish to Negotiate Agreements involving a Delegation of Authority for Course Validation and Review, 29 October 1985; Reviews Co-ordinating Sub-Committee, Institutional Agreement: key issues, 29 October 1985 (both with CAIP papers 14 November 1985).

50 Letter of 28 November 1985 (CDP Paper 85.230).

51 Cmin, 16 October 1985; Pilkington, HS interview.

52 Sir Keith Joseph, Statement to House of Commons, 17 March 1986; Degree Courses in the Public Sector: Quality and Validation — The Government's Response to the Lindop Report.

53 Sir Keith Joseph to Sir Alastair Pilkington, 17 March 1986.

54 Sir Norman Lindop, HS interview.

55 *Development Services Briefing No. 3: Institutional Agreements and the Validation Process*, 1987; Clem Adelman and Janet Powney (1986) Institutional Self-Validation and Course Validation, paper to SRHE Conference.

56 Reviews Co-ordinating Sub-Committee, Proposed Common Wording and Format for an Institutional Agreement involving Delegated Authority for Course Validation and Review (with CAIP papers, 11 June 1986); Agreement between the CNAA and Institution involving Delegated Authority for Course Validation and Review, September 1986.

57 CAIP, Developments Following the Government's Response to the report of the Lindop Committee (with CAIP papers, 11 June 1986).

58 CN (1986), *Quality and Validation: Future Relationships with Institutions. A Consultative Document*, 1986.

59 CN, Responses to Consultative Document on 'Quality and Validation: Future Relationships with Institutions' — Main Points Emerging from the Responses, 20 January 1987 (with Council papers, 5 February 1987).

60 CN (1987) *Future Strategy: Principles and Operation*, February.

61 Cmin, 12 March 1987.

62 Cmin, 17 December 1987.

63 CN *Handbook 1988*, p. 143.

64 *ibid.*, pp. 152-3.

65 *Future Strategy*, p. 4.

66 Malcolm Frazer to Directors and Principals, 11 June 1987.

67 Newcastle upon Tyne Polytechnic, Application to Become a CNAA Accredited Institution, April 1987.

68 Sir Denis Rooke, HS interview.

69 Sir Alastair Pilkington, speech at dinner to mark his retirement as Chairman of the Council, 13 July 1987; Pilkington, HS interview.

70 The phrase is Edwin Kerr's, HS interview.

71 Overy, HS interview.

72 Kerr, HS interview

73 *Academic Validation in Public Sector Higher Education*, 1985, p. 77.

74 *The Economist*, 'Valediction for validators', 30 November 1985.

75 CN (1985) Summary of Price Waterhouse Associates Report on Management and Organisation of the CNAA (as at October 1984) and a Note on Implementation, circulated to Council members, 28 January.

76 Eric E. Robinson (1988) 'The polytechnics: 20 years of "social control"', *Higher Education Review*, 20, 2, pp. 22-3.

77 *Times Higher Education Supplement*, 'Reshaping the CNAA', 29 August 1986.

78 Sir Bryan Nicholson, 'Chairman's statement', *Annual Report 1987-88*, p. 11.

79 CN (1984) Consultative Paper on Future Arrangements for Relationships between the CNAA and the NAB, June.

80 Committee for the Built Environment minutes, 5 March 1986.

81 CN (1987) Review of Relationships between the CNAA and the National Advisory Body for Public Sector Higher Education (with Council papers, 8 April).

82 Committee for Arts and Humanities (1986) Review of the Effects of Council's Policy Statement on the Implications of Developments in Information Technology for Undergraduate Courses (1982), with CAIP papers, 24 June.

83 DES (1985) *An Assessment of the Costs and Benefits of Sandwich Education*, HMSO; Kerr to Leslie Wagner, Deputy Secretary of the NAB, 7 May 1986.

84 Committee for Teacher Education, Initial Teacher Education Board (1986) Notes on the Validation of Initial Teacher Education Courses in the Context of the Application of Externally Devised Criteria.

85 CN *Annual Report 1985-86*, p. 16; *Annual Report 1987-88*, p. 18.

86 *Managing Design: An Initiative in Management Education*, CNAA, 1984; *Managing Design: An Update*, CNAA, 1987; *Art and Design Papers 1: Professional and Business Awareness in Art and Design Degree Courses*, 1986.

87 CN, *Annual Report 1987-88*, pp. 34-42.

88 Quoted in John Fairhall (1986) 'Baker promises expansion of higher education', *The Guardian*, 24 March.

89 Anne Caborn (1986) 'If our universities were animals, they'd be pandas', *Today*, 23 September.

90 Secretary of State for Education and Science *et al.* (1987) *Higher Education: meeting the challenge*, HMSO, passim.

91 NATFHE, Letter to academic staffs in polytechnics and major providers of higher education, 20 May 1987.

92 Sir Ron Dearing to Secretary of State, 15 April 1987.

93 DES (1987) Changes in Structure and Planning for Higher Education: Polytechnics and Colleges Sector, April.

94 CN (1987) Changes in Structure and Planning for Higher Education: comments of the Council on the government's consultative documents on the polytechnics and colleges sector, May (with Council papers, 14 July).

Chapter 11

Pasts and Futures

Reconstructing a history involves choosing emphases. In the case of the CNAA, as in others, there are inevitably perceptions, interpretations, silences, that are not shared or are differently understood by other participants and onlookers. Some emphases, however, command a large degree of shared attention and agreement, even if there are differences of judgment about why events and processes took shape, whether they might have been shaped or timed differently, and what roles particular people or structures played or might have played. With those reservations it is clear that the CNAA has not been merely a figure in changing landscapes, it has itself been a major contributor to the changes. It has been, as it was intended to be, centrally concerned with widening access to higher education and maintaining and raising standards — two inseparable elements in its work. It has therefore been involved in extending and reinterpreting the curricula of higher education, and creating and taking advantage of the opportunities presented. It has addressed the difficult balance between exercising its own responsibilities and enabling its related institutions to shoulder theirs — with how many cheers for its record in doing so at different times in its twenty-five years of activity is probably the issue most open to differences of emphasis and interpretation. It has taken a process of peer validation and review pioneered by the NCTA and developed it into an instrument which has been at work for institutions and courses serving a majority of the country's higher education students — an instrument which in the late 1980s has been adapting to new relationships. It has made peer validation and review part of the culture of public sector institutions, even in those institutions no longer subject to formal validation by the CNAA. Against the background outlined in the first two chapters it has — together with its related institutions — established new dimensions and characteristics for the 'higher education' which — in the space of a quarter of a century — the universities have come to share with a range of other institutions. Future historians may further find that it also had significant impacts on the universities themselves.

The broadening of access to higher education has been a constant preoccupation of the CNAA in a number of respects. It has been instrumental particularly in establishing the polytechnics and colleges as an alternative sector of higher education, with the increasing numbers of students that we have seen entering the new higher education institutions and the expanded and new areas of study that they have represented. It has pioneered new areas of study — such as business studies and computer studies — before they have appeared in the universities. It has consistently emphasized the importance of the development of provision for non-standard and mature students, and has emphasized the need for its institutions to take advantage of the opportunities offered by the CNAA's liberal regulations on mature students. From the very beginning it recognized the traditions of public sector institutions in catering for part-time as well as full-time students. After expressing its interest in 1965 in hearing from 'any colleges which have proposals for part-time degree courses in mind, particularly those arranged for mature students', it described its 'considerable pleasure' the following year in being able 'to approve one part-time course leading to its degree of B.Sc., and two part-time courses leading to its degree of M.Sc.'. There was clearly a need for 'part-time courses specially designed for mature students including teachers'.[1] The CNAA has taken up the challenge to acknowledge 'experiential' or 'prior' learning as a contribution to higher education qualifications, and it has developed a capacity to accredit the in-house education and training activities of industrial, commercial and professional bodies. The Credit Accumulation and Transfer Scheme has been a major breakthrough of the 1980s towards broader opportunities for these and other kinds of potential students. The CNAA has also regularly liaised with other bodies — including the Business and Technician Education Council — to examine the mesh between further and higher education courses of study. As one aspect of this interest one of the projects supported by the CNAA's Development Fund and conducted at the Roehampton Institute of Higher Education in 1986–88 was a study of different models of the relationship between further and higher education through 'access courses', the selection and assessment of access course students, access course curricula and management, and the dissemination of 'good practice'.[2] When the government decided to plan for a national framework for such access courses as a mode of transition to higher education it invited the CNAA to act as 'handling agent' for the initiative on behalf of the polytechnics and colleges, and the universities, in partnership with the CVCP. A statement of principles and an invitation to intending validating agencies to apply for a franchise under the scheme were both published in 1989.[3] The concern of the CNAA and its related institutions to widen access has meant greater diversity of institutions, opportunities, courses, and paths through higher education. This has been a central way in which the CNAA has implemented its Charter, and inextricably related to it have been the processes by which it has sought to establish, maintain and enhance standards.

While 'standards' and 'quality' have been the heart of the CNAA's concerns, neither it nor other organizations which provide or are concerned with higher education have been eager to define or to debate the concepts too closely. The National Advisory Body addressed the question directly in 1984 in a paper on 'Quality', acknowledging that it had hitherto been making judgments about quality but 'it has not defined, nor stated explicitly, what that quality is, or consists of'. This Secretariat paper began to fill the gap by summarizing discussions that had taken place, emphasizing 'role or function', the achievement, or otherwise, of declared objectives and processes' (which is very much the basis on which the accreditation of institutions has taken place in the United States). At the same time it emphasized that quantification and measurement were dangerous proxies for judgments of quality, and that such measures were only a part of quality assessment, which is 'ultimately, at least in large part, subjective'. Christopher Ball, as Chairman of the NAB Board, continued the debate with a paper entitled 'What the hell is quality?', and the Society for Research into Higher Education ran a conference on questions of standards.[4] Within the CNAA, especially in the late 1970s and 1980s, officers and committees wrestled with the definition of standards in relation to the Council's terminologies and procedures regarding validation and review, appraisal and evaluation. Summarizing earlier analysis, David Billing in 1983 underlined that standards had to do with more than the level of performance — they were also concerned with 'the calibre and potential of the students at admission; the quality of the students' learning experience promoted by the institution; the final level of achievement of the course aims as reflected in the assessment of students' performance'. The CNAA was therefore concerned with 'the quality of the educational process and its environment, as well as its products, and it is important to note that any estimate of the quality of the process rests largely on the perceptions and judgments of staff, students, examiners, and employers'.[5] A good deal of the CNAA's interest in questions of standards across the years has therefore focussed both on attempts to clarify criteria and on the needs and experience of grappling with them in operation.[6] The CNAA and others have in various ways tried to detect how the validation and related procedures have in precise terms influenced behaviours which affect the standards of course provision and monitoring. An HMI commentary in 1983 on degree courses in public sector higher education, underlined, for example, that 'the processes by which the CNAA scrutinises course proposals before validation have encouraged staff to formulate more explicitly the means and teaching methods through which a measure of integration in the curriculum is achieved'.[7] It is not so much questions of integration that are important here as the pressures towards definition, explanation, explicitness, in relation to those processes which affect the learning experience and its outcomes — teaching methods, attention to curriculum design, assessment, course review... It is this that explains the central interest of the institutions and of CNAA committees and visiting panels over the years in questions of professional development or institutional machineries for dealing with the processes which underlie the concern with standards. In 1979, to take a single example, the subject boards of the Committee for Science and Technology, while reviewing course approvals, had detected 'signs of falling academic health, either through original promise not being fulfilled, or through a failure to maintain previously acceptable levels of provisions and performance', and this had to do with resource levels and a range of other particular problems. The academic health of courses had to be 'a matter of continuing concern to all partners in the complex processes of higher education . . . it is no less important to sustain and develop the quality of demonstrably successful courses'. The Committee was therefore invited to give its attention to the matter 'by considering the indicators of academic health and present problems connected with them'.[8]

These are no more than pointers to the CNAA's necessary and continuing concern not only with implementing procedures intended to safeguard standards, but also with analyzing and understanding the nature of the exercise itself. The range of elements in the CNAA's approach to standards is perhaps best illustrated, however, by Sir Michael Clapham's opening address to the degree congregation in 1976. What, he asked, is quality in higher education? And he answered:

> It is the quality of those who teach and those who plan the courses which are taught. It is the quality of those who are admitted to a course of study, and the quality of those who assess and examine them. It is the quality of the academic environment in which teachers and taught alike move and have their being: that unquantifiable, ideal blend of intellectual freedom and intellectual discipline in which ideas multiply and are cross-fertilised, learning flourishes and sciolism wilts. It is an atmosphere which encourages a broad diversity of interests combined with a profound depth of penetration. To some extent it may be enhanced by the non-academic pursuits available . . . Least important but never to be disregarded, it is the quality of the physical environment; the resources available, the facilities for using them.

Applying this comprehensive statement to the work of the CNAA, he emphasized that it was only the last item in the list that was amenable to other than subjective judgment: 'it thus becomes the Council's task to organise subjective judgment on a vast scale'. He went on to ask whether and how this should in fact be done, in the CNAA's 'complex system of visitations and discussions, both at course level and college level'.[9] In relation to all of the elements in Sir Michael Clapham's list, in fact, the CNAA has had to concern itself with the purposes and operational details of the environment of institutions and the content of courses, the work of external examiners and changing levels of resources, the balance of curricula and the relationship of academic organization and delivery to the pressures of local and national control.

Whatever reservations individuals may have about specific procedures or decisions (or absence of decisions) of the CNAA, it is commonly agreed that the impact of the CNAA on British, and not only British, higher education has, over the past quarter of a century, been in terms of its sustained concern with the expansion of student access and the enhancement of standards. One or the other or both of these elements feature in response to the question: what you would most want to record about the CNAA from its creation in 1964? Jean Rossiter, for example, as one of the CNAA's earliest officers and concerned with the development of new subject areas in former colleges of technology, emphasized that without the CNAA there could have been no polytechnics, given its influence on resources for institutions and their structures — notably the role of academic boards: 'democratization stems from the CNAA'. Cynthia Iliffe, a long-serving officer of the CNAA, notably as Registrar for Business and Management Studies, describes the 1970s as enormously exciting precisely because the work of the CNAA was worthwhile in 'broadening access and expanding the system of higher education as a whole'. Ann Ridler, concerned over a long period of time with the arts and with policy issues, also emphasized the strengthening of the polytechnics in the early years, the development of course review as a major strength of the system, and the contribution to quality in higher education of the encouragement of courses as 'logical, progressive wholes', and the building of a tradition of 'thinking about why'. Roger Woodbridge, Assistant Registrar for Science, with thirteen years experience of the CNAA, emphasized both the conflicts that had been a thread in the CNAA's history, but also the gradual build-up of public awareness of the CNAA and the public sector, especially of the latter. The CNAA had played a large part in this by setting the standards. Although universities were still seen as 'preferable' in the public eye as places to send one's children the public sector had established itself as credible. Edwin Kerr, Chief Officer for fifteen years, picks out the ability of the CNAA to respond to policy developments and influence the system; the contribution to the expansion of provision in subject areas such as teacher education, art and design and management studies — and therefore to innovatory approaches in those areas and such new or newly developing ones as computer science or the creative and performing arts; the development of the institutions' academic boards; opportunities for mature students, and for independent study; modular courses and credit accumulation; in general the planning and coordination of a sector contributing to increases in scale and variety in higher education. Bill Gutteridge, as a university professor and one of the longest-serving members of the Council, including as Chairman of the Committee for Arts and Social Studies, stresses the operation of the CNAA as an informal network within which university and polytechnic people could meet and 'come to terms with each other', as they did for example in the Political Studies Board with which he was associated. For him the success of the CNAA lies in its having set out on the 'tightrope' of standards and opportunities for higher education, and in walking it successfully — 'better, in fact, than anywhere in the world, to ensure that higher education expanded without lowering quality', to ensure that an honours degree, a II(i) or whatever meant something. Marion North, Director of the Laban Centre for Movement and Dance, reflecting on the difficulty of surmounting the first hurdle in obtaining CNAA approval for a degree course, underlines the CNAA's concern with staffing and resources alongside conceptual questions, and judges that the CNAA was ultimately 'asking the right things'. If a degree was to be the first of its kind 'it had to be good'. George Tolley, first Director of Sheffield Polytechnic, long active in the CNAA, including as Chairman of the Management Board, while severely critical of the CNAA's partnership in validation policy and the operation of the subject boards from the late 1970s, underlines the considerable development of quality in degree courses to which the CNAA contributed. One of its great contributions was the development of peer evaluation, and as the 'guardian of standards' it was instrumental in establishing the credibility of the public sector and its degrees within higher education and with employers. Sir Norman Lindop, former Director of Hatfield Polytechnic, long active in the CNAA, including as Chairman of the Committee for Education, and then Chairman of the Committee of Inquiry on Academic Validation, also sharing some of the criticism of CNAA procedures from the late 1970s, considers that the CNAA 'changed the face of higher education in this country' — which is particularly clear if one looks back at the external degree system and compares it with the 'extraordinary developments' which followed. The process of validation was fundamental, a 'critical mechanism', and he has 'not the least doubt of its overwhelming influence for progress'. It 'materially assisted academic development' in those institutions which would never have achieved the maturity and status that they did without the CNAA. The National Advisory Body, commenting on 'the Lindop Report', underlined — as we have seen — the CNAA's contribution to higher education, and it is worth recalling the terms of the NAB's comments:

> There can be no doubting the beneficial effects the CNAA has had over the past twenty years on both the standard and the standing of qualifications from public sector institutions . . . these standards have been achieved while encouraging and accommodating curriculum innovation, more flexible course structure, development into new subject areas, wider access for students . . . [10]

Clearly concern with standards and access has to be broken down into the specifics of policy and operation, and from the mid-1960s we have traced many of the elements involved in both of these. Analysis and judgment of the CNAA's role therefore involves consideration of the nature of its responsiveness, including for example to the opportunities opened up by the James report on teacher education or the Finniston report on engineering. 'Responsiveness' has also to do with perceptions of the state of development of institutions, of disciplines, of existing and emergent needs in the professions, industry and commerce. It has to do with opportunities of the kind associated, for example, with the CNAA's role in developing interest in design management or credit transfer. The concern with standards has also had to relate both to the CNAA's own procedures in 'guaranteeing' them, and to the range of institutional characteristics we have considered. Included, and of central importance to the CNAA from its creation, has been its concern with research, with emphasizing its relationship to the academic health of courses and institutions, with monitoring its development or its failure to develop, in general and in specific areas,[11] with establishing policies for research, with supporting it when opportunity has arisen, and with acting as advocate on behalf of public sector institutions in relation to the research councils and other bodies which support research. The specifics of standards have also involved the CNAA in continuous efforts to use its networks to promote subject and curriculum development, through the mechanism of seminars and workshops, conferences and working parties, as well as through the activities of its officers and committees.

In its concern with the curriculum and its delivery, the CNAA has had to confront not only questions of standards within individual course and programme structures, but also questions of desirable 'balance' and the relationship of students' experience of courses to their employment intentions or opportunities. 'Balance' in the early years of the CNAA meant the controversial area of complementary and contrasting studies, or the definition of appropriate objectives for courses of study in the polytechnics and colleges of higher education. It also meant a continuing interest in the nature and provision of sandwich courses. The interest in employment outcomes has been a matter not only of relationships with employers and the labour market, but also close attention to those of institutions and their courses. There has invariably been an assumption in the CNAA's approach to validation that employment opportunities should to one degree or another be a concern of institutions in appraising their course proposals and their implementation. Subject boards have at different times — particularly at times of shrinking graduate employment — laid considerable stress on the 'market research' aspect of course proposals. In 1982 the CNAA indicated that the points which boards had found to be 'of particular value' within institutions' critical appraisal of their courses were 'statistics of student cohort admission and progression and career outlets'.[12] In the 1980s the CNAA commissioned and supported work intended to provide data on the career experience of graduates with CNAA awards, both in general and in specific subject areas.[13] The CNAA and its institutions developed over the years an approach to courses of study which sought to bring together the traditions of the 'public sector', with its strong interest in the labour market and employment outcomes, and the wider characteristics of a 'liberal' higher education. A 'liberal vocationalism' was the outcome, one in which the vocational intentions of courses were not narrowly conceived, and in which the generally accepted aims of higher education were not divorced from the world of employment.[14]

In all of these characteristics of the CNAA, as we have seen, a dominant one has been its explicitness, and its encouragement of its related institutions to be equally so. The validation of courses and the review of institutions produced an emphasis on documentation which was often regarded in the polytechnics and colleges — particularly by those responsible for producing it — as laborious or ritualistic. What it accomplished at the same time, however, was a constant concern for explanation, for what was often called the 'rationale' of courses, for the definition of institutional purposes which we have seen emphasized by different institutions at different times. The CNAA's own operations have been highly documented, as a result of the accounts of debate in working parties or committees, working papers by officers and reports widely circulated within and beyond the CNAA. The CNAA's record of published policy statements, guidelines, research-based information, consultative documents, reports and the like is considerable. Most of the CNAA's decisions, intentions, debates, responses, controversies or concerns had their reflection in documents circulated to institutions or other forms of public statement. Subject boards and committees not only received detailed documentation, they also recorded and explained their discussions and decisions in detail. Between institutions and the CNAA an intensive communication often developed — whether seeking or giving explanations, making or discussing proposals — which may or may not have related to courses and parochial concerns, disseminating information, making response and counter-response, expressing anxiety, anger or gratitude. The NCTA established and the CNAA further developed procedures which almost inevitably produced such levels of explicitness. The CNAA and its institutions operated from the 1960s in a context of public accountability — whether to Ministers or the DES, or in the general context of the responsibilities placed upon it by its Charter — which made its processes intensely and deliberately open to scrutiny and debate. The very concept of validation, review or evaluation made this true both of the CNAA and of any institution which came into association with it. It was to a large extent this characteristic of the CNAA and its associated institutions that also made the CNAA internationally visible, not only with regard to its role in Hong Kong, but also in the interest shown by institutions, academics, administrators and governments in other countries in its operation. The CNAA similarly often saw itself in international perspective, as when, for instance, the Working Party on Longer Term Developments in 1982 'received information about the systems employed for the assurance of academic standards in other countries — particularly Australia and the USA'.[15]

In the case of the CNAA, as with all institutions, there are difficulties in interpreting and judging the persistence of characteristics — the same features at different times, the confidence that may be both strength and weakness, the procedure that may be both innovatory and conservative, the virtues of continuity and of discontinuity. There is also the difficulty of angle of vision, and as we have seen in precise cases very different judgments may be made of events as experienced from the Council, from the boards, from the institutions, by officers or members, by college principals or course teams, by the CNAA itself and by other agencies. What was clearly consistent strength for some was for others dirigisme or worse. The work of the boards was for some both the essential mechanism for safeguarding standards and promoting subject development, and for others the main obstacle to necessary change in the operations of the CNAA. The role of the Council in providing the necessary benchmarks for quality and comparability was for some an outdated role almost as soon as it took effect, and from then on could be interpreted as a brake on institutional development. Somewhere in the late 1970s and early 1980s is a point at which critics detect what some see as a loss of confidence, and others a failure to grasp opportunities or understand realities. It is only by placing such judgments of strength or weakness in the historical complexities of the time, in the nature of the competing values and constituencies, in the competing claims for attention and priority, that the judgments can be made without excessive portrayal in black or white.

The principal context and component for the history of the CNAA has been the redefinition of 'higher education'. The new contexts developing at the end of the 1980s did not make it easy to interpret the changing roles of the CNAA, but a configuration of well-established, recently changed and new directions for its activities was rapidly taking shape. By the end of the decade some 90 per cent of students in the polytechnics and colleges sector would be in 'accredited' institutions, and eighty-five or so institutions — mainly smaller or specialist institutions or those with only a small proportion of their work at or above degree level — would remain as 'associated' institutions — all of them in vastly changed circumstances. Even by the end of 1988 the Committees for Art and Design and for the Performing Arts, for example, were reporting that 'only a tiny number of colleges remained in a traditional relationship with CNAA',[16] and these 'traditional relationships' were themselves substantially changing. Following the 1987 White Paper and the 1988 Education Reform Act, the institutions were having to tackle simultaneously the new responsibilities of their corporate status, and the implications of their changed academic status vis-à-vis the CNAA. John Brennan interpreted the new position of the institutions in terms of the continuing but changed external accountability of the polytechnics and colleges, and the relationship between their two new sets of responsibilities:

The messages of incorporation are of financial responsibility, of efficiency, of contracts and markets, and of competitiveness. The messages of accreditation are of academic responsibility, of collective responsibility for standards, of peer review and the institution's place within the wider academic community.

Between the two sets of messages lay those of quality, to which competition was not necessarily antithetical. Shoddy products might not survive in the market place, but in higher education 'the nature and quality of the product is not easy to assess':

> In an increasingly competitive setting, academic institutions may find themselves needing to present ever better evidence about the quality of their work for intending students, for employers of graduates, for funding bodies.

However institutions were viewed, 'rather than being the source of conflict between the competitive and community models of higher education, quality is part of the essential linkage between them'.[17]

Part of the CNAA's continuing role was clearly to be that of providing the system with such 'evidence', and with the intelligence on which national and institutional judgments and policies might be based. The Council in fact now saw itself as 'a national centre for the collection and dissemination of information about academic standards and developments in higher education',[18] and in addition to its work of validation and re-accreditation it was shaping a programme of seminars, meetings and conferences that would contribute to the promotion of enhanced standards. In 1987–88, for instance, a series of regional seminars on the humanities and employment was held at commercial and industrial venues — Wedgwood, the IBM Research Centre and British Steel. The Committee for Life Sciences sponsored a meeting of external examiners, in association with the British Psychological Society, the Association of Heads of Psychology Departments and Plymouth Polytechnic. The Committee for Health Studies held a series of meeting with representatives of professional and registration bodies, the first being with the College of Radiographers.[19] For the following year the CNAA was planning induction meetings for new members, workshops for newly-appointed external examiners and a series of validation workshops to supplement a successsful series already conducted. It intended organizing an annual programme of workshops and conferences on questions relating to the maintenance and enhancement of quality. It saw the development of the Credit Accumulation and Transfer Scheme as a priority, as more institutions introduced schemes based on CATS, and as increasing interest was being shown from many directions. In 1987–88, for example, the scheme was discussed with some 200 representatives of the universities at seminars at Warwick, York, Strathclyde and Oxford universities.[20] By 1989 the CAT scheme had established procedures 'for the allocation of credit towards CNAA awards for in-company training programmes, and about fifteen employing organizations have received credit in this way'.[21] In changed circumstances the CNAA was to continue its dual concern for access and for standards.

As in previous stages of its history the CNAA was also continuing to explore new subject areas or possibilities of awards that would embody this concern. In 1989, for example, the Chief Executive, Malcolm Frazer, was outlining developments in the area of initial education programmes for new managers, in connection with the Council for Management Education and Development. In association with the Training Agency the CNAA commissioned five pilot programmes for such managers, operating at four English polytechnics and one Scottish college, with the aim of 'meeting the requirements of employers and employees for high-quality education based on workplace skills, abilities and competence, while also incorporating an appropriate level of academic rigour'. The outcome was intended to be a new certificate award and, following a review of the Diploma in Management Studies and the MBA, a new hierarchy of CNAA awards in management education.[22] Joint conferences or seminars with other bodies in such fields as media studies also pointed to the possibility of new departures. In relation to established areas of study what the CNAA planned for a beginning in 1988 was a rolling programme of 'subject and course development reviews', to examine changes in courses and their responsiveness or otherwise to academic and social change. These reviews were intended to consider: the number, variety, aims and structure of courses; data about students (from enrolment to employment); developments and trends in the curriculum; innovations in teaching methods and in methods of assessment; links with industry and the professions; developments and trends in research. Information would be collected and collated and disseminated through publications, workshops and conferences. These subject reviews, including topic-based reviews across subject areas, were to take place at five-yearly intervals.[23] The CNAA's continued commitment to resourcing development projects was for work in four priority areas: quality assurance; higher education and work; continuing education, and extending opportunities.[24] The configuration of developing activities remained United Kingdom-wide, with a particularly strengthened development in Scotland. By 1987–88 the adaptation of CATS to the needs of Scotland was the subject of advanced consultations. A newly-reconstituted Committee for Scotland was designed to play a 'more positive and proactive role in CNAA's work in Scotland', and it pressed successfully in 1987 for 'a permanent officer presence' in Scotland,[25] and such an officer based in Scotland was in fact appointed in 1989. In 1989 the Council was actively developing a 'Five year development plan', containing a 'mission statement' embodying the CNAA's commitment to three principal objectives: 'to guarantee standards; to enhance standards; to promote innovations and more flexible approaches to higher education without loss of quality'. It spelled out in some detail how the CNAA intended from this point to pursue its aims and commitments in the changed contours of higher education, the polytechnics and colleges, and the CNAA itself.[26]

'Public sector higher education', and higher education in general, were no longer what they were in 1964, or even in 1984, and nor was the CNAA. While its relationships with the institutions had changed, it had retained a major role as a guarantor of maintained and enhanced standards, and it was defining and developing activities consonant with that role. 'Standards', 'quality assurance', 'access', 'developing opportunities', 'flexibility' . . . the CNAA, its scale, strategies and structures, its related institutions, 'higher education', had all changed markedly across the quarter-century and with particular speed in the 1980s, but the essential vocabulary and purposes had remained the same.

Notes

1 CN *Annual Report 1987–88*, p. 8.
2 CN (1989) *Development Services Briefing 9. Access Courses in Higher Education: Dimensions of Quality Assurance. An Overview.*
3 CN and CVCP (1989) *Access Courses to Higher Education. A Framework of National Agreements for Recognition*; *ibid.*, *Procedures for the Approval of Authorised Validating Agencies and an Invitation to Apply*, 1989.
4 NAB, 'Quality' (report by the Secretariat), 1984; Christopher Ball, (1984) 'What the hell is quality?' in Dorma Urwin (Ed.) (1985) *Fitness for Purpose: Essays in Higher Education by Christopher Ball*, Society for Research into Higher Education; Graeme Moodie (Ed.) (1986) *Standards and Criteria in Higher Education*, Society for Research into Higher Education.
5 David Billing (1983) 'Practice and criteria in validation under the CNAA' in Clive H. Church (Ed.) *Practice and Perspective in Validation*, Society for Research into Higher Education, pp. 32–3.
6 See R.A. Barnett (1987) 'The maintenance of quality in the public sector of UK higher education', *Higher Education*, p. 16.
7 DES (1983) *Degree Courses in the Public Sector of Higher Education: An HMI Commentary*, HMSO, p. 24.
8 CST (1979) The Academic Health of Courses, 24 October.
9 Sir Michael Clapham, Opening Address, CNAA Degree Congregation, 1976.
10 Rossiter, Iliffe, Ridler, Woodbridge, Kerr, Gutteridge, North, Tolley, Lindop — HS interviews; 'NAB's response to the Lindop report', *NAB Bulletin*, summer 1985, pp. 14–15.
11 For example, Harold Silver (1988) *Education and the Research Process — Forming a New Republic* , CNAA.
12 CN (1982) *Procedures for the Validation of Courses*, 1982.
13 John Brennan and Philip McGeevor (1988) *Graduates at Work: Degree Courses and the Labour Market*, Jessica Kingsley; CN Information Services (1988) *'Outcomes' Paper 1: Social Science Graduates: Degree Results and First Employment Destinations*, and (1989) Papers 2 and 3 on art and design graduates and humanities graduates.
14 Harold Silver and John Brennan (1988) *A Liberal Vocationalism*, Methuen.
15 CN *Annual Report 1982*.
16 CN *Annual Report 1987–88*, p. 15.
17 John Brennan (1989) 'Fewer fears over standards', *Times Higher Education Supplement* 27 January.
18 CN *Annual Report 1987–88*, p. 13.
19 *ibid.*, pp. 16–17 and 20.

20 *ibid.*, p. 19.
21 Malcolm Frazer (1989) 'On-site training', *Times Higher Education Supplement*, 10 March; CN (1989) *Development Services Briefing 15. New Initial Award in Management Education*.
22 *ibid.*
23 CN (1989) Draft Five Year Development Plan, 20 March.
24 *ibid.*
25 CN *Annual Report 1987–88*, pp. 20 and 22; Cmin, 17 December 1987.
26 Draft Five Year Development Plan.

Appendix A: An Outline Chronology

1945   Percy Committee Report on *Higher Technological Education*.

1946   Barlow Committee Report on *Scientific Manpower*.

1955   Creation of NCTA (Lord Hives, Chairman: Frank Hornby, Secretary).

1956   White Paper on *Technical Education*; designation of CATs.

1963   Robbins Committee Report on *Higher Education*, including proposal to create CNAA; government accepts proposal; meeting of Ministry of Education, SED, UGC and CVCP to discuss establishment of CNAA.

1964   (September) First meeting of Council (Lord Kings Norton, Chairman; Frank Hornby, Chief Officer); receipt of Charter; invitation to Duke of Edinburgh to become President accepted.

            Crick (NACEIC) Report on *A Higher Award for Business Studies*.

1965   (March) First meeting of the Business Studies Board.

            (September) First courses approved by CNAA begin.

            (November) First meeting of the Committee for Arts and Social Studies (to parallel Committee for Science and Technology).

First discussions CNAA and NCDAD.
Crosland announces 'binary' policy at Woolwich Polytechnic.

1966   White Paper on *A Plan for Polytechnics and Other Colleges.*
Sub-committee to discuss courses in Education (becomes
Committee for Education in 1967).

1967   Secretary of State issues list of proposed polytechnics.

1968   Provisional designation of first polytechnics.

1970   Committee of Directors of Polytechnics established.

1971   Michael Clapham becomes Council Chairman.

1972   Edwin Kerr becomes Chief Officer.
Committee of Officers established.
First delegations of authority to register MPhil students.
James Committee Report on *Teacher Education and Training.*
White Paper on *Education: A Framework for Expansion.*
CNAA-NCDAD agreement in principle to amalgamate.

1973   *Procedure for Validation of Courses of Study.*
First CNAA-approved courses in Education.
Joint CNAA-UGC conference on BEd and DipHE.

1974   Merger of CNAA and NCDAD.
CNAA declines to validate University College Buckingham courses.

1975   *Partnership in Validation.*

1976   Transfer of DMS to CNAA.

1977   The Prince of Wales becomes President.

1978   Sir Denis Rooke becomes Chairman.
Committee for Academic Policy established.
Institutional review visit to Teesside Polytechnic.
Report of the Oakes Working Group on *The Management of Higher Education in the Maintained Sector.*

1979   *Developments in Partnership in Validation.*
Committee for Institutions established.
Committee for Scotland established.
Council agrees advisory role in Hong Kong (first review takes place 1981).

1980   Finniston Report on *Engineering Our Future.*
Joint validation agreement between CNAA and Newcastle-upon-Tyne Polytechnic (followed by agreements with Sheffield City Polytechnic and Kingston Polytechnic).
Development Services Unit created.

1982   Creation of National Advisory Body for Local Authority (later Public Sector) Higher Education.

1983   (February) Letter to CNAA alleging bias at PNL.

(April/May) HMI visit to PNL.

(July) Council receives report on its own enquiry into allegations.

(October) HMI report on PNL made public.

(December) Council responds to HMI report on PNL.
Response to NAB on town and country planning.
Agreement to continue joint validation with Newcastle-upon-Tyne Polytechnic.
Future Development of CNAA's Academic Policies at Undergraduate Level.

1984   Sir Alastair Pilkington becomes Chairman.

(April) Secretary of State appoints Lindop Committee of Enquiry on Academic Validation.

(July) Chairman's Study Group established.

(July) Letter from Parliamentary Under-Secretary of State on credit transfer.

Committee on Academic and Institutional Policy replaces CAP and Committee for Institutions.

Working Party on Relationships with NAB established.

Research and Related Activities.

Council agrees Development Fund.

(November/December) Consultative paper on the development of the Council's relationship with institutions.

1985   (March) Chairman's Study Group reports to Council on responses to consultative paper.

(April) Lindop Committee Report.

(May) Green Paper on *The Development of Higher Education into the 1990s.*

(June) CNAA responds to Lindop Committee Report.

(July) CNAA invites institutions to apply for 'special agreements'; special agreements with Newcastle and Sheffield as first step.

(November) *Economist* article on CNAA.

(December) STEAC report on *Future Strategy for Higher Education in Scotland.*

1986   Malcolm Frazer becomes Chief Executive.

(March) Secretary of State's response to the Lindop Committee Report.

(October) Council's consultative document on *Quality and Validation: Future Relationships with Institutions.*

Launch of Credit Accumulation and Transfer Scheme.

1987   Sir Ron Dearing becomes Chairman.

(February) *Future Strategy: Principles and Operation.*

'Accredited' and 'associated' institutions.

Supplemental Charter received.

(March) Council agrees new CNAA structure.

(May) White Paper on *Higher Education: Meeting the Challenge*.

(June) Institutions invited to apply for accreditation.

1988   (September) Operational date for first group of accredited institutions.
The Princess Royal becomes President.
Sir Bryan Nicholson becomes Chairman.

1989   (April) Designated polytechnics and colleges receive corporate status.
Council prepares a Five-Year Development Plan.

Appendix B: A Note on Sources

The primary documentary source for the history of the CNAA is, of course, the voluminous collection of the CNAA's own records. Many of these, especially the more recent ones, are in the possession of the CNAA — on paper or microfilm — but the earlier records have been gradually transferred to the Public Record Office. At the time of this research the PRO and the CNAA library have lists of the PRO holdings.

The main documentary research for this study focussed on the minutes and related papers of meetings of the Council and its main committees (particularly CST, CASS, CAP and CAIP). The papers of the boards were sampled and consulted in ways that are reflected in the priorities allocated in the structure of this history. Many of the CNAA's publications were helpful — including its annual reports, *Commentary* published in the 1970s, accounts of, and documents from, working parties and conferences, consultative documents, handbooks, accounts of the work of the Council, and so on. The publications of the Development Services Unit in the 1980s were especially useful. The publication by the CNAA of Robert Strand's account of the development of art and design in the public sector, including the merger with the CNAA and its ensuing position in the CNAA, in *A Good Deal of Freedom* (1987) proved timely and helpful.

There were, however, kinds of material not always directly related to specific committees or boards or to discussion in the Council itself. The most important of these included the large number of 'office papers', discussion documents, working party material, draft proposals, surveys and analyses of various kinds — as well as related correspondence, memoranda and the like. Some of these surfaced in the files other than those related to committee and boards or to the validation of individual institutions. Some surfaced in the papers of the Committee of Officers, or in collections of such material — particularly draft documents and proposals — in the possession of individual officers responsible for the drafting. A number of serving officers made collections of this kind available.

In addition to the interviews listed in appendix C there were also a considerable number of discussions, fleeting or substantial with officers and members, often pointing in the direction of a topic and source materials. Former officers were often willing to help in this way, sending copies of papers in their possession, or a written gloss following an interview or discussion.

Background material for higher education during this period can be traced through the notes to the chapters. Some of the main events and developments across this period have been widely documented and discussed — including, for example, the Robbins Report, the binary policy and the establishment of the polytechnics. The thesis and dissertation literature in this field is slender, and in fact only two theses proved valuable. John Heywood's University of Lancaster MLitt thesis (1969), *An Evaluation of Certain Post-War Developments in Higher Technological Education*, was important for the early period, particularly the context for the emergence of the NCTA. Martin Davis's 1979 Loughborough University thesis on *The Council for National Academic Awards, 1964–1974: A Study of a Validating Agency* (see also appendix C) was an invaluable resource in placing the first ten years of the CNAA in context. A number of other publications underlining particular interpretations of changes in higher education are cited in the notes.

The NCTA records are located at the PRO, and of particular importance in this connection were the minutes of the Governing Body, the collection of material contained in the Lord Hives Education Miscellaneous file, and the various reports and policy papers.

The records of the institutions whose relationships with the CNAA were explored were in the possession of the institutions concerned. The CNAA's own files of material relating to these institutions were not consulted, but in all cases the institutions gave unrestricted access to their own records. The records of Brighton, Bristol and Newcastle-upon-Tyne Polytechnics, Bulmershe College of Higher Education, Reading, and King Alfred's College, Winchester, are therefore cited at appropriate points in the chapter notes, particularly chapter 8, and the file location of the material used is indicated in the notes.

The files of the CVCP were consulted in connection primarily with the establishment and early work of the CNAA, and the file locations are also indicated in the notes as appropriate. The records of the CDP are extensive, and access was made particularly easy by the existence of an index at the CDP to its papers. In this case the material consulted was both the collection of minutes and the files of documents, and locations are indicated in the notes for the many such sources used.

It should be possible, with few exceptions, to identify the location of any source from the information given in the notes, although the disposition of records between the CNAA and the PRO changes over time. The exceptions are the small number of documents cited where the sources may not be obvious, and in these cases the source is in the possession of the author.

Surprisingly little has been written about the work of the CNAA itself. The only previous book was Michael Lane's *Design for Degrees: New Degree Courses under the CNAA — 1964-1974* (Macmillan, 1975), which detailed the operation of the CNAA at that time. An indicative, beginning bibliography of publications relating to the CNAA could be as follows:

ADELMAN, C. and ALEXANDER, R. (1982a) 'Internal evaluation and external validation', *Higher Education Review*, 14, 2 .

ADELMAN, C. and ALEXANDER, R.J. (1982b) *The Self-Evaluating Institution: Practice and Principles in the Management of Educational Change*, London, Methuen.

ALEXANDER, R. (1979) 'What is a course? Curriculum models and CNAA validation', *Journal of Further and Higher Education*, 3, 1.

AUSTIN, R. (1983) 'Evaluation and review: Current policy', *Studies in Higher Education*, 8, 2.

BARNETT, R.A. (1987) 'The maintenance of quality in the public sector of UK higher education', *Higher Education*, 16.

BILLING, D. (1983) 'Practice and criteria of validation under the CNAA' in CHURCH, C.H. (Ed.) *Practice and Perspective in Validation*, Guildford, Society for Research into Higher Education.

BRIGGS, B.F.N. (1985) 'By CNAA degrees', *IEE Proceedings*, 132, Pt A, 4.

CHAMBERS, P. (1975) 'Course validation and curriculum innovation: A critique of the influence of the Council for National Academic Awards on the colleges of education', 97.

CHURCH, C. (1976) 'Not up to par? Some problems in comparing the validation of degree courses outside the universities', *Higher Education Bulletin*, 5, 1.

DAVIS, M.C. (1980) 'Performance at national level: The CNAA as validating agency' in BILLING, D. (Ed.) *Indicators of Performance*, Guildford, Society for Research into Higher Education.

DAVIS, M. (1981) 'Prelude to partnership: The CNAA and the polytechnics 1964-74', *Higher Education Review*, 13, 2.

FRANCIS, D.C. (1975) 'CNAA involvement in adult education', *Adult Education*, 47, 6.

FRANCIS, D. (1985) 'Validation: Perceptions of partnership', *Journal of Further and Higher Education*, 9, 2.

FRANCIS, D. (1986) 'An exploration of aspects of the traditional board structure of the CNAA and the implications of current changes', *Journal of Further and Higher Education*, 10, 1.

GOODACRE, E. (1981) 'Advanced courses outside the universities: The contribution of the CNAA' in ALEXANDER, R. and ELLIS, J. (Eds) *Advanced Study for Teachers*, Guildford, Society for Research into Higher Education, Teacher Education Study Group.

HARGREAVES, J. (1979) 'CNAA validation and course evaluation: The state of the art', *Evaluation Newsletter*, 3, 2.

HARGREAVES, J. (1982) 'A valediction for validation? "Partnership" and power in the current educational climate', *Journal of Further and Higher Education*, 6, 2.

HIGHER EDUCATION REVIEW (1979) 'Editorial: Partnership in validation', *Higher Education Review*, 12, 1.

LANE, M. (1975) *Design for Degrees: New Degree Courses under the CNAA — 1964-1974,* Macmillan.

MCGETTRICK, B.J. (1980) 'CNAA validation as a contract: Some influences on evaluation', *Evaluation Newsletter*, 4, 2.

MCNAY, I. and MCCORMICK, R. (1982) *Case Study 3: The CNAA* (Educational Studies: A Third Level Course), Milton Keynes, Open University Press.

PRATT, J. (1983) 'Co-ordination in the public sector: The Council for National Academic Awards' in SHATTOCK, M. (Ed.) *The Structure and Governance of Higher Education*, Guildford, Society for Research into Higher Education.

RIDLER, A.M. (1975) 'CNAA and the polytechnics', *Coombe Lodge Reports*, 8, 9 (*Polytechnic Perspectives*).

ROBINSON, E.E. (1968) *The New Polytechnics*, London, Cornmarket (especially chapter 5).

STRAND, R. (1987) *A Good Deal of Freedom: Art and Design in the Public Sector of Higher Education*, London, CNAA.

WALKLEY, H. (1972) 'Evaluation in the CNAA curriculum process', *Evaluation Newsletter*, 3, 2.

There are, additionally, the files of *The Times Higher Education Supplement*, and the publications of the CNAA's Development Services Unit, many of them reporting on projects carried out under the auspices of the CNAA's Development Fund.

Appendix C: Interviews

Conducted for This Study

Dr Rita Austin	29.10.1986
Dr Ron Barnett	14.12.1988
Mr Peter Brinson	11.12.1987
Sir Derman Christopherson	10.12.1987
Sir Michael Clapham	2.10.1987
Dr John Clark	29.7.1987
Dr Martin Davis	30.11.1986
Mr David Francis	3.3.1988
Dr Martin Gaskell	31.3.1987
Mr Hugh Glanville	6.3.1987
Professor William Gutteridge	16.2.1988
Mr Francis Hanrott	14.6.1988
Mrs Cynthia Iliffe	4.3.1987
Dr Edwin Kerr	6.1.1987, 15.10.1987 and 8.9.1989
Lord Kings Norton	22.7.1988
Dr Michael Lane	2.10.1987
Sir Norman Lindop	25.2.1988
Mr Geoffrey Melling	18.10.1988
Mr Graham Middleton	14.12.1988
Dr Marion North	17.6.1988
Mr Bryan Overy	25.2.1988
Sir Alastair Pilkington	25.8.1989
Mr James Porter	10.6.1987
Sir Alan Richmond	31.10.1988
Dr Ann Ridler	25.3.1987
Miss Bridget Rogers	19.7.1988
Sir Denis Rooke	18.9.1989
Miss Jean Rossiter	8.8.1988
Mr Maxwell Smith	1.4.1987
Revd Dr George Tolley	23.5.1988
Dr Roger Woodbridge	23.4.1987

Conducted by Martin Davis in 1973–77 for a Thesis on "*The Council for National Academic Awards, 1964–1974: A Study of a Validating Agency*" (Loughborough University PhD, 1979): Tapes, Transcripts and Notes made available and Used with the Permission of the Interviewees

Dr G.S. Bosworth
Sir Derman Christopherson
Sir Cyril English
Professor H.C. Edey
Mr H.W. French
Mr F. Gorner
Professor W.F. Gutteridge
Mr F.G. Hanrott
Mr F.R. Hornby
Mr G.A. Hunting
Mr I. Kane
Mr A.J. Jenkinson
Lord Kings Norton
Sir Norman Lindop
Dr G.A. Moore
Sir Antony Part
Mr E.G. Peirson
Mr J.E. Proctor
Sir Walter Puckey
Sir Alan Richmond
Professor G.D. Rochester
Mr E.E. Robinson
Dr C. Rogers
Miss J.F. Rossiter
Sir Lionel Russell
Dr J. Topping
Mr L. Wharfe

Index

Academic Advisory Committees
    (AACs) 61, 146
Academic Boards 93-4, 101-2,
    105-6, 146, 147, 230, 231, 235
access, student 260-1, 264, 270, 271
access courses 261
accountability 1, 267
'accredited institutions' 203, 240-2,
    244, 268
accreditation 146, 148, 162, 201,
    205-8, 213, 214, 233-45, 249,
    253, 268-9
    Instrument of Accreditation 243-4
    obtained 244
Accreditation Committee 242
Adams, Roger 193
Adelman, Clem 239
agricultural engineering 52
Anderson Committee 7
Andrew, Sir Herbert 44
Annan, Lord 185
Anne, Princess Royal 249
Area Training Organizations 80, 115
art 81-2, 96
    colleges of art 81-2, 123-4
arts 50-1, 85-6, 96, 222, 223
    courses 76
    creative and performing
        arts 125-8, 133
    provision 220-1
    see also Committee for Arts and
        Social Studies
Ashby, Eric
    Technology and the Academics 12,
    18
'associated institutions' 241, 268
Association of Teachers in Technical
    Institutes 66, 72
asterisked degrees 53-4

Austin, Rita 227
Australia 62, 109-10, 255
autonomy of institutions 60, 106-8,
    113, 147, 167, 205-6, 233
    universities 9

BA* 553-4
Baker, HMI 78
Baker, Kenneth 239, 251
Ball, Christopher 185, 206, 262
Barden, Laing 181
Barlow Committee 15, 16
Battersea College of Technology 29
BEd 80, 114-17
Beloff, Max 137
Berkshire College of Education see
    Bulmershe
Berrill, Sir Kenneth 115, 118
Bethel, David 150, 161-2
Billing, David 207, 262
binary policy 14, 16, 60-2, 65-74,
    87
Birmingham University 80
Bleach, Barrie 227
Bolton Institute of Technology 57
Booth, Clive 221
Borough Polytechnic 101
Bosworth, George 98
Boyle, Sir Edward (later Lord) 7-8,
    61, 66, 69, 70, 155
Bradshaw, Alan 153-4
Brennan, John 268-9
Brighton 71, 84
Brighton Polytechnic 102-3, 166-70
Brinson, Peter 126-7
Bristol Polytechnic 82, 101-2
Brixton School of Building 92
Brogan, Colm 96-7

Brooke, Peter   225, 237
BSc*   53–4
Buckingham, University College
    of 136–7
Bulmershe College of Higher
    Education
    (Berkshire College of Education)
    116, 119, 170–2, 256
Burgess, Tyrrell   39, 100
Burnham Technical Committee   33
business studies   47, 48, 50, 51, 76,
    77, 129
Business Studies Board (CNAA)   47,
    50, 77–8, 129–30

Caine, Sir Sydney   13
Carlisle, Mark   186–7
Carswell, John   60, 68, 70
Central Institutions (CI)   24, 45, 47,
    49, 96, 124
Central London Polytechnic   191
Chairman's Study Group
    (CNAA)   212–13, 229–31
Chambers, Peter   138
Charles, Prince of Wales   139–40,
    161, 249
Charter (CNAA)   45–6
  supplemental   243
Chelmer-Essex Institute of Higher
    Education   191
Chorley Day Training College   51
Christopherson, Sir Derman   52, 54,
    70, 80, 109, 115–16, 174
City and Guilds of London
    Institute   17
City of London Polytechnic   83, 159
civil engineering   58
Clapham, Sir Michael   46, 94, 109,
    123, 139–40, 160–1, 187, 233,
    244, 263
Clark, John   177–81
Cockcroft, Sir John   17–18
College Research Degrees Committees
    (CRDCs)   242
colleges of art   81–2, 123–4
colleges
  compared with universities   194
  relations with CNAA   55, 56, 57–60
  relations with universities   57
  see also further education colleges;
    polytechnics; technical
  colleges; *names of colleges*
Colleges of Advanced Technology
    (CATs)   11, 24–7, 32–4, 38–9,
    48, 50, 56, 65–6

Combined Studies (Creative and
    Performing Arts) Board
    (CNAA)   125–6, 127
Combined Studies (Humanities) Board
    (CNAA)   121, 122, 125–6
Combined Studies (Science) Board
    (CNAA)   132
Committee for Academic Affairs (CAA;
    CNAA)   242
Committee for Academic and
    Institutional Policy (CAIP;
    CNAA)   22–3, 228
Committee for Academic Policy
    (CNAA)   135, 194–5, 197, 199,
    207, 226
Committee for Art and Design
    (CNAA)   124, 231, 268
Committee for Arts and Humanities
    (CNAA)   250
Committee for Arts and Social Studies
    (CASS; CNAA)   47, 51, 59, 76–7,
    85–6, 91, 209, 231
Committee for Business and
    Management (CNAA)   231
Committee for Education (CNAA)   51,
    114–17, 122, 157, 232, 250
Committee for Engineering
    (CNAA)   250–1
Committee for Institutions
    (CNAA)   135, 150, 156, 180,
    197, 202, 203
Committee for Science and
    Technology (CST; CNAA)   47,
    58–9, 75–6, 85–6, 131, 195, 263
Committee for Scotland (CNAA)   198,
    232, 242, 270
Committee of Directors of
    Polytechnics (CDP)   75, 99, 106,
    123, 134–5, 144, 146, 176, 181,
    199–200, 208, 213, 236–7, 245
  comments on CNAA report on
  Teesside   154–5
  papers   ix, 279
  response to *Developments in
    Partnership
    in Validation*   155–8
  response to *Partnership in
    Validation*   148–9
Committee of Officers
    (CNAA)   135–6, 230
Committee of Vice-Chancellors and
    Principals (CVCP)   33, 44, 54,
    55, 72, 79, 95, 222
Committee on Longer Term
    Developments (CNAA)   184

Commonwealth 9
complementary and contrasting
    studies 60, 85–6, 169, 266
computer science 105, 139–1
Computer Weekly 131
Congress of Commonwealth
    Universities 16–17
Constantine College of
    Technology 57, 58, 91, 101,
    151
Cook, Sir James 72
Coombe Lodge Conferences 55,
    60–1, 84, 108, 146
Cooper, W.M. 73
Cotgrove, Prof. 209
Council for National Academic
    Awards (CNAA)
    proposed 39–40
    preliminary discussion
        meeting 44–5
    first meeting 48–9
    Statement No. (1) 48–50
    transition from NCTA 47–50
    achievement and role 260–71
    Chairmen 34
    committee membership 94
    conferences 132–3
    finances and management 95,
        227–9, 231, 245–8
    membership 45, 46
    records 4–5, 278–9
    premises 95
    Presidents 139–40, 249
    publications on 280–1
    research and development 226–9
    Royal Charter 45–6
        supplemental 243
    staff structure 95, 200–1
        reductions, 1987 249
    Statutes 46
    title 49, 94–5
    see also degrees; *names of boards
        and committees*
Council for the Accreditation of
    Teacher Education 250
course approval 79–9, 90–2, 107,
    145, 156, 233, 235–6
    1966–7 57–9
    education 79–81
    King Alfred's College 173–6
    polytechnics 68
    social studies and
        sociology 209–11
    see also validation
course review 177–80

Coventry *see* Lanchester
Cox, Sir Harold Roxbee *see* Kings
    Norton, Lord
creative and performing arts 125–8,
    133
Creative and Performing Arts Board
    (CNAA) 125–6
Credit Accumulation and Transfer
    Scheme (CATS) 224–6, 252, 261,
    269
Crewe and Alsager College 119
Crick, W.F. 50, 129
Crick Committee 47, 50, 77, 78
Crispin, Alan 228
Crosland, Anthony 39–40, 61, 62,
    65, 66–7, 74–5
Crowther-Hunt, Lord 185–6

Daily Mail 153, 210
Daily Telegraph 153, 210
dance 125, 126–7
Dartington College of Arts 126, 127
Davis, Martin ix–x, 279, 283
Dearing, Sir Ron 249
degrees 44, 46, 47, 48, 49, 51–3,
    86–7
    asterisked 53–4
    external 14–15, 21, 22, 94
    higher 44–5, 55
    honours and ordinary 53, 76–7,
        87, 132
    NCTA 21
    part-time 77, 261
    polytechnics' own 205–6
    research 87
    two-year 137
Delft Technical University 7
demography 49, 51, 61–2, 186–7,
    221, 222
Dent, H.C. 7, 30
    Universities in Transition 13
Department of Education and Science
    (DES; *formerly* Ministry of
    Education) 47–8, 60, 69–70, 74,
    77, 82–3, 91–2, 95, 100, 105,
    122, 238, 250, 255
    relations with CNAA 54
    teacher education policy 79–80
Department of Scientific and
    Industrial Research 33
design 81, 82, 96, 123–5, 227, 229,
    251
Development Fund (CNAA) 227–9,
    231, 261, 281

Development of Higher Education into the 1990s (Green Paper) 220-3, 252
Development Services Unit (DSU; CNAA) 226-7
Developments in Partnership in Validation ('the blue book') 151, 156, 157, 161, 179, 180, 181, 198, 208
Didsbury College 80-1, 116, 171, 173
Diploma in Higher Education (DipHE) 113-16, 118-20, 121, 131, 175
 Study Group 119
Diploma in Management Studies (DMS) 47
Diploma in Technology (DipTech) 23-4, 26-31, 33, 34-5, 37-8, 47-8
diversification 12, 61, 120-3
documentation 145, 267
drama 125

Ealing College of Technology 129
Earls, Jack 210-11
Economist, The 193, 246
economy 185-7, 222
 see also expenditure; funding
Edey, Harold 52, 109
Edinburgh, Duke of 49, 139, 249
Edinburgh 139
Edinburgh College of Art 125
Education 35
Education: A Framework for Expansion (White Paper) 116
Education Act 1988 255
education courses 51, 79-81, 113-20, 121-2, 131, 170-3, 250
 see also Committee for Education; Diploma in Higher Education
Educational Studies course 114-17
Electrical and Electronic Engineering Board 54-5
Elvin, Lionel 73
employment 98, 194, 266-7
Enfield College of Technology 80, 170
engineering 15, 22, 23, 27, 33, 34, 35-6, 85, 195-6, 249, 250-1
 civil engineering 58
 courses 75-6
 mechanical engineering 58, 59
Engineering Our Future 195

Evans, Norman 225
examiners, external 34, 94, 269
expenditure 68
 cuts 185-7, 212, 221-2, 251-2
 see also funding
external degrees 14-15, 21, 22, 30, 94

faculty visits 177
Fedden, Sir Roy 35-6
Federal German Republic 62
Files on Courses in Institutions (FOCII) 198
Finniston Committee 195-6
food science 131
Ford, Boris 70, 72, 73
Ford Motor Co. 91
Fowler, Gerry 160
France 62
Francis, David 182, 205
Frazer, Malcolm 244, 245, 248-9, 270
French, H.W. 31, 49, 54
funding 21, 186-90, 227-9, 251-2, 254-6
further education colleges 12, 48, 66, 68, 261
Future Strategy: Principles and Operation 241-2, 244, 256

General Committee (CNAA) 137, 227, 242
general education' 197
Glamorgan College of Technology 106
Glanville, Hugh 150, 151
Gloucester College of Arts and Technology 191
Goldman, Arnold 211
Gould, Julius 209
government policies 65, 205-6
 1956 White Paper 22, 24, 28, 37
 1966 White Paper 67-8
 1972 White Paper 116
 1979-80 184, 186-8
 1980 Select Committee 184
 1985 Green Paper 220-3, 252
 1987 White Paper 251-6
 Labour 185-6, 187
 response to Lindop Report 237-9
 see also Department of Education and Science; Ministry of Education and Science
grants 21, 56, 189

Grants to Students 7
Guardian, The 54, 70, 153, 211
Gulbenkian Foundation 125, 126, 133
Gutteridge, William 59, 100, 119-20, 122, 206, 264-5

Hailsham, Lord (*formerly* Quintin Hogg) 12, 48
Hall, Geoffrey 150, 167
Hampson, Keith 123
Hanrott, Francis 52, 81, 86, 93, 101, 108, 109, 170
Hatfield Polytechnic 65, 91, 93-4, 103-5, 116, 131
Hatt, Frank 124
Hencke, David 122
Her Majesty's Inspectorate (HMI) 68, 78, 188, 199, 210-11, 262
Scottish 199
Heywood, John 26-7, 279
High Wycombe College of Technology 94
Higher Award in Business Studies, A (Crick report) 47, 50, 77 ?
higher education
concept 7-18, 48
in other countries 62, 67
pattern 21-4, 40, 48-9, 87, 99
redefined 268-270-1
resource allocations 68
see also binary policy
Higher Education into the 1990s 186
Higher Education: Meeting the Challenge (White Paper) 251
Hives, Lord 21, 23, 24, 25, 26, 28, 34, 35-7
Hogg, Quintin *see* Hailsham, Lord
Holden, John 125, 127
Home Universities Conference 12
Hong Kong 198-9, 267
Hornby, Frank 24, 31-2, 34-5, 38, 40, 49, 51, 52, 54, 55-6, 59, 79, 60, 74, 79, 92-3, 106, 107-8, 109, 110, 161, 247, 248
Houghton, John 151-3
House of Commons 46, 61, 66, 70, 138, 237
housing studies 131
Huddersfield College of Technology 78
human movement studies 133

humanities 121, 122, 222, 223
see also arts; liberal studies
Hunting, Gordon 52

Iliffe, Cynthia 129-30, 264
industrial training 24-5, 26-7, 33, 84-5
industry 34, 35-6, 97, 98
see also National Advisory Council on Education for Industry and Commerce
information technology 250
Inner London Education Authority 72
Institution of Mechanical Engineers 33-4
institutional review 93, 147, 156, 157, 175, 177, 184-5, 197-8, 199, 200-1, 205, 207, 230-42, 267
Brighton 169
'faculty' 177
PNL 209-12
Sheffield 235
Teesside 151-6
institutions
accredited 203, 238, 239, 240-2, 268
associated 241, 268
relations with CNAA 106-7, 137-9, 144-62, 166, 181, 184-5, 229-35
Modes A and B 212-13, 214, 230
see also autonomy of institutions; colleges, Committee for Institutions; partnership in validation; *names of institutions*
Instrumentation and Control Board (CNAA) 132
interdisciplinary courses 83
Interfaculty Studies Board (CNAA) 131, 197

Jahoda, Marie 27
James Committee 81, 94, 113-114, 118
joint validation 180-1, 201-4, 235
Joseph, Sir Keith 208-10, 212, 215, 220, 231, 236, 237, 246, 247

Kerr, Edwin 81, 109, 114, 115, 118, 122, 123-4, 128, 137-8, 145, 146, 151-2, 161, 169, 179, 187,

195, 200, 205, 208, 212, 213,
224, 225, 227, 233, 235, 239,
245, 247-8, 264
King Alfred's College,
Winchester 173-6
Kings Norton, Lord (*formerly* Sir
Harold Roxbee Cox) 23, 34,
37-8, 42, 52, 72, 93, 94, 106,
109
Kingston Polytechnic 180, 203
Kogan, Maurice 60, 155, 197

Laban Centre for Movement and
Dance 126, 127
Labour policies 21, 39, 66, 68-9,
185-6, 187
Lanchester Polytechnic,
Coventry 57, 71, 91, 101,
105-6, 191
Lane, Michael 95, 280
Leeds College of Technology 57
Leeds Polytechnic 99
legal education 131, 137
Leicester College of Technology 57
Leicester Polytechnic 204
Lewis, Michael ix
liaison committees 95
*Liberal Education in a Technical
Age* 28
*Liberal Education in Technical
Colleges* 28
liberal studies 24-5, 27-9, 77, 85-6,
99
librarianship 79, 86
Librarianship Board (CNAA) 79
libraries 122
Lindop, Sir Norman 103, 105, 117,
122, 131, 150, 201, 204,m 206,
207, 212, 239, 265
Lindop Committee 201, 208,
212-13, 237, 244, 245
Report 213-15
response 229, 231-4, 236,
237-8, 239, 247
Liverpool Polytechnic 82, 93, 177
Livingstone, Sir Richard 16
Lloyd Jones, David 83
local education authorities (LEAs) 66,
69, 70, 97, 188-9, 255
control of colleges 93, 253-4
expenditure 68, 187-9, 254, 256
relations with CNAA 56
see also National Advisory Body
for Local Authority Higher
Education (NAB)

Locke, Michael 100
London Colleges Alliance 82-3
London University
external degrees 14-15, 21, 22, 94

MacArthur, Brian 70, 99
MacRae, Donald 109, 128
management studies 128-30, 270
Management Studies Board
(CNAA) 128
managing design 227, 229, 251
Manchester Polytechnic 80, 116,
117, 204, 244
Mason, Stewart 82-3, 123
mathematics 59
mature students 196-7, 223, 261
McGettrick, B.J. 157-8
mechanical engineering 58, 59
media studies 270
Membership of the College of
Technologists (MCT) 31, 47
Middlesex Polytechnic 125
Milton Keynes College of
Education 170
Ministry of Education 13-14, 21,
29-30, 31, 40, 44-5, 49
see also Department of Education
and Science
Moberly, Sir Walter 9-10
modular courses 83-4, 159
Moodie, Graham 12
Morris, Sir Charles 14, 17
Morris, Sir Philip 18
MPhil degrees 107, 148
music 78, 125, 127

Napier College, Edinburgh 97, 125
National Advisory Body for Local
Authority Higher Education
(NAB) 187-94, 195, 200, 213,
234, 249, 254, 262, 265
National Advisory Council on
Education for Industry and
Commerce (NACEIC) ? 17, 21,
24, 47
National Council for Diplomas in Art
and Design (NCDAD) 1, 81-2,
123-4, 167
National Council for Technological
Awards (NCTA) 1, 2, 18, 21-40,
44
papers 279
proposed 15-16

transition to Council for National
Academic Awards   40, 47–8, 50,
52, 59–60
Nature   12, 18
nautical studies   52
New Statesman   193
Newcastle University   173, 251
Newcastle upon Tyne
Polytechnic   127, 176–81, 201–3,
204, 208, 234, 236–6, 238, 243–4
Nicholson, Bryan   249
Nokes, Geoffrey   174
Norman, Sir Arthur   98
North, Marion   265
North East London Polytechnic   119,
131
North London Polytechnic
(PNL)   116, 208–12, 244, 245
North Staffordshire College of
Technology   54
Northern Ireland   194, 195
Notre Dame College   80, 81
Nuffield College, Oxford   10–11
nursing   131

Oakes, Gordon   187–8, 224
Oastler College, Huddersfield   51
Observer, The   39
Open University   39, 84, 108, 109,
134, 184, 228
Overy, Bryan   131, 227, 246
Oxford College of Technology   101
Oxford Polytechnic   83, 101, 159,
191

Paisley   93, 97
Parliament
House of Commons   46, 61, 66,
70, 138, 237
Select Committees   184, 186 ?
Part, Sir Anthony   29–30, 32
part-time courses   77, 261
partnership in validation   144–51,
155–62, 169, 175, 176–81,
191–2, 199–205, 235
see also *Developments in
Partnership in Validation*;
Working Party on Partnership in
Validation
Partnership in Validation   147, 148,
149, 158–9, 170, 199
peer review   158–9, 188, 192, 206,
207, 230–2, 240–2, 244, 260
Percy Committee   11, 15–16, 21
performing arts   125–8

Perry, Sir Walter   119
Peston, Maurice   109, 138
Peterson, A.D.C.   63
Pharmaceutical Journal   79
pharmacy   78–9
PhD degrees   148
Philip, Duke of Edinburgh   49, 139,
249
Pilkington, Sir Alastair   212, 227,
233, 235, 238, 244, 245, 247
Pimlott, John A.R.   40, 45, 46, 49,
54, 74
planning   46–7, 61–2, 189–91, 253–6
Planning Committee (CNAA)   46–7
Pocock, Maurice   129, 130
Pollard, Derek   224
polytechnics   138, 179
1960s designation   65, 67–8, 72,
74–5, 100–6
art and design   81–2
autonomy   106–8, 113, 162,
167–70, 205–6, 233–7
charters   144, 146, 162
CNAA's view of   166–70
compared with
universities   97–100, 160, 193–4
corporate status   253–6
mergers   57, 101–2
relations with CNAA   106, 157,
159–60, 166–70
teacher education   115, 116–17
see also Committee of Directors of
Polytechnics *and names of
colleges*
Polytechnics and Colleges Funding
Council (PCFC)   249, 254, 255,
256
Porter, James   119, 120, 170–3
Portsmouth College of
Technology   78
Portsmouth Polytechnic   203–4
postgraduate work   30, 56, 98
Powney, Janet   239
Pratt, John   39
Prentice, Reginald   74, 186
Price Waterhouse   246
Princess Royal   249
*Procedure for Validation of Courses
of Study*   145
*Procedures for the Validation of
Courses*   207
professional education   11, 15
projects   27
public expenditure   186–7, 212,
221–2, 251–2

public sector 60, 65–74, 223
Puckey, Sir Walter 26, 27, 31

quality 262, 269
'Quality' 262
*Quality and Validation: Future
    Relationships with
    Institutions* 240–1
  response to 241

Reading University 170, 256
Recreation and Sports Studies Board
    (CNAA) 133
Regional Advisory Councils
    (RACs) 68, 91, 100, 188
Regional Colleges 30, 39, 50, 56
research 30, 44, 55, 59, 74, 134,
    221, 250, 266
  polytechnics 67, 87
Research and Related Activities 250
research degrees 148, 242
*Resources for Research in
    Polytechnics and other
    Colleges* 134
Reviews Co-ordinating Sub-Committee
    (CNAA) 232, 234–5
Richmond, Sir Alan 58, 84, 85
Rickett, Ray 224
Ridler, Ann 122, 125, 126, 136, 170,
    264
RISE Report 250
Robbins Committee 7, 8, 12, 13,
    14–15, 27, 31, 32–3, 38–40, 45,
    48–9, 51, 52, 53, 54, 56, 60, 61,
    62, 65–6, 73
Robinson, Eric 66, 69, 73, 98
Rochester, G.D. 46, 52
Roehampton Institute of Higher
    Education 261
Rooke, Sir Denis 140, 155, 161–2,
    188, 199, 205–6, 211, 227, 244–5
Rose, Martial 175–6
Rossiter, Jean 52, 109, 129, 264
Royal, Princess 249
Rugby College of Engineering
    Technology 57
Rugby College of Technology 25
Russell, Sir Lionel 31, 34, 40, 46,
    49, 52, 60, 72, 109

Salmon, John 224
sandwich courses 24, 25–7, 33,
    37–8, 84–5, 250
  award for 53–4

science 8, 10, 15–18
  combined studies 132
  courses 75–6
  university students 37
  see also Committee for Science and
    Technology
Scotland 49, 96–7, 133–4, 198, 270
  art colleges 124–5
  Central Institutions (CI) 24, 46,
    47, 49, 96, 124
Scotsman, The 96–7
Scottish College of Textiles 125
Scottish Council for the Validation of
    Courses for Teacher's
    (SCOVACT) 198
Scottish Education Department
    (SED) 44, 80, 124
Scottish Tertiary Education Advisory
    Council (STEAC) 220, 223, 254
Scottish Tertiary Education
    Council 198
Scottish Woollen Textile College 81,
    96
seminars 269
Sheffield City Polytechnic 103, 180,
    234–6, 238
Short, Ted 97
Shrivenham Military College 131–2
Simon of Wythenshawe, Lord 12
Skinner, Joyce 119
Smith, Sir Alex 138
Smith, Maxwell 92–3, 109
Snow, C.P. 12
social science 80
social studies 50–1, 85–6, 222, 223
  courses 76
  North London Polytechnic 208–11
  see also Committee for Arts and
    Social Studies
Social Studies Board (CNAA) 209
Sociological Studies Board
    (CNAA) 80, 158
sociology 209–11
Southampton University 173, 174
sports studies 133
St Osyth's College of Education 78,
    116
standards 46, 159, 232, 262–4, 265,
    266
  see also validation
Standing Conference of Principals and
    Directors of Colleges and
    Institutes in High Education 135
starred degrees 53–4

Statement No. 1, CNAA   48-9
Stewart, Michael   66, 69
Strand, Robert   124, 278
Strategy Group (CNAA)   239-40
students
    mature   196-7, 223, 261
    'non-standard'   196-7
    numbers   186-7, 221, 251, 252
    part-time   77, 261
    science and technology   37
subject boards, CNAA   47, 51, 75-6,
    95-6, 145-6, 185, 206-8, 213,
    241
    see also names
subject committees (CNAA)   241, 242
subject range   11, 51-2, 60, 75-6, 96,
    113, 131-3
subject review   178, 270
Sunday Times, The   153
Sunderland   91, 116
Surveying Board (CNAA)   92
Sussex University   13, 71

Taylor, G.   60
Taylor Committee   38
teacher education   51, 73, 79-81,
    113-23, 132, 170-3, 250
    Scottish   198
technical colleges   15-16, 22-35
    see also Colleges of Advanced
    Technology; *names of colleges*
Technical Education (White
    Paper)   22, 24, 28, 37
technology   8, 15-18, 21, 23-32,
    36-40
    courses   75-6
    diversity of studies   131
    university students   37
    see also Diploma in Technology;
    National Council for
    Technological Awards
Technology   26
Teesside College of Education   151,
    153
Teesside Polytechnic   101, 151-6
textile design   81, 96
Thatcher, Margaret   114, 144, 186
Times, The   99
*Times Educational
    Supplement* (TES)   7, 31, 78-9,
    123, 153, 211
*Times Higher Education Supplement
    (THES)*   108-9, 122-3, 152-3,
    211, 235, 248, 281

Tolley, Revd. Dr George   128, 206,
    265
Topping, Dr James   52, 60, 69, 105
'topping up'   254, 256
town and country planning
    courses   191, 192, 249
Town Planning Board (CNAA)   249
Toyne, Peter   224, 226
training *see* employment; industrial
    training
Training Agency   229, 270
    Training Panel (CNAA)   84
Trent Polytechnic   116, 125, 249
Twentieth Century   12

Ulster College, the Northern Ireland
    Polytechnic   96, 100-1, 133
United States of America   9, 56, 62
universities
    1960s perception of   69-73
    education course validation   114,
        115, 117
    expansionism   12-16, 61-2, 184-5
    expenditure cuts   251-2
    Green paper, 1985   220-2, 252
    mergers with colleges   57, 173
    nature and purpose   8-18
    and polytechnics   97-100, 160,
        193-4
    relations with CNAA   44-5, 54, 56,
        73
    science and technology
        students   37
Universities Funding Council   254
Universities Quarterly   9, 12, 17-18
University and Polytechnic Grants
    Committee (UPGC)   198
University Grants Committee
    (UGC)   ix, 8, 9, 16, 44-5, 55, 95,
        193, 221-2, 254
University of the Air, A   39

Vaizey, John   12
validation   87, 90-1, 113, 210-11,
    232, 265, 267
    'autonomy in'   214
    Chairman's Study Group   212-13,
        229-31
    'internal'   146-8, 178-80, 205
    interdisciplinary and modular
        courses   83
    joint   180-1, 201-4, 235
    Lindop Report   213-15

Mode A   230
Mode B   212-13, 214, 230
of creative and performing
    arts   125-8
of education courses   51, 55-6, 81,
    113-17, 173-250
of textile design   82
of town and country
    planning   191-2, 249
partnership in   144-51, 155-62,
    169, 175, 176-81, 191-2,
    199-205, 235
    Newcastle   176-81, 208, 235-6
polytechnics   74, 75
self-validation   146-9, 159, 168-70,
    214, 253
simplification   144-8
by universities   144, 115, 117, 173
    *see also Developments in
    Partnership in Validation*;
    institutional review; partnership
    in validation; *Partnership in
    Validation; Procedure for
    Validation of Courses of Study;
    Procedures for the Validation of
    Courses*; Working Party on
    Partnership in Validation
Venables, Sir Peter   31, 32, 72, 73
vocational studies   17, 99, 221-2,
    266-7

Waldegrave, William   193
Walden, George   224
Wales   96, 106, 131, 133, 134
Walker, Patrick Gordon   97
Warwick University   57, 71
Watford College of Technology   57
Weaver, Sir Toby   70, 71-2, 146
West England College of Art   82
Wilson, Harold   39
Winchester School of Art   173
Wolfenden, Sir John   44
Wolverhampton and Staffordshire
    College of Technology   57-8
Woodbridge, Roger   264
Woolwich Polytechnic   91
Worcester College of Higher
    Education   80, 81, 116, 126
Working Group on Relationships with
    the NAB(CNAA)   192
Working Party on Longer Term
    Developments (CNAA)   199-200,
    201, 205, 208, 213, 267
Working Party on Partnership in
    Validation   149-50, 155, 161-2
World War II   8

Young, Michael (*later* Lord)   38-9
Young, Michael F.D.   209

Ziman, John   119